SELECTED PLAYS
OF
DENIS JOHNSTON

chosen and with an introduction by
Joseph Ronsley

Irish Drama Selections 2

COLIN SMYTHE
Gerrards Cross, Bucks.

THE CATHOLIC UNIVERSITY
OF AMERICA PRESS
Washington, D.C.

Copyright 1929, 1931, 1935, 1954 by Denis Johnston
Copyright © 1958, 1960, 1977, 1979 by Denis Johnston
All Rights Reserved
This selection copyright © 1983 by Denis Johnston
Introduction copyright © 1983 by Joseph Ronsley

This selection first published in 1983 by
Colin Smythe Limited, Gerrards Cross, Buckinghamshire

British Library Cataloguing in Publication Data

Johnston, Denis
    Selected plays of Denis Johnston.—(Irish drama
    selections, ISSN 0260–7964; 2)
    I. Title   II. Ronsley, Joseph
    III. Series
    822′.912   PR6019.0397

    ISBN 0–86140–123–9
    ISBN 0–86140–086–0 Pbk

First published in North America in 1983 by
The Catholic University of America Press, Washington, D.C.

Library of Congress Cataloging in Publication Data

Johnston, Denis, 1901-
    Selected plays of Denis Johnston.
    (Irish drama selections; 2)
    Contents: The old lady says 'No! ' — The moon in the
    Yellow River — The golden cuckoo — [etc.]
    I. Ronsley, Joseph.   II. Title.
    III. Series.
    PR6019.0397A6   1983   822′.912   82–9443
    ISBN 0–8132–0576–X (Catholic University) AACR2
    ISBN 0–8132–0577–8 (Catholic University : pbk.)

Produced in Great Britain
Set by Grove Graphics, Tring, Herts., and printed
and bound by Billing & Son Ltd., Worcester

Contents

Introduction

DENIS JOHNSTON is a Dubliner. This has been important personally
for Johnston, a Protestant whose parents came from the North.
Unlike many of his Dublin literary and theatre contemporaries,
moreover, Johnston in his youth was relatively affluent and well-
dressed, educated and able to travel abroad, and generally had a
cosmopolitan air about him that did not endear him to some of
his less privileged and more provincial colleagues and acquain-
tances who referred to him hostilely as a 'West Briton'. In the long
run, however, his credentials as an Irishman, and especially as a
Dubliner, are unquestionable. Despite the satire in his writings (or
partly, perhaps, in light of it), and the fact that much of his active
career was spent outside the country, his devotion to Ireland is
manifest both in his work and his life, the closing speech of his
first play, *The Old Lady Says 'No!'*, being only the most lyric
expression of this devotion.

Like his father, who had chosen the Law rather than the
Ministry, Johnston disappointed his father in turn by preferring
the Theatre to the Law. 'We all disappoint our fathers,' he has
said. William Johnston, Denis's father, was a Supreme Court
Judge. His eldest son, William Denis Johnston, was born on 18
June 1901, was educated first at St. Andrew's College, Dublin, then
at Merchiston Castle, Edinburgh. He attended Christ's College,
Cambridge, from 1919 to 1923, was President of the Cambridge
Union and studied Law, graduating with a B.A. and LL.B. In
1923-24 he was Pugsley Scholar at Harvard Law School, where
he wrote his thesis for the LLM degree on 'The Implementing of
the Anglo-Irish Treaty' of 1922 under the direction of Felix
Frankfurter, later famous as a Chief Justice of the American
Supreme Court. He was called to the English and Irish Bars in
1925, and practised Law from 1926 to 1936. So he began by
pleasing rather than disappointing his father.

Even while at Harvard, however, he extended what had already been an avid interest in the Theatre. Upon his return from America he joined the Dublin Drama League which had been created to explore new and experimental dramatic forms and to produce foreign plays which were outside the Abbey's chosen domain. Here he began acting and directing, and having become acquainted with German Expressionism in London, he soon began directing expressionist plays. He discovered Expressionism, he says, along with his companion in the audience, Sean O'Casey. It appears that both Johnston and O'Casey sat down about the same time to write plays which, if not entirely expressionistic, certainly contained expressionist elements. O'Casey of course was already a highly successful playwright, *The Plough and the Stars* having just had its first tumultuous run at the Abbey, while for Johnston the newly discovered expressionist techniques were being incorporated into a first play. Both *The Old Lady Says 'No!'* and *The Silver Tassie* were rejected by the Abbey. The controversey over O'Casey's play is well known; after Johnston's play, entitled in this first version 'Shadowdance,' was submitted to Lady Gregory for judgment, it was returned to the author by the Abbey's Director, Lennox Robinson, with the words scribbled on the first page of the manuscript, 'The old lady says No.'

Yeats suggested revisions, having gone over the manuscript with some care, and secured a small subvention from the Abbey for the play's production if Johnston could get it produced elsewhere. Johnston rejected the suggested revisions, though he did revise the play considerably himself, and took it to Mícheál MacLiammòir and Hilton Edwards whose fledgling Dublin Gate Theatre was devoted to the production of original Irish plays as well as of international masterpieces. Here in 1929 the play with its new title (and with the Abbey subvention — £15) was given a production directed by Edwards, and with MacLiammòir playing 'Emmet,' which was to become nearly as established a part of the play as the script. *The Old Lady Says 'No!'* became Johnston's most popular play in Ireland and Johnston became the Gate Theatre's first notable playwright 'discovery'; essentially the same production, with MacLiammòir in the lead role, was revived periodically at the Gate for over forty years.

Johnston's next play, *The Moon in the Yellow River*, is in a more conventional realistic mode, and hence more suitable for the Abbey, where it appeared in 1931. It was later produced by the New York Theatre Guild, where it caused considerable controversy among the critics, some of whom were bewildered by the play's themes and motivations. This play has become Johnston's best known work outside Ireland. *A Bride for the Unicorn*, his third play, produced at the Gate in 1933, was even more eccentric in technique than *The Old Lady Says 'No!'*. In many ways this play, though flawed, is Johnston's most exciting work for the theatre. The play was extensively revised for publication in the 1979 edition of Johnston's *Dramatic Works*, but it is doubtful that the needed solutions were found.

Storm Song, written in 1934 and intended to be a commercial success, was in fact not very successful commercially. The play is considerably better than this would suggest, however. It is partly about film-making, and Johnston himself about this time directed a silent film version of Frank O'Connor's story 'Guests of the Nation.' *Blind Man's Buff* was written in 1936 at the urging of the German expressionist playwright Ernst Toller. The play is an adaptation, or more accurately an alteration, of Toller's *The Blind Goddess*. Johnston was reluctant to write the play, explaining to Toller that all Toller's heroes would become Johnston's villains, and the other way round, and Johnston was never happy with the result; he rewrote it almost entirely in 1956 as *Strange Occurrence on Ireland's Eye*. The Golden Cuckoo was written in 1939, and *The Dreaming Dust*, originally entitled *Weep for Polyphemus* and written for radio, in 1940.

By the mid 1930s Johnston was considered by many people to be the most brilliant and original playwright writing for the Irish stage. In 1937, however, he left the Theatre and went into broadcasting. Until this time he had been combining his law practice with playwriting and serving on the Board of Directors at the Gate. Now he was intrigued by the new medium of television, and with a place in this field as his objective, he became a features writer and director with the BBC in Belfast. Shortly afterwards, he moved to London to join the BBC Television Service. He also dropped his law practice, though in later years he has been fond of recalling the Law as his 'favorite profession.'

During World War II developmental work by the BBC in television was suspended, and Johnston became a BBC war correspondent, first in the Middle East, then, moving with the allied armies, in Italy, France, and Germany. He was imaginative and creative in this occupation as he had been in the others, being one of the first journalists to obtain news directly from the front line of action rather than from commanding generals' press releases. He made a secret and unapproved visit to Tito's partisans in Yugoslavia, and was the first correspondent to record a report from a bomber during a bombing mission. The War was for Johnston, as for many others, a crucial time in his own spiritual development, to which he gave expression in his moving book, *Nine Rivers from Jordan.*

After the war, Johnston returned to BBC television, which had now started up again in earnest, and became Head of Programmes. In 1947, finding the bureaucracy stifling, he went to the United States to become a play adapter for the New York Theatre Guild of the Air, and directed its first television programme. It was, of course, an exciting time in the new medium, when directors, producers and technicians were learning a new craft. But in 1950 Professor Curtis Canfield of Amherst College in Amherst, Massachusetts, offered Johnston a one-year term as visiting professor. Academic life evidently appealed, because for the following sixteen years he taught, first at Mount Holyoke College, then at Smith College where he was appointed Chairman of the Department of Theatre and Speech. He retired in 1967, and a few years later moved back to Ireland, but continued for several years to teach in various universities and colleges as a visiting professor. During his academic years he wrote books on Swift and Synge, directed plays for summer theatre, wrote *Tain Bo Cuallnge: A Pageant of Cuchulain* (produced under the auspices of the Irish Tourist Board in Croke Park, Dublin, as part of the Tostal Festival of 1956), two opera librettos, numerous articles and reviews, and *The Scythe and the Sunset.* Since retirement he has continued to write reviews and articles, has completed his philosophical-biographical book, *The Brazen Horn,* and revised several of his plays extensively for the 1977-79 two-volume edition of his *Dramatic Works.*

* * *

Seen in terms of realistic, narrative chronology, virtually the entire action of *The Old Lady Says 'No!'* takes place in a matter of a few moments. The play opens with a play-within-a-play, a romantic piece comprised almost entirely of fragments from sentimental and patriotic 18th and 19th century Irish verse,* and depicting the farewell of Robert Emmet to his beloved, Sarah Curran, following his abortive Rising of 1803, with his consequent apprehension by the British garrison commanding officer, Major Sirr. The historical Emmet was subsequently tried, hanged, drawn and quartered, but we never learn how far along in this sequence

* See pp. 87–89.

of events the play intends to proceed because the action is interrupted when an actor playing a British soldier is over zealous in
his part, accidentally knocking 'Emmet' unconscious. A doctor is
called from the audience, who after examining the hurt actor
departs in search of a rug with which to cover him, and returns
with it at the very end of the play. All the action taking place
between the doctor's departure and his return does so in the disoriented subconscious mind of the injured actor, who is referred to
in the text as the 'Speaker'.

Naturally, the various personages, themes, and ideals embodied
in the playlet emerge in the mind of the actor who has been
immersed in them through his role. Thus *The Old Lady Says 'No!'*
contains a basic psychological realism. And since the protagonist's
mind is disoriented, the world he perceives takes a surrealistic
form; realistic images are distorted and exaggerated as in a dream,
or for the most part in this case as in a nightmare. The romantic
ideals embodied in Emmet, who becomes their symbol, are in-
congruously interwoven with the ordinary 20th-century Dublin life
in which the actor himself exists, and are also set against the more
rational vision represented by the statue of Henry Grattan, which
in the actor's hallucinatory perception comes to life. Historically,
the risings of 1798 and 1803, for all their patriotic fervour, did
much to destroy the real progress toward Irish independence that
Grattan had achieved through painstaking, parliamentary work. It
is symbolically important that the same actor play Major Sirr and
the statue of Grattan, since together they project an essence of
opposition to Emmet's fanatic idealism. Likewise, it is important
that the same actress play Emmet's sweetheart, Sarah Curran, and
the old flower woman representing Ireland, or Cathleen ni
Houlihan, the 'Old Lady' of the title. These figures merge as the
object of Emmet's nightmarish quest, and as the femme fatale
leading her lovers to death. The purpose of the other double roles
is readily apparent. As to depicting Emmet as a play-actor, the
historical personage, as Johnston implies in his preface, actually
exists more as a romantic make-believe figure than as a real human
being in the modern imagination.

Johnston's satire in the play strikes out in all directions. But for
all his ridicule of contemporary Dublin life – its fickleness, super-
ficiality, and paucity of ideals – affection for Dublin is displayed
nevertheless, most poignantly in the Speaker's final lines. And for
all Robert Emmet's silly and destructive, sentimental and fanatic
patriotism that sacrifices human blood so easily to a personal

vision of truth, there is an inclination to admire the visionary who can dedicate himself to an ideal.

Dramatic action as portrayal of disturbed dream provides a realistic basis for use of the expressionist techniques: normal restrictions on time, space and behavior are eliminated since the audience's perspective is the disoriented one of the Speaker's hallucinatory condition; special theatrical effects of music, light, and shifting scenes interrupt or are interwoven with dialogue, and convey a sense of disturbed and fragmented thought processes; and the characters lose their realistic individual identities, becoming stylized types or symbols, an abstraction actually begun with the highly artificial dialogue of the opening playlet. But Johnston eliminates the ponderous, humourless atmosphere characteristic of the German expressionists, while sounding echoes of Strindberg's *A Dream Play* and of the other plays mentioned by the author in his preface. There is probably more influence of Joyce than Johnston admits, *Ulysses* rather than *Finnegans Wake*, especially the 'Circe' episode, and the counterpoint of the salon scene at the beginning of Part II was inspired by the second act of O'Casey's *The Plough and the Stars*. Of course it is important that the audience be familiar with Yeats's little play, *Cathleen ni Houlihan*, which inspired much of Johnston's satire.

For all its topicality, *The Old Lady Says 'No!'* deals with universal themes, and with a few programme notes should be accessible to audiences everywhere.

While *The Old Lady Says 'No!'* has been Johnston's most popular play in Ireland, *The Moon in the Yellow River* has received most attention abroad. *The Old Lady* can be set nowhere but in Dublin, in spite of the universality of its themes; *The Moon in the Yellow River*, while its setting suggests the Liffey or the Shannon, and while a generally Irish atmosphere and historical condition prevails, deals with issues that are more immediately universal: conflicting visions of the quality of life, a simple, apparently basic need of certain temperaments for a cause to which they can devote themselves, and the difficulty of choosing between subjective, idealistic vision and objective, practical action.

Darrell Blake, like Robert Emmet, is an impractical, romantic idealist who is personally attractive, even inspiring, but whose obsession with his own truths leads to death and destruction. Tausch is a good-natured and rational man, cultured and enlightened, but is in his own way just as limited in his vision as Blake; he is too myopic to see that an absolute devotion even to reason can lead to catastrophe, and his self-righteous good intentions consequently do not take into account the inevitable conclusions of his own logic. The play is neither primarily about politics, then, nor about the advantages and disadvantages of industrial progress, but about human behaviour, about people's dreams and their responses to other people's dreams. Tausch dreams of scientific and industrial advances making life more comfortable for the people, Blake of a green arcadia unmarred by industrial blight.

Dobelle, too, once had a dream. Given a willingness to accept the subjective realities that people generally, and especially the characters in the play, inhabit, it is not difficult for the audience to understand Dobelle's present cynicism, and to feel compassion for him. Blanaid, who for her father is a symbol of his own harsh awakening, has needs which evoke more ready sympathy however, further enhanced perhaps by her charm. The reconciliation of father and daughter at the end of the play has been viewed by some critics as too melodramatic, but I believe this response depends largely on the individual performance.

Not without ideals himself, Commandant Lanigan says things of which Johnston himself morally disapproves, and is certainly not a likeable character. The characters in a play, Johnston would say, take on lives of their own. They must be let to speak for themselves, and if the playwright does not like what they say or do he may invent another character to contradict them, but he should not impose upon them himself. For all his dislike, however, Johnston cannot deny the rightness of Lanigan's logic. But an absolute devotion to logic, by Lanigan or by Tausch, does not count for wisdom, and in certain circumstances can be as lethal as Blake's pursuit of his illusions, his attempt to embrace 'the moon in the Yellow River.' Johnston's plays may sometimes appear bewildering as to his character's motivations, and to the issues of right and wrong – which side the audience is supposed to be on – because of the very profundity of his human realism.

If we are uncertain whether to be on the side of Robert Emmet, in his idealistic but death-serving conflict with a 20th-century Irish populous of bourgeois values without ideals, or of Darrell Blake in his conflict with 'progress,' stable government, and the good-natured Tausch, there can be no question that our full sympathy lies in *The Golden Cuckoo* with Mr Dotheright (whose name is intended to combine 'do-the-right' with 'dithery,' pronunciation being somewhere between the two), for all the questionableness of his sanity. His very madness, of course, embodies a profound sagacity in a well-established literary tradition of enlightened madness; most obvious is the echo of Shaw's Saint Joan.

The Golden Cuckoo was extensively revised by Johnston for the 1979 edition of his *Dramatic Works* (vol. II). The most important of several changes was the introduction of the little boy, who Johnston felt was needed to reflect the sensibilities of the audience, somewhat, he has said, as Blanaid does in *The Moon in the Yellow River*. But the little boy, I believe, is not an integral part of the play, as Blanaid is, and injects a clever but irrelevant and distracting element. A further revision was made in the name of realism (thereby, it would seem, being at cross-purposes with the introduction of the little boy), because instead of the 'cock' laying an egg at the end of the play, as it does in the earlier version, Johnston has the little boy, in a rather slapstick gesture, crack the egg over Paddy's head. The element of fantasy in this otherwise realistic but high-spirited play did not spoil the mood, and in fact was compatible with the fine strain of madness with which the realism of the play is infused. The version of the play I prefer, then, is that of the Jonathan Cape edition of 1954, but the one included in this volume is that of the 1979 edition of the *Dramatic Works*, representing the final intention of the author.

The Old Lady Says 'No!' is written essentially in a surrealistic mode using various expressionist techniques, *The Moon in the Yellow River* and *The Golden Cuckoo* are primarily realistic, though the realism of the latter is delicately touched with fantasy. *The Dreaming Dust* combines several modes. A group of dramatic players enters St. Patrick's Cathedral in Dublin just after performing a masque of 'The Seven Deadly Sins,' and at a time coinciding with the replacement of the skulls of Swift and Stella in their tomb beneath the church floor, from which they had been removed to allow for repair of the church's foundation, and at the same time, conveniently, to be examined by a group of phrenologists then meeting in Dublin. It is not surprising that a discussion begins about the characters of Swift and Stella, and Vanessa. The present Dean of St. Patrick's arrives amidst debate on the subject, and inspired by the troubled spirit of Swift which pervades the place, he suggests that the group dramatise Swift's life in relation to the two women, each scene according to the notion of one of the players, and corresponding to the 'deadly sin' he or she represents. Thus the audience is engaged alternately on two levels of reality, that of the players as they argue over their conflicting theories, and that of the dramatised segments of Swift's life. But the pattern is further

14

complicated in each of the scenes by the symbolic emphasis pro-
jected in the view of the player dominating, and by the different sin
which characterises Swift's actions in each scene. It is remarkable
how quickly and fully, in a good production, the audience can be
engaged in a short scene begun abruptly and to be cut off just as
abruptly by conversation of the players, and replaced by another,
set at a different time and place. What emerges cumulatively is a
poignant drama of Jonathan Swift, an heroically brilliant figure
tragic in his humanity, and of the two women not simply as
adjuncts to Swift, but as human beings in their own right.

The Dreaming Dust followed two other plays about Swift
written and produced in Ireland, The Earl of Longford's *Yahoo* of
1933 and Yeats's *The Words Upon the Window-Pane* of 1934,
both of which contain non-realistic elements. Johnston objected,
among other things, to the biographical assumptions in both plays,
though they are different from each other. His own extensive
scholarly pursuit of the subject was begun before but extended
after he wrote the first version of *The Dreaming Dust*, and resulted
in the intriguing biographical study *In Search of Swift*, published in
1959, a book confirming the biographical thesis of the play. It
should be read by anyone seriously interested in the dramatic
work.

Uncertainty as to the favorable side of the dramatic conflict is
as pronounced in *The Scythe and the Sunset*, Johnston's play deal-
ing with the Rising of 1916, as in any of the plays. Johnston is
quite even-handed in presenting the arguments of the two principal
rivals, Tetley representing the Irish rebels, and Palliser representing
the British Empire. Tetley shares both the attractiveness and the
shortcomings of his dramatic predecessors Emmet and Blake, possibly even of Dotheright. Palliser evokes certain biographical
associations with Johnston, but this fact hardly protects the
dramatic character from the author's satire. On the whole, the
strengths and weaknesses of both sides as described by Johnston
in his preface are developed dramatically in the play. Whereas
characters and issues associated with the rebel cause are objects
of mockery and ridicule in the first act, the audience is gradually
shifted in its attitude toward sympathy and respect as the play
progresses, its focus of attention correspondingly moving from
Roisin and Dr. MacCarthy to Tetley and Palliser. Thus, as in
all the plays, lively comedy verges on issues that are deadly
serious. The result is an artful exploration of the human need to
discover truths, and of the consequences of too full a commitment

15

to them once they are found, a universal theme running through most of Johnston's plays and in this case using the Easter Rising for symbolic purposes, as both Yeats and O'Casey had used it.

Johnston mentions in his preface that Tetley bears a certain resemblance to Pearse. It should also be noted that there is a similar resemblance between the character Williams and the historical James Connolly, between O'Callaghan and Plunkett, and between Emer and Constance Markievicz. There is also a resemblance between Dr. MacCarthy and Dr. Oliver St. John Gogarty, and Endymion is a real-life character celebrated by Gogarty in the opening pages of *As I Was Going Down Sackville Street* and by Joyce as Cashel Boyle O'Connor Fitzmaurice Tisdall Farrell in *Ulysses*. Endymion, the sagacious fool, functions in the play as a kind of Greek chorus reporting and commenting on events.

While it is to be expected that the reader will disagree with some of the views Johnston expresses in his prefaces, these prefaces on the whole should be taken quite seriously. Like Shaw's, they are witty and satiric, but their intention is to express genuine viewpoints, and they can be quite useful to a fuller understanding of the plays. Johnston's plays tend to make substantial intellectual demands upon their audiences, but though the modes in which they are written are quite diverse, as this collection attests, they are all highly theatrical in the best sense. All make extensive use of rich dialogue, whether comic or serious, sometimes verging on poetry; the characters are for the most part convincing and appealing and are psychologically realistic; the plays are visually interesting and sometimes downright exciting; and the issues are handled with extraordinary sensitivity and with a sincerity that often does not allow for the easy answers that contribute to popularity.

Joseph Ronsley

THE OLD LADY
SAYS 'NO!'

*A Romantic Play in Two Parts
with Choral Interludes*

OPUS ONE

ONE of the best loved figures of Irish romantic literature is Robert Emmet. The story of his rebellion of 1803 has all of the elements that make for magic. It was very high-minded, and completely unsuccessful. It was picturesquely costumed and insufficiently organized. Its leader – a young protestant university man of excellent social background – having failed to achieve anything more than an armed street riot, remained behind to bid goodbye to his forbidden sweetheart, instead of taking flight as any sensible rebel should do. In consequence of this, he was captured by an ogre of melodrama called Major Sirr, and was hanged after making one of the finest speeches from the dock in the annals of the criminal courts – and we have had some pretty good ones in Ireland.

So we all love Robert Emmet. Yeats and De Valera loved him, each in his own fashion. I do too; and so did Sarah Curran. Even the hoardings along the Canal have been known to display a chalked inscription, 'UP EMMET'. We all agree that it was a pity that some of his supporters had to murder one of the most liberal judges on the bench, Lord Kilwarden, and that the only practical outcome of his affray was to confirm the Union with England for about a hundred and twenty years. Our affection is not affected by these details.

The tragedy of his love has been immortalized by Tom Moore in one of his finest ballads:

> She is far from the land
> Where her young hero sleeps,
> And lovers around her are sighing.
> But coldly she turns from their gaze, and weeps,
> For her heart in his grave is lying.

Who cares that this reason for her absence from the land is the fact that she subsequently married an English officer, and ended her days happily with him elsewhere? For us, her heart will always be lying in Robert's grave. And lying is the operative word.

19

The whole episode has got that delightful quality of story-book unreality that creates a glow of satisfaction without any particular reference to the facts of life. To put it into conflict with those facts ought to be an easy proposition in the theatre, and particularly so back in 1926, when several years of intermittent and unromantic civil war had soured us all a little towards the woes of Cathleen ni Houlihan. It was inevitable that such a play would be written in Ireland by someone or other at about that time.

Although it is by no means my favourite play, and is my only work that might fairly be described as anti-Irish, it is by far the best spoken-of in its native habitat. In Dublin it is now generally regarded as a strongly nationalistic piece, full of sound popular sentiments and provided with a title calculated to annoy Lady Gregory and the Abbey Theatre. It is true that on the occasion of its first production at the Gate, some tentative efforts were made to have me prosecuted – for what, I cannot at present remember. But those days are long past, and the only acrimony that the play evokes today is among the cast, the older members of which argue strongly during rehearsals over business and movements that were used on previous occasions, and must not now be altered.

As for the title, I cannot be held responsible for this. It was written by somebody on a sheet of paper attached to the front of the first version, when it came back to me from the Abbey. Whether it was intended to inform me that the play had been rejected, or whether it was being offered as an alternative to my own coy little name for the play – *Shadowdance* – is a question that I never liked to ask. So it remained, thereafter, as the title of the work – a definite improvement for which I have always been grateful. Lennox Robinson used to complain bitterly about any suggestion that Lady G. was against the play, but all I know of the matter is the distaste she expressed to me in the back sitting-room of her hotel in Harcourt Street. I was never invited to Gort.

It is, of course, a director's play, written very much in the spirit of 'Let's see what would happen' if we did this or that. We were tired of the conventional three-act shape, of conversational dialogue, and of listening to the tendentious social sentiments of the stage of the 'twenties, and we wanted to know whether the emotional appeal of music could be made use of in terms of theatrical prose, and an opera constructed that did not have to be sung. Could dialogue be used in lieu of some of the scenery, or as a shorthand form of character-delineation? Could the associations and thought-patterns already connected with the songs and slogans of our city be used deliberately to evoke a planned reaction from a known audience?

The opening playlet – which was felt by Lady G. to be an all-too-brief preliminary to a vein of "coarseness" that was to follow – is made up almost entirely from lines by Mangan, Moore, Ferguson, Kickham, Todhunter, and the romantic school of nineteenth-century Irish poets, still well known to everybody although no longer imitated. So too, the final speech of the play contains some easily recognizable sections of Pearse's funeral oration for O'Donovan Rossa, together with a large portion of Emmet's actual speech from the dock, which concludes:

'When my country takes her place amongst the nations of the earth, then, and not till then, let my epitaph be written.'

There are both handicaps and benefits to be derived from writing for so specialized an audience. A phrase such as 'When in the course of human events' will spontaneously call up an association-pattern when uttered in the United States, where it belongs. An Englishman, prodded with the expression 'Kiss me, Hardy', may react in a variety of ways, but some response is usually noticeable. On the other hand, outside Ireland, a reference to 'my four beautiful green fields' will not wring any withers, but becomes instead a mere literary reference that may or may not be recognized as an echo from Yeats.

Thus, although written in a language common to all three countries, *The Old Lady* is not quite the same play in London or New York as it is in Dublin. Across the sea its intentional clichés are no longer clichés, and the various daggers concealed within its lacy sentiments find no flesh into which to probe. For this reason, apart from one production in New York, a couple in London, and a few presentations in colleges with *avant garde* theatre departments, it has never been performed outside Ireland. There the pattern devised by Hilton Edwards and Micheál MacLiammóir for its first production in 1929 has become as much an integral part of the play as is the text.

Although many of its expressionist tricks are now commonplace, especially in radio production, it was, at the time of writing, a fairly original type of play, and technically it owes less to other dramatists than anything that I have written since. The play's actual foster parents are neither Evreinov, O'Neill nor Georg Kaiser. Nor has Joyce got much to do with it, although I gratefully acknowledge the presence of his finger in the stirring of some of my later

21

pies. I have once or twice been written to by students of the drama who feel that they can trace the influence of *Finnegans Wake* upon *The Old Lady*. This is a book that I first attempted to read through about ten years ago, and the only part of it that has got into my play did so by a most circuitous route. This is the *Thuartpeatrick* phrase, misspelled *St Peetrick* by me in the party scene. Its presence there is a surprising reminder that Tuohy, the artist who painted both Joyce and his old father, had sentences from Joyce's own lips that he was bandying around Dublin as early as the Nine Arts Ball of 1925. In this very second-hand condition the expression has found its way into my text, as a quotation from a section of a book that had then hardly been begun. There are, of course, two short quotes from *Ulysses* in *The Old Lady*, together with a phrase or two, such as 'Jacobs Vobiscuits'. But any resemblances to the *Wake* have nothing to do with me.

The two plays to which this experiment does owe something are, firstly, Kaufman and Connelly's *Beggar on Horseback* – a superb piece of American expressionism that I have always admired – and secondly, a Continental satire called *The Land of Many Names* that I once saw in the 'twenties. Who wrote it, and where it came from, I have often since wondered. I think it may have been one of the Capeks.

The Old Lady Says 'No!'

Cast of Characters

(in this Version)

SARAH CURRAN *and* FLOWER WOMAN*
THE SPEAKER (ROBERT EMMET)
FIRST REDCOAT *and* GENERAL*
SECOND REDCOAT
MAJOR SIRR *and* GRATTAN*
STAGE HAND *and* MINISTER FOR ARTS AND CRAFTS*
DOCTOR
BLIND MAN
CHORUS: VOICES AND FORMS, NEWSBOYS, PASSER-BY, BUS MAN, FLAPPER, MEDICAL, WELL-DRESSED WOMAN, BUSINESSMAN, CARMEL, BERNADETTE, AN OLDER MAN, TWO TOUTS, HANDSHAKERS, YOUNGER MAN, A MAN, SECOND MAN, JOE, MAEVE, LADY TRIMMER, O'COONEY, O'MOONEY, O'ROONEY, MINISTER'S WIFE, HE, SHE.
FIRST SHADOW, SECOND SHADOW, THIRD SHADOW, FOURTH SHADOW.

* Both characters to be played by the same performer.

The action of the play opens in the garden of The Priory, the home of John Philpot Curran, close to Rathfarnham (now a suburb of Dublin), on the night of August 25th, 1803.

This play was first produced by the Dublin Gate Theatre Studio at the Peacock Theatre on July 3rd, 1929, with the following cast:

The Speaker (Robert Emmet)	MICHEÁL MACLIAMMÓIR
Sarah Curran	MERIEL MOORE
Major Sirr	HILTON EDWARDS
First Redcoat	JOHANN MANNING
Second Redcoat	MITCHELL COGLEY

The Other Ones: GEARÓID O'LOCHLAIN, CORALIE CARMICHAEL, MICHAEL SCOTT, DOROTHY CASEY, FRED JOHNSON, HAZEL ELLIS, DUDLEY WALSH, FLORENCE LYNCH, ART O'MURNAGHAN, IDA MOORE, DOM. BOWE, KAY SCANNELL, PAULINE BESSON, SUSAN HUNT, SHEILA CAREY.

The play produced and lit by Hilton Edwards; the settings designed and executed by Micheál MacLiammóir; costumes designed by Micheál MacLiammóir and made up by Bougwaine Wilson.

PART ONE

To the left the dark gable of a building can be seen with a light burning behind the blind in the first-floor window. It is the house of John Philpot Curran, The Priory, close to Rathfarnham, a village outside Dublin. To the centre and to the right are the trees of the garden, and behind them the profile of Kilmashogue and the hills beyond. It is the night of August 25th in the year 1803, and the sound of men's voices is dying away into the distance as the Curtain rises.

VOICES.

> With their pikes in good repair,
> > Says the Shan Van Vocht,
> To the Curragh of Kildare
> The boys they will repair,
> And Lord Edward will be there,
> > Says the Shan Van Vocht.

(*The window opens and* SARAH CURRAN *gazes out towards the mountains.*)

SARAH.

The air is rich and soft – the air is mild and bland.
Her woods are tall and straight, grove rising over grove.
Trees flourish in her glens below and on her heights above,
Oh, the fair hills of Eire, oh.
Down from the high cliffs the rivulet is teeming
To wind around the willow banks that lure him from above.
Ah, where the woodbines with sleepy arms have wound him . . .
(*She starts.*)
Who is there? I heard a rustling in the trees!
Who is there, I say?

(*The* SPEAKER *emerges from among the trees. He is dressed as Robert Emmet in a green tunic, white-plumed hat, white*

25

breeches and Wellington boots with gold tassels. At his side hangs a large cavalry sword.)

SPEAKER (*with an appropriate gesture*). Hush beloved, it is I.

SARAH. Robert! I think, oh my love, 'tis thy voice from the kingdom of souls!

SPEAKER. Was ever light of beauty shed on loveliness like thine!

SARAH. Oh, Robert, Robert, why have you ventured down? You are in danger.

SPEAKER. My bed was the ground, my roof the greenwood above: and the wealth that I sought, one far, kind glance from my love.

SARAH. My love, for a vision of fanciful bliss to barter thy calm life of labour and peace!

SPEAKER. What matters life! Deirdre is mine: she is my queen, and no man now can rob me!

SARAH. The redcoats are everywhere. Last night they were around the house and they will come again.

SPEAKER. Let them come! A million a decade! Let me be persuaded that my springing soul may meet the eagle on the hills, and I am free.

SARAH. Ah, go, forget me. Why should sorrow o'er that brow a shadow fling?

SPEAKER. My strong ones have fallen from the bright eye of day. Their graves are red, but their souls are with God in glory.

SARAH. Ah, love, love! Where is thy throne? It is gone in the wind!

SPEAKER. A dark chain of silence is thrown o'er the deep. No streak of dawning is in the sky. It is still unriven, that clanking chain. Yet, am I the slave they say?

SARAH. A lost dream to us now in our home! Ullagone! Gall to our heart!

SPEAKER. But there is lightning in my blood – red lightning tightening in my blood! Oh, if there was a sword in every Irish hand! If there was a flame in every Irish heart to put an end to slavery and shame! Oh, I would end these things!

SARAH. It is too late! Large, large affliction unto me and mine, that one of his majestic bearing, his fair and stately form, should thus be tortured and o'erborne – that this unsparing storm should wreak its wrath on head like this!

SPEAKER (*softly*). My earthly comforter, whose love so indefeasible might be! Your holy, delicate, white hands shall girdle me with steel. You'll pray for me, my flower of flowers! You'll think of me through daylight hours, my virgin flower!

SARAH. At least I'll love thee till I die.

26

SPEAKER. How long, ah, Sarah, can I say how long my life will last?

SARAH. Cease boding doubt, my gentlest love; be hushed that struggling sigh.

SPEAKER. When he who adores thee has left but a name, ah say, wilt thou weep?

SARAH. I shall not weep. I shall not breathe his name. For my heart in his grave will be lying. I shall sing a lament for the Sons of Usnach.

SPEAKER. But see, she smiles, she smiles! Her rosy mouth dimples with hope and joy; her dewy eyes are full of pity!

SARAH. Ah, Robert, Robert, come to me.

SPEAKER (*climbing up*). I have written my name in letters of fire across the page of history. I have unfurled the green flag in the streets and cried aloud from the high places to all the people of the Five Kingdoms: 'Men of Eire, awake to be blest! Rise, Arch of the Ocean and Queen of the West!' I have dared all for Ireland and I will dare all again for Sarah Curran. Ah, it is a glorious thing to dare!

(*He is about to touch her outstretched hand when – *)

A VOICE. Halt! Who goes there?

SARAH. Ah God! The yeomen!

VOICES. The countersign.
      Stand.
      Front point.
      Advance.

SPEAKER. The flint-hearted Saxon!

(*He makes a gesture to her. She disappears and the light goes out.*)

SARAH. . . . in their fearful red array!

FIRST REDCOAT (*rushing forward*). Hold! Surrender or I fire!

SECOND REDCOAT. We hold this house for our lord the King.

FIRST REDCOAT. Amen, says I. May all traitors swing.

SPEAKER. (*springing down and folding his arms*). Slaves and dastards, stand aside!

(MAJOR SIRR enters.)

SIRR. Spawn of treason, bow down thy humbled head to him, the King!

SPEAKER. A nation's voice, a nation's voice, 'tis stronger than the King.

SIRR. Silence rebel! Do you not know who I am?

SPEAKER. A jackal of the Pale.

27

SIRR. Major Sirr.

SPEAKER. Who trapped Lord Edward?

SIRR. The same.

SPEAKER (*drawing his sword*). I am honoured. Ireland will remember. Look well to your soul, Major Sirr, for the dawn of the Gael is still to break; when they that are up will be down and they that are down will be up. I tell you, Major Sirr, we'll be a glorious nation yet – redeemed, erect, alone!

(*He leaps upon them. One of the* REDCOATS *clubs his musket and strikes him a resounding blow upon the head. The lights flicker momentarily and he lies still.* SARAH CURRAN *appears once more at the window.*)

SARAH. A star is gone! There is a blank in heaven. The last great tribune of the world is dead.

SIRR (*seemingly a little surprised*).

The sport of fools – the scoff of knaves,

Dead ere they blossomed, barren, blighted.

They came, whose counsels wrapped the land in foul rebellion's flame,

Their hearts unchastened by remorse, their cheeks untinged by shame,

To sue for a pity they shall not – shall not –

Er –

(*One of the* REDCOATS *kneels beside the* SPEAKER *and shakes him by the shoulder.* SIRR *looks helplessly into the wings from which he receives a whispered prompt.*)

PROMPT. Find.

FIRST REDCOAT. Ay!

SECOND REDCOAT. What's up?

SIRR (*to the wings*). Curtain . . . curtain . . . I say.

STAGE HAND. Is he hurted?

VOICES. He's hurt. Hurt. He's hurt. Hurted.

FIRST REDCOAT. It wasn't my fault. I only . . .

SIRR. Curtain, please. Do stand back for a moment and give him a chance.

VOICES. Loosen his collar. What do you think you're doing? How did it happen? What's the matter? He'll be all right. Give him brandy. Take those boots off. Stand back, please. Did you see the skelp he gave him? Can I help?

(*The Curtain comes jerkily down and there is a heavy tramping behind upon the stage. Presently* SIRR *comes through the Curtain. House lights up.*)

28

SIRR (*beckoning to someone in the audience*). Is there a doctor in ... I say ... can you?

DOCTOR. Me?

SIRR. Just come through for a minute. I think he'll be all right.

DOCTOR. It looked a heavy enough ...

SIRR. I don't think it is ...

DOCTOR. ... blow from the front.

SIRR. ... very serious, really.

DOCTOR. I hope not. Anyhow you had better see whether you can't ...

(*They disappear through the Curtain, talking. Presently* SIRR *re-appears.*)

SIRR. Ladies and gentlemen ... he ... er ... the doctor would like the curtain up again ... the draught blows through from the scene dock when it's across. We're really very sorry that the performance should be held up ... but you see ... it's nothing really ... He ... er ... says he will be all right in a moment if he's kept quiet and not moved ... if you would only be so good as to keep your seats and stay perfectly quiet for a few moments ... just a few moments ... while the doctor is ... er ... busy ... I'm sure we'll be able to go on ... if you don't mind ... curtain please ... quite quiet please ... just for a few minutes ... thank you so much.

(*He hurries off. The Curtain is slowly drawn again, disclosing the* SPEAKER *where we left him, now attended by the* DOCTOR, *the* STAGE HAND *and one of the* REDCOATS. *A black gauze curtain has been drawn behind him through which we can see dim figures moving about and hear the thumping of heavy weights.*)

DOCTOR. That's better now. Can you get them off?

STAGE HAND. Yes, sir. They're coming now.

(*He draws off one of the* SPEAKER'S *boots.*)

REDCOAT. How could I know anyway? It wasn't my fault. I tell you I only ...

DOCTOR. That's all right. Hold up his head a little. That's better. Oh, they've got it up.

(*He refers to the Curtain.*)

REDCOAT. Ah, God, isn't it awful!

DOCTOR. Ask those people to keep quiet there while he's coming round.

STAGE HAND. Ay, Barnie, tell them to shut up! Give us a hand with this boot. I can't get a grip on it at all.

29

REDCOAT. I don't know how it could have happened at all. You pull now.

STAGE HAND. Ah, will you hold on? How the hell . . .

DOCTOR. Sssssh!

STAGE HAND. There she comes.

DOCTOR. See if you can get something to cover his legs with. He must be kept warm. And ask them to turn down that light a bit. He'll be all right soon if he's kept quiet and allowed to come round.

(The STAGE HAND *goes out obligingly.)*

REDCOAT. I swear to God I hit him no harder than I was shown yesterday. I only . . . look . . .

DOCTOR. Ah, be quiet you, and be off. You're more of a hindrance than a help.

REDCOAT. It's all very well blaming me, but I only did what I was shown bef . . .

DOCTOR. Sssssss!

(The REDCOAT *goes off muttering protestations. The lights are dimmed, making the forms behind the gauze clearer still. Presently the* STAGE HAND *enters with a pair of gaudy carpet slippers.)*

STAGE HAND. Would these be any use? They were all I could find. They belong to Mr . . . er . . .

DOCTOR. He's stirring a little.

(He examines the SPEAKER *while the* STAGE HAND *puts the slippers on his feet.)*

STAGE HAND. Is the lights O.K. now?

DOCTOR. What's that? Oh, fine. You'd better . . .

STAGE HAND. I brought a sup of brandy.

DOCTOR. Brandy! Good heavens, no! He has a slight concussion.

STAGE HAND. Is that a fact? A what?

DOCTOR. But I tell you what. Go and see if you can manage to get a little ice.

STAGE HAND *(dubiously)*. An ice?

DOCTOR. Yes. You know. In a basin of cold water. For a compress.

STAGE HAND. Oh, for a . . . Oh I see.

(He goes out slowly.)

DOCTOR. And . . . *(He notices the slippers.)* My God, what are those? I told you to bring something for his legs. Do you hear? A rug. *(He rises and crosses).* Has anybody got a rug? *(He goes off and his voice is heard faintly.)* A rug for his legs. Ah, thanks so much. That will . . .

30

(*Silence. The figures behind the Curtain have ceased to move and are clustered in a silent group peering through towards the spot where the* SPEAKER *is lying. Presently the latter stirs and his lips begin to move. There is a dim and distant boom-boom-boom as of someone tapping on a big drum. The lights pulse.*)

SPEAKER. Redeemious . . . Oh . . . be a redeemious . . . re . . . warmest core I said . . . we'll (*He opens his eyes and stares weakly ahead.*) . . . I love thee . . . love thee bosom my head bosom my head's all . . . Oh, God! (*There is a pause while he stares out into the auditorium.*) They that are down will be down . . . down . . . up . . . erect . . . redeemiable . . . love thee, Sarah . . . redeemiablecurran . . . I see you. (*Pause – then with a great effort*) I am the Speaker . . . Deadbosom I see you.

THE FORMS (*answering on behalf of the audience with unctuous friendliness*).

A.	Quirke	present
B.	Quinn	present
C.	Foley	present
D.	Byrne	present
E.	Ryan	present
F.	Carrol	present
G.	Lynch	present
H.	Dwyer	present
I.	Burke	present
J.	Farrell	present
K.	Gleeson	present
L.	Mooney	present
M.	Quigley	present

SPEAKER (*holding up his hand peremptorily*). Stop! (*Pause. He bows solemnly.*) Thank you.

THE FORMS (*whispering in rhythm*).

Poor poor poor poor
Hit him hit him
With a gun
Butt end butt end
Dirty dirty
Give him water
For a compress
Calf's foot jelly
Fever fever
Ninety-nine point ninety ninety

31

Fahrenheit Centigrade
Centigrade Fahrenheit
Very unsettled unsettled unsettled
Take his boots off
Milk and soda
Patrick Dun's and
Cork Street Mater
Adelaide and
Vincent's Elpis
Baggot Street and
Mercer's Meath and
Is he better?
How's the headache?
Ambulance ambulance
S.O.S.
S.O.S. S.O.S.
Tut tut tut tut
Tut tut tut tut
Poor poor poor poor . . .

SPEAKER (*with an impatient flap of his hand*). Slaves and dastards stand aside, a nation's voice . . . nation's voice is stronger than a Speaker . . . I am an honoured gloriable nationvoice your Sirrflinthearted Saxons . . . Oh! . . . if it would only stop going round . . . round . . . round . . . up . . . down . . . up will be down . . . O God, I am the Unspeakerable.

THE FORMS (*relentlessly*).
On with the performance
Programmes Tenpence
No Smoking
Spitting Coughing
Nobody admitted
Till after the Performance
After nine
Point ninety ninety
For further particulars
Apply to the Manager
N.   Moore
O.   Callan
Q.   O'Reilly
R.   Donovan
S.   Muldoon

SPEAKER (*with the rhythm*). Yes . . . yes . . . yes . . . yes . . .

THE FORMS.

> T. Cosgrave
> U. O'Toole
> V. Kelly
> W. Fogarty

SPEAKER.

Red lightning tightening through my blood
Red tightening lightning tightening through my blood
My tightening blood . . .

> (*The voices are merged in a clanking, shrieking concatenation that swells up . . . the throb of petrol engines, the hoot of motor horns, the rattle and pounding of lorries, and, above all, the cry of the newsboys.*)

NEWSBOYS.

> Hegler Press
> Late Buff Hegler Press
> Weekly Honesty
> Hegler Press

SPEAKER. (*commencing to act again, at the top of his voice*). Their graves are red but their souls are with God in glory. A dark chain of silence is thrown o'er the deep. Silence . . . silence I say. O Ireland, Ireland, it is still unriven, that clanking chain . . . still unriven. O Ireland, Ireland, no streak of dawning is in the sky.

> (*As he has been declaiming the crowd breaks up and passes to and fro as in the street. The gauze parts. Headlights of motor cars. A policeman with a white baton is directing the traffic, while behind him upon a pedestal stands* GRATTAN *with arm outstretched. He has the face of* MAJOR SIRR.)

SPEAKER (*now in the midst of the traffic.*) Men of Eire, awake to be blest! Do you hear? (*He fiercely accosts a* PASSER-BY.) Do you hear? Awake!

PASSER-BY (*politely disengaging himself*). Sorry. The banks close at half two.

SPEAKER. At the loud call of freedom why don't they awake? Come back! . . . Rise Arch of the Ocean . . . Let me be persuaded that my springing soul may meet the eagle on the hills . . . the hills . . . the hills . . . I say . . . (*He shouts.*) I say! Look here!

> (*The* STAGE HAND *enters with the script.*)

STAGE HAND. What's the trouble?

SPEAKER. The hills!

STAGE HAND. What hills?

SPEAKER. Yes, what hills? Where?

STAGE HAND. Where's which?

SPEAKER. Don't be so stupid. You know I must have them. The eagle on the . . .

STAGE HAND. Did the Artistic Director say you were to have hills?

SPEAKER. I don't know what you mean. I can't go on like this. This is not right.

STAGE HAND. Well it's the first I heard of it. Wait now till I get the place.

SPEAKER. Down from the high cliff the rivulet is teeming. Go away! Be off!

STAGE HAND. Where had you got to?

SPEAKER. Not very far. I was with Sarah. She was up there. I was talking to her.

STAGE HAND (*producing a dirty programme*). Scene One. Wait now till I see. Who did you say you were?

SPEAKER. Robert Emmet. See there.

STAGE HAND. Oh is that you? I thought I rekernized the unyform.

SPEAKER. 'The action of the play opens in the garden of "The Priory", the home of John Philpot Curran close to Rathfarnham.' You see. This is not Rathfarnham.

STAGE HAND. No. I suppose not.

SPEAKER. I can't go on here. Can't you stop this noise?

STAGE HAND. Well you know I'd be glad to do all I can, but . . . well, you see, it's all very well telling me now.

SPEAKER. The air is rich and soft, the air is mild and bland, her woods are tall and straight, grove rising over grove . . .

STAGE HAND. Yes, I know, but I don't know what I can do. You should have told me sooner. You see the shops is all shut now . . .

SPEAKER. And Sarah . . . Sarah Curran is gone too. Clear all this away!

STAGE HAND. Ay, you can't touch that! That's wanted for the dancing class.

SPEAKER. Stop them! My play! Rathfarnham!

STAGE HAND. Ah you know I'm doing my best for you. But as a matter of fact I have to be off now.

SPEAKER. Off where?

STAGE HAND. I'm due at my Irish class this half hour.

SPEAKER. And what am I to do?

STAGE HAND. Ah sure aren't you doing well enough. You're very particular all of a sudden.

34

SPEAKER. Come back, damn you!

STAGE HAND. Ah, they won't know the difference. It's good enough for that gang. Ta-ta now or I'll be late.

SPEAKER. Stop! You must tell me . . .

STAGE HAND. You'll get a Rathfarnham bus over there at the corner. Goodbye-ee!

(*He goes.*)

SPEAKER. Here! Oh my head! At the corner where? Rathfarnham.

BUS MAN. Rathfarnham bus. No. 17 Rathfarnham. Step along now please.

SPEAKER. Are you going to Rathfarnham?

BUS MAN. This bus's full. Full, I tell ya. You'll have to wait for the next.

SPEAKER. Nonsense . . . there's lots of room. See . . .

BUS MAN. The bus's full. D'ye want to get me into trouble? Let go the bar now there's room for no more here. There'll be another along behind.

SPEAKER. I tell you there's nobody there.

(*Ding Ding Ding.*)

BUS MAN. Fares please. (*And he moves off mysteriously*).

SPEAKER. There's nobody there! Liar! Cheat! You're all a lot of . . . a lot of . . . I shall speak to the stage manager about . . . (*His voice breaks.*) Oh my head! I wish I wasn't so tired. I wish I wasn't so terribly tired!

(*He sinks down upon something in the centre of the stage. The passers-by thin out and the noise dies away, first into a low hum and then into complete silence. There is nobody left but the figure of* GRATTAN *and an old tattered* FLOWER WOMAN *in a black straw hat who sits crouching at the base of the pedestal.*)

SPEAKER (*mumbling*). My bed was the ground – my way the greenwood above, and the wealth I sought . . . I sought . . . the wealth . . . Oh, what is it?

GRATTAN. How long, O Lord, how long?

(*Pause.*)

SPEAKER (*without looking round*). What was that?

GRATTAN. This place stifles me. The thick, sententious atmosphere of this little hell of babbling torment! Sometimes the very breath seems to congeal in my throat and I can scarce keep from choking.

SPEAKER (*nodding gravely*). I might have known it.

WOMAN. Penny a bunch th' violets.

35

GRATTAN. God forgive me, but it is hard sometimes. Very hard.

SPEAKER. All the same I will not allow this. It is the voice of Major Sirr. It is not my part.

GRATTAN. Your part? Ah yes! More play-acting. Go on, go on.

SPEAKER. I am Robert Emmet and I . . .

GRATTAN. A young man playing Robert Emmet! Yes, yes, they all come here.

SPEAKER. I am Robert Emmet. I have written my name in letters of fire across the page of history. I have unfurled the green flag . . .

GRATTAN. Letters of fire?

SPEAKER. Their graves are red but their souls . . .

GRATTAN. Ah yes, the graves are red . . . the grave of one poor helpless old man, the justest judge in Ireland . . . dragged from his coach by the mob and slaughtered in the road.

SPEAKER. Kilwarden!

GRATTAN. Kilwarden's grave is red.

SPEAKER. Who said that? I did my best to save him, but the people were mad . . .

GRATTAN. 'Let no man perish in consequence of my death,' he cried, as his lifeblood stained the cobbles crimson . . .

SPEAKER. . . . . maddened by long centuries of oppression and injustice. I did my best to save him. What more could I do?

GRATTAN. 'Let no man perish, save by the regular operation of the laws.' And with that, pierced by a dozen patriot pikes, he died, at the feet of his gallant countrymen.

SPEAKER. It was horrible. But it was war.

GRATTAN. Eighty tattered turncocks from the Coombe; a plumed hat, and a silver sword. War, for the liberation of Erin!

WOMAN. Me four bewtyful gre-in fields. Me four bewtyful gre-in fields.

SPEAKER. Men of Eire, awake to be blest!

GRATTAN. The full long years of my life I gave for her, with the harness weighing on my shoulders and my heart bleeding for my country's woes.

SPEAKER. Rise, Arch of the Ocean!

GRATTAN. Full fifty years I worked and waited, only to see my country's new-found glory melt away at the bidding of the omniscient young Messiahs with neither the ability to work nor the courage to wait.

SPEAKER. I have the courage to go on.

GRATTAN. Oh, it is an easy thing to draw a sword and raise a barricade. It saves working, it saves waiting. It saves everything

36

but blood! And blood is the cheapest thing the good God has made.

WOMAN. Two apples a penny. Penny a bunch th' gre-in fields.

SPEAKER. Listen! Something is telling me that I must go on. I must march proudly through to the final act. Look! (*Pointing.*) The people are waiting for me, watching me.

GRATTAN. Fool, fool, strutting upon the stage! Go out, into the cold night air, before you crucify yourself in the blind folly of your eternal play-acting.

SPEAKER (*to the audience*). He is an old man. He does not understand the way we do. He can only doubt . . . while we believe . . . believe with heart and soul and every fibre of our tired bodies. Therefore I am not afraid to go on. I will kiss my wounds in the last act. I will march proudly through, head high, even if it must be to my grave. That is the only test.

GRATTAN. Ah, the love of death, creeping like a mist at the heels of my countrymen! Death is the only art in which we own no masters. Death is the only voice that can be heard in this distressful land where no man's word is taken, no man's message heeded, no man's prayer answered except it be his epitaph. Out into every quarter of the globe we go, seeking for a service in which to die: saving the world by dying for a good cause just as readily as we will damn it utterly by dying for a bad one. It is all the same to us. It is the only thing that we can understand.

(*The* WOMAN *laughs shortly and shrilly and breaks into a wheezy cough.*)

SPEAKER. What is that woman doing here?

WOMAN. God bless ye, lovely gentleman, spare a copper for a cuppa tea. Spare a copper for yer owin old lady, for when th' trouble is on me I must be talkin' te me friends.

GRATTAN. A copper, lovely gentleman, for your own old lady.

SPEAKER. Go away! There is something horrible about your voice.

GRATTAN.
 Young she is, and fair she is
 And would be crowned a Queen.

SPEAKER. What can I do in this place? I can't even remember my lines!

WOMAN. Yer lines, ducky. Ay Jack, pull them up on ye!

SPEAKER. I must go back to Rathfarnham. They will understand there.

GRATTAN. A shadowy land has appeared.

SPEAKER. Sally!

GRATTAN.
> Men thought it a region of Sunshine and Rest,
> And they called it 'Rathfarnham', the Land of the Blest.

SPEAKER. Oh if the will had wings, how fast I'd fly to the home of my heart!

GRATTAN. Poor weary footsore fool. And we are all the same, every one of us, whether we look to the foreigner for our sovereign or for our salvation. All of us fit to lead, and none of us fit to serve.

SPEAKER.
> If wishes were power, if words were spells,
> I'd be this hour where my true love dwells!

GRATTAN. Driven blindly on by the fury of our spurious moral courage! Is there to be no rest for Ireland from her soul? What monstrous blasphemy has she committed to be condemned to drift for ever like the wandering Jew after a Heaven that can never be?

WOMAN (*crooning softly to herself*).
> She's a darlin', she's a daisy,
> She has all the neighbours crazy,
> And she's arrums an' legs upon her like a man.
> But no matter where she goes,
> Sure everybody knows
> That she's Mick Magilligan's daughter, Mary Ann.

GRATTAN. In my day Dublin was the second city of a mighty Empire. What is she now?

SPEAKER. No! No!

GRATTAN (*with unutterable scorn*). Free!
> (*He bursts into a wild peal of laughter.*)

SPEAKER. You are lying! It is the voice of Major Sirr! You are trying to torment me . . . torture me . . . Ghosts out of Hell, that's what you are.
> (*The figures are blotted out by black curtains which sweep across behind the* SPEAKER, *entrapping him in their folds.*)

SPEAKER. But I'm not afraid! Heads up! One allegiance only! Robert Emmet is not afraid! I know what I want and I'm going on. (*Feverishly fumbling with the folds.*)
> God save Ireland cried the heroes,
> God save Ireland cry we all,
> Whether on the scaffold high –
> Whether on the scaffold high
> The scaffold high . . . !

Come out! Come out! Where are you? Oh, where am I? Come

out! I . . . can't . . . remember . . . my lines . . . !

(*An old blind man, tap-tapping with his stick, passes slowly across the stage, a mug outstretched and a fiddle under his arm.*)

SPEAKER. If only I could get through. Where's the way through?

(*A* FLAPPER *and a* TRINITY MEDICAL *appear.*)

FLAPPER. No, I don't like the floor there, the Metropole's much better. As for that Buttery basement up and down and down and up Grafton Street. Tea for two and two for tea on one enchanted evening in the Dewdrop Inn. Do you like my nails this shade? Heart's Despair it's called.

MEDICAL. Play wing three for Monkstown. Four caps in the last couple of seasons. Pity they've put those glass doors in the Capitol boxes.

FLAPPER. Brown Thomas for panty-bras and Elizabeth Arden to rebuild drooping tissues. Max Factor, Chanel Number Five and Mum's the Word. Has your car got a strap round the bonnet?

MEDICAL. Well let's go up to Mother Mason's and hold hands. She needs decarbonizing probably. Botany Bay, you can be sure. Number twenty-one is my number.

SPEAKER. Can I get through here?

FLAPPER. Brittas Bay in a yellow M.G.

SPEAKER. I beg your pardon.

MEDICAL. Would you like a part in the Trinity Players?

SPEAKER. What?

FLAPPER. Tennis at Fitzwilliam all through the summer. We all go to Alexandra where the Lady Ardilaun lectures on Gilbert and Sullivan are quite indescribable. See you at the Carrickmines Mixed Singles. The Aga Khan is playing.

MEDICAL. Tyson's ties tie tightly. Going to crew next week for Dr Snufflebottom. Coming in left, Wanderers. Use your feet!

BOTH (*singing as they disappear*).

Kitty she was witty, Kitty she was pretty,
Down in the valley where they tried to pull her leg.
One of the committee thought he would be witty,
So he hit her on the titty with a hard boiled egg.

SPEAKER. What was that?

(*A* WELL-DRESSED WOMAN *and a* BUSINESSMAN *appear.*)

WELL-DRESSED WOMAN. This is the way to the Ringsend Baby Club. Double three Clubs. You are requested to attend a meeting of the Peamount After-care Committee. Ballsbridge, at 11.30 a.m. (*She yawns loudly.*)

39

BUSINESSMAN. Dame Street to Clarinda Park East Kingstown not Dun Laoghaire. Second National Loan Deferred Preference is now at thirty under proof. And only last Saturday I went round the Island in twenty-five and a bisque. Service not self I always say. Telegrams: 'Stability' Dublin. Have you got a *Herald*?

SPEAKER. Please . . . please! Can't you tell me the way out of here?

WELL-DRESSED WOMAN. Cover the milk. Do keep the milk covered, there's a good man.

    (*Goes.*)

BUSINESSMAN (*making a secret sign*). Past Grand High Deacon for the Fitzwilliam Lodge. Honorary Treasurer of the Sandycove and District Philatelic Society. House Committee, Royal St George. Assistant District Commissioner, South County Dublin Boy Scouts. Achievement. (*Goes.*)

    (TWO YOUNG THINGS *from somewhere up Phibsboro' way appear.*)

CARMEL. Down at the Girls' Club a Parnell Square. Janey Mac, such gas as we had!

BERNADETTE. Ah God, if I'd only a known! I couldn't get out a Tuesday. Were the fellas in?

CARMEL. They were. The Grocers' and Vintners' Assistants Association. D'ye know?

BERNADETTE. An' I suppose you had the Wet Dreams to play?

CARMEL. We had. The Gorgeous Wrecks were on in the Banba Hall. But listen. D'ye know the fella out a Cusack's a Dorset Street?

BERNADETTE. Is it that awful-lookin' iabeck with the red hair?

CARMEL. He ain't an awful lookin' iabeck, Bernadette, an' his hair's auburrin.

BERNADETTE. Yer taste's in yer mouth, duckie. Anyway . . . eyes off. He's walkin' out with Sarah Morrissy for I seen them meself last Sunday week a-clickin' on the Cab-ar-a Road.

CARMEL. Well wait now till I tell ya. He asked me for an A.P. at the Depot next Sunday an' he said to bring a pal an' he'll get her a fella, will ye come?

BERNADETTE. Will I come? Te th' Depot? Looka Carmel, I'll be there in me best Viyella.

CARMEL. Looka I'm off up to meet him a half five a Doyle's. He said th' Phib, but I think he has one eye on the Courtin' Park if I know that laddo. Do ye know?

BERNADETTE (*giggling*). Ah such gas! Sarah'll be wild when I tell her.

CARMEL. That one! You'd think she was someone.

SPEAKER (*politely*). I beg your pardon.

(BERNADETTE *nudges* CARMEL.)

SPEAKER. Did I hear you mention Sarah?

BERNADETTE. There's a fella tryin' to click.

CARMEL. Where? What sort of a fella?

BERNADETTE. Behind you. A queer-lookin' skin.

SPEAKER. If you would be so good? I'd be very much obliged.

(CARMEL *queries* BERNADETTE *with her eyebrows. The latter thinks not.*)

BERNADETTE. Give him the back of yer hand, Carmel. I'm not on.

SPEAKER. Could you tell me . . . ?

CARMEL (*turning with great dignity*). Chase yerself Jiggs or I'll call the Guards.

SPEAKER. Please don't misunderstand me. I only want to make an inquiry.

(*The two girls look knowingly at one another.*)

BERNADETTE (*in a hoarse whisper*). One of the Foresters.

CARMEL. Aw yes, well ye didn't meet me in Bray last summer. So goodbye-ee.

SPEAKER. In Bray? I said . . .

(BERNADETTE *giggles hysterically.*)

CARMEL (*to* BERNADETTE). That's th' stuff to give th' trupes. Well, I'll have to be off now or I'll be late. He'll be wild as it is. So long love.

BERNADETTE. Corner a Prussia Street a Sunday?

CARMEL. Mind yer there a half seven. Ta-ta so.

SPEAKER. Listen . . . I must speak. I will not have this!

CARMEL. Egs-scuse me! But may I ask who you're addressin' in that tone a voice?

BERNADETTE (*fluttering*). Ay – ay!

SPEAKER. I can't have this.

(*He tries to restrain her with a hand.*)

BERNADETTE. Ay, give us a hand someone!

CARMEL. Oh ye can't have this so ye can't, then listen to me, me Mountjoy Masher, ye'll have the flat of me fist across yer puss if ye can't conduct yerself when addressin' a lady, an' I'll thank ye to take that big slab from fingerin' me bawneen before I have ye run in the way God knows ye ought to be pesterin' an' pursuin' a pair a decent girls in th' public thoroughfare!

41

SPEAKER. Stop! For God's sake!

BERNADETTE. Ay-ay! Help! Help!

CARMEL. It's not safe for a respectable woman to leave th' shadda of her own door, so it's not, for the dirty gowgers that would be after them like . . . (*He tries to place his hand over her mouth. She bites him.* BERNADETTE *screams.*) Looka, I suppose you think yer face is yer fortune, but God knows at that rate some of us should be on the dole!

VOICES. Ay, what's up? What's the matter?

CARMEL. I declare to God I'd be ashamed of meself. A big lowsey yuck the like of you, why can't ye get a job a honest work and not be annoyin' young girls in th' street. It's lucky for your skin me fella's on th' far side of the Tolka River this minnit d'ye hear that now!

VOICES.
What did he do?
Is that him?
What's up?
Ay, can't ye leave the girl alone?
(*Rows of heads, hatted and becapped. The Curtains part again, disclosing a street.*)

BERNADETTE (*breathlessly*). Laida – laid aholt of us he did . . . an' says he, didn't I meet you in Bray last summer? says he, didn't I meet you in Bray? . . . An' then he takes her by the arm and says he . . .

SPEAKER. I did nothing of the sort!

VOICES.
Hold that fella.
Disgusting.
Put him out.

SPEAKER. I was only asking the way.

CARMEL (*choking*). Askin' th' way! Now d'ye hear that? . . . only askin' th' – looka what sort of a brass neck has that one got at all!

BERNADETTE. Look at what wants to ask th' way!

VOICES (*raucously – laughing*). To ask the way! 'Will any lady show a gentleman how who doesn't know the way?'

AN OLDER MAN. Ay, see here now. You ought to know better at your age. You'd better leave the girls alone or maybe some of these days you'll be finding your way where you least expect. This is a decent country.

42

VOICES.

    Still dear. No longer dirty.

    Keep to the right.

    Does your mother know yer out?

SPEAKER.

      How shall I reach the land that I love?

      Through the way of the wind, the high hills above?

      Down by the blue wide ways of the sea?

      (*Pause.*)

OLDER MAN. What's that?

CARMEL. God blessus, he's up the spout!

SPEAKER. That this unsparing storm should wreak its wrath . . .

OLDER MAN. Ay, give over. What's up with ye?

CARMEL. Well ye won't see me in his bewty chorus!

    (*General laughter.*)

OLDER MAN. Be quiet youse! I'm lookin' after this. What's yer name?

SPEAKER. I am Robert Emmet.

A VOICE. Robert Emmet?

A VOICE. Who?

A VOICE. Any relation to Paddy Emmet of Clonakilty?

OLDER MAN. Ssssh!

VOICES. Ssssh!

SPEAKER. I could explain it all in a moment if only you thought it worth while to give me a chance.

OLDER MAN. Oh if you're Robert Emmet you'll get every chance you want here. This is a free country. Is this true what you say?

SPEAKER. It is.

BERNADETTE. Well, d'ye hear that?

CARMEL. Who did he say?

BERNADETTE. Emmet. D'ye know. That fella.

A VOICE (*as fingers point*). That's Robert Emmet.

VOICES.

    Emmet.

    Emmet.

    That's him.

    Ay, d'ye know.

OLDER MAN. If yer Robert Emmet it must be all right.

SPEAKER. Won't you let me explain?

OLDER MAN. You can speak yer mind here without fear or favour.

VOICES.

    Nor sex, nor creed, nor class.

One for all and all for one.
Can laws forbid the blades of grass
From growing as they grow?
That's right.
A free country.
Up freedom!

SPEAKER. I knew it would be all right when I told you. And it will be so much better for all of us.

OLDER MAN. Let him have his way. I'll see that justice is done.

VOICES.
Without fear or favour.
That's right.
It's Robert Emmet.
Fair play for all.
Let him have his way.
He's all right.
Be reasonable.
Justice.
Free speech.
All right. All right.

OLDER MAN (*fussing round as if putting everybody into their seats*). Sit down now all. Be easy. I'll look after this. I'll see you through. Leave it all to me now an' we'll fix it all up for you in half a jiffy. Isn't that right?

(*General clapping. The* OLDER MAN *assumes an air of platform importance, coughs, and comes forward to address the audience.*)

OLDER MAN. Ladies and gents . . . we are very fortunate . . . in having with us tonight . . . one, who . . . I am sure . . . will need no introduction from me to a Dublin audience . . . His fair fame . . . his manly bearing . . . his zeal in the cause of the Gael . . . his upright character . . . his unbounded enthusiasm for the old cause . . . whatever it may or may not have been . . . his Christian charity . . . his wide experience . . . his indefatigable courage . . . his spotless reputation . . . and his kindness to the poor of the city . . . have made his name a household word wherever th' ole flag flies.

CARMEL (*shrilly*). Who wounded Maud McCutcheon?

OLDER MAN (*tolerantly*). Now, now, we mustn't touch on controversial matters . . . In introducing him to you this evening . . . I can say with confidence . . . that you will one and all listen to what he has to say . . . whatever it may be . . . and I am sure we are all looking forward to it very much indeed . . . with the greatest interest and with the deepest respect . . . The views which he has at heart . . . are also very near to the hearts of every one of us in this hall . . . and before calling upon him to address you I would just like to say that the committee will be glad to see any or all of you at the Central Branch Whist Drive in Ierne Hall next Friday and the treasurer will be waiting in the passage as you pass out for those members who have not yet paid their subs. Ladies and gents, Mr — er – er –

A VOICE. Emmet.

OLDER MAN. Mr Robert Ellis.

(*Applause.*)

SPEAKER. Don't gape at me like that. It is you who are confused – not I. It is only in this place that I am mocked. But I will carry you away to where the spirit is triumphant . . . where the streets have no terrors and the darkness no babbling torment of voices . . . where all will be plain . . . clear and simple . . . as God's sky above, and the chains will fall from your souls at the first sound of her voice from the lighted window. Which of you would not be free?

BERNADETTE. Up the Repubbelick!

SPEAKER. We know only one definition of freedom. It is Tone's definition; it is Mitchell's definition; it is Rossa's definition. Let no man blaspheme the cause that the dead generations of Ireland served, by giving it any other name and definition than their name and their definition. Life springs from death, and from the graves of patriot men and women spring living nations. Men and women of Eire, who is with me?

VOICES.
Up Emmet!
We are with you! Up the Partisans!
Fuck a bal la! Emmet leads!

SPEAKER. But hark, a voice in thunder spake! I knew it. Slaves and dastards, stand aside!

VOICES (*with great waving of arms*). Rathfarnham! Rathfarnham! (*Singing.*)

> Yes, Ireland shall be free
> From the centre to the sea,
> Then hurrah for Liberty!
> Says the Shan Van Vocht.

(*Terrific enthusiasm. A queue forms.*)

OLDER MAN (*ringing a hand-bell*). Line up, line up, ladies and gents.

45

This way for Rathfarnham. All aboard for the Priory. Leaving An Lar every three minutes. Plenty of room on top. No waiting. This way ladies and gents. Seats for Rathfarnham.

TWO TOUTS (*distributing handbills*). Next bus leaves in ten minutes. All aboard for Tir-na-n'Og. Special reduced return fares at single and a third. The Radio Train for Hy Brasail. No waits. No stops. Courtesy, efficiency and punctuality. Joneses Road, Walsh Road, Philipsburg Avenue, Clontarf, Clonturk, Curran's Cross and the New Jerusalem.

OLDER MAN. Now then, quietly, quietly please. There is room for one and all. Step this way please. All those in favour will say 'Taw'.

> Put your troubles on the shelf.
> Country life restores the health.

(*Many gentlemen and ladies shake hands with the* SPEAKER *as they file past.*)

TWO TOUTS. Schoolchildren, under twelve half price. Senior Citizens free. Uniformed social workers will meet young girls travelling alone. Special Whit facilities when not on strike. Penalty for improper use, five pounds. Empyrean Express, Park in Paradise. Hearts' Desire Non-stop picks up and sets down passengers only at the white pole. Please do not spit in or on the conductor.

HANDSHAKERS.
Proud to meet you, sir.
Look us up any time you're in Sandymount.
Jacobs Vobiscuits.
The country is with you.
My! how you've grown!
Remember me to the boys.
D'ye vanta vuya vatch?
Magnificent, sir!
Would you sign a snap?
Have ye e'er a Green Stamp?

TWO TOUTS. Excursions for schools and colleges. Boy Scouts and Girl Guides in uniform admitted free. Tea and boiled eggs may be had from the conductor. Special comfort facilities on all vehicles, except when standing in the station.

(*The queue queues. Presently the* SPEAKER *finds himself shaking hands with the old* FLOWER WOMAN. *There is silence.*)

WOMAN. Wait, me love, an' I'll be with ye.

SPEAKER. You!

46

WOMAN. I thought I heard th' noise I used to hear when me friends come to visit me.

> Oh, she doesn't paint nor powdher,
> An' her figger-is-all-her-owin.
> Hoopsie-daisie! The walk of a Quee-in!

SPEAKER. Hurry on please.

WOMAN (*patting him roguishly on the shoulder*). Ah, conduct yer-self. We're all friends here. Have ye nothing for me, lovely gentleman?

SPEAKER. What do you want?

WOMAN. It's not food or drink that I want. It's not silver that I want. Ochone.

SPEAKER. I have no time to waste talking to you.

WOMAN. What is it he called it? . . . the cheapest thing the good God has made . . . eh? He-he-he. That's all. For your own old lady.

SPEAKER. I've nothing for you.

WOMAN. Gimme me rights . . . me rights first!

SPEAKER. Go away!

WOMAN. Me rights! Me rights first . . . or I'll bloody well burst ye!

VOICES. Get on! Get on!

WOMAN (*turning on the crowd*). Aw ye have a brave haste about ye. Ye have a grand wild spirit to be up an' somewheres, haven't ye! Ye'll be off to a betther land will yez? Ye will . . . in me eye!

VOICES.
Ah, dry up!
What's she talking about?
Up Emmet!

WOMAN. An' a nice lot a bowsy scuts youse are, God knows! Emmet! He-he-he! Up Emmet! Let me tell youse that fella's not all he says he is!

VOICES. What's that? Not Emmet?

WOMAN. Look at him, ye gawms! Use yer eyes an' ask him for yourselves.

A VOICE. But the costume?

WOMAN. Five bob a day from Ging.

> (*She disappears into the crowd, whispering and pointing.*)

SPEAKER. My friends . . .

OLDER MAN. Is this true?

SPEAKER. My friends . . . we must go on . . . at once.

OLDER MAN. I asked you a question.

47

VOICES.
> Look at him.
> Well, what about it?
> Perhaps she's right.

SPEAKER. We can wait no longer.

VOICES. Can't you answer the gentleman's question?

OLDER MAN. Are these charges true?

SPEAKER. What are you talking about?

YOUNGER MAN (*in a beret*). What's all this?

OLDER MAN. This chap says he's Robert Emmet.

SPEAKER. I am.

OLDER MAN. Oh, you are, are you?

SPEAKER. I am.

OLDER MAN. Well answer me this then. *What's happened to your boots?*

VOICES.
> Ah-ha!
> Look!
> What about his boots?

SPEAKER. My boots!

OLDER MAN. He comes here an' says he's Robert Emmet, and where are his boots?

VOICES.
> That's right.
> Such an idea.
> He's an impostor.
> Throw him out!

SPEAKER. I don't know . . . I thought they were . . . I see your point . . . I . . .

VOICES. Well?

SPEAKER. Perhaps I had better explain . . . You see . . . someone took them from me when I was playing Robert Emmet and . . .

OLDER MAN (*with heavy sarcasm*). Oh so you were *playing* Robert Emmet? A play-actor are you? Some of this high-brow stuff I suppose?

SPEAKER. Oh no, not at all.

VOICES. High-brow! Ha!

OLDER MAN. I suppose you consider yourself a member of the so-called Intelligentsia? One of the Smart Set.

SPEAKER. Me?

VOICES. Smart Set! Ha! Ha!

OLDER MAN. A self-appointed judge of good taste, eh?

SPEAKER. I don't want to judge anything.

VOICES. Good taste. Ha! Ha! Ha!

OLDER MAN. You want to pose before the world as representative of the Irish people? Eh?

SPEAKER. I only want to . . .

VOICES. Representative. Ha! Ha! Ha! Ha!

OLDER MAN. Tell me (*suddenly*) how much do you get for this?

SPEAKER. That's none of your business!

VOICES.

A job! A job!

He does it for a job!

He's related to someone!

And has a job!

OLDER MAN. Honest friends and anti-jobbers! This so-called leader, this self-appointed instructor of the Irish people, is owney linin' his pockets at the expense of the poor. His downy couch, debauched with luxury is watered with the sweat of the humble. A traitor's pillory in the hearts of his countrymen would be a proper reward for such an abattoir of licentiousness.

SPEAKER. (*assuming a Parnellesque attitude*). Who is the master of this party?

OLDER MAN. Who is the mistress of this party?

SPEAKER. Until the party deposes me I am leader.

A VOICE. You are not our leader. You are a dirty trickster.

A VOICE. Committee Room Fifteen!

SPEAKER. So you won't follow me any longer?

VOICES. No!

SPEAKER (*after a pause*). Very well. I shall just have to go on by myself.

OLDER MAN. Oh no you don't. You're not going out of this.

SPEAKER. Who's going to stop me?

OLDER MAN. We are. You're not going to be allowed to hold up this country to disgrace and ridicule in the eyes of the world. Throwing mud and dirt at the Irish people.

VOICE. Give him a taste of backwoodsman's law.

SPEAKER (*to* YOUNGER MAN). Tell him to get out of my way. You won't allow this.

YOUNGER MAN. It's nothing to do with me. The army has no interest in civilian affairs. All the same I don't like to see my country insulted by indecent plays.

OLDER MAN. That's right.

YOUNGER MAN. A high-spirited race resents being held up to scorn

49

before the world, and it shows its resentment (*He takes out a revolver and hands it to the* OLDER MAN.) in various ways. But as I say it has nothing to do with me.

(*He walks away.*)

OLDER MAN (*with revolver*). Take off that uniform.

SPEAKER. Put up that revolver. I warn you, I am serious.

(*He stretches out his hand and gently takes it from him. The crowd slowly closes in upon him with sheeplike heedlessness.*)

SPEAKER. Stand back or I will have to shoot. I warn you I won't be interfered with, I am going on at all costs.

VOICES. Traitor. Spy. Cheat. Cur.

SPEAKER (*hidden in their midst*). Back! Back! Slaves and dastards, stand aside! Back! Back! or I'll . . .

(*The revolver emits a dull pop. The crowd melts away to the side and he is disclosed standing there alone with the smoking weapon still clenched in his fist. There is a deathlike silence.*)

A VOICE. Oh, my God!

OLDER MAN (*very quietly*). Now you've done it.

SPEAKER. Done what?

OLDER MAN. You've plugged somebody.

A VOICE. Oh, my God! My God!

SPEAKER. I've what?

A MAN (*looking out*). It's Joe.

SECOND MAN. Joe?

FIRST MAN. He's got it in the breast.

YOUNGER MAN (*reappearing*). Who fired that shot?

OLDER MAN. Joe's got it. Right through the left lung. He can't last long.

SECOND MAN. Christ!

FIRST MAN. It wasn't any of us, Tom. It was this chap.

SPEAKER. Stand back, stand back, I tell you. I'm fighting. This is war.

YOUNGER MAN (*quite unperturbed*). There's a man out there. You've put a bullet through his breast.

OLDER MAN. God rest his soul!

SPEAKER. I warned you – I warned you all.

YOUNGER MAN. He's going to die. You did it. That's what comes of having guns.

VOICES.
He's going to die.
You did it.

50

You did it.

SPEAKER. I had to. It wasn't my gun.

(*Two men appear bearing between them the body of another. The people take off their hats and stand mutely with bowed heads.*)

JOE. It's welling out over me shirt, boys . . . Can't anybody stop . . . it?

YOUNGER MAN. A good man . . . a true man . . . That is what you did.

OLDER MAN. That is what he did.

VOICES.

You did.

He did.

Robert Emmet did.

Who did it?

He did it.

He there.

SPEAKER. I had to . . . (*All hands point.*)

JOE. Give me . . . me beads . . . before the life . . . has ebbed out of me . . . I can't breathe . . . oh, lads, I'm going . . .

SPEAKER. What could I do? I ask you, what could I do? It was war. I didn't mean to hurt him.

OLDER MAN. Joe, old scout. We're sorry . . . we're . . . O God!

JOE. God bless you boys . . . sure I know . . . I know well . . . it wasn't any of . . . you . . .

SPEAKER (*flinging down the revolver*). Shoot back then! It is war. Shoot! I can die too!

YOUNGER MAN. Will that give him back the warm blood you have stolen from him?

OLDER MAN. Ah, leave him alone, Tom, leave him alone.

VOICES (*whispering*).

Leave him alone.

He shot Joe.

Through the breast.

Poor Joe.

Leave him alone.

JOE (*as he is carried off, followed by the crowd*). O my God . . . I am heartily . . . sorry . . . for having offended . . . Thee . . . and . . . I . . .

VOICES (*chanting*).

> *Lacrymosa dies illa*
> *Qua resurget ex favilla*
> *Judicandus homo reus.*

51

Huic ergo parce Deus;
Pie Jesu Domine
Dona eis requiem
Amen.

FLOWER WOMAN (*appearing in the shadows, but speaking with the voice of* SARAH CURRAN).

Do not make a great keening
When the graves have been dug tomorrow.
Do not call the white-scarfed riders
To the burying . . .

(*Hoarsely*). Ay misther – spare a copper for a cuppa tea – spare a copper for a poor old lady – a cuppa tea – (*Whisper.*) a copper for your own ole lady, lovely gentleman.

(*She fades away.*)

SPEAKER. Sally! Sally! – where are you? – where are you? Sally!

THE CURTAIN FALLS

PART TWO

Through the Curtain, amidst a hearty round of applause, comes the MINISTER'S *talented daughter,* MAEVE. *She has on a nice white dress with a white bow to match in her long, loose, black hair which reaches quite to her waist. Around her neck on a simple gold chain hangs a religious medal. She curtsies in charming embarrassment and commences to recite.*

MAEVE.

> Kingth Bweakfatht.
> The King athed de Queen
> And de Queen athed de Dar-med
> Could – I (*a little breathlessly*) – se – butter
> For-de-roy – – – thlaice – a – bwead?
> Queen athed de Dar-med
> De Dar-med thed Thertinley
> Ah goan tell – Cow now
> For he goeth tebed . . .

(*She continues this amusing piece to the very end, when the Curtain parts amid general applause disclosing a fantastically respectable drawing-room loud with the clatter of tea things. A party is in progress under the aegis of the* MINISTER FOR ARTS AND CRAFTS *and his nice little* WIFE. *The guests consist of one of the* REDCOATS, *now a* GENERAL *in a green uniform, the Statue of* GRATTAN, *rather a nice woman called* LADY TRIMMER – *one of those people whose expression of pleased expectancy never for a moment varies, the old* FLOWER WOMAN *who is seated unobtrusively in the background eating an orange, and a small but enthusiastic* CHORUS. *Side by side upon the sofa reading from right to left are* O'COONEY *the well-known dramatist,* O'MOONEY *the rising portrait painter, and* O'ROONEY *the famous novelist.* O'COONEY *wears a cloth cap, blue sweater and a tweed coat.* O'MOONEY *has a red shirt and horn-rimmed spectacles, while* O'ROONEY *is dressed in*

53

full saffron kilt together with Russian boots. The MINISTER
himself bears a strange resemblance to the STAGE HAND. *It
is all very nice indeed.*)

CHORUS.

Oh very nice nice
Oh very nice nice nice
How old how nice how very nice don't you think so
Oh yes indeed yes very nice indeed I do think so indeed don't
you indeed.
(*Teaspoons clink.*)

LADY TRIMMER. What was that one, my dear?

MAEVE. Kingth Bweakfatht pleathe.

LADY TRIMMER. Very nice indeed, Maeve. I must teach that one to
my two chicks. Where do you learn, my dear?

MAEVE. The Banba Thcool of Acting, Lower Abbey Thweet.

CHORUS. The Banba School of Acting, Lower Abbey Street.

O'COONEY. Wasn't that bloody awful?

O'MOONEY. The question is, is she an aartist? A real aartist?

O'ROONEY. O'Mooney sounds better with his mouth shut.

WIFE. Of course, she hasn't been learning very long. But she has
the language, and that's half the battle these days. Show them,
Maeve.

MAEVE. *Caed mile failte.*

LADY TRIMMER. Oh very good indeed. But of course, she has her
father's talent.

MINISTER. Ah, well, now . . .

WIFE (*pleased*). Oh, Lady Trimmer!

MINISTER. Well, now, all the same I don't know about that. But
mind you I do say this, Talent is what the country wants.
Politics may be all O.K. in their way, but what I say to *An
Taoischach* is this, until we have Talent and Art in the country
we have no National Dignity. We must have Talent and Art.
Isn't that right?

CHORUS. We must have Art have Talent and Art.

LADY TRIMMER. Quite. And cultivated people of taste. You musn't
forget them, Mr Minister. Art cannot live you know by taking
in its own washing – if I may put it that way.

O'COONEY. Aw Holy God!

O'MOONEY (*ruminatively*). The reel aartist must be fundamental.
Like Beethoven. Now, *I'm* fundamental.

O'ROONEY. Fundament, all right.

MINISTER. Now see here. I'm Minister for Arts and Crafts, you see.

Well, a young fellow comes along to me and he says, Now look, Liam, here's some Art I'm after doing . . . it might be a book you see, or a drawing, or even a poem . . . and can you do anything for me, he says? Well, with that, I do . . . if he deserves it, mind you, only if he deserves it, under Section 15 of the Deserving Artists' (Support) Act, No. 65 of 1926. And there's none of this favouritism at all.

CHORUS. The State supports the Artist.

GRATTAN. And the Artist supports the State.

CHORUS. Very satisfactory for everybody and no favouritism at all.

MINISTER (*confidentially*). And of course, then you see, it helps us to keep an eye on the sort of stuff that's turned out, you understand.

CHORUS. Clean and pure Art for clean and pure people.

LADY TRIMMER. What we need most is a small Salon.

GENERAL. That's right. A small Art Saloon.

WIFE. We often have people in on Sunday evenings for music and things. Won't you sing something now, General?

GENERAL. Aw, I have no voice at all.

O'COONEY. He's bloody well right there.

O'MOONEY. The question is . . . Is he fundamental?

LADY TRIMMER. Just somewhere where the nicest people . . . the people one wants to meet . . . like Mr O'Cooney and Mr O'Mooney . . .

O'ROONEY (*suspiciously*). And Mr O'Rooney.

LADY TRIMMER. *And* Mr O'Rooney, can get together quietly and discuss Art and common interests.

WIFE. Haven't you brought your music?

CHORUS. You must have brought your music.

GENERAL. Well now . . . if you insist. Maybe I might find something.

O'COONEY (*to* O'MOONEY). Ay, have *you* put my cap somewhere?

WIFE. Do, General.

GENERAL. I don't know for sure, mind you. I might . . . just happen to have something on me.

(*He produces a roll of music from inside his tunic.*)

CHORUS. The General's going to sing.

GENERAL. Ah, but . . . sure there's no one to play th' accompanyment.

WIFE. Maeve will play. Won't you, darling?

MAEVE. Yeth mammy.

(*Signs of distress from the sofa.*)

WIFE. Of course you will dear. Give her the music, General.

CHORUS. Ssssh!

> (*The* GENERAL *gives her the music rather doubtfully and they are opening the performance, when there comes a loud, peremptory knock at the door. General surprise.*)

WIFE (*bravely but apprehensively*). What can that be?

LADY TRIMMER. Strange!

MINISTER. A knock at the door?

GENERAL. Ah now, isn't that too bad!

CARMEL (*entering*). There's a gentleman at the door, ma'am, looking for the Rathfarnham bus.

WIFE. What kind of a gentleman, Carmel?

CARMEL. A gentleman in a uniform, ma'am.

MINISTER. A uniform? Tell me, does he look like the start of a Daring Outrage?

CHORUS. Possibly the Garda Síothchána.

CARMEL. He has a sword, sir.

MINISTER. A sword?

CARMEL (*primly*). And a pair of slippers.

WIFE. Slippers?

GENERAL. I don't think I know that unyform.

CHORUS. Can't be the Garda Síothchána after all.

WIFE. Did he give any name, Carmel?

CARMEL. Yes, ma'am. A Mr Emmet.

LADY TRIMMER. Not *the* Mr Emmet?

CARMEL. I don't know I'm sure, ma'am.

MINISTER. Ah, yes I remember. That's him all right.

GENERAL. Aw, the hard Emmet.

MINISTER. The old Scout.

WIFE. The gentleman who is far from the land. Show him up at once, Carmel.

CARMEL. Yes, ma'am. (*She goes, muttering.*) Doesn't look like a sailor to me.

LADY TRIMMER. How nice of him to call.

WIFE. Yes, indeed, but you know we can't be too careful since the Trouble.

MINISTER. Emmet's all right. I know him well. Used to work with him in the old days.

GENERAL. Aw, the rare old Emmet.

LADY TRIMMER. You know I've wanted to meet him for such a long time. My husband always says that we of the old regime ought to get into touch with those sort of people as much as

56

possible. We can assist each other in so many ways.

MINISTER. That's right. We must all get together for the good of the country.

WIFE. I wonder has he brought his music too?

GRATTAN. I expect he has.

(CARMEL *enters, cocking her head contemptuously towards the* SPEAKER, *who follows her with a strange, hunted look in his eye. He glances round apprehensively as though prepared for the worst and yet hoping against hope.*)

CHORUS. Oh how do you how do you how do you how do you how . . .

WIFE. How do you do? Bring another cup, Carmel.

CARMEL. Yes, ma'am. (*She goes, muttering.*) I'll have to wash one first.

SPEAKER. Excuse . . . me.

WIFE. Come and sit down and let me introduce you to everybody. It was so nice of you to call. Liam has just been speaking about your work.

SPEAKER. I only came in to ask . . .

CHORUS. Have you brought your music?

WIFE. This is Lady Trimmer, Mr Emmet.

CHORUS. Of the old regime.

LADY TRIMMER. Dee do.

SPEAKER (*after peering closely into her face*). No, ah, no.

LADY TRIMMER. You must come and visit us too, Mr Emmet. First Fridays. Now promise.

WIFE. And General O'Gowna of the *Oglaigh na h-Eireann*.

GENERAL (*affably*). And many of them.

SPEAKER. It was you who hit me.

WIFE. And of course you know my husband, the Minister for Arts and Crafts.

CHORUS. Vote *Fianna na Poblacht*.

MINISTER. *A chara.*

(*The* SPEAKER *tries to remonstrate but is hurried on.*)

WIFE. And Mr Grattan's statue from College Green.

GRATTAN. Welcome Don Quixote Alighieri. Did I speak the truth?

(*The* SPEAKER'S *head goes up.*)

WIFE. And this is Mr O'Cooney, the great dramatist.

SPEAKER. Cap?

WIFE. Oh, Mr O'Cooney always wears his cap in the drawing-room.

O'COONEY. And why the bloody hell shouldn't I wear my cap in the drawing-room?

(*General laughter.*)

SPEAKER. I see.

O'MOONEY. Now me.

WIFE. This is Mr O'Mooney, the artist, if you can remember everybody.

O'MOONEY. The reel Aartist.

O'COONEY. The owl cod.

WIFE. Oh, please, Mr O'Cooney!

CHORUS. I love the way he talks, don't you?

O'MOONEY. Oh, don't mind O'Cooney. He's a great friend of mine, really.

O'COONEY. He is not!

WIFE. And this is Mr O'Rooney, the well-known novelist. Now I think you know everybody.

SPEAKER (*indicating the costume*). You play the pipes?

(O'MOONEY *laughs shrilly.*)

O'ROONEY. I do not. I do not believe in political Nationalism. Do you not see my Russian boots?

WIFE. Mr O'Rooney believes in the workers.

O'ROONEY. I do not believe in the workers. Nor do I believe in the Upper Classes nor in the Bourgeoisie. It should be perfectly clear by now what I do not believe in, unless you wish me to go over it again?

LADY TRIMMER (*archly*). Mr O'Rooney, you dreadful man!

SPEAKER. I'm sorry.

WIFE. Sit down now and have a nice cup of tea.

(CARMEL *meanwhile has been back with a dirty cup.*)

CHORUS. I do like a nice cup of tea.

SPEAKER. So she is here, too!

WIFE. What's that?

SPEAKER. That damned old flower woman who turned them all against me!

WOMAN. Ay, mister, have ye e'er an old hempen rope for a neck-cloth?

WIFE. You're joking, Mr Emmet. There's no old flower woman.

SPEAKER. I mean . . . look there.

WIFE. Have some tea, Mr Emmet. You're a little tired, no doubt.

SEMICHORUS. Delightful drink.

SEMICHORUS. Pity it tans the stomach.

WIFE. You'll feel much the better of it. And we'll have a little music afterwards. We often have music in the evenings.

MINISTER. Are you interested in Art, Mr Emmet?

LADY TRIMMER. I suppose you're a member of the Nine Arts Club?

WIFE. And the Royal Automobile Academy?

CHORUS. Celebrity Concerts. The Literary Literaries.

SPEAKER. I don't feel very . . . Did you say that statue of Grattan was there?

WIFE. Oh yes, that's Mr Grattan's statue from College Green. We always have a few of the nicest statues in on Sunday evening. My husband is Minister for Arts and Crafts, you know.

LADY TRIMMER. Just to form a little group you know. A few people of taste.

WIFE. Of course we're only amateurs, but we're doing our best.
    (*Pause.*)

SPEAKER (*suddenly*). Let me be persuaded that my springing soul may meet the . . .
    (*Pause.*)

LADY TRIMMER. I beg your pardon?

SPEAKER. Let me be per— (*He shakes his head hopelessly.*) I am Robert Emmet.

GRATTAN. You are not.

SPEAKER. Who are you to question me?

GRATTAN. You are only a play-actor.

SPEAKER. Look well to your own soul, Major Sirr!

GRATTAN. Have you found your Holy Curran, Galahad?

WIFE. I always say to Liam, Liam you really *must* get a proper statue of Mr Emmet. It's positively disgraceful that we haven't got a good one, don't you think?

MINISTER. Ah, well, dear, you know, expense, expense.

LADY TRIMMER. What a nice uniform! Tell me, do you admire the plays of Chekhov?

WIFE. Perhaps he acts for the Civil Service Dramatics.

SPEAKER. Act? . . . No. No cake, thank you.

CHORUS. Benevente Strindberg Toller Euripides Pirandello Tolstoy Calderon O'Neill.

LADY TRIMMER. I'm sure you'd be good.

CHORUS. An annual subscription of one guinea admits a member to all productions and to all At Homes.

MINISTER (*confidentially*). Say the word and I'll get you into the Rathmines and Rathmines. I know the man below.

LADY TRIMMER. Now do tell us, Mr Emmet, about your wonderful experiences in the Trouble.
    (*The* SPEAKER *spills his tea and looks around wild-eyed.*)

SPEAKER. What do you mean?

59

GRATTAN. Ah – ha!

WIFE. Never mind. It's quite all right. I'll pour you out another cup.

LADY TRIMMER (*hastily*). You must have had such interesting times all through the fighting.

SPEAKER. I shall never fight again!

    (*He buries his face in his hands.*)

MINISTER. Oh come, Mr Emmet! What's the matter?

WIFE. Are you not felling well?

LADY TRIMMER (*aside*). Ssssh! Don't pay any attention. I understand. Do tell us about it, Mr Emmet. Talk. Talk someone.

SPEAKER. God have pity on me.

CHORUS. Oh the fighting everyone talk don't pay any attention wonderful experiences those were the attention fighting days how wonderful do tell us about the fighting days interesting and wonderful.

SPEAKER. It was I who shot him and you all know it! You all know! Isn't it enough for you? Haven't I suffered enough?

CHORUS (*louder*). Oh tuttut poor man don't talk do talk as hard as you can fighting wonderful pay no attention shellshock probably to have seen it all wonderful is he better yet poor man everybody pretend not to fighting notice.

SPEAKER. They trapped me! A good man . . . a true man . . . and I did it!

WIFE. Well what if you did shoot somebody? Everybody's shot somebody nowadays. That'll soon be over.

LADY TRIMMER. Yes, yes; of course we didn't approve of it at the time, but it's all so interesting now.

SPEAKER. Interesting!

CHORUS. Perhaps we had better how is he change the subject change the subject getting on what's the wonderful experiences matter with him matter with him at all?

WIFE. How about a little song?

CHORUS. How about a little little song song song?

WIFE. Do you sing, Mr Emmet?

SPEAKER. What do you all want with me?

LADY TRIMMER. Nothing, nothing at all, Mr Emmet. Perhaps you'd like to act us a little snippet from your play?

WIFE. We often have plays on Sunday evenings. Poor man. There, there. We are all friends here.

LADY TRIMMER. The General has just obliged us.

GENERAL. I have not. I was interrupted before I got going.

WIFE. You're better now, I'm sure. Of course you are. Aren't you?

MINISTER. Well, I believe in supporting Art and acting's Art. So you have *my* consent anyhow.

WIFE. You'll act something for us, Mr Emmet, won't you?

GRATTAN. Ah, leave him alone. Can't you see he's beaten.

SPEAKER. That voice! That voice!

GRATTAN. I said that you were beaten. You should have taken my advice from the first; but you would go on with your play-acting. Now, perhaps you know better. Rathfarnham! Ha! Sarah Curran! Ha-ha-ha!

SPEAKER (*slowly rising*). I am not beaten. I still believe. I will go on.

CHORUS. Oh good, he's going to do something for us.

WIFE. Oh do, Mr Emmet.

GENERAL. But look here . . .

GRATTAN. Don't be a fool. Do you imagine that they'll listen to you if you do?

MINISTER. Nothing political. That's barred of course.

O'COONEY. For God's sake make it short anyhow.

O'MOONEY. Nothing Iberian. There's no Iberian real Art.

O'ROONEY. See that it's not pompous. That would be an insult to the people of this country.

GENERAL. Hey, what about my song?

GRATTAN. Go on. Tell them all to go to hell.

SPEAKER. Please, please . . . if you want me to do it . . .

CHORUS. Oh yes yes, do Mr Emmet.

MINISTER. I suppose it will be all right. I wouldn't like anything by somebody with the slave mind, you know.

SPEAKER. Nobody can object to my play.

MINISTER. Or calculated to excite you-know-what.

CHORUS. Emmet's play is all right.

GENERAL. Well you needn't expect me to sit down quietly under this sort of behaviour. When you ask a man to sing . . .

SPEAKER (*advancing towards the audience*). It's very hard without Sally. It may seem a little strange here . . . but I'll do it.

GRATTAN. Very well. Have it your own way.

LADY TRIMMER. Did I hear him mention somebody called . . . er, Sally Somebody?

WIFE (*confidentially*). I think it must be his young lady.

LADY TRIMMER. How charming.

GENERAL (*determinedly*). One of Moore's Melodies entitled 'She is Far from the Land'.
        (*He bows.*)

O'COONEY. Aw, this'll be bloody awful. (*Settles down.*) D'ye remember that night, Liam, when the two of us hid in the chimbley from the Tans?

MINISTER. Will I ever forget it? Ah, those were the days, Seamus.

SPEAKER. I had got to the part where I am arrested, hadn't I? No. I think I was . . .

WIFE. We always have music and things on Sunday evenings.

LADY TRIMMER. Just a nucleus. A few nice people.

GENERAL (*to* MAEVE). Have you got the place?

MAEVE. Mammy.

WIFE. Yes, dear?

MAEVE. Why ith that man wearing hith thlipperth in the dwawing woom?

WIFE. Hush, dear, you mustn't ask questions. You must be a good girl.

MAEVE (*plaintively*). You never let me –

GENERAL. Ah, go on when I tell you!

> (MAEVE *commences the introduction to 'She is Far from the Land'*.)

SPEAKER.

> The air is rich and soft – the air is mild and bland.
> Her woods are tall and straight, grove rising over grove.
> Trees flourish in her glens below and on her heights above,
> Oh, the fair hills of Eire, oh.

O'ROONEY. Will you move up on the sofa and breathe into yourself.

O'MOONEY. We'd be better off if your hips were as soft as your head.

> (*Simultaneously.*)

SPEAKER.	GENERAL (*singing*).
Down from the high cliffs the rivulet is teeming	She is far from the land where her young hero sleeps
To wind around the willow banks that lure me from above;	And lovers around her are sighing:
Ah, where the woodbines with sleepy arms have wound me.	But coldly she turns from their gaze and weeps
	For her heart in his grave is lying.

MINISTER (*solo*). And do you remember the day, Seamus, of the big round-up in Moore Street when the 'G' man tried to plug me getting out of the skylight?

> SPEAKER, GENERAL, *and* O'COONEY (*simultaneously.*)

SPEAKER (*louder*).	GENERAL
But there is lightning in my blood; red lightning tighten-	She sings the wild songs of her dear native plains,

ing in my blood. Oh! if there was a sword in every Irish hand! If there was a flame in every Irish heart to put an end to slavery and shame! Oh, I would end these things!

Every note which he loved awaking.
Ah! little they think, who delight in her strains,
How the heart of the ministrel is breaking.

O'COONEY.

Aw, Jesus, and the evenings down in the old I.R.B. in Talbot Street, picking out the 'Soldiers' Song' on the blackboard.

SPEAKER, MINISTER, and GENERAL (*simultaneously*).

I have written my name in letters of fire across the page of history. I have unfurled the green flag in the streets and cried aloud from the high places to the people of the Five Kingdoms: Men of Eire, awake to be blest! to be blest!

He had lived for his love, for his country he died,
They were all that to life had entwined him;
Nor soon shall the tears of his country be dried,
Nor long will his love stay behind him.

MINISTER.

Sometimes I wish I was back again on the run with the old flying column out by the Glen of Aherlow.

(O'MOONEY *and* O'ROONEY *join in in low undertones.*)

O'ROONEY

My good woman, I said, I'll tell you what's wrong with you. Virginity, my good woman, that's all. And believe me, its nothing to be proud of.

O'MOONEY

Saint Peetric d'ye see because Saint Peter was the rock and Saint Patrick was the seed. That makes Saint Peetric, d'ye see. For the rock is underneath and the seed lies above, so Saint Peter and Saint Patrick are Saint Peetric.

(*At the same time.*)

O'COONEY

And that night waiting up on the North Circular for word of the executions. Ah, not for all the wealth of the world would I give up the maddenin' minglin' memories of the past . . .

SPEAKER.   GENERAL

Rise, Arch of the Ocean and

63

Queen of the West! I have
dared all for Ireland, I will
dare all again for Sarah   O! make her a grave where
Curran. Their graves are red.   the sunbeams rest
O make her a maddening   When they promise a glorious
mingling glorious morrow . . .   morrow . . .

> (*The black curtain closes behind the* SPEAKER, *blotting out
> the room, and the voices fade away. The* SPEAKER *himself
> has somehow chimed in upon the last few lines of the song,
> and is left singing it by himself.*)

SPEAKER.

They'll shine o'er her sleep like a smile from the west,
From her own loved island of sorrow . . .

> (*The* BLIND MAN *comes tap-tapping with a fiddle under his
> arm and a tin mug in his hand. He bumps lightly into the*
> SPEAKER.)

BLIND MAN (*feeling with his stick*). Peek-a-boo! Peek-a-boo!

SPEAKER. Damn your eyes!

BLIND MAN (*looking up*). That's right.

SPEAKER. You're . . . blind?

BLIND MAN (*with a chuckle*). That's what they say.

SPEAKER. I didn't know. I didn't mean to hurt you.

BLIND MAN. Ah, not at all. I'm not so easy hurted. (*Feeling him
over.*) Oh, a grand man. A grand man. A grand man surely,
from the feel of his coat.

SPEAKER. Do you know where I am?

BLIND MAN. Well, isn't that a rare notion now! Asking the way of
an old dark fiddler, and him tip-tappin' over the cold sets day
in and day out with never sight nor sign of the blessed sun above.

SPEAKER. I give it up.

BLIND MAN. And where might you be bound for, stranger?

SPEAKER. The Priory.

BLIND MAN (*with a start*). Ah, so! So you're bound for them parts,
are you, stranger dear?

SPEAKER. Yes.

BLIND MAN. Up the glen maybe as far as the edge of the white mist,
and it hanging soft around the stones of Mount Venus, eh
stranger? He-he-he!

SPEAKER. That's right.

BLIND MAN. Oh, I know you. I know you. Sure all the Queer Ones
of the twelve counties do be trysting around them hills beyond
the Priory.

SPEAKER. The blessed hills!

BLIND MAN. It's sad I am, stranger, for my light words of greeting and the two of us meeting for the first time. Take my arm now, and walk with me for a while and I'll put you on your way. Come – take my arm! Why should you not take my arm, stranger, for I'm telling you, my fathers are Kings in Thomond so they are.

SPEAKER (*taking his arm gingerly*). There.

BLIND MAN. That's better now. He-he-he. 'Tis proud I am to be walking arm in arm with the likes of you, stranger. Tell me now, or am I wrong? Would you by any chance be Mr Robert Emmet?

SPEAKER. You know me?

BLIND MAN. Uh! I thought I recognized them words I heard you singing.

SPEAKER. Yes. I am Robert Emmet. He said that I wasn't. But I am. It was the voice of Major Sirr.

BLIND MAN. Ah, poor Bob Emmet. He died for Ireland. God rest his soul.

SPEAKER. He died. I died?

BLIND MAN. You did indeed. You remember the old song we used to sing?

(*They sit down together.*)

SPEAKER. You mean 'The Struggle is Over'.

BLIND MAN. That's right. Ah, the rare old lilt of it. How does it go, now? (*He sings.*)

The struggle is over, our boys are defeated,
    And Erin surrounded with silence and gloom.
We were betrayed and shamefully treated
    And I, Robert Emmet, awaiting my doom.
Hanged, drawn and quartered, sure that was my sentence,
    But soon I will show them, no coward am I.
My crime was the love of the land I was born in.
    A hero I've lived and a hero I'll die.

BOTH.

Bold Robert Emmet, the darling of Erin,
Bold Robert Emmet will die with a smile.
Farewell companions, both loyal and daring,
I'll lay down my life for the Emerald Isle.

(*Pause. From somewhere comes faint dance music.*)

BLIND MAN. Ah, them are the songs. Them are the songs.

SPEAKER. He died for Ireland. I died. I?

BLIND MAN. High Kings in Thomond, my fathers are. Lords of the Gael. You'll know them, stranger.

SPEAKER. How can I have died for Ireland? What is that I hear?

BLIND MAN. Ah, never mind that. That's nothing. Nothing at all.

> (*A young man in evening dress and a pretty girl are walking out of the darkness into the edge of the light. It is the* TRINITY MEDICAL *and his friend, now a little older. They are smoking and laughing together.*)

SPEAKER. Go away.

BLIND MAN. Never heed them stranger. That's nobody at all.

SPEAKER. And I am dead this hundred years and more?

BLIND MAN. What would the likes of you have to do with the likes of them? He-he-he.

HE. I remember when I was a kid in Clyde Road how wonderful I thought a private dance was.

SHE. Now I suppose you've quite grown out of us all.

HE (*laughing*). Oh, well, I wouldn't say that. But of course when one's lived abroad things do seem a little different, when you come back.

SHE. I suppose so.

HE. Small in a way and rather provincial. But that's to be expected.

SPEAKER. I wonder is Sally dead too?

BLIND MAN. Dust to dust and ashes to ashes.

HE. Of course, there have been a lot of improvements. But over there . . . well, after all, it takes over an hour and a half to get into the country.

SHE. And you like that?

HE. Well, you know how it is. It makes one feel one's sort of *in* the world. Everything seems more serious, somehow.

SHE. While we and the old days never seemed serious at all.

HE. Oh well, I didn't quite mean it that way.

SPEAKER. O God help me!

BLIND MAN. Coming and going on the mailboat. And they thinking themselves the real ones – the strong ones! I do have to laugh sometimes and I hearing the wings of the Queer Ones beating under the arch of the sky.

HE. Of course I liked the old days. We had some jolly good times together, didn't we?

SHE. I liked them too.

HE. I was crazy about you.

SHE. My eye and Betty Martin.

HE. I was. I was, really. I often think about it all. It's a bit lonely sometimes over there, and often – Oh, I don't know. Do you ever think about me?

SHE. Sometimes.

HE. I hope you do. You know, Daphne, sometimes I wonder whether you and I oughtn't to have . . .

SHE. Have what?

HE. I think we ought to have . . . maybe we still could . . .
      (*The music stops. There is a pause.*)

HE. Hello. The music's stopped.

SHE. Yes. I suppose it has.

HE. Like to go in and have a drink?

SHE. I think we might as well.

HE (*briskly*). Funny, you know, how the old place can get you for a bit. But after all, one can't get away from the fact that it's all so damned depressing – (*They vanish.*)

SPEAKER. O God, make speed to save us! I cannot tell what things are real and what are not!

BLIND MAN. Oh, but it is not myself that is dark at all, but them – blind and drunk with the brave sight of their own eyes. For why would they care that the winds is cold and the beds is hard and the sewers do be stinking and steaming under the stone sets of the streets, when they can see a bit of a rag floating in the wild wind, and they dancing their bloody Ceilidhes over the lip of Hell! Oh, I have my own way of seeing surely. It takes a dark man to see the will-o'-the-wisps and the ghosts of the dead and the half dead and them that will never die while they can find lazy, idle hearts ready to keep their venom warm.

SPEAKER (*up*). Out of the depths I have cried to Thee, O Lord: Lord, hear my voice!

BLIND MAN. In every dusty corner lurks the living word of some dead poet, and it waiting for to trap and to snare them. This is no City of the Living: but of the Dark and the Dead!

SPEAKER. I am mad – mad – mad! Sally!
      (*During his speech the stage darkens until both figures are blotted out and the* SPEAKER *is left groping in the dark.*)

SARAH'S VOICE. Robert! Robert!

SPEAKER. What was that?

SARAH'S VOICE (*singing*).

> She stretched forth her arms,
> Her mantle she flung to the wind,
> And swam o'er Loch Leane
> Her outlawed lover to find . . .

67

SPEAKER. Sally! Sally! Where are you?

SARAH'S VOICE. Why don't you come to me, Robert? I have been waiting for you so long.

SPEAKER. I have been searching for you so long.

SARAH'S VOICE. I thought you had forgotten me.

SPEAKER. Forgotten you! Forgotten you, Sally! Is that your hand, dear? *A cuisle geal mo chroidhe* – 'Tis you shall have a silver throne – Her sunny mouth dimples with hope and joy: her dewy eyes are full of pity. It is you, Sally – Deirdre is mine: she is my Queen, and no man now can rob me!

> (*The lights go up. He is in the dingy room of a tenement house. The plaster is peeling off the walls. On a bed in the corner a young man with the face of* JOE *is lying with an expression of serene contentment upon his pale, drawn features. Two men – the* OLDER *and the* YOUNGER MAN – *are playing cards at a table opposite, upon which stands a bottle with a candle perched rakishly in the neck. The* SPEAKER *himself is affectionately clasping the arm of the old* FLOWER WOMAN. *When he sees her he bursts into hysterical laughter.*)

WOMAN. Ah, me lovely gentleman, is it me yer calling?

SPEAKER. Well done! Well done! The joke is on me! Well done!

WOMAN. The Lord love ye, an' how's the poor head?

SPEAKER. Robert Emmet knows when the joke is on him! Kiss me, lovely Sarah Curran!

WOMAN (*archly*). Ah, go on owa that! D'jever hear the like!

OLDER MAN (*looking up from his game*). Drunk.

YOUNGER MAN. Aw, disgustin'.

WOMAN. Sit down now. Ah, go along with ye! Sit down now there, an' take no heed a them ignerant yucks . . . an' I'll get ye a small drop.

SPEAKER. My lovely Sarah Curran! Sweet Sally!

WOMAN (*aside to the* OLDER MAN). Ye bloody rip! I'll twist the tongue of ye, that's what I will.

SPEAKER. Her sunny mouth dimples with hope and joy.

YOUNGER MAN. Ho, yes, you'll do the hell of a lot, ma . . . in me eye!

WOMAN. Don't heed them. Don't heed them at all mister. He's no son of mine that has ne'er a soft word in his heart for th' old mudher that reared him in sickness and in sorra te be a heart-scaldin' affliction an' a theef a honest names.

OLDER MAN. Now ye can say what ye like, but there's a Man! There's a Man! Drunk, an' it's hours after closin'! Drunk, an' in th' old green coat! (*Singing.*) Oh, wrap the green flag round me, boys.

SPEAKER (*joins in.*) Ta-ra-ra-ra-ra-ra, Ra! Ra!

WOMAN. Sure, he's not drunk are ye, gentleman, an' if he was itself it's none a your concern. (*To* SPEAKER.) Isn't that right, son?

OLDER MAN. And why the hell shouldn't he be drunk? Tell me that. We're a Free State, aren't we? Keep open the pubs. That's my motto. What man says we're not a Free State?

YOUNGER MAN. I say it, ye drunken bastard!

OLDER MAN. Drunken bastard . . . hell! I declare to God I'm sober'n you are, me bold, water-drinkin' Diehard. God knows I'm cold an odd time, but sure a true Patriot is always drunk.

YOUNGER MAN. Have you no love for Ireland?

SPEAKER. God save Ireland!

OLDER MAN. Ho yes – 'The Republic still lives'. Aw – go te hell!

YOUNGER MAN. I've been to hell all right, never fear. I went down into hell shouting 'Up the living Republic', and I came up out of hell still shouting 'Up the living Republic' .Do you hear me? Up the Republic!

SPEAKER. Up the Priory!

OLDER MAN. Oh, I hear you well enough. But you'll not convince me for all your bridge blasting. Looka here, I stand for the status q-oh, and I'll not be intimidated by the gun.

WOMAN (*handing the* SPEAKER *a precious black bottle*). Here, have another sup and never heed that old chat of them!

SPEAKER. A health, Sarah Curran! A toast to the woman with brave sons!

WOMAN. Aw God . . . If I was young again!

YOUNGER MAN. And who needs to convince you?

OLDER MAN. Oh, you needn't think . . .

YOUNGER MAN. Every day and every night while you were lying on your back snoring, wasn't I out in the streets shouting 'Up the living Republic'?

OLDER MAN. Ah, don't we remember that too well.

SPEAKER. Up the living Departed!

YOUNGER MAN. Every morning and every night while you were sitting in the old snug, wasn't I out on the hills shouting 'Up the living Republic'?

SPEAKER. Up the pole!

OLDER MAN. Well?

YOUNGER MAN. Every hour of the day that you spent filling your belly and gassing about your status q-oh, wasn't I crying 'Republic, Republic, Republic'?

OLDER MAN. May God give ye a titther a sense some day.

SPEAKER. Up the blood-red Phlegethon! Up Cocytus, frozen lake of Hell!

OLDER MAN (*turning for a moment*). Aw, wouldn't that languidge disgust ye!

YOUNGER MAN. So one day, me laddo, you woke up and found that the Republic did live after all. And would you like to know why?

OLDER MAN. 'Tell me not in mournful numbers' . . .

YOUNGER MAN. Just because I and my like had said so, and said so again, while you were too drunk and too lazy and too thick in the head to say anything at all. That's why. And then, with the rest of your kidney you hunched your shoulders, spat on your hands, and went back to your bed mumbling 'Up the Status q-oh'. So why the hell should I try to convince you?

SPEAKER. A long speech. A strong speech. A toast to the son that speaks. A toast to the son that swills!

OLDER MAN. Aw, that's all words. Nothing but bloody words. You can't change the world by words.

YOUNGER MAN. That's where you fool yourself! What other way can you change it? I tell you, we can make this country – this world – whatever we want it to be by saying so, and saying so again. I tell you it is the knowledge of this that is the genius and glory of the Gael!

SPEAKER. Up the Primum Mobile! Up the graters of verdigreece. Up the Apes Pater Noster.

JOE.
> Cupping the crystal jewel-drops
> Girdling the singing of the silver stream . . .

(*He tries to scribble on the wall.*)
> What was it? . . . the singing of the silver stream.
> Damp acid-cups of meadowsweet . . .

SPEAKER. Hello! There's the fellow I shot. Is he not gone yet? A toast to the son that dies!

WOMAN. Ay . . . are ye lookin' for a bit of sport tonight?

SPEAKER. I have had brave sport this night!

WOMAN. Aw, mister . . . have a heart!

SPEAKER (*flaring up.*) A heart!

(JOE *gives a short, contented laugh.*)

SPEAKER. Do not do that. That is not the way to laugh.

YOUNGER MAN. I tell you, what the likes of me are saying tonight, the likes of you will be saying tomorrow.

OLDER MAN. Is that a fact? And may I be so bold as to in-quire what awtority you have for makin' that observation?

YOUNGER MAN. Because we're the lads that make the world.

OLDER MAN. You don't say!

SPEAKER (*passionately*). Then why have you made it as it is? Then will you stand before the Throne and justify your handiwork? Then will you answer to me for what I am?

YOUNGER MAN. What are *you* talking about? You're only a bloody play-actor. If you were a man and not satisfied with the state of things, you'd alter them for yourself.

OLDER MAN (*holding out a bottle*). Aw, have a sup and dry up for God's sake!

(JOE *laughs again*.)

SPEAKER. That blasphemous laugh! Do you not know you're going to die?

JOE (*laughing again*).

       Soft radiance of the shy new moon
       Above the green gold cap of Kilmashogue
       Where . . .

SPEAKER. Kilmashogue!

JOE.

       Where of a summer's evening I have danced
       A saraband.

SPEAKER. What of Kilmashogue? Look around you. Here! Don't you know me? I shot you.

JOE. Well, please don't interrupt. (*He coughs*.)

WOMAN. It's the cough that shivers ye, isn't it, son? Me poor lamb, will ye tell the gentleman . . . (*She goes as if to touch him*.)

JOE (*through his teeth*). Strumpet! Strumpet!

WOMAN. Blast ye! ye'd use that word t'yer own mudher, would ye! God, I'll throttle ye with me own two hands for the dirty scut ye are!

SPEAKER. Go back!

YOUNGER MAN (*seizing her from behind and flinging her away*). Away to hell, ye old trollop!

OLDER MAN. Ah, leave her alone.

WOMAN. Awlright, awlright! Yer all agin me. But it won't be th' cough will have th' stiffenin' of him not if I lay me hands on his dirty puss before he's gone. When I get a holt a ye I'll leave me mark on ye never fear.

71

YOUNGER MAN. Aw, shut yer mouth, ma!

JOE. I'd like to do it all again . . . That's right . . . Again . . . It's
good . . . to feel the wind . . . in your hair . . .

(*He laughs weakly.*)

SPEAKER. Don't! Don't do that I tell you!

JOE.

> Stench of the nut-brown clay
> Piled high around the headstones and the yews,
> My fingers clotted with the crusted clay,
> My heart is singing . . . in the skies . . .

(*He coughs again. The* BLIND FIDDLER *enters slowly through
the door.*)

OLDER MAN. You know, some of that stuff is very hard to follow.
I'd sooner have the old stuff any day.

> 'Oh I met with Napper Tandy
> An' he took me by the hand.'

SPEAKER. Sssssh!

YOUNGER MAN. What do you want here?

BLIND MAN. Wouldn't I have a right to pay my respects to one,
and he passin' into the ranks of the Government? Isn't it a
comely thing for me to be hopin' that he'll remember a poor
old dark man an' he sittin' in the seats of the mighty in his kingdom out beyond?

JOE (*very soft*). Well . . . so long, lads. It was . . . a grand life . . . so
long, lad . . . that plugged me . . So long . . . (*He dies.*)

WOMAN. Burn ye! Burn ye!

BLIND MAN. Be silent now, and a new shadow after being born! Do
you not know, woman, that this land belongs not to them that
are on it, but to them that are under it.

YOUNGER MAN. He's gone. Stiffening already, poor chap. Hats off,
lads.

SPEAKER. Gone! And I am only a play-actor – unless I dare to
contradict the dead! Must I do that?

BLIND MAN. Let them build their capitols on Leinster Lawn. Let
them march their green battalions out by the Park Gate. Out
by Glasnevin there's a rattle of bones and a bit of a laugh where
the presidents and senators of Ireland are dancing hand in hand,
with no one to see them but meself an' I with the stick an' the
fiddle under me arm.

OLDER MAN. Well . . . a wake's a wake, anyhow. So pass over the
bottle and give us a tune on the ole instrument.

BLIND MAN (*tuning up*). It's many's the year an' I fiddled at a wake.

72

WOMAN. One son with th' divil in hell, an' two more with th' divils on earth. (*She spits.*) God forgive me for weanin' a brood a sorry scuts!

(*The* SPEAKER *is seated silently at the foot of the bed, staring at the body with his back to the audience. There is a knock at the door.*)

WOMAN. Wha's that?

(*The* YONGER MAN *goes to the door, pauses, and flings it open. On the threshold stands* MAEVE.)

MAEVE. My mammy thez...

WOMAN. Ah love, is it yerself?

MAEVE. My mammy thez I'm to play the accompaniment of 'The Thruggle Ith Over'.

WOMAN. Come on in, duckie. God love ye an' welcome. The ole pianner's waiting for ye, love.

MAEVE. Yeth pleathe. My mammy...

(*She comes in and, catching sight of the* SPEAKER, *she points, and bursts into tears.*)

WOMAN. There, there! What's the matter, lamb? Ah God help her! What ails ye at all?

MAEVE (*gulping*). Thlipperth...

WOMAN. There, there now...

OLDER MAN. Aw, will ye dry up?

WOMAN (*with an impatient flap of the hand*). There's the pianner, so do what yer mammy says before I slaughter ye.

BLIND MAN. Play on now, young one. And when you've played, 'tis meself will fiddle for the shadows and they dancing at the wake.

MAEVE (*sniffling*). My mammy thez...

(MAEVE *sits at an old cracked piano, upon which presently she commences to thump out carefully 'The Struggle Is Over'.*)

WOMAN. There now. Ah God, hasn't she the gorgus touch on th' ole instrument!

(*Another knock at the door. The* YOUNGER MAN *opens it. The* MINISTER FOR ARTS AND CRAFTS *is on the threshold in top hat, frock coat, and carrying one of those hemispherical glass cases full of white flowers.*)

MINISTER. Deep concern – Government grieved to learn – struck down in prime – Requiem Mass – life for Erin – send a gunboat – bitter loss – token of our regard. (*He presents the case.*)

73

WOMAN (*very unctuous*). Ah, aren't ye the kind-hearted Government, and isn't them th' gorgus flowers. God will reward ye, sir; He will indeed at the next election, for th' blessed pity ye've shown to a poor woman in her sorra.

(*Another knock at the door. The* YOUNGER MAN *opens it.* LADY TRIMMER, *dressed in widow's weeds, enters.*)

LADY TRIMMER. So sad! So sad indeed! I can't simply say how sad it is. Quite a poet, too, I hear. Can any of his books be purchased?

WOMAN. At Hodges an' Figgis ma'am. Be sure ye get the name right. Come in, come in!

(*Before the* YOUNGER MAN *has the door properly closed there comes another knock. He abandons it, leaving it open. The* STATUE OF GRATTAN *is on the threshold.*)

GRATTAN. A word-spinner dying gracefully, with a cliché on his lips. The symbol of Ireland's genius. Never mind. He passed on magnificently. He knew how to do that.

WOMAN (*her head quite turned*). An' he was me favrit', too lady . . . never a bitter word . . . never a hard glance. Sure, it's them we love th' best is took th' first, God help us. Ullagone! Ullagone! Ochone-a-ree!

(*Enter the* GENERAL *with crape upon his arm.*)

GENERAL . . . a grand song called 'Home to Our Mountains'. No. 17 bus passes the door or a bus to Ballyboden, whenever the road's not up. But of course if you don't want me to sing, I won't force myself on you. Won't I?

WOMAN.

> Low lie your heads this day
> My sons! My sons!
> The strong in their pride go by me
> Saying, 'Where are thy sons?'

(O'COONEY, O'MOONEY *and* O'ROONEY *enter, all in black gloves and top hats.*)

ALL THREE. Who's a twister? I'm a twister? You're a twister? He's taken a header into the Land of Youth. Anyhow, he was a damn sight better man than some I could name, and there's no blottin' it out.

LADY TRIMMER. So yellow-haired Donough is dead! Dear, dear!

(*A few more stray figures crush in, chattering and pressing forward in file before the body.*)

WOMAN.

> Gall to our heart! Oh, gall to our heart!

Ullagone! Ochone-a-ree!
A lost dream to us now in our home!

MAEVE (*stopping her playing*). Will that do, Daddy?

BLIND MAN (*mounting upon a chair*). The shadows are gathering, gathering. They're coming to dance at a wake. An' I playin' for them on the gut box. Are yez ready all?

(*He tunes up. The lights in front have dimmed, leaving a great sheet of brightness flooding from the sides upon the back-cloth. The walls of the room seem to fade apart while the crowd draws aside and seats itself upon the floor and upon all sides of the stage. The* SPEAKER *has vanished.*)

THE VOICES OF THE CROWD. The Shadows are gathering, gathering: he says they must dance at a wake. Seats for the Shadows the gathering Shadows . . . The Shadows that dance at a wake.

(*The* BLIND MAN *commences to fiddle a jig in the whole-tone scale.*)

THE VOICES.
Overture started
Seats for the Shadows
Gathering, gathering
Dance at a wake
Loosen his collar
Basin of water
Dance Shadows
Oooooooh!

(*Upon the back-cloth two great* SHADOWS *appear gesturing and posturing in time with the music.*)

THE FIRST SHADOW (*stopping his dance and striking an attitude*).
Come clear of the nets of wrong and right;
Laugh, heart, again in the grey twilight,
Sigh, heart, again in the dew of the morn.
Your Mother Eire is always young . . .

(*Hand clapping. The* SECOND SHADOW *jostles the* FIRST *aside and points one long arm vaguely in the direction of the* FLOWER WOMAN.)

THE SECOND SHADOW. Stone traps of dead builders. Warrens of weasel rats! How serene does she now arise! Queen among the Pleiades, in the penultimate antelucan hour: shod in sandals of bright gold: coifed with a veil of gossamer.

(*Applause. Amidst shrieks of laughter the* FLOWER WOMAN *rises, curtsies and dances hilariously once round the fore-*

ground. Two more SHADOWS *have elbowed the first pair aside and are now dancing to the music.*)

THE VOICES.

Dance! Dance!

Speak, Shadows, speak!

THE THIRD SHADOW. It is difficult not to be unjust to what one loves. Is not He who made misery wiser than thou?

(*Applause, mingled with some booing. The* THIRD SHADOW *throws up its arms and flees.*)

THE FOURTH SHADOW. Every dream is a prophecy: every jest an earnest in the womb of time.

(*Shouts of laughter and applause. The* SHADOWS *change into a tumbling mass of blackness.*)

THE VOICES.

Dance! Dance!

Speak, Shadows, speak!

A VOICE. There are no Shadows left to speak.

BLIND MAN. Speak, great Shadow! Shadow of Ireland's Heart.

VOICES (*whispering*). We see him. He is here.

(*The shadow of the* SPEAKER *precedes him as he comes slowly in from the back.*)

BLIND MAN. Speak, shadow of Robert Emmet.

SPEAKER. I know whom you are calling. I am ready.

BLIND MAN. The eyes of the people are fixed on your face.

VOICES. Justify! Justify! Shadow of the Speaker, speak!

VOICES. Sssh!

SPEAKER. The souls in the seven circles of Purgatory cry out, Deliver us O Lord from the mouth of the Lion that Hell may not swallow us up. The Word Made Flesh shall break the chains that bind me. Three armies may be robbed of their leader – no wretch can be robbed of his will.

Yes, there is darkness now, but I can create light. I can separate the waters of the deep, and a new world will be born out of the void. A challenge, Norns! A gage flung down before you! Justify! Justify!

VOICES. Justify! Justify!

(*The* SPEAKER *continues to address the audience.*)

SPEAKER (*continues*). Race of men with dogs' heads! Panniers filled with tripes and guts! Thelemites! Cenobites! Flimflams of the law! Away! while Niobe still weeps over her dead children. I have heard the angels chanting the Beatitudes to the souls in Malebolge, and I have done with you.

76

I do not fear to approach the Omnipotent Judge to answer
for the conduct of my short life and am I to stand appalled here
before this mere remnant of mortality? I do not imagine that
Your Lordships will give credit to what I utter. I have no hopes
that I can anchor my character in the breast of this court. I only
wish Your Lordships may suffer it to float down your memories
until it has found some more hospitable harbour to shelter it.

(*Voices, shuffling, applause.*)

SPEAKER (*continues*). For now is the axe put to the root of the tree.
My fan is in my hand, and I will burn the chaff with unquench-
able fire.

VOICES.

Up Emmet!

Up Rathfarnham!

Up the Up that won't be Down!

(*He draws his sword and turns upon them all. During the
following commination the* VOICES *give the responses in unison
and the* FIGURES *in turn fling up their arms and take flight
before him. The light fades, gradually blotting out all vestiges of
the room.*)

SPEAKER. Cursed be he who values the life above the dream.

VOICES. Amen.

SPEAKER. Cursed be he who builds but does not destroy.

VOICES. Amen.

SPEAKER. Cursed be he who honours the wisdom of the wise.

VOICES. Amen.

SPEAKER. Cursed be the ear that heeds the prayer of the dead.

VOICES. Amen.

SPEAKER. Cursed be the eye that sees the heart of a foe.

VOICES. Amen.

SPEAKER. Cursed be prayers that plough not, praises that reap not,
joys that laugh not, sorrows that weep not.

VOICES (*dying away*). Amen. Amen. Ah – men.

(*The last of the* FIGURES *fling up their arms and vanish. As
the* SPEAKER *comes down stage they come creeping back
again, crouching in the darkness and watching him with many
eyes. It is dark.*)

SPEAKER. I will take this earth in both my hands and batter it into
the semblance of my heart's desire! See, there by the trees is
reared the gable of the house where sleeps my dear one. Under
my feet the grass is growing, soft and subtle, in the evening dew.
The cool, clean wind is blowing down from Killakee, kissing

my hair and dancing with the flowers that fill the garden all around me. And Sarah . . . Sarah Curran . . . you are there . . . waiting for Robert Emmet.

I know this garden well for I have called it into being with the Credo of the Invincibles: I believe in the might of Creation, the majesty of the Will, the resurrection of the Word, and Birth Everlasting.

(*He flings aside his sword and looks around him in triumph. It is very dark, so dark that for all we know perhaps it may be the garden of the first scene. Perhaps those may be the trees and the mountains beyond the Priory. For a moment we hear the tramp of feet and the distant sound of the Shan Van Vocht. His voice falters and he staggers wearily.*)

SPEAKER. My ministry is now ended. Shall we sit down together for a while? Here on the hillside . . . where we can look down over the city, and watch the lights twinkle and wink to each other . . . Our city . . . our wilful, wicked old city . . .

(*The gauze curtains close slowly behind him.*)

I think . . . I would like to sleep . . . What? . . . On your shoulder? . . . Ah, I was so right to go on!

(*His head sinks drowsily and his eyes stare out into the auditorium. He is lying just where the* DOCTOR *left him some time ago.*)

Strumpet city in the sunset
Suckling the bastard brats of Scots, of Englishry, of Huguenot.
Brave sons breaking from the womb, wild sons fleeing from their Mother.
Wilful city of savage dreamers,
So old, so sick with memories!
Old Mother
Some they say are damned,
But you, I know, will walk the streets of Paradise
Head high, and unashamed.

(*His eyes close. He speaks very softly.*)

There now. Let my epitaph be written.

(*There is silence for a moment and then the* DOCTOR *speaks off.*)

DOCTOR. . . . . do, fine.

(*He appears bearing a large and gaudy rug. He looks towards the audience, places one finger to his lips, and makes a sign for the front curtains to be drawn. When last we see him he is*

78

covering the unconscious SPEAKER *with his rug. That is the end of this play.*)

BLOOMSBURY, 1926 – DALKEY, 1976.

A NOTE ON WHAT HAPPENED

(The following note was originally written nearly fifty years ago in advance of the production of the play in the United States. It is published here for the first time.)

Walking back from Sorrento with Mr Yeats he gave me what was probably the most incisive criticism this play has received. 'I liked your play,' he said, 'but it has one or two faults. The first is, the scenes are too long.' He was silent for a time, while we both gazed with some signs of embarrassment at a cargo boat rounding Dalkey Island. 'Then', he added finally and after considerable thought, 'there are too many scenes'.

Needless to say I was grateful for this opinion.

To say that the scenes are too long and that there are too many of them goes right to the root of the matter. Why do it at all? And if it does mean anything, isn't it better left unsaid?

A distinguished member of the audience who sat through most of the performance with his eyes closed remarked very aptly as he took himself home, 'I suppose people must have nightmares, but why inflict them on us?' I am afraid I can supply very little in the way of an answer. Perhaps nightmares – or dreams, if you're that kind – don't really mean very much, and probably a good many of them would be better left unremembered. Ireland is spiritually in a poor condition at the moment and I don't know that homoeopathic treatment is the best for her complaint. A young lady having seen the play said of it that it made her blush. Not because of its vulgarity – ordinary vulgarity was a commonplace on the stage. But this was different. She had blushed for me – that such thoughts should ever have entered my head.

This play, if plays must be about something, is about what Dublin has made a good many of us feel. And if it is a very wrong and vulgar feeling that could only have been experienced by people with nasty minds, we aren't worth bothering about anyway. But it

80

is no good saying that it isn't true, because we happen to know that it is.

I was warned during rehearsals by various friends that the play would be denounced as anti-National, or as Republican propaganda, or as a personal reflection on so-and-so – opinions which were given with the best of good will but whose only common denominator was that the play would be denounced. In this they were right, but only in their conclusions. For as it turned out when the production was complete the assault came from a most unexpected quarter. It was well patronised by *l'ancien regime* and was stoutly defended in the press and elsewhere by more than one physical force Intransigentist. But exception was taken to the play on the ground that it was blasphemous.

It appeared that the language of the Holy Writ was used in obscene circumstances – ranted and raved by a mad actor to the accompaniment of a chorus of curses and swearwords – that the scene in which some of these lines were spoken was a brothel – and that the final Commination was a ribald parody of Jesus driving the money-changers from the Temple.

I need hardly say that I was not prepared for this, although I was ready to be philosophic about the charge that I was trying to write a silly lampoon of living persons. But now that I come to think of it, I have noticed before that the words of Holy Writ when used in circumstances in which they are liable to be taken seriously sometimes incur the suspicion of being either insanity or blasphemy.

I can quite appreciate the point of view which holds that the ethics of religion are solely a matter for the pulpit and have no place upon the stage.

But granted that we have persuaded all those members of the audience to leave the theatre if they are the kind who experience a shock on discovering that their own theological ideas have a human and a dramatic meaning as well as a symbolic one; how then, are we to express on the stage the idea of the triumph of the Word over environment – the dogma of the Resurrection? It seems to me that the most straightforward way – especially in a play where all other ideas are conveyed by the thematic method – is to call up the desired association of ideas by suggesting the words of the Liturgy.

Whether or not I have succeeded in doing this myself is another matter, but the fact that I appear to have suggested to the minds of some of my critics the picture of the expulsion of the money-changers from the Temple – an analogy which was not before my own mind – would indicate that I have not entirely failed.

And lest it should be thought that criticisms of this kind are not of much consequence these days, I should add that nearly every night indignant women walked out during the last act, and strong representations were made to the authorities to have a blasphemy prosecution set on foot. Needless to say the authorities had no time to waste on such small fry as the little Gate Theatre or myself, but the threat had high ramifications and results that it would be amusing but totally wrong of me to disclose.

* * * *

I think that it must be a result of the long predominance of narrative drama to the exclusion of all else that people get so worried when one cannot tell them what a play is about. Yet the dithyrambic outbursts from which both western and eastern theatrical conventions have developed had nothing to do with a plot. It would be difficult to interpret the religious ecstacy of a mediaeval miracle play or the intricacies of a No Play of Japan for inclusion in French's 'Guide to Selecting Plays'.

It seems to me that the real play must be regarded as what goes on in the mind of the audience. What, therefore, a play is about depends entirely on who is listening to it.

Anybody who has done any acting will know that a performance to an audience is quite a different affair from the most complete Dress Rehearsal – as different as War is from Salisbury Plain. And furthermore, a good play – that is to say, a play which is succeeding in registering its effect whether we personally approve of it or not – is a different play from night to night according as the reflex of the House varies.

And these ideas and emotions can be stimulated without the assistance of a narrative plot at all, whether melodically as in music, by direct statement as in continental Expressionism, or by simple association of ideas. Strindberg in some of his later work provides one of the best modern examples of the fact that dramatic experience is not dependent on physical actuality and is in fact hampered by it. In the 'Spook Sonata' there is for example, the wretched wife who sits all day in a dark cupboard from which she cries like a parrot, 'Pretty Polly! Pretty Polly!' This genius with which he conveys an attitude of mind in terms of a fantastic physical reality has, on me at any rate, a most real and horrifying effect, but the intention of the author is completely defeated if the audience insists on regarding the picture as one of narrative fact.

82

The melodic method has been greatly developed since the War by the Russians, principally in the Constructivist Theatre of Meierhold and in the Moscow Jewish Art Theatre, where an attempt is made to stimulate the desired attitude of mind by means of acrobatics and dancing and the elimination of all unnecessary detail in the way of stage decor or scenery. The development of electric lighting has of course opened up limitless possibilities in all those directions.

Toller and Kaiser taking the dangerous course of direct statement have so simplified the stage by throwing out unnecessary lumber that nothing will convince a British audience, schooled to the loud technical camouflage of Mr St. John Irvine, that they are really saying anything at all. They have however discredited their school to some extent in the eyes of non-industrial audiences by a complete absence of humour and by the Frankenstein complex that seems to have dominated the stage of Central Europe ever since the War.

In English-speaking countries on the other hand, the tradition of Pinero, Barker and Shaw, culminating in the 'Problem Play', is still well entrenched in the path of any further development of the theatre. We have the Play that leaves you with a Thought. What would I do if I met an Escaped Convict? How would I like it if Father married a Prostitute? Is War Right? I need hardly say that as a natural consequence nobody can go to an ostensibly serious play without feeling that he must concentrate upon what it is all About.

But surely this is all wrong, just as it would be in the case of music! All that is needed to enjoy and appreciate a work such as E. E. Cummings' 'Him' is a simple faith, a little human experience, and a receptive state of mind attained by a process the reverse of concentration. This being the normal condition of my own mind I need hardly say that I find little difficulty in preferring Strindberg's 'Dream Play' to 'Emperor and Galillean'.

*   *   *   *

'The Old Lady says "No"!' is not an expressionist play and ought never to have been mistaken for one. I have attempted to evolve a thematic method based on simple association of ideas, a process which has as many disadvantages as the opposite. For it presupposes at the start a set of recognisable figments in the minds of the audience – figments which from their very nature are bound to be somewhat local. In consequence of this, the play to be intelligible to a non-Irish audience requires to some extent to be translated.

The theme of the Romantic temperament seeking for an environment in which to express himself is a universal one, but everybody cannot be expected to know about Robert Emmet. When an old lady appears upon the stage and maunders about her four beautiful green fields, it is too much to expect of a London audience that it will recognise the traditional figure of romantic Nationalism for whom Mangan and Pearse sighed. It is only in the Free State that the O'Donovan Rossa speech and Committee Room 15 (where Parnell was betrayed) can be relied upon to call up any recollections without the aid of a footnote.

Yet the search for the Land of Heart's Desire is as old and as universal as the Holy Grail. The tale might also be the tale of such diverse figures as Juan Ponce de Leon, of the great Danton, of Abelard, of John Brown of Harper's Ferry and even of poor William Blake. Every land has had its store of Emmets, preaching their burning messages to the accompaniment of farmyard noises, and Ireland has more than her share.

It was Plato who first told us that if we don't like our environment it is up to us to alter it for ourselves, and the vigorous philosophy of Nietzsche's Man-Gott and the biology of Buffon and Lamarck are in somewhat the same line of business. If the Emmets in particular or if intransigent Irish Republicanism in general are to be taken as having made any contribution to the world of applied philosophy I feel that it is this characteristic attitude of mind. 'The Republic still lives' is not the expression of a pious hope, but is in itself a creative act, as England knows to her cost.

I understand that there is a correct psychological explanation of all this. Ned Stephens, for instance, tells me that the play represents the breaking down of something called a 'synthetic personality' by contact with reality and the creation of a new one in its stead. I am much too scared of Freud, Adler and McDougall ever to have attempted any such thing, but I feel that if a play is true to experience in its emotional aspect it may well have a sound psychological meaning thrown in as well. As a small boy I used to make pictures for myself with a box of blocks. When the work was completed I used to find that by turning the whole over you found another finished picture constructed on the other side.

But I should add that all this is not intended to be by way of explanation. All that I do wish to do is to answer the objection levelled at much of the post-war spirit both in art and in letters;

that it is insincere, intentionally obscure and that it lacks fundamentality. Lucidity seems to me to be the *sine qua non* of any effort of this kind. It has not been my desire to detract attention from my lack of craftsmanship by muddling people's minds. Neither have I any desire that the play should be unjustly enhanced by the 'false glitter of quotations', as one critic very threateningly put it. The method is thematic and a motif in the realm of thought is carried best by a name or a quotation.

Some years ago I used to have to play a game where some large, blindfold person, groping round with a cushion, would sit on my knee and tell me to 'Make a noise like a camel'. Well in this play when I want to make a noise like the Old Ireland, I do it in what seems to me to be the easiest way – by means of a potted anthology of the 'Erin a tear and a smile' school that preceded Geoffrey Phibbs. The play with which the first part opens, and which crops up again at intervals, is almost entirely composed of well-known lines from Mangan, Moore, Callinan, Blacker, Griffin, Ferguson, Kickham, Todhunter and a dozen more. The voices of the Shadows are the easily recognisable words of some of Dublin's greatest contributors to the World's knowledge of itself. The long speech with which the play concludes contains suggestions from Emmet's speech from the dock, the resurrection thesis of the Litany, and the magnificent, though sadly neglected, Commination Service of the Anglican Church.

I have already drawn attention to the Old Woman's lines. For the rest I have not consciously or wilfully bowdlerised anybody, except one line of Blake's which I freely admit I am not entitled to, but which is too apt to be surrendered. You may have it if you can find it!

But whatever may be said of the play, there can be no two opinions as to the merits of Hilton Edward's production. It was staged on a space roughly 16 feet by 12 feet – an incredible feat, when it is remembered that at several points there are mass movements of crowds that have to be carried out in a manner not dissimilar to a ballet, and that sets have to be changed while the action is proceeding.

The rhythmatic chanting of the Choruses was carried out to the throb of a drum, for which purpose a considerable portion of the dialogue had practically to be scored – the parts coming in one on top of the other as in instrumental music or a madrigal. It was an unusual and amusing sight at rehearsals to see the spoken lines being conducted from the front by the Producer. It would be invidious to refer to the players. The elan of Michael MacLiammoir as the Speaker, the virtuosity of Meriel Moore in the difficult double role of Sarah Curran and the old woman, and the very trying work of the Chorus were the real cause of the play's success.

May I respectively thank them – not forgetting to include my friend Kate Curling for her help and for her contribution.

Pertisau, 1929.

86

TITLES AND AUTHORS OF POEMS USED IN THE PROLOGUE

CURTIS CANFIELD

Many of these poems are included in *The Dublin Book of Irish Verse*, 1728–1909, edited by John Cooke.

1. *The Shan Van Vocht*—a famous patriotic ballad written in 1796. "Shan Van Vocht" (Sean Bhean Bhocht) means "the poor old woman" and is symbolic of Ireland. Hence the significance of the play's title.
2. *"The air is rich and soft.... Oh, the fair hills of Eiré, oh."* "The Fair Hills of Eiré, O!" by James Clarence Mangan (1803–1849). The original has *"The soil is rich and soft ... etc."*
3. *"Down from the high cliffs ... sleepy arms have wound him."* "Serenade of a Loyal Martyr" by George Darley (1795–1846).
4. *"I think, oh my love, 'tis thy voice from the kingdom of souls!"* "At the Mid Hour of Night" by Thomas Moore (1779–1846).
5. *"Was ever light of beauty shed on loveliness like thine!"* "An Ancient Tale" by John O'Hagan has *"... was ever light of evening shed ... etc."*
6. *"My bed was the ground ... kind glance from my love."* "The Outlaw of Loch Lene," translated from the Irish by Jeremiah Joseph Callanan (1795–1829).
7. *"... for a vision of fanciful bliss ... labour and peace!"* "High Brasail—the Isle of the Blest" by Gerald Griffin (1803–1840) has *"Rash fool! For a vision ... etc."*
8. *"Let them come! A million a decade!"* "The Exodus" by Lady Wilde (1820?–1896).
9. *"Let me be persuaded ... hills and I am free."* "Sonnet Written during His Residence in College" by Charles Wolfe (1791–1823).
10. *"Ah, go, forget me. Why should sorrow o'er that brow a shadow fling?"* "Go! Forget Me" by Charles Wolfe.
11. *"My strong ones have fallen from the bright eye of day."* "Oh, Say, My Brown Drimin" by J. J. Callanan.
12. *"Their graves are red ... with God in glory!"* "Plorans Ploravit" by Sir Aubrey De Vere (1814–1902).

87

13. *"Where is thy throne? It is gone in the wind!"* "Gone in the Wind" by James Clarence Mangan.

14. *"A dark chain of silence is thrown o'er the deep."* "Eiré' by William Drennan (1754–1820).

15. *"No streak of dawning . . . that clanking chain."* "To Erin" by Mary Eva Kelly.

16. *"Yet, am I the slave they say?"* "Soggarth Aroon" (Priest dear) by John Banim (1798–1842).

17. *"A lost dream to us now is our home! Ullagone! Gall to our heart!"* "The Swan's Lament for the Desolation of Lir" by John Todhunter (1839–1916).

18. *"But there is lightning in my blood-red lightning tightening in . . . etc."* "Dark Rosaleen" by James Clarence Mangan (from the Irish). The Speaker's excitement evidently causes him to misquote here. The original has *". . . red lightning lightened through my blood . . . etc."*

19. *"It is too late! Large, large affliction . . . its wrath on head like this!"* "O'Hussey's Ode to the Maguire" by James Clarence Mangan.

20. *"My earthly comforter, whose love so indefeasable might be!"* "True Loveliness" by George Darley. This poem is known also by the title, "It Is Not Beauty I Demand."

21. *"Your holy, delicate, white hands . . . daylight hours my virgin flower!"* "Dark Rosaleen" by James Clarence Mangan.

22. *"At least I'll love thee till I die . . . hushed that struggling sigh!"* "Dry Be That Tear" by Richard Brinsley Sheridan (1751–1816).

23. *"When he who adores thee has left but a name . . . etc."* When He Who Adores Thee" by Thomas Moore.

24. *"I shall not weep. I shall not breathe his name."* "Oh! Breathe not his Name" by Thomas Moore.

25. *"For my heart in his grave will be lying."* "She Is Far from the Land" by Thomas Moore.

26. *"I shall sing a lament for the Sons of Usnach!"* John Todhunter is the author of a poem "Deirdre's Great Lamentation for the Sons of Usnach."

27. *"But see, she smiles, . . . dewy eyes are full of pity!"* "The Benumbed Butterfly" by Sir Aubrey De Vere (1788–1846).

28. *"Men of Eiré, awake to be blest. Rise, Arch of the Ocean . . . etc."* "Eiré" by William Drennan.

29. *"The countersign.*
    Stand.
    Front point.
    Advance." "Rory of the Hill" by Charles Joseph Kickham (1828–1882).
30. *"The flint-hearted Saxon!"* "Oh, Say, My Brown Drimin" by J. J. Callanan.
31. *". . . in their fearful red array!"* "Kathleen bán Adair" by Francis Davis (1810–1885).
32. *"We hold this house . . . may all traitors swing."* "The Croppy Boy, a Ballad of '98" by William B. McBurney.
33. *"Slaves and dastards, stand aside!"* "Fag an Bealach" (Clear the Road) by Charles Gavan Duffy (1816–1903).
34. *"Spawn of treason."* "Oliver's Advice" by Colonel William Blacker (1777–1855).
35. *". . . bow down thy humbled head to him, the King!"* "The Land Betrayed" by Sir Stephen E. De Vere (1812–1904).
36. *"A Nation's voice, a Nation's voice, 'tis stronger than the King."* "Nationality" by Thomas Osborne Davis (1814–1845).
37. *"When they that are up will be down . . . etc."* These sentiments are expressed in the well-known play, "The Rising of the Moon" by Lady Gregory.
38. *". . . we'll be a glorious nation yet—redeemed, erect, alone!"* "Ourselves Alone" by John O'Hagan (1822–1890).
39. *"A star is gone! There is a blank in Heaven."* "The Fallen Star" by George Darley.
40. *"The last great Tribune of the world is dead."* "The Great Tribune" by Denis Florence McCarthy.
41. *"The sport of fools . . . blossomed, barren, blighted."* "The Land Betrayed" by Sir Stephen E. De Vere.
42. *"They came whose counsels . . . cheeks untinged by shame."* "Oliver's Advice" by Colonel William Blacker.
43. *"To sue for a pity they shall not . . ."* "The Ballad of the Bier that Conquered; or O'Donnell's Answer" by Sir Aubrey De Vere.

Reprinted with permission from Curtis Canfield, *Plays of Changing Ireland*, New York, Macmillan, 1936.

THE MOON
IN THE YELLOW RIVER

A Play in Three Acts

LET THERE BE LIGHT

An Irish play, taking its title from an American poet's translation from the Chinese, a play in which the references range from Slovakian convents to Paraguayan railway bridges, in which the commentator is a German, and the theme is international industrialism, can hardly be considered to have the same limited target as *The Old Lady*. Indeed, I have sometimes wondered whether the fact that its setting suggests the Liffey or the Shannon, and that it contains incidents drawn from the conflict of Irregular and Free Stater, is sufficient to constitute *The Moon in the Yellow River* as an Abbey play at all.

Although there is a good deal of talk about theology in the course of the dialogue, it is not as easy as it should be in an Irish play to determine the religious persuasion of most of the principal characters. It may also be noticed that the only reference to England is a passing sneer at the lion as 'a very middle-class beast'. So without either the odour of sanctity or of England, it may be asked what this play has got to do with the Emerald Isle. Yet in Dublin it has always been suspected of harbouring a superior ascendancy smile at the expense of the noble native, and it has never been popular there on that account.

It was gently sabotaged by most of its original Abbey cast who until 1938 played it with that subtle air of distaste with which experienced actors can dissociate themselves from the sentiments expressed in their parts. On its first night it had one of those very mixed receptions that usually presage a riot on the second. However, this never quite materialized, although I waited in some apprehension in the green room for another of those summonses to the stage that have nothing to do with a curtain call. All that it got was a rough deal from the newspapers, which complained that its humour was feeble, that it had no visible plot, and that it 'introduced some coarse levity on the subject of childbirth'.

In fairness to Dublin, it must be admitted that the play does propound a problem which was difficult, in those days, to face

93

without a certain feeling of depression. Although no physical assault was ever actually launched against the Shannon Hydro-electrical Power Plant, a very determined effort had been made by an armed minority to make majority government unworkable. This had been effectively stopped by the use of methods equally rough, but very practical in their results. In short, the recrudescence of murder as a political argument had been brought to a sudden stop by means of the counter-murder of prisoners in the hands of the new native Government. There was no legal or moral justification for such measures on the part of the infant Free State. But the melancholy fact remained that it had worked, and that an Irish Government had proved to be much tougher with the Irish than the English had ever dared to be. Nor did the glamour of patriotic martyrdom attach itself to the victims. This was all very sobering and disgusting. Yet it is hard to see what other answer could have been made to a continuance of underground warfare, provided of course that we were to have any government at all.

When Captain Jack White, the founder of the Irish Citizen Army, accosted me outside the theatre and accused me of justifying these methods in my play, I invited him to tell me what the proper answer was, and I would put it in.

'There is no answer,' said Jack White, 'and you know it. That's why you are a traitor and a renegade.'

So I wrote the operative part of this remark into the play, where it is still to be found in the last act.

As I have already mentioned, *The Moon* was the first, and is still the only one, of my works to have undergone the standard processing by which a script is rendered fit for Broadway production. Whether this is a good or a bad thing is a question that has long puzzled me. I have little doubt that, as a rule, it is a very good thing when practised by producers who are themselves either writers or directors. But the trouble is that this so seldom is the case. One of the two moments in the theatre when the Nuisances are most in evidence is whenever a dramatist is being told how to rewrite his script. The other, of course, is during casting, which is heaven for these chaps, but is hell for most of the regulars, who understand the heartburnings that are involved.

In my own case I was lucky in having only to deal with a committee of reputable theatre people. Even so, the sense that was talked with regard to making the play intelligible outside

Ireland was sometimes outweighed by the vulgarity of some of the technical suggestions as to how this excellent purpose was to be effected.

I was summoned to New York – as many a writer has been before and since, with much the same experience. It was explained to me that here was a more sophisticated audience than any that I was probably used to – an audience that had been trained by my present producers to expect a high state of care and accuracy in anything that they were to see upon the stage. Would I therefore please begin by drawing a plan of the fort in which the play was set, and add to this a sketch-map of the countryside for some miles around.

This was a pleasure. I drafted out a plan of the Pigeon House, together with all the topographical aspects of the surrounding slob-lands of Sandymount. But there were other things that they wanted to know. How many people were hurt in the explosion? How far away did the life-saving exercises take place? How old was Blanaid's mother when she died?

This was in the days before the Method, and – ponderous as it may seem – it was not a bad test by which to find out whether an author had really visualized what he was writing about. Indeed, a few more direct quotes from these conversations – which I wrote down in the Taft Hotel after each session – may be the simplest way of commenting upon some of the main points of the play, on how it first struck Broadway, and on how I failed to answer some of Broadway's more searching probes. The verbiage today is, of course, different from that of the days of the soup queues in Times Square, at which date 'Motivation' was one of the great Things. Nor is the catch-phrase 'I'm from Missouri' still in current use. But the same longing to leap to melodramatic assumptions, and to misinterpret human behaviour in terms of what is imagined to be Good Theatre (but is usually only Good Cliché) is still prevalent today – a fact that suggests that we are none of us probably quite as sophisticated as we like to imagine.

MR L. Well, I think this last Act is interesting philosophically, but it seems to me that nothing further happens. Just explain to me what this scene between the father and the daughter has to do with the play about the power house.

ME. The play isn't about a power house. It's a play about people.

MR L. Don't be afraid to say that it has nothing to do with it. I was reading a play of Dryden's last night that had three plots, and none of the characters in each ever meet each other.

ME (*doggedly*). It's not that I'm afraid to say it. All my characters meet each other.

MR M. What's missing is the motivation. This playing for time by Tausch has got to be motivated. The shooting of Blake must be motivated. You see, I'm from Missouri. Do you know what that means?

ME (*lying*). Yes. But I'm not sure that I know what 'motivated' means.

MR M. Well for example, how about Blake making some taunting remark after his song to Lanigan to make Lanigan mad at him so that he shoots him?

ME. But he doesn't shoot him because he's mad at him.

MR M (*surprised*). He doesn't? Then why does he shoot him?

ME. He shoots him because it is the only thing to do.

MR M. Splendid! That's a great idea. But why don't you say so?

ME. I thought I did say so. I'll say it again if you think I should.

MR M. Do. Always remember, we're all from Missouri.

MISS W. I don't understand what exactly Blake wants. I mean – why exactly should he *wish* to blow up the works?

MR M. I have no difficulties with that. You see, they're all after some sort of Arcady. That's why the aunt objects to factories and says that . . .

ME. No, no! The aunt doesn't want any Arcady. All that she objects to is being dominated by people like Tausch.

MR M. That's all right by me. Only why don't you say so?

ME (*frantically turning over some pages*). But I *do* say so. I mean – what about this speech here?

MR M. Doesn't come across. Simply doesn't come across, old man.

ME. Will it be all right if I give her an encore?

MR L. This still doesn't answer Helen's question about Blake. Doesn't he want Arcady?

ME. Not exactly. But he *is* against industrialism.

MR L. Why?

ME. Why? I suppose because he's that kind of person.

MR L. You mean because he's not very bright? He can't see all the good it would do to the country?

ME (*getting cross*). I doesn't necessarily follow that industrialism

96

does good. That's like assuming that everybody wants to live in New York, which is far from being the case.

MR L. (*after a pause*). Oh.

MR M. Well apart from all that, I'd like to know what *side* Dobelle is on?

ME. Neither side.

MR L. He must be on some side. Does he or does he not want the works to be blown up? Answer me that.

ME. He would say that there's no point in wanting either, because whatever happens will happen anyhow. If they don't belong in Ireland they will go. What he really objects to is Tausch's attitude of mind.

MR M. Of course. Don't you see, he objects to being patronized. He doesn't like to hear Tausch calling the country backward.

ME. No, no! He doesn't feel the slightest patronized. By some damn German who reads his old magazine articles! Why should he give a damn what Tausch thinks about Ireland? It's something far more important than that. Tausch is what he calls a Servant of Righteousness, and those are the most dangerous people of all. He feels that all that they ever bring is misery.

MR M. Grand, grand! But . . .

ME. I know! I know! Why can't I say so?

A few years ago, I happened to pass through a reception room in the handsome premises of my old friends, and stopped to admire a plaque celebrating the jubilee of their organization, and listing some of their memorable past productions. My own play was there, but with the title misquoted. This is what I find so endearing about the American theatre. It is so right about motivation, and so wrong in its facts. It thrives on a series of crises that would never be permitted in a less businesslike community. And after all, why couldn't I have *said* what the title of my play was?

In addition to these operations in the United States, *The Moon* has been translated into Polish, French, Scandinavian and German, and been performed in these several tongues. It slipped into London by the back-door of the Malvern Festival, and if its varying reception over the years can be regarded as any index of audience receptivity it may be of interest to note that in England nowadays there are noticeably many more complaints and mutterings of 'What is all this about?' than there used to be twenty-five years ago. Maybe this is a sign of the times; or perhaps it is just another peculiarity of *The Moon,* that it becomes less familiar with longer acquaintance.

In the course of its productions on many stages and in various mediums, its cast has included such distinguished names as Claude Rains, Donald Wolfit, James Mason, Cyril Cusack, Barry Fitzgerald, F. J. McCormick, Errol Flynn, Jack Hawkins, Esmé Percy and Jean Anderson – though never, be it regretted, all in the same production. It blew a hole in the roof of one theatre, and on another occasion an efficient stage manager discovered just before Lanigan's entrance that his gun, by some error, had been loaded with live ammunition.

Occasionally the curtain falls on the second act without as much as a clap of a hand from the audience. And, oddly enough, this phenomenon is regarded by those who know the play well, not as a disgrace, but as an indication of a really fine performance.

The Moon in the Yellow River

This play was first produced at the Abbey Theatre, Dublin, on April 27th, 1931, with the following cast:

Agnes	MAUREEN DELANY
Blanaid	SHELAH RICHARDS
Tausch	FRED JOHNSON
Aunt Columba	EILEEN CROWE
George	ARTHUR SHIELDS
Captain Potts	MICHAEL J. DOLAN
Dobelle	F. J. MCCORMICK
Willie	U. WRIGHT
Darrell Blake	DENIS O'DEA
Commandant Lanigan	P. J. CAROLAN

The action of the play takes place in an old fort, now used as a dwelling-house, near the mouth of a river in Ireland.

ACT ONE	The Living-room
ACT TWO	The Armoury
ACT THREE	The Living-room

Time: About the year 1927.
    The play opens on an evening in late September.
    Act Two overlaps Act One by about five minutes.
    Several hours elapse between Acts Two and Three.

ACT ONE

The house was once the officers' quarters of the fort covering the river mouth. But it is now a long time since racks of small arms decorated the stone walls, and for a number of years it has done duty as a fairly comfortable, if out-of-the-way, modern residence. The room is furnished sparsely with good heavy furniture upon which the sea air has left its mark, and it is shockingly untidy. A large book-case is filled with books on technical engineering mixed with a hotchpotch of modern and classical literature. A cupboard filled with old blue-prints hangs open, and a small heap of fishing-tackle lies in the corner. To one side of the rear wall the massive door opens on to the court. It still carries some of the relics of its warlike past in the shape of rusty chains and bolts. To the centre the original aperture has been enlarged into a big window with iron shutters, opening outwards and hung with heavy curtains. These now stand open and we can see out and across the court to a whitewashed wall in which is a cannon port. Shortly after the scene opens it grows dark outside. Whenever the hall door is open, the distant hum of turbines can be heard. To one side of the room a short flight of stairs runs up to a gallery, off which the bedrooms open, of which the door of the first is visible. And down towards us, on one side, is an unpainted wooden table, running off stage out of sight, upon which is a toy railway station, signal box, signals and siding and a set of tracks which emerge from an aperture and disappear again.

As the Curtain rises a ship's siren can be heard from the river. It is an evening in late September, and an enormous red-faced woman wearing an apron is laying a few plates on the centre table. Although she has strong, domineering eyes and a commanding voice, there is nothing masculine about her. Quite the reverse, for her ample breasts and figure bear witness to a triumphant, all-enveloping matriarchy. Through the open door of the first bedroom we can see an angular, elderly lady who is

*seated at a typewriter on which she slowly clicks. In the window
seat a young girl of about thirteen dressed in a short cotton frock
is reading a book. She is an incredibly thin, solemn, untidy little
girl with short, tangled fair hair and bright, intelligent eyes.*

SERVANT. Well, about Mrs Mulpeter. Did I tell you about Mrs
Mulpeter, the poor lamb? (*She goes to the sideboard and then
returns.*) Ttt-ttt-ttt. Three days she's been now and three long
nights. Think of that now, isn't it a shocking, oh, a shocking
thing! (*She works vigorously for a time.*) Such a time as we've
had. God knows it's a terrible thing to be a woman. (*There is
a knock at the door.*) That was a knock at the door. (*But she
pays no attention to it.*) If some of them fellows could be
made to suffer half what a woman has to put up with! Oh,
my blood boils whenever I think of poor Mrs Mulpeter lying
there in pain. Ttt-ttt-ttt.

(*She goes out. The click of the typewriter, which had
stopped during her remarks, recommences and continues
until her return with the tray.*)

Well, I censed the room a bit then, and I gave her a spoonful
of holy water. 'Take this, Mrs Mulpeter,' says I, 'take this
between your poor lips and it'll be as good as a novena to the
blessed St Margaret, the friend of all women in your condition.' (*The knock is repeated louder.*) There's that knock
again. Maybe there's someone at the door. (*She goes as if to
open it, but stops on the way.*) Isn't it a terrible thing for me
to be quietly laying the supper-table here as if there was no
trouble in the world to torture and torment a decent woman!
I think I'll go across now and see her, supper or no supper.

(*She goes out again and the typewriter recommences. The
girl peers out the window. Presently the* SERVANT *comes
back with her hat and coat on.*)

SERVANT. Yes, I'm off now, supper or no supper, and you can
tell them that with my compliments.

(*The knock is repeated still louder. The girl draws the
curtains about her. The* SERVANT *goes to the hall door and
flings it open.*)

Now, now, what's all this? What's going on here?

VISITOR. Excuse.

SERVANT. Are you the ignorant bosthoon that's banging and
hammering away at my knocker?

102

(*Upon the threshold is a pleasant-faced gentleman whose clothes suggest his continental origin. He has close-cut, greyish-fair hair and steady blue eyes. He is in the early forties, and a general air of physical well-being is set off by the punctilious charm of his manner. He has a scar upon one of his cheeks and speaks excellent English with a clipped, meticulous pronunciation, occasionally accenting the wrong syllable and having a little difficulty with his 'th' and his 'w'.*)

VISITOR. Pardon, I hope that I have not inconvenienced the Herr Doktor?

SERVANT. You ought to know better at your age than to be clattering and thumping on respectable people's hall doors.

VISITOR. But, excuse. I am a visitor. I wish to come in.

SERVANT. Not to speak of the clattering racket of them mechanicalisms out there driving the blessed sleep from her poor tired eyes.

VISITOR. Perhaps you will kindly take my card.

SERVANT. Oh it's little I can do to ease you in your trouble, poor Mrs Mulpeter, little and all.

VISITOR. Pardon?

SERVANT. Ttt-ttt-ttt! Shocking, shocking!

(*She goes out, leaving the door open. He stares after her in some bewilderment. He peers into the room and slowly enters.*)

VISITOR. Herr Doktor.

(*A sudden click of the typewriter makes him start. Finally he goes across and proceeds to examine the toy railway in a tentative manner. The GIRL emerges from behind the curtain and approaches him silently.*)

GIRL. Nobody's allowed to touch that.

VISITOR (*with a start*). *Himmel!*

GIRL. What does that mean?

VISITOR. It means, my dear young lady, that you gave me a surprise.

GIRL. I suppose you don't know who I am?

VISITOR. I am afraid not. But they say that Beauty is a good letter of introduction, eh?

GIRL. I thought you wouldn't know me, but I know you. You're the man from the Power House. Sometimes I look in through the windows and see you working.

VISITOR. So? You do?

GIRL. Hh-hh!

VISITOR. I will certainly look out for you tomorrow.

GIRL. You're a German, aren't you?

VISITOR. That is so, indeed.

GIRL. I was born in Germany.

VISITOR. *Ach!* Then we are compatriots. You are perhaps the daughter of the Herr Doktor?

GIRL (*nods*). At least it was somewhere out there. I'm not very good at geography. Perhaps you know a place called Bratislav?

VISITOR. I know the place well. I have passed by in the boats many times on the trip to Budapest. So that is where you were born!

GIRL. Well, there's a convent near there. Father was doing something to a bridge at the time, but of course I was too young to remember. I say, aren't you going to sit down?

VISITOR. *Bitte sehr.* But, as you say, Ladies first!

GIRL. Oh, I'm not a lady.

VISITOR. *Nicht wahr!* but a very charming one.

GIRL. I'm afraid not. But it's my father's fault. He calls me a little slut, but I think it's calling people things that makes them it, don't you? Oh, what's that little thing on the back of your hat?

VISITOR. This? Oh, it is nothing. We wear them so at home.

GIRL. It's awfully funny. (*She takes his hat.*) Just like a little brush . . . Oh, it comes in and out!

VISITOR. *Nein – Nein!* It . . . *Ach,* yes. I see now that it comes in and out.

GIRL. Isn't it meant to? I haven't broken it?

VISITOR. Not at all, my dear young lady. It is quite all right.

GIRL. I'm afraid I *have* broken it. You're not telling me the truth.

VISITOR. Please do not bother. *Das macht nichts.*

GIRL. Can you mend it?

VISITOR. I can procure another. It is nothing.

GIRL. I'm rather unlucky with things, but it's not really my fault, you know. At least, hardly ever. They always say it is, though.

VISITOR. One's parents never do understand, do they?

GIRL. I haven't any parents.

VISITOR. No parents? But . . .

GIRL. Not unless you count Father.

VISITOR. One usually counts one's father.

GIRL. Not ones like mine. We don't get on very well, I'm afraid. I can't remember my mother.

VISITOR. So.

GIRL. But there's a picture of her out in the armoury. She has fair hair and the loveliest hands. I think she's pretty, but we don't know much about her. Except Father, and of course he says nothing. Have you got any parents?

VISITOR. No, I am afraid not.

GIRL. Then, I suppose we're both orphans in a sense. But I daresay you've been better brought up than me?

VISITOR (*laughing*). Well, that is a very difficult question. What would you say was being . . . well brought up?

GIRL. Oh, going to a proper school instead of being taught by Auntie and George. That's Auntie typing up there. She knows medieval history and Latin, and George knows a lot of awfully good sea shanties. But you can't go far on that, can you? Nowadays, I mean.

VISITOR. Well, it all depends upon what you want.

GIRL. I think that every girl needs an education nowadays in order to prepare her for the battle of life. She wants to be taught deportment and geography and religious knowledge and – oh – mathematics. I adore mathematics, don't you?

VISITOR. *Ach,* but you are the daughter of a great engineer. Most young ladies of my acquaintance try to avoid these things and to stay away from school.

GIRL. Perhaps that's because they have got more suitable parents. My father says that education poisons the mind, but I say he was educated himself, so his mind must be poisoned, and if it's poisoned, how can he know what's good for me?

VISITOR. And what has he got to say to that?

GIRL. Nothing. He just looks at me – the way he always does. I don't know why. Don't you think it must be wonderful to have proper lessons and sleep in an enormous dormitory with twenty other girls and go for walks in a long line like geese? Tell me, have you ever looked through a convent keyhole?

VISITOR. *Ach!* No – I have not had that experience!

GIRL. Well, you can see them in there. Walking about in the garden, always in threes – never in pairs. That's how I know all about it. I wish you would take a look some day. Then you might be able to tell me whether you think they're very much more advanced than I am.

VISITOR. But have you no other young friends?

GIRL. No. There isn't anybody much out here except the men going out the wall to the lighthouse. I think that Darry Blake is my only real friend. Do you know him?

VISITOR. No.

GIRL. He used to come across the bay a lot when he had the water-wag, and sometimes he'd take me up to the pictures. But he hardly ever comes now. I think he must have dropped us. We're not awfully good, you know – socially, I mean.

VISITOR. I am sure that it cannot be that. But perhaps, when we are better acquainted, I may be permitted to take you up to the pictures instead.

GIRL. Oh, would you? How lovely! When? Tomorrow?

VISITOR. I would be charmed. But first we must ask the permission of your distinguished father.

GIRL. Oh, he won't care.

VISITOR. *Ach,* but you see, I do not know the Herr Doktor very well. This is the first time I have had the honour of his invitation to supper.

GIRL. Oh, supper! Is that why you called?

VISITOR. Then, you do not expect me?

GIRL. Oh, I'm sure it's all right. People do sometimes come to supper. Perhaps I'd better go and tell Father.

VISITOR. You are very kind. But if I am not expected . . .

GIRL. Oh, I wouldn't mind that. (*Turning at the bottom of the stairs.*) I think you were wonderful about the pictures. I do hope you're not annoyed about that little thing I broke?

VISITOR (*distressed*). Not at all, I assure you. Perhaps it would be well for me to call another time.

GIRL. I didn't think you would be annoyed, really. But don't tell Father, please. He'd only say it was what he expected of me or something. I'll get him now.

(*She goes upstairs. He takes a step after her, but decides to wait, and sits down uncomfortably in a big chair with his back to the stairs.*)

AUNT (*from her room*). Blanaid!

GIRL. Yes, Auntie?

AUNT. Who's that?

BLANAID. The man from the Power House.

AUNT. What does he want?

BLANAID. He wants to stay to supper, and for me to come to the pictures tomorrow.

AUNT. Was he asked?

BLANAID. He says so.

AUNT. I don't believe it for a minute.

BLANAID. Hush, Auntie! He's listening.

AUNT. Well, listeners never hear any good of themselves.

BLANAID. I'm supposed to tell Father.

AUNT. Well, if he stays, I go.

BLANAID. Ss-ssh! (*With a glance at the speechless foreigner*) It's all right. I don't think he heard.

(*She goes off down the gallery. Presently the* AUNT *emerges from her bedroom and comes quietly downstairs. She is a lean and vigorous woman of about fifty, with bright fanatical eyes. She wears a tweed skirt and a Fair Isle sweater that comes to the throat. Her hair, once very beautiful and still uncut, is now streaked with grey and is untidily done. She comes to the table in the centre and removes a silver flower vase which, with a look of deep suspicion at the* VISITOR, *she brings back to her room. She is almost at the table before he notices her and springs to his feet bowing politely. After she has gone he decides to steal away, but before he has got as far as the open hall door, there is a sound of voices outside and two men enter. They are* GEORGE *and his friend and crony,* CAPTAIN POTTS. *They are both well-seasoned and weather-beaten salts – the former a tall, lean man with brown wrinkled skin, dressed in a loose-fitting double-breasted grey tweed suit. He still has the face and carriage of an incurable romanticist, which he has never ceased to be since he ran away to sea from a comfortable home and a good family fifty years ago. Since then he has been all over the world, fought in half a dozen campaigns and come through them all unscathed both in mind and in body. The only regular feature in his life has been its unvarying lack of money, for on the occasions on which he has managed to acquire any, he has always lost it promptly, thanks to his uneconomic enthusiasms and his impulsive habit of backing bills for insolvent friends. For the last seven of his ripening years he has more or less settled down in a Government appointment that takes him about the coast, drilling crews and inspecting the life-saving*

107

apparatus. His old friend, CAPTAIN POTTS, *is storekeeper. The latter, a fat old Cockney with a heavy grey moustache, is dressed in his best blue serge with collar and tie and a sailor's cap and has a black crape band on his sleeve. He carries a large bunch of flowers. Neither of them at first takes any notice of the foreigner.*)

GEORGE and POTTS (*singing off*).

           O whiskey is the life of man,
           O whiskey Johnny!
           I'll drink whiskey when I can,
           Whiskey for my Johnny.

           O whiskey makes you feel so gran',
           O whiskey Johnny!
           Whiskey from an old tin can,
           Whiskey for my Johnny!

GEORGE (*as he enters*). Bring 'em in, Potts, bring 'em in. Don't be shy, old man, there's nobody here. We'll get something for them over here. (*He goes to a cupboard and selects a glass jar.*) Perhaps we'd better put some water in it.

POTTS. Ri'. (To VISITOR.) Better for a drop o' water, y' know.

GEORGE (*filling the jar from the carafe on the table*). There now, shove 'em into that, old man. Much too late, don't you think?

POTTS. Sure. Gent 'ere, George.

GEORGE. What's that? Who? Why, so there is, b'gad. Friend of yours, Potts?

POTTS. Nope.

GEORGE (*as they carefully arrange the flowers*). Suppose we'd better have a word with the fellow. No good in being stand-offish, eh?

POTTS. Just as you say, George.

GEORGE. Meet my friend Captain Potts. In charge of my store.

VISITOR. I am delighted to meet you, Herr Kapitän.

POTTS. 'At's aw ri'.

GEORGE. You're the fellow from the Power House. I know you. Like to shake hands?

VISITOR. With pleasure.

GEORGE. *Gooden tag!* Shake hands with Potts, too. Shake hands with him, Potts, old man. These fellows love shaking hands.

(POTTS *does.*)

POTTS. *Gooden tag.* (*Laughter.*)

VISITOR. I know you and your friend by sight. You manage the rocket apparatus. You save lives from the ships in distress, eh?

GEORGE. That's right. Do you like these flowers? (*Whispering.*) Say you do. For the old man.

VISITOR. You are fond of flowers?

GEORGE. They're not for himself, you know. (*Whispering.*) His wife's dead.

VISITOR. *Ach,* I am so sorry! A recent demise?

GEORGE. About sixteen years. Sixteen – is that right, Potts?

POTTS. Sixteen eggsackly.

GEORGE. Very sad for the poor old fellow.

VISITOR. (*rather at a loss*). Oh . . . yes. Er, I like your flowers, Herr Kapitän.

POTTS. Think they'll do?

VISITOR. *Sehr schön.*

GEORGE. Say you like his suit, too. Only puts it on once a year. Wife's anniversary. It was her favourite suit. Poor old Potts. (*He sniffs.*) I wonder is there anything in here. (*He inspects the cupboard again and produces a whiskey bottle.*) How about it, Potts, old man? Drink, Herr Splosch?

VISITOR. Tausch is my name.

POTTS. Ri'. I'll 'ave a small 'un.

GEORGE. You'll have to share a glass with Potts, I'm afraid. Mind sharing a glass with Herr Splosch, Potts?

POTTS. Naw. 'Salls same.

TAUSCH. I thank you, but I do not take spirits.

GEORGE. What? No spirits?

TAUSCH. No, thank you.

GEORGE. Really?

TAUSCH. Unfortunately they do not agree with me.

GEORGE. Most extraordinary! Well, you know yourself best. There you are, old man.

POTTS. 'At'll do.

GEORGE. Pour it down, Potts.

POTTS. Well – 'ere's looking at yer.

GEORGE. We got as far as the Scotch House, you know. But I said to Captain Potts here, 'Potts, it's all very well, old man, but I think we've started too late. Take a taxi and we'll have no damn money to get home. Take a tram and the damn cemetery'll be closed by the time we get there. It's no good bringing flowers to a cemetery when it's closed, is it?'

TAUSCH. You bring these flowers to the tomb?

GEORGE. Yes, you know the poor old fellow's wife's dead. Anniversary. We always go.

POTTS. Yes, mush too late.

GEORGE. So when we left the Scotch House, I said, 'Come on back to the store, Captain Potts, and we'll put these flowers in water and try again tomorrow.'

POTTS. 'Ave to go again.

TAUSCH. The Scotch House is closed tomorrow, I suppose?

GEORGE. Oh no, Sunday. Different hours, that's all. Well, when we saw the door open on our way back, we thought we'd come in to look for some water. And, by God, we got it, eh, Potts old man?

POTTS (*refreshed*). You betcher life!

GEORGE. Good thing we came in, Potts, or we wouldn't have met Herr Splosch. Are you sure now you won't have a splash, Splosch?

TAUSCH. No, thank you.

GEORGE. Well, you must step across to the store some time and we'll give you a rosner. You know – just next door in the old armoury.

TAUSCH. I think that I know the place.

GEORGE. Everybody welcome. Just like in this house. Eh, Potts?

POTTS. Liberty 'All.

GEORGE (*singing*). 'Sally Brown, she's a bright Mullatter.'

BOTH. 'Way – ay – y, roll and go.'

GEORGE. 'She drinks rum and chews tobacker.'

BOTH. 'Spend my money on Sally Brown.'

GEORGE. Steady, Potts old man, steady. Can't make a row in other people's houses, you know.

POTTS (*abashed*). 'At's ri', George. Shouldn't do that.

GEORGE (*mysteriously*). Listen! You're a foreigner. Are you at all interested in guns?

TAUSCH. Guns?

GEORGE. Don't mention it much. But come along some time and I'll show you something will surprise you. Just next door in . . .

(*The* HOST *and his* DAUGHTER *appear at the top of the stairs. He is a distinguished-looking elderly gentleman with a refined sensitive face and the delicate nervous hands of an*

110

artist. There is a certain ruthlessness – one would almost say, cruelty – about his fastidious lips and chin that seems to be perpetually at war with his eyes, which are imaginative and sympathetic. He dresses carelessly in tweeds, but with good taste, and his manner betokens an inborn restlessness. He comes down the stairs quickly, his hand outstretched.)

HOST. Why, my dear sir, I had no idea that you were here. You must accept my sincerest apologies. Put on the light, Blanaid.

TAUSCH. Good evening, Mr Dobelle. I am afraid I have called unawares.

DOBELLE. Not at all, not at all. I was buried in the library, and nobody dreamt of telling me you were here. Deuced unmannerly house this.

TAUSCH. *Im gegenteil.* I have been entertained most charmingly by your daughter.

(BLANAID *from the stairs flings him a smile, points to her head and places a finger to her lips.*)

GEORGE. We thought you'd like us to give him a drink. So we did.

DOBELLE. Well, thank God for that! I hope there was enough. (*He lifts the empty decanter and looks at* TAUSCH *in some surprise.*)

GEORGE. Oh yes, lots, old man, lots.

DOBELLE. You have met George, then?

TAUSCH. We have introduced ourselves. Oh, I assure you, I have – how you say – I have been done proud.

DOBELLE. Let me take your coat.

TAUSCH. Believe me, sir, since first I came to reside at the Power House, I have been looking forward to the pleasure of this visit.

DOBELLE. Very handsome of you to say so, I'm sure. We haven't much to offer, I'm afraid.

BLANAID. You can't stay to supper, George. There's only just enough as it is, and Agnes has gone off somewhere.

GEORGE. That's all right, my dear. We're not staying. Only dropped in to entertain Herr Splosch. Come along, Potts, old man.

POTTS. Well . . . Bye . . .

GEORGE. So long, everyone.

TAUSCH. *Auf Wiedersehen.*

GEORGE. *Auf Wiedersehen?* Did you hear that Potts? That was German. And don't forget what I told you. Any time you're passing. Like to show you what I mentioned. Wiedersehen! Ha-ha! Ha-ha! Damned silly language. Ha-ha-ha!

(*They go and are heard singing off for a moment,* POTTS *after a moment's hesitation in the door coming back for his flowers and removing them vase and all.*)

DOBELLE. Do sit down, sir.

TAUSCH. With pleasure.

DOBELLE. I'm very glad George gave you a drink. He's a dear fellow, but rather a rolling stone. Very good company out here where company is scarce.

TAUSCH. It is farther from the town than I had imagined. This place is very old?

DOBELLE. No, just a relic of the Napoleon scare. Derelict for about fifty years before I took it for my hermitage. Darrell Blake could tell you all about its history.

TAUSCH. I do not think that I have met him. But your daughter mentioned his name.

DOBELLE. He's one of our few regular visitors. But lately he's got a little involved in other things and we don't see him so often. It is a pity. I find, Herr Tausch, that there are very few people in this world that are at all tolerable to talk to.

TAUSCH. I respectfully agree. That is why I feel so honoured in being invited to share your hospitality, Mr Dobelle. You – a distinguished railway engineer – I have so often in my student days read your articles in the technical journals. Little did I think that one day I would have you as my neighbour.

DOBELLE. Tut, tut. No man should be reminded of the articles that he has written.

TAUSCH. When first I decided to come to this part of the world my friends they all say: 'But why do you wish to go there?' I answer, 'Ha-ha, I know what I am doing.' And now I write home and I say, 'I told you so. I am the neighbour of the man whose works I have studied for so many years – Mr Dobelle.'

DOBELLE. Still, that scarcely answers their question, does it? Why should you wish to come here?

TAUSCH. *Ach,* how can one say. It is the call of the west wind. One grows tired of those places where everything has been done already. Then one day comes the call of romance. I answer. You understand.

DOBELLE. I certainly do not. It sounds like nonsense to me.

TAUSCH. *Ach,* but I cannot believe that. You wish me to believe that you smile at sentiment, but that is only a charming conceit. I know that you can appreciate the charm of the West, Mr Dobelle, and I had spent but a very few weeks upon my course before I realized how right I had been.

DOBELLE. Oh, you took a course?

TAUSCH. But naturally. When one goes to live in a strange land, one should try to acquaint oneself with the customs of the people.

DOBELLE. We have some customs here that I fancy it would be difficult to understand in München. But be specific now and tell me frankly what is there here that can possibly interest an intelligent hydro-electrical engineer?

TAUSCH. Might I not put that question to you, Mr Dobelle? You seem to find something to interest you.

DOBELLE. My wander-years are over. I have come home to renounce them.

TAUSCH. Precisely. You have travelled the world and have come to the conclusion that your own place is the best after all.

DOBELLE. No, I doubt if I could explain to you, Herr Tausch. It's a purely personal point of view. But I find that the world you speak of maddens me.

TAUSCH. I think I understand. You prefer the life of the spirit. You long for – how does it go? –

'. . . magic casements opening on the foam
Of perilous seas in faery lands forlorn.'

DOBELLE. Ridiculous. Nobody but a Cockney could have conjured up such a picture. Don't be deceived, Herr Tausch. Here by the waters of Lethe we may believe in fairies, but we trade in pigs. No. I think it was those very pigs that called me back. It takes one a long time to find one's spiritual home, but revelation comes at last, my friend. Isn't it Goethe who tells us that when we are old we must do more than when we are young? Don't believe a word of it, my dear sir. Once I served Righteousness with that intense desire for service that one has in one's youth. I studied hard, read everything that came my way, and built railway bridges anywhere from Hungary to the Gran Chaco. But since my revelation I amuse myself with toy trains instead of real ones and read little else but the *Encyclopaedia*. And, believe me, I find it much more satisfactory.

TAUSCH (*smiling*). I suspect, Mr Dobelle, that you visited China as well as the Gran Chaco.

DOBELLE. I suppose every cock crows loudest on its own dunghill. Here it is still possible to live on one's own mind. Even if usually it proves a mighty poor diet. And speaking of diet, I did ask you to supper, didn't I?

TAUSCH. If it inconveniences you in any way . . .

DOBELLE. No, no; he who works may eat. Agnes! I wonder where Agnes is?

(*The* AUNT *appears at the top of the stairs. She has put on her hat and coat.*)

AUNT. Agnes has gone. (*She goes away again.*)

DOBELLE. Gone! Damnation!

BLANAID. It's all right. The table's nearly laid. Mrs Mulpeter is going to have a baby.

DOBELLE. Not again? I never heard of such a thing!

BLANAID. The supper is on the range. (*To* TAUSCH) Do you mind finishing the table while I go and get it?

TAUSCH. *Ja gewiss.* With pleasure.

DOBELLE (*making no effort to help*). This is too bad! too bad! Leaving the table half laid! And the supper on the range! Without as much as with your leave or by your leave!

TAUSCH. It is a privilege, I assure you. I enjoy the helping very much indeed.

DOBELLE. Servants are insufferable. Why can't we do without them? (*The* AUNT *appears again at the top of the stairs carrying a bicycle which she brings down with her.*) What the devil has happened to supper? I ask Herr Tausch here to supper. I give notice to you all. He comes. There is nothing to eat and he has to lay the table himself. Don't answer me back.

AUNT. Who cares about supper! Maybe there'll be more than supper to bother about by the time this night is out.

DOBELLE. A nice way to treat a guest. Oh, Herr Tausch, may I introduce my sister, Columba.

TAUSCH (*bowing*). *Gnädige Frau.* I think that we have met already tonight.

AUNT. I daresay you expect me to shake hands with you; but even if I would, I can't with this bicycle.

TAUSCH. Perhaps you will allow me to assist you with it.

AUNT. Leave it alone, please. I know how to look after my own bicycle.

TAUSCH. I am so sorry.

DOBELLE. She doesn't like people to touch her things, Tausch. That's why she keeps it in her bedroom.

TAUSCH. I see.

AUNT. And take my advice, my good man, don't leave any of your property round here if you ever want to see it again. A word to the wise.

DOBELLE. Columba, you're not going out before supper?

AUNT. I am. I have work to do. Sometimes there are too many strangers in this house.

DOBELLE. Oh well, have it your own way. Better let her go, Tausch, if she wants to.

TAUSCH. My dear sir, I had no intention of interfering with her departure.

AUNT. I'd just like to see you try. (*She pauses at the door and feels in her pocket.*) You'd better take one of these. They'll all be gone when I get back. (*She hands him a typewritten pamphlet.*)

TAUSCH. *Danke sehr.*

AUNT. Ah yes, the turbines are humming merrily now. The dynamos are turning and the water piles up behind the sluices. You think you have done well. But you haven't accounted for everything. No, you haven't accounted for everything, my good man.

(*The* AUNT *goes.* BLANAID *enters with a tray.*)

TAUSCH. *Grüss Gott.*

BLANAID. Supper!

DOBELLE. At last. Sit down, Tausch, and let us atone for our laxity with a bottle of hock. Where's the corkscrew? (*He takes a bottle from the cupboard.*)

TAUSCH (*reading*). 'Our existence is not the aftermath of a past revolt. It is the presage of a future one. We shall rise again.'

DOBELLE. What's that? Where's the corkscrew?

TAUSCH. 'We shall rise again.' What is this?

DOBELLE. Oh, that? Just propaganda. She types them herself and pastes them up on the tram posts in town.

TAUSCH. *Ach, Fliegende Blätter.* Politics.

DOBELLE. Here's the corkscrew. Yes, she's been in jail once or twice. You mustn't mind it.

TAUSCH. In jail? So interesting.

DOBELLE (*drawing the cork*). Oh yes. In and out. But she's not typical of the country.

TAUSCH. I do not think that I have met many people who have been often in jail.

DOBELLE. It's one of the best qualifications for a public appointment. Hock?

TAUSCH. With pleasure.

DOBELLE (*filling his glass*). I always say it's a pity she never got married; but her only serious affair ended in rather a row. Something about a mowing machine. And, by the way, while I remember, better not mention the matter to her. She's rather sensitive on the subject.

TAUSCH (*drawing another typewritten document from his pocket*). My dear sir, I would not think of doing so. But I wonder does what you tell me throw any light upon a strange communication which I received a few days ago?

DOBELLE. Let me see. (*He takes it.*) Oh-ho! A threat to the works! You got this a day or two ago?

TAUSCH. Yes. One of my men found it pinned to the door of the switch house.

DOBELLE. Were you at all put out by this?

TAUSCH. I did not understand it, my dear sir. Some people object because I supply power and light to the military barracks. I did not think it of much consequence, because when I notify the police they say that it will be quite all right. I am more than relieved to learn that it may only be your charming sister.

DOBELLE. I wonder. The situation is a little different from what you are accustomed to. In most countries the political idealist is merely a bore, but here he has a disconcerting tradition of action. He usually has his own Government and his own army as well, you see.

TAUSCH. You mean to say that he does not recognize the machinery of democracy?

DOBELLE. He would say that you don't understand democracy. The Will of the People is a tender delicate bloom to be nurtured by the elect few who know best. The icy blasts of a general election are not for it. There's some sense in it – when you know that you know best.

TAUSCH. That is a little metaphysical for me.

DOBELLE. Metaphysical? My dear fellow, it's simply Christian Science applied to politics. If you don't like the Government you deny its existence – a state of affairs which is sometimes a little embarrassing for the likes of you and me.

BLANAID. Willie's out tonight. I saw him go off with his whistle and his water-bottle.

DOBELLE. Oh? I suppose it's useless to say anything to Darrell.

TAUSCH. And your other acquaintance – the gentleman whose friend has suffered the so sad bereavement – would he be one of these too?

DOBELLE. Who? George? Well, not really. He's a barbarian, but an amiable one. When did Willie go off?

BLANAID. About half past six.

DOBELLE. Oh well, there's nothing can be done now. A little more hock, Tausch?

TAUSCH. With pleasure. And what will you have, young lady?

BLANAID (*taking the carafe*). Only this, thanks.

TAUSCH. 'And Roman women were of old for drink content with water.' Eh?

DOBELLE. Prosit. (*They rise.*)

TAUSCH. Prosit.

(*They drink.*)

Go muh shocht noora nees farr hoo bleeun oh nyoo.

DOBELLE (*after a surprised pause*). Part of your course, no doubt?

BLANAID. That's Irish. He was only trying to say, 'May you feel better next year.'

TAUSCH. And this is the little Miss who pretends to have no education!

(DOBELLE *looks at her silently for a moment and then sits down.*)

DOBELLE. I suppose that's what Columba teaches you. Well, after this display of erudition, perhaps we may get on with supper.

(AGNES *enters by the hall door.*)

AGNES. Tt-ttt-tt-tt.

DOBELLE. So here you are!

AGNES. Yes, here I am. I thought I'd come back for a short bit. But she's very bad.

DOBELLE. I'm afraid there's not much more for you to do.

AGNES. That's just as well. They may want me back any minute. They've sent for the doctor. So I propped her up on the pillows and I wrapped a vinegared handkerchief round her poor head. 'Poor Mrs Mulpeter,' says I, 'isn't that nyummy nyumm? God help you, it won't be long now.' And neither it will. I'd be ashamed and me a man to be quietly eating supper and drinking strong drink and poor Mrs Mulpeter so near to her great trouble. (*She goes into the kitchen.*)

DOBELLE. Well, I suppose we must be thankful for small mercies.

TAUSCH. I understand. A lady is in childbirth. It is a very trying time. Yes. One can excuse a lot at such moments. I remember when my dear wife was –

AGNES (*putting her head in the door*). Now, now! I'll have none of that sort of talk while I'm about, if you please. Think shame to you – a couple of men to be gostering and making chatter about the trouble and misfortune tormenting a poor woman.

TAUSCH. Pardon.

(*They eat in silence for a few minutes.* AGNES *enters again.*)

AGNES (*putting a plate on the table*). I made them move her downstairs, so I did. In the top room of the gate-house she was. But I said No. That child must not be carried downstairs until it's carried upstairs first or I'll know the reason why, and if the poor mite starts at the top of the house, how can it go upstairs first? So down to the sitting-room poor Mrs Mulpeter had to come. The agony the poor creature suffered! Tt-tt-tt – (*She goes.*)

DOBELLE. Oh, by the way, Tausch, I should have mentioned it before, but do be careful what you say in front of Agnes. She's very puritanical. You understand?

TAUSCH. I will try to remember that too.

DOBELLE. We find it best to attune our conversation to the tastes of our servants. Let's go back to George. He's quite a noncommittal subject. Have a sausage? George, you know, is the best of fellows. Calls himself a Christian Communist and wants everybody to be free and happy and at peace. But every time that the people try to be free and happy and peaceful it seems to George that somebody comes along and stops them with big guns.

TAUSCH. So?

DOBELLE. Well, a few years ago George, the most practical of men, decided to make a big gun for himself so that the next time the people won't be so badly off. He's been at it on and off ever since.

TAUSCH. To *make* a big gun?

DOBELLE. Exactly. And with quite surprising results. Of course nobody knows what will happen when it's fired. But we all hope for the best. Naturally, this is all in the strictest confidence. You must get him to show it to you the next time you're passing the armoury.

TAUSCH. I certainly will. But what industry! What enthusiasm!

DOBELLE. And why not, if one believes as George does? If you, Herr Tausch, a complete stranger, can come here to harness our tides for us, why be surprised when George tries to do something for the country too?

TAUSCH. But, my dear sir – to make a big gun! It is a year's work!

DOBELLE. About four years, as a matter of fact. And about a year extra for each projectile. Yes, they started on the fourth shell in the spring.

TAUSCH. Colossal!

DOBELLE. Oh yes, in about twenty years' time we'll be getting quite formidable.

TAUSCH. Ah now, sir, I am afraid you are jesting. Of course it is not the application that I admire. I am not so materialistic. But the spirit – the praxis – it is an example. Please excuse while I make a note in my book for my next letter to my son Karl.

DOBELLE. Well, well, I'm sure George would be delighted to know that he had been a help to Karl. You have a large family?

TAUSCH. Not very large. Four children only. They are still young and at school. That is why I have to leave them behind when I come here.

DOBELLE. You must miss them all.

TAUSCH. I confess that sometimes I do. In the evenings especially I miss the music.

DOBELLE. You are fond of music?

TAUSCH. But naturally. We all love music in Bavaria. You are musical, too, perhaps?

DOBELLE. Oh, very.

TAUSCH. What instruments do you play?

DOBELLE. None, I'm afraid.

BLANAID. We had a piano once, but it got stuck.

TAUSCH. Stuck?

BLANAID. Yes. It's out in the armoury now.

TAUSCH. The sea air, I suppose?

DOBELLE. You play yourself, of course?

TAUSCH. Oh yes. We all play. I play the 'cello and my dear wife she plays very beautifuly upon the piano. My daughter – the eldest one, Lotte – she is the violinist of the family.

DOBELLE. Quite a little orchestra, in fact.

TAUSCH. Oh, that is not all. Karl, my first son, he plays the viola, and Herman, the second boy, plays the flute. And even my little Greta – she is only five years – we are teaching her to accompany us upon the triangle.

DOBELLE. Charming.

TAUSCH. We were to buy an electric organ when I decided to come away. Just a small organ, but a beautiful instrument. However, we found that the vibration would be dangerous for a wooden house. So this winter they are laying down a concrete foundation and that will make it all right, I think.

DOBELLE. A concrete foundation? For the organ, you mean?

TAUSCH. Yes.

BLANAID. Oh, how lovely!

TAUSCH. Each evening in my room at the works I play to myself when I can afford the time, just to keep in practice. I am afraid you will think me a little sentimental. But the melodies that we are fond of, what else can bring back to us in the same way the mountains, the lakes, the wife and children that one loves? You understand.

DOBELLE (*after a pause*). I don't think you should ever have come here. I shudder to think what is before you.

TAUSCH. I only hope that I may be able to help you. I love your country and would serve it even in some small way.

DOBELLE. Yes, that is what I feared, and I know that I should resent it, but I haven't the heart. You are in higher hands. Still, I can't help being sorry for you.

TAUSCH. Sorry for me? May I ask why?

DOBELLE. Because, Herr Tausch, I like you, and at the same time I see with infinite pathos the not far distant date when, if you stay here, you will find yourself out. And that to my mind is always a pity.

TAUSCH. I do not understand.

DOBELLE. It is not the destiny of a man like you to be buried in this accursed hole. Take my tip before it is too late. Leave your Power House and go.

TAUSCH. Leave my Power House? What joke is this?

DOBELLE. Have you ever heard of the bogey man, Herr Tausch?

Well, here we have bogey men, fierce and terrible bogey men, who breathe fire from their nostrils and vanish in the smoke.

TAUSCH. You have what?

DOBELLE. And we have vampires in shimmering black that feed on blood and bear bombs instead of brats. And enormous fat crows that will never rest until they have pecked out your eyes and left you blind and dumb with terror.

TAUSCH. Come, come, Mr Dobelle.

DOBELLE. And in the mists that creep down from the mountains you will meet monsters that glare back at you with your own face.

TAUSCH. Ah now, Mr Dobelle, you cannot frighten me with parables. You forget that I am a German, and what you say only convinces me how much you really need my work.

DOBELLE. I know that nobody will ever listen to me; but, remember, I have warned you.

TAUSCH. I think, if I may say so, that you are a little afraid of life and that is why you live here. But we are not like that in Germany. There we still have the virile youth of a new nation: hope, courage, and the ability to rise again. Put Germany in the saddle and you will find that she can ride. Just a little organization here and you will see the change. Do not please think that I am preaching the doctrines of material prosperity. That matters nothing. (*The sound of a motor-car comes from outside and headlamps throw a beam of light on the blinds of the window.*) It is here, in the brain, that we find all that is of any value. It is the change of mind that only power can bring that will be the justification for all my work here. As Schiller tells us, freedom cannot exist save when united with might. And what might can equal electrical power at one farthing a unit? (*On the blinds appears the shadow of a man in an overcoat holding something in his hand that closely resembles a revolver.*) I see in my mind's eye this land of the future – transformed and redeemed by power – from the sordid trivialities of peasant life to something newer and better. Soon you will be a happy nation of free men – free not by the magic of empty formulae or by the colour of the coats you wear, but by the inspiration of power – power – power. And in that day I shall say in the words of Horace . . .

(*He notices the silence of the other two and follows their eyes to the window. Presently a* GUNMAN *enters silently*

121

through the door. He wears a waterproof coat and a soft cap and the lower part of his face is masked by a handkerchief. He carries a revolver. The two men sit in silence, the HOST *limply, the* VISITOR *rigid. Then the older man eats a piece of bread.*)

GUNMAN. All the men in this house will have to be searched for arms.

(*Silence.* BLANAID *at last rises and runs out. For a terrible moment it looks as though she may be shot.*)

GUNMAN. Have you any arms or ammunition?

(*Silence. The* GERMAN *makes a move, but the other with a quick movement restrains him.*)

GUNMAN. Come on, now.

DOBELLE. Now, we're not going to have any shooting here, are we?

GUNMAN. Oh, I'm not so sure of that.

DOBELLE. Well, perhaps you'd better come back another time. When supper's over, maybe, or when I haven't any visitors.

GUNMAN. I'm sorry. I have my orders – from battalion headquarters.

DOBELLE (*standing*). Well . . .

GUNMAN. The house is surrounded.

DOBELLE. Probably. (*He rings the bell on the table.*)

GUNMAN. Leave that bell alone.

DOBELLE. Certainly. I just thought that as you have to search the men, you might like to see the women, too.

GUNMAN. I don't want to see the women.

DOBELLE. Then you can send them away.

(*There is a pause during which the* GUNMAN *shifts uneasily, and the* COOK *enters.*)

DOBELLE. Oh, Agnes, here's somebody who says he wants to search us all for arms.

GUNMAN (*gruffly*). Everybody ought to put up their hands.

AGNES. If I put up my hands, it'll be to take you across my knee and give you a good skelping where you least expect it.

DOBELLE. An excellent suggestion.

AGNES. Take that old rag off your face at once, Willie Reilly. And who, may I ask, let you in here with them boots on?

GUNMAN (*sheepishly removing his mask and displaying an honest, pink face*). Aw, I didn't know you knew me.

AGNES. Do you hear me asking who let you in with them dirty boots?

GUNMAN. I have me orders, Ma.

AGNES. Well, you have your orders now, and out you go before I lam you with the flat of my fist.

WILLIE. Ay, easy now, Ma.

DOBELLE. Just a moment, Agnes. It seems that Willie's here on military business, and I think it's scarcely fair to pack him off without hearing what it's all about.

WILLIE. That's right, Mr Dobelle.

AGNES. Military business! Indeed! And what sort of military business gives him the right to come trapesing into my clean living-room with the mud of three counties on his boots, I'd like to know? Go 'long owa that, ye ignorant yuck, before I military business your backside.

WILLIE. Ay, keep off me, Ma.

DOBELLE. Agnes, please. If you don't mind. There's no use being violent. Personally, I'd like to hear what it's all about.

WILLIE. That's right. Now, violence never did any good, Ma. You know that.

AGNES. Oh, very well, very well. Have it your own way. It's no concern of mine if you turn the place into a pigsty. But don't ask me to clean up after you. You can do that for yourselves. (*She goes off with a slam into the kitchen.*)

WILLIE. God looka what can a man do with a mother the like of that, tormenting and disgracing him and he on active service! Looka now, I ask you what harm in God's name is my boots doing?

(*The* GERMAN *rises and mops his brow.*)

DOBELLE. Not much, I'm sure, Willie. Don't mind your mother. I'll put in a word for you and any mess you make you can sweep up before you go. (*The* GERMAN *whispers to him.*) Oh yes, and Willie, now that we're talking on a friendlier basis, don't you think that you might put that revolver away?

WILLIE. Ah sure, there's nothing in it. But I'll put it in my pocket if you like, sir.

DOBELLE. That's good. This is Mr Tausch of the Power House. Herr Tausch, Willie Reilly, Agnes's first-born.

TAUSCH. I see – Good day.

WILLIE. How-are-ye?

DOBELLE. Won't you sit down, Willie?

123

WILLIE. Ah no, I can't, thank you very much, sir. I have to be off in a tick. The boys is all outside.

DOBELLE. And what have the boys got on hand, Willie?

WILLIE. Well, the idea is to blow up the works.

TAUSCH. *Gott in Himmel!*

WILLIE. You know – the Power House.

TAUSCH. You are going to blow up the Power House!

WILLIE. Yes. D'ye know.

TAUSCH. *Almachtiger Gott!* What is all this?

DOBELLE. Just a moment, Tausch. Perhaps you'd better let me talk to him.

TAUSCH. Perhaps I had better!

DOBELLE. Listen, Willie. Why are you proposing to blow up the Power House?

WILLIE. I'm sure I don't know, sir. Battalion orders, d'ye know.

TAUSCH. But it is monstrous! Outrageous! There must be some mistake.

DOBELLE. You realize, Willie, that this is all rather upsetting for Mr Tausch. They are his works, you know.

WILLIE. Indeed, I'm sure he'd have a right to be a bit put out, and I'm sorry indeed to be fixed the way I am. But I have my orders as a soldier, d'ye know, and I've got to obey orders, sir. But there's no ill will at all.

DOBELLE. I know, Willie, I know. I suppose it can't be helped.

WILLIE. You know that, Mr Tausch, don't you? There's no ill will at all.

TAUSCH. Ill will? What is that? I think I go mad!

WILLIE. We'll do the least damage we can, you may be sure.

DOBELLE. I'm sure of that, Willie. But this doesn't explain what you want here. These aren't the works, you know.

WILLIE. Well, sir, the fact is the stuff we have is a bit damp. I think somebody must have left it out last night, because we can't touch it off at all. So some of the boys thought if we were for to burn the place a bit first it might go up that way. D'ye know!

DOBELLE. That seems quite a practical notion.

WILLIE. So they sent me up to commandeer a few tins of petrol. There's a couple in the shed by the sea wall, we thought was Mr Tausch's.

DOBELLE. I see.

WILLIE. We'll pay for them, of course. That's what I want to do.

124

DOBELLE. Just what I would have expected of you, Willie.

WILLIE. Let me see now. 1s. 3d. a gallon – two gallons a tin – two times 1s. 3d. is . . .

DOBELLE. 1s 3d. from the pump, Willie. 1s. 3½d. in the tin.

WILLIE. Aw, that's right. One and threepence ha'penny, it is. Two one and threepence ha'pennys is two and seven, and two tins will be twice seven are fourteen, one and two – five and twopence. Isn't that right? (*He counts the money.*)

TAUSCH (*pulling himself together*). I think I ought to say that one of the tins is not quite full.

DOBELLE. Very handsome of you, Tausch, I'm sure.

WILLIE. Oh, is that so? (*He considers.*) Ah, well, we'll take it all the same. Or supposing we make it the even five bob? (TAUSCH *inclines his head and receives the money.*) And I'm sure you know how sorry we are to have to trouble you, sir. But orders is orders. D'ye know. (*Confidentially.*) And you can have the fire brigade out in no time.

TAUSCH. I see. (*He looks round the room and notes the telephone.*) You say you are a soldier. May I speak to your commanding officer?

WILLIE. Oh, I don't think so, sir. This is all very secret, d'ye know.

DOBELLE. Don't be silly, Willie. We all know who it is. Ask Mr Blake to come in and have a drink.

WILLIE. Well, sir . . . I don't know if . . .

DOBELLE. Come in, Darrell, for God's sake.

(DARRELL BLAKE *enters. He is a young man of about twenty-eight with great grace and charm of manner. He is well dressed in an ordinary lounge suit and wears an overcoat, but no hat. He has an air of reckless indifference which – at a distance – is rather fascinating. There is no external evidence of any weapon about his person. The quick nervous movements of his hands betray a highly-strung and sensitive disposition. He carries a small parcel under his arm.*)

BLAKE. Did somebody mention refreshments? Well, that's always a pleasure. (*He bows.*) Ah! (*He blesses the decanter.*) Benedictus benedicat.

DOBELLE. Herr Tausch – Mr Blake. Let me pour you out something.

BLAKE. *Sehr angenehm,* Herr Tausch.

TAUSCH (*crossly*). Good day.

BLAKE. Enough, enough, coz. What will the visitor think of me?

DOBELLE. Sit down, Darrell. (*He goes to the model railway and works with it.*)

BLAKE. Thank you, but I only sit on formal occasions. This is a strictly informal one. Herr Tausch will appreciate.

TAUSCH. I quite appreciate.

BLAKE. I knew you would. Here's health. (*He drinks.*) I'm sorry now we sent Willie in to you. I can see that there's only been a sordid family scene. By the way, I hope you don't think that Willie is our show desperado? Did you, Herr Tausch?

TAUSCH. I hardly know what to think.

BLAKE. Then don't bother at all. Thought is shocking bad for the brain. You should be a man of action like me, Herr Tausch. Terribly desperate, I assure you. You should see the blood I've spilt in my time!

TAUSCH. Mr Blake, I am in no mood for flippancy. I insist upon knowing at once whether it is seriously intended to interfere with my Power House?

BLAKE. Why, most seriously. Hannibal is at the gates! You didn't think we were pulling your leg, I hope?

TAUSCH. Then it is true what this man says?

BLAKE. That the wicked shall be burned with fire? Oh yes! Unfortunately it rained last night, and rain is damn bad for explosives, when left in Willie's charge. So you see us temporarily embarrassed.

TAUSCH. Then I go to the Power House, and I will see that nothing of the kind occurs.

BLAKE. Back, back! Regretfully not. Please regard that as out of the question.

TAUSCH. You propose to hold me by force?

BLAKE. That's right.

TAUSCH. But – but why?

BLAKE (*airily*). Oh, Revolution.

TAUSCH. What do you mean?

BLAKE. Just that.

TAUSCH. Revolution! What do you mean? That is just a word!

BLAKE. A beautiful word. So few people appreciate beautiful words nowadays!

WILLIE. Up the rebels! That's all, d'ye know.

BLAKE. Willie, I think we've had enough of you. Outside and guard something. We've got a better idea than we had. Where's George, coz?

(WILLIE *goes out.*)

DOBELLE. I'm not sure. Across in the armoury, I suppose.

BLAKE. This will be a great night for George. Excuse me, while I bring good news to Aix.

(*He goes.* TAUSCH *is galvanized into activity. He springs to the door and makes sure that nobody is about. Then a finger to his lips he beckons to* DOBELLE.)

TAUSCH. S-sh! There are men out there. Keep them engaged three minutes, and I will call assistance. See. *Wo ist das Telefonbuch?*

(*He hurries to the telephone and* DOBELLE *indicates the directory on a side table.* TAUSCH *feverishly turns over the pages and then waves* DOBELLE *away. The latter goes to the door, pauses, looks out, then in, shakes his head and finally disappears.* TAUSCH *throws the book away impatiently and takes up the receiver. After a while he glances out of the window and rattles the instrument.*)

TAUSCH. *Allo, Allo! Mein Gott!*

(*He rattles again. The* AUNT *enters carrying her bicycle. He slams down the receiver and turns away in affected innocence.*)

AUNT. Oh no, nobody would pay any attention to me. But maybe they'll listen now. The hour of the poor and the defenceless and the down-trodden comes sooner or later. The dynamos are turning. (*Shouting as she goes upstairs.*) But the proud in their pride shall be laid low. They didn't account for everything. Not for everything!

(*She goes into her room. The* GERMAN *makes sure that she is gone and returns hastily to the telephone. From upstairs the click of the typewriter starts once again. At last he gets a response.*)

TAUSCH (*in a loud whisper*) *Allo! Allo!* Yes, give me the police – caserne. No, I cannot speak louder . . . What? I do not know the number. Surely you can – No – *Gott in Himmel!* Never mind the Inquiries . . . I want the military – troops – *hilfe* – I say, are you listening? *Allo!* (*There is a distant burst of laughter from outside. Disconcerted, he glances out of the window before continuing.*) *Allo!* . . . Are you there? . . . *Allo? Allo!*

(WILLIE *enters quietly.* TAUSCH *holds the receiver behind*

*him, breathing heavily, with thoughts of violence in his
mind.*)

WILLIE. Did you press button 'A'? (*Pause.*) Maybe I could get it
for you. I know the girl below. What is it you want? The fire
brigade, I suppose? (*He takes the receiver from the speechless*
GERMAN.) Well, take my tip and – and – Hello, miss, is that
you? Oh, I'm well, how are ya? . . . Oh, I will indeed. Looka,
will you give me double two double two one . . . thanks very
much . . . (*To* TAUSCH) And I tell you what, you'd better give
a call to the guards. There's often a lot of rough sorts and
tinkers, you know, that comes hanging around the place where
there's a fire. They'd be out in half an hour. Would you like
to speak to them yourself? Hello, miss . . . (*He bangs the*
receiver.) Ay, for God's sake, can you not get me the fire
brigade!

(*The* GERMAN *drops into a chair with a string of expletives.*
A ship hoots in the river. The turbines hum merrily in the
distance through the open door.)

S W I F T   C U R T A I N

ACT TWO

This room was once the premises of the Army Ordnance Corps, but it is now used (officially) as a store of the Coast Life Saving Service and (unofficially) as a dumping place for old trunks and furniture belonging to the Dobelle family. There is a wide stone hearth over which the Royal Arms are still to be seen. To the rear is a big double door and a high barred window. Numerous Government circulars relating to distress signals at sea, fog-horns, and the like are pinned and pasted upon the walls, together with a picture of a full-rigged sailing ship cut from a tobacco advertisement. There is a desk against the wall near the window on which are a couple of ledgers. On the one side, opposite the fireplace, is a workman's bench covered with tools, amongst which stand four polished four-inch projectiles. From a door upon this side protrudes something that might be the muzzle of a gun. The room is full of coils of tarred rope, collapsible wooden tripods, a few big life-saving rockets and numerous lanterns of all sizes and shapes. Amongst the stored furniture is a cottage piano, and one or two pictures, all of which are covered with sacking, and on the wall, plainly visible to all, is a large kitchen clock. It stands at five to nine, and keeps going throughout the scene.

When the Curtain rises, CAPTAIN POTTS *is seated on a high stool with his back to the audience, making entries in one of the ledgers, and* GEORGE *is seated near the bench binding the stopper of a glass bottle, into which has been inserted a model of a full-rigged ship.* BLANAID *is seated on the ground beside him. The scene commences about six minutes before the conclusion of* ACT ONE.

GEORGE. Well, kid, we got into Cape Town, and the captain he drew a chalk line across the deck abaft the fiddley door and he said to me: 'Quartermaster,' he said, 'the doctor and I are going ashore on important business. See that none of those

129

women cross that line.' 'Ay, ay, sir,' said I. So off he and the doctor went in a hansom cab.

BLANAID. And how many women had you on board?

GEORGE. Hundred and thirty-two. All cooks and housemaids. Government emigrants for Sydney. Never such a cargo known before, my dear.

BLANAID. Well, what happened then?

GEORGE. Well, I sat at the end of the gangway chatting with the little brown-eyed one, and by and by along comes the one called Scotch Annie, at the head of twenty-five whopping great females. 'Annie,' said I, 'you can't go ashore. Captain's orders.' 'George,' said Annie, 'we like you. You're a good sort. And me and these girls don't want to have to sock you one on the jaw.' 'O.K., Annie,' said I, 'I like you too.' And with that up the gangway and ashore they went and the whole hundred and thirty-two after them. All but the little brown-eyed one who stayed chatting with me.

BLANAID. And did they ever come back?

GEORGE. Come back! About an hour later up drives a hansom cab at the gallop with the captain and the doctor hanging out and shouting bloody murder. 'Quartermaster,' yells the captain, 'what the hell does this mean? Whole town's had to close down. Those damn women are everywhere.' And then up drives another hansom cab with two policemen and one cook in it. (*He gets up and acts the part with many gestures.*) 'Emigrant from the *Triumph*, sir.' Shove her on board. Salute. Off. Another hansom cab. Two more policemen. Two housemaids. 'Emigrants from the *Triumph*, sir.' Shove 'em on board. Salute. Off. All night. Hansom cabs. Policemen. Cooks and housemaids. Shove 'em on board. Salute. Off. Sailed next morning twenty-nine short. Next year the Boer War.

POTTS. Will you fire a rocket at the Greystones drill?

GEORGE. Greystones? When's that?

POTTS. Wednesday is when you said. Them rockets cost seven pounds apiece.

GEORGE. Um. Lots of kids at Greystones usually. Better let them have a rocket, old man. They like 'em.

BLANAID. May I come and watch you practising, George?

GEORGE. Delighted, kid. Like to go across in the breeches buoy? It's quite safe.

BLANAID. Oh, I'd love to. May I?

GEORGE. Wednesday, then, at Greystones. Artificial respiration too.

(WILLIE *enters and* BLANAID *rises.*)

WILLIE. May I come in?

GEORGE. Of course. Take a seat.

WILLIE. Ah, I won't sit down, thanks very much. I'm on active service, d'ye know.

BLANAID. I knew it was only you, Willie. What's happening?

WILLIE. Nothing much, miss. Mr Blake is over there now – talking.

BLANAID. Oh, Darry? Who to?

WILLIE. Ah, to no one special, miss. They were all talking when I left them.

BLANAID. What were they talking about?

WILLIE. They didn't say, miss.

BLANAID. Then I'm going over to see. Oh, hello!

(*She meets* BLAKE *in the doorway.*)

BLAKE. And how is my friend Blanaid?

BLANAID. Very well, thank you. You haven't been to see us for ages.

BLAKE. I know. But I want to atone for my past with a present. (*He hands her a small parcel.*)

BLANAID. Oh, Darry. (*She examines it.*) I'm so glad there's paper round it. Do you mind if I don't open it for a little?

BLAKE. Of course not. That's much the best part of a present.

BLANAID. I can't imagine what it is. It feels very interesting.

BLAKE. It's really most commonplace. Hello, George. Good evening, Captain.

GEORGE. Well, Blake, old man. Some time since we've seen you.

BLAKE. Yes, I've been rather busy lately. And, by the way, it's you I really want.

GEORGE. Anything to oblige, Darry.

BLAKE. Concerning this loud speaker of yours we've heard so much about.

AUNT (*off*) . . . proud in their pride shall be laid low. They didn't account for everything. Not for everything.

GEORGE. The gun you mean? Why, man, she's a beauty. Want to see her?

BLAKE. What do you suppose that was?

BLANAID. It sounds like Auntie. (BLAKE *smiles.*) What's the joke, Darry?

131

BLAKE. She must be abusing poor Tausch. Can you see?

(BLANAID *goes to the door and looks out to the side*.)

BLAKE. Have you met Tausch, George?

GEORGE. Oh yes. Potts and I were just giving him a drink about half an hour ago. Peculiar chap, I thought. Still we've got to make allowances for these foreigners. Come on, Potts. Let's get the cover off the gun for Darrell. (*They go off*.)

BLAKE. Listen, Willie, never mind the petrol. This job is worthy of a bit of style, so we're going to land a shot in the place with the gun. Besides, we want to please the old men.

WILLIE. The gun? Oh, that'll be very interesting for the boys.

BLAKE. Well, what's happening?

BLANAID. He's telephoning.

BLAKE. No! (DOBELLE *enters*.)

DOBELLE. Really this is too bad. I will not have my guests baited like this. The man's ringing up town.

BLAKE. Marvellous. (*They all crowd round the door and look out*.)

DOBELLE. It mayn't be so marvellous for you when somebody comes out.

BLAKE. By God! He's telephoning all right.

BLANAID. Golly, isn't he excited.

BLAKE. Willie, go across and ask if you can help.

WILLIE. I will indeed, Mr Blake. (*He goes*.)

BLAKE. Watch now everybody. Three to one in pounds that he hits Willie on the jaw. (BLANAID *and* BLAKE *laugh heartily*.)

DOBELLE. It's all very well to laugh. But what's going to happen when Lanigan gets out?

BLAKE. I don't give a damn for Lanigan. What sort of a fool do you suppose that German takes me for? Ringing up town when he thinks he's got me out of the way. And now I suppose he'll come across and try to distract us for half an hour with bright, helpful conversation until the lorries can get out with the Staters. I do dislike having my intelligence insulted.

DOBELLE. Darrell, this is intolerable behaviour. You know quite well what it will mean in the end.

BLAKE. Listen, I've got an idea. Is the tide out, my dear?

BLANAID. Yes. Why?

BLAKE. Then I think I'll give Mr Tausch all the cat and mouse he wants and bit to spare. We'll get the gun out on the sea wall, loaded and trained on the works, and then, by God, Tausch shall have all the distracting conversation he asks for.

132

We'll keep him on the hop for ten, fifteen, twenty minutes until we hear the rumble of the lorries. God, what a scheme! I'll be laughing for months. The rumble of the lorries, and the Bosch thinking he's caught us. And then bang goes the gun, up go the works to hell, and off we trot across the sand to the shore on the far side. What do you think of that?

DOBELLE. Exactly. And leave us to take the consequences.

BLAKE. They can't take the lorries off the road. We'll have them on toast.

DOBELLE. You know perfectly well what it will mean. The ruin of our privacy for weeks. The inquiries – the cross-examination – the statements – the alibis! Some of these days, my boy, I damn well will make a statement and where will you be then?

BLAKE. Don't worry. You'll have much the best part of the evening's entertainment. You'll be able to see the German's face. I'd give my soul for that. I do hope Willie hasn't discouraged him.

BLANAID (*opening her parcel and disclosing a small book*). Oh, how lovely! Did you have to buy it, Darry?

BLAKE. There. That's all the thanks a criminal ever gets! I always said you were badly brought up.

BLANAID. The Girl Guide's Diary. (*Laughing.*) Oh, it's perfect.

DOBELLE (*grumbling round amongst the Dobelle impedimenta*). Insufferable! Monstrous! Nobody ever has any consideration for me.

(*A ship hoots in the river.*)

BLANAID. With a pencil and everything. It's full of useful information.

BLAKE. Come on, George. About this gun. May I show it to the boys?

GEORGE (*reappearing*). Only too delighted, old man. Know anything about guns?

BLAKE. No, but I'm always ready to learn. This is the dangerous end, I suppose?

GEORGE. In theory, old man. At present we can't say more. Come along, Potts. We'll have to show him.

(POTTS *appears.*)

BLANAID. I suppose I could be a Lone Guide if I learnt all these knots?

DOBELLE. Of course, you must upset the fellow when he's my guest. Some of these things seem familiar.

GEORGE. This gun is what we call a muzzle-loading, four-inch-slow-firing-Potts-shot. Now explain, Potts. You've got it all learnt off.

POTTS (*in a steady sing-song*). Well, sir, beginning at this end, first the steel barrel is strengthened with wrought iron 'oops shrunk over one another so that the inner toob or barrel is placed in a state of compression and the outer portions is in a state of tension.

BLAKE. You don't say.

POTTS. Furthermore, by forming the outer parts of wrought iron bar eviled round a mandrel and then welding the coil into a solid 'oop, the fibre of the iron is arranged what we calls circumferentially, and is thus in the best position to resist the stress.

DOBELLE. Who the devil brings all these things of mine over here? No wonder I never can find anything!

BLAKE. One moment – just before you go any further. You mentioned a mandrel. Now, what exactly is that?

POTTS. A mandrel?
(*An uncomfortable pause.*)

GEORGE. Better come inside, old man. Able to explain better there. Eh, Potts?

POTTS. Inside? Oh, yaw. Much better inside.
(*They go out.* DOBELLE *has taken the sacking partially off one of the pictures, disclosing the portrait of a young woman dressed in the clothes of about thirty years ago.* POTTS *returns to collect a corkscrew and a couple of glasses from the bench.*)

POTTS. Forgotten something, George. (*He goes.*)
(*There are sounds of movement off followed by the clink of glasses.* BLANAID *stands looking at her father.* WILLIE *enters.*)

WILLIE. Where's Mr Blake?

BLAKE (*off*). Busy, Willie. (*Pop of a cork.*)

WILLIE. Oh, are you there? He doesn't seem to want anything. He sent me across and says he'll be after me.
(*He goes into the adjoining room. There is the sound of flowing liquid.*)

DOBELLE. Now there's something I've been looking for for months. How did it get here?

BLANAID. I don't know, Father. A lot of the things from the house get left over here.

DOBELLE. Well nobody has any business to do it no matter how full the place is.

(DOBELLE *stares out of the window. Siphon off.* BLANAID *approaches him tentatively.*)

BLANAID. Father . . . Did you see what Darry gave me?

DOBELLE. No.

BLANAID. It's a diary . . . I love it.

DOBELLE. You'll lose it, I expect.

BLANAID. No, I won't. Guides don't lose things . . . Father, do you think that giving presents to a person is a sign of friendship?

DOBELLE. I really don't know.

BLANAID. I think so. I haven't very many friends, I'm afraid . . . (*Silence.*) . . . Daddy, would this diary be of any use to you?

(DOBELLE *turns his head and looks at her for a moment.*)

BLANAID. You don't want it?

DOBELLE (*shakes his head and turns away*). No, thank you.

BLANAID. I see. (*Choking it back.*) Well . . . I think . . . I want something . . . in my room.

(*She turns and runs out.*)

POTTS (*off*). The castings are annealed by placing them in a furnace or hoven until red 'ot, then allowing them to cool gradyerly. The exterior of the body must be ground by a hemery wheel or turned on a lathe. (*Pop of a cork.*) 'Ere's looking at yer. (*Pause. Then briskly.*) The groove for the driving band is also turned an' the fuse 'ole fitted with a gunmetal bush.

BLAKE (*off*). And the same to you.

(TAUSCH *enters. He has an air of suppressed excitement and crosses swiftly to* DOBELLE.)

TAUSCH. Ach, so you are here! (*He whispers loudly.*) Listen, *Fünf-und-zwanzig Minuten.* When I have got rid of the young man I call the barracks. They come in lorries. Twenty-five minutes and all will be well.

DOBELLE. I expected as much. This is all most distasteful. (*He goes to the door.*)

TAUSCH (*misunderstanding him*). Nein, nein. Courage, *mein Freund.* Courage! See, until nine hours thirty! *Frisch gewagt ist halb gewonnen, eh, Kamerad!*

(*Enter* BLAKE, GEORGE, POTTS *and* WILLIE. *They go to the shell cases.*)

BLAKE. How many did you say you've got?

TAUSCH (*conversationally*). *Ach,* so here we are!

GEORGE. Hello, Splosch, old man. Four.

POTTS. The last one needs a bit o' greasing. We only got it done last week.

BLAKE. Four. A beautiful number. Like the gospels.

DOBELLE (*calling.*) Columba, come over here, please.

GEORGE. We'll have more in a year or so. Takes time to get down to them, you know.

BLAKE. Four are quite enough to save our souls. Do you mind if we take everything outside?

GEORGE. Not at all, old man. What's it all about?

BLAKE. Crime, George! Enough said, for your own sake. Tonight I am Dick Deadeye, the boy burglar! I'll call the boys to help to get it out the door. Willie, you bring one of those things.

DOBELLE. Columba, will you kindly come when I call you.

(*He disappears out the door, carrying the picture with him.*)

TAUSCH. Er, perhaps I also can assist in some way.

BLAKE. Of course, Herr Tausch. We were just saying you would. Bright, helpful conversation.

WILLIE. Will I take this one?

BLAKE. Any one. And for God's sake be careful. Remember they go off.

WILLIE. Oh, I'll walk like a cat.

(*Half-way to the door, the shell spins in his grasp, he catches it again, loses it once more, and finally lets it fall.* TAUSCH *drops flat on his face.* BLAKE *covers his head with an arm.* GEORGE *and* POTTS *fall into a locked embrace. The shell bounces dully and then lies still. Pause.*)

WILLIE. Oh! I dropped it.

BLAKE. He dropped it! He tells us he dropped it.

(GEORGE *and* POTTS *come slowly forward and bend over the object on the ground.*)

GEORGE. That was strange, Potts.

POTTS. Don't understand that, George. (*They prod it gingerly. Nothing happens.*)

WILLIE. Did it not go off?

BLAKE. O God, give me patience!

GEORGE. Ought to do better than that, old man. (*He picks it up*

and shakes it to an ear.) I don't know. Some carelessness somewhere.

POTTS. Watcher mean, carelessness?

GEORGE. Did you bring the water to the boil?

POTTS. Of course I brought the water to the boil.

GEORGE. Doesn't look like it, old man.

WILLIE. I hope I didn't break it on you.

POTTS (*indignantly gets out a dog-eared notebook*). There's the
nitrate, ain't it – mercurous nitrate, sol-soluble in 'undred an'
thirty times its weight o' boiling water.

GEORGE. Well let's bring it over and have a look.

POTTS. 'Ave as many looks as you like, but I don't like them
insinuations, George. D'ye think I don't know 'ow ter boil
water?

GEORGE. Now, now, Potts, there's no use crying over spilt milk.
Maybe the stuff's not shaken down in the bag.

POTTS. Well, it's not my job to shake it, is it?

BLAKE (*dusting himself*). So much for Matthew. I suppose we may
expect equally good performances from the other three?

GEORGE. No, no, not at all. You see, this one was the first we
made. Probably a bit on the old side by now. Or maybe Potts
here . . .

POTTS (*threateningly*). Atcher!

BLAKE. In any event, we'll excuse you, Willie. Go and help the
boys to get that thing out. I'll handle the next myself.

WILLIE (*most willingly*). Right ye are, Mr Blake. Where's it to
go?

BLAKE (*in a low voice*). Across the yard behind that parapet. And
then you're to train the muzzle very carefully through one of
those loopholes on to the roof of the turbine house. Now, do
you understand me? Because say so, for God's sake, if you
don't.

WILLIE. Oh, I do indeed. That'll be very interesting. (*To the
earnest workers at the bench, as he passes*) I hope it'll be all
right. (*He goes.*)

TAUSCH. *Alles zu seiner Zeit,* Mr Blake. You think it is necessary
for us to risk our poor lives again?

BLAKE. It's all for the cause, you know. Did you see my glass
anywhere?

(TAUSCH *fetches it and fills another for himself, which, however, he does not drink.*)

TAUSCH. I would like so much to talk with you for a little. To ask you some questions about yourself.

BLAKE (*smiling*). Well, why not. There's no hurry, is there?

TAUSCH. Oh no. No hurry at all.

GEORGE. Try the screw in the base plug.

POTTS. D'ye not know that's the centrifugal bolt.

BLAKE. I suppose they're all right with that damn thing?

TAUSCH. We are in the hands of One above.

VOICES (*off*).

Come on in boys.

That's right, get the door open.

Ay, will you look where you're going?

BLAKE. Well, what do you want to know about me?

TAUSCH. Mr Blake, I am very glad I have met you. I think you are the most interesting person I have known since I have come to your most interesting country.

BLAKE. Oh, come now. Flattery.

TAUSCH. Yes, indeed. But, believe me, it is not quite the compliment. For, you see, I am much more interested in my enemies than in my friends. And I feel that you are my enemy.

BLAKE. I only hope, Herr Tausch, a foeman worthy of your steel.

TAUSCH. I think so. I think so.

BLAKE (*raising his glass*). Then may the worst man win. (TAUSCH *bows and drinks a sip also.*)

GEORGE. Take the needle pellet out of another one. This is no good.

POTTS. Picric, ain't it?

TAUSCH. You see, I have every sympathy with your National Movement.

BLAKE. Ah, national movements are only a means to an end. We're not such parochial politicians as you seem to take us for.

TAUSCH. But why, then? Why all this?

BLAKE. Why not? Look here, Herr Tausch, you are our guest, and I declare that in a way I like you. Let me give you a word of advice. Don't let yourself be deceived by life. She's fooling you.

TAUSCH. In what way, pray?

BLAKE. My God, man, go out and take a look at your works and then ask yourself that question again. Listen to the noise of your turbines and then come back and give me any adequate reason for it all. The rest of the world may be crazy, but there's one corner of it yet, thank God, where you and your ludicrous machinery haven't turned us all into a race of pimps and beggars.

TAUSCH. Machinery, my dear sir, does not make pimps and beggars.

BLAKE. It makes proletarians. Is that any better?

(*For some time* WILLIE *has been pushing vigorously at the muzzle of the gun.*)

A VOICE (*off*). Say when you're ready to shove.

WILLIE. Ah God! haven't I been shoving for the last ten minutes.

(*The gun is heaved out of sight.* WILLIE *falls after it.*)

TAUSCH. But, Mr Blake, must we not have some regard for progress?

BLAKE. My good man, how do you know what progress is? Tell me, if you dare.

TAUSCH. Well, perhaps I may put it this way without offence. Surely you must admit that there are such things as backward countries?

BLAKE. There are countries where, incredible as it may seem to you, some of us prefer to live.

WILLIE (*off*). If you go through there you'll be stuck in the jamb of the door.

BLAKE. If man has anything to boast of that the ant, the bee and the mole haven't got, surely it's his greater capacity for enjoying life. To me it is progress just to live – to live more consciously and more receptively. Herr Tausch, do you never see yourself as rather a ridiculous figure trying to catch life in a blast furnace?

TAUSCH. It seems to me that the blast furnace is just the thing that leaves us all the freer to enjoy life.

BLAKE. Excuse me – does it leave *you* any the freer? Does it leave your dirty workmen any the freer? That's just where you allow yourself to be deceived. It's just another shackle on your limbs, and a self-inflicted one at that. I might be like you, Herr Tausch, if I chose, and this country might be like yours if you had your way. But I don't choose, and you won't have your way. Because we intend to keep one small corner of the globe safe for the unfortunate human race.

TAUSCH. Very interesting. And so you are a machine wrecker? We are engaged in a *Kulturkampf*. Well, I have heard of such before. You are a man of courage, Mr Blake.

BLAKE. To challenge you? Tausch said 'Let there be light,' And the evening and the morning were the first day.

TAUSCH. There have been others.

BLAKE. Elsewhere maybe. But here we believe that the dawn will break in the west. You bring us light from the wrong direction.

(GEORGE *is holding the shell, and* POTTS *is rapping it smartly on the nose with a wooden mallet.*)

GEORGE. Give it a good hard one, Potts old man.

BLAKE. Really, I do think this has gone far enough. Can't you do that somewhere else?

GEORGE. Quite safe, old chap.

BLAKE. If it goes off it'll spoil that suit of yours, Potts.

POTTS. My suit? You know, George, I'd forgotten all about the poor old missus.

GEORGE. There now, you've reminded the old fellow!

BLAKE. Anything to stop him fiddling with that damn bomb. And look here, what have you been doing to this other one? It's all in bits.

GEORGE. Had to take out the needle pellet. And she just came apart in my hands.

BLAKE. Damn it, then there's only two left!

POTTS. Think I'll have to go and have a drink, George.

GEORGE. I don't blame you, Captain. I'm going to get one myself. Come along. (*He leaves by a door on the fireplace side.*)

BLAKE. Oh, do cheer up, Potts. Did you ever tell Herr Tausch the story?

POTTS (*hesitating in the door.*) I don't think as 'ow I did.

TAUSCH. I am sure it would be very painful for the Herr Kapitän on such a day as this.

BLAKE. Not at all. We often discuss it. You should listen to this, Tausch. It's rather illuminating. Go on, Potts. Here's a fresh cosmopolitan mind for you.

POTTS. Well, you see, sir, we was all out in the old *Mermaid,* and we found out we only 'ad the one lifebelt as soon as she turned out to be sprung. Well, I was for drawing lots for it. But George, 'e says, 'No, Potts, women and children first, Potts,' 'e says. So I says, 'You're right, George.' So we fixes the lifebelt around the old missus and pitches her overboard.

TAUSCH. Ah, your ship was sinking!

POTTS. Well, yes, sir, in a way. So we thought at the time. But

140

that's just the queer thing, sir, for when the fog lifted and we could see what was what, there we was aground in about 'alf a fathom 'ard by Fairview.

TAUSCH. Ach, so. That was fortunate for you. You escaped?

POTTS. Sure. We just waded ashore. All but the old missus, poor soul. We didn't get 'er till the next day.

TAUSCH. She was safe in the lifebelt?

POTTS. Sure she was safe in it. Floating a cable or two off Salthill. The wrong ways up. Poor Maggie. I often wonders whether we was wrong, sir. George 'e says not, and 'e ought ter know. But sometimes on 'er anniversary I thinks of poor Maggie, and, you know, I 'as my doubts. I do indeed. (*He shakes his head and follows* GEORGE *off.*)

BLAKE. Well? You don't feel inclined to laugh?

TAUSCH. Mr Blake, I never feel inclined to laugh at a man because his wife is dead. I am amazed that a man of some sensibility such as yourself could be so cruel.

BLAKE (*thinks for a moment and at last raises his glass.*) To death, Herr Tausch, that makes the whole world kin. (*He drinks.*) There's nothing cruel about her. (*He sits.*) Quite the reverse. (*There is another pause while he sinks into a brown study.*)

TAUSCH. Come, my friend. Perhaps I have been unjust. I am sorry.

BLAKE. It's all right. I'm partially intoxicated, that's all. (*Angry voices rise outside.*)

VOICES:

A bucketful will do.

Try it the other way round.

Ah, will you leave it alone?

Etc.

BLAKE. (*pulling himself together*). What are those damn fellows up to now?

TAUSCH. Wait, I will see. (*They both look at the clock.*)

BLAKE (*rising*). We can't fool about here any longer. *Fronta capillata,* as the elder Cato says. If Matthew and Mark fail us, then Luke must do the trick.

(BLAKE *takes the third shell and goes out.* TAUSCH *hastily fills his glass from the bottle and hurries after him.*)

TAUSCH (*following*). Mr Blake, you have forgotten your glass.

WILLIE (*off*). Ay, will ye looka. I say the bloody thing goes the other way round. (*Altercations till* BLAKE'S *voice quietens them. After a moment* DOBELLE *and* AUNT COLUMBA *come in.*)

DOBELLE. I don't care how full the house is. Nobody has any business to leave any of my things over here.

AUNT. Don't raise your voice at me, please. You can't intimidate me with loud speeches.

DOBELLE. I wish to God I could intimidate somebody in the house.

AUNT. Well, now that we're on the subject of intimidation, what have you been saying to Blanaid?

DOBELLE. Nothing. Why?

AUNT. She's retired to her room in tears. Whatever it is this time, I've had to tell you before that you're doing that child a great injustice.

DOBELLE. Well, hasn't she done me an injustice?

AUNT. You mean – Mary? How can you blame her for that? She didn't ask to be born.

DOBELLE. It seems to me that she was most insistent about being born.

AUNT. Roddy, you're unbalanced on that subject.

DOBELLE. Next you're going to tell me that I'm off my head, I suppose.

AUNT. Sometimes I wonder. But that doesn't make any difference to your duty to instruct her.

DOBELLE. Don't I leave that to you?

AUNT. Yes. But you don't allow me to teach her about you-know-where. (*She points downwards.*)

DOBELLE. I don't see why that should be an essential part of her instruction.

AUNT. Don't be ridiculous, Roddy. Doesn't the Bible say: 'Suffer the little children to come unto me'? Well, if one adopts your absurd attitude, supposing they won't come, where can you tell them to go to?

DOBELLE. My dear Columba, if your instruction depends on that – as indeed all instruction ultimately does – then it only confirms what I say – that ignorance is bliss.

AUNT. She's entitled to be told.

DOBELLE. Well, I won't have it. And if I find she knows, you can leave this house.

AUNT. It is every parent's duty and privilege to tell his child about that.

DOBELLE. I deny all duties and privileges where Blanaid is concerned. I will feed and clothe her, but there my interests end.

AUNT. What possible complaint can you have against her? She's a most mild-mannered child.

DOBELLE. Her existence . . . that was bought and paid for at Pressburg. Isn't that enough?

AUNT. That's a most outrageous thing to say. I'd like to know what Mary would think.

DOBELLE. Columba, you're a most unscrupulous woman. What right have you to bring Mary into it when you know I can't bear the subject?

AUNT. Well I can't say I've ever noticed any great tact on your part where my feelings are concerned. Aren't you always hinting to me about mowing machines?

DOBELLE. Be quiet. They're coming back.

AUNT. I won't be quiet.

DOBELLE. S-sh!

> (*They continue to converse in low undertones amongst the luggage.* TAUSCH *enters. He smiles nervously as they glare at him, and he crosses swiftly to the door through which* GEORGE *and* POTTS *have gone out. He looks out and then closes it, coming back centre as* BLAKE *enters rather loquaciously tipsy.*)

BLAKE. Come and show us which way up this – oh! Where's George?

TAUSCH. He is not here. (BLAKE *looks out the wrong door.*)

BLAKE. Oh, hell!

TAUSCH. Well, Mr Blake. You were to tell me what you thought of me.

BLAKE. Was I? Well, I'll tell you how I regard you. As a demon pantechnicon driver. Old worlds into new quarters, by road, rail and sea.

TAUSCH (*with a look at the clock*). But surely that is a most praiseworthy occupation?

BLAKE. Maybe. Do what you like with your own world. But I insist that you leave me mine. I am Persephone, weary of memory, putting poppies in my hair.

TAUSCH. This world is neither yours nor mine. It belongs to all these people. Have you the right to say that I may not help them?

BLAKE. Nobody wants your help, Tausch. Why can't you just go away?

143

TAUSCH. How do you know they don't want it? Have you ever asked them?

BLAKE (*incredulous*). Asked them? (*Then with a laugh.*) Well, ask them. I don't mind.

TAUSCH. The verdict of democracy.

BLAKE. God bless the dear old people. The majority is always right. O.K. Let's try.

TAUSCH. Mr and Miss Dobelle, may we put this question to you?

DOBELLE. Still fishing the troubled waters of a dry well, eh?

BLAKE. We ought to get them all. (*Shouting at the door*) Willie! Blanaid! Come over here.

TAUSCH. It is a matter of great importance. (*Whispers*) Twelve minutes more.

(*Enter* GEORGE *and* POTTS.)

BLAKE. Come on in, George. You'll enjoy this.

GEORGE. Hullo, Splosch, old man, still here?

BLAKE. I think Potts should take the chair. He's the most impartial.

POTTS. What's all this? (*He sits and smokes his pipe, phlegmatically.* WILLIE *enters.*)

AUNT. I suppose we must have that door open all night regardless of the temperature.

(BLAKE *and* WILLIE *close it.*)

BLAKE. Have you been able to fix that, Willie?

WILLIE. Oh, I think so. It looks all right to me now.

BLAKE (*opening the window and again speaking in a low voice*). Well, stand there by the window and listen for you-know-what. And the minute you hear them coming tell me at once.

WILLIE. But are we not going to . . .

BLAKE. Do what I tell you, and stop making remarks, Willie. I know what I'm doing.

(WILLIE *stands at the window. For some time* TAUSCH *has been speaking earnestly to* GEORGE.)

GEORGE. But did I ever call you 'Splosch', old man?

TAUSCH. It is a small matter. Just if you can remember.

GEORGE (*ruminatively*). Tosh – Tush – (*He puts the bottle beside Blake's chair.*) Good for the voice, old man.

BLAKE. Thank you, George. How about keeping some minutes, Aunt Columba? An affair like this will be nuts and wine to you.

AUNT. Many a minute I've kept that people have regretted when sober.

> (*She draws forward a small chair and sits down.* BLANAID *comes quietly in and sits on the ground. She takes out her diary and starts to write in it.*)

BLAKE. Dearly beloved, the situation is a straightforward one. Our German brother stands indicted before the bar of this court on the gravest of charges. He has outraged the sacred person of our beloved mother – Cathleen ni Houlihan. I say let him be condemned and his works be a deodand. In other words, I propose to blow them up. We leave it to you.

TAUSCH. To express your views without force or unfair influence.

BLAKE. *Nihil obstat.* What are you working at, my dear?

BLANAID. I'm filling in my personal memoranda. (*She produces a tape and takes a few measurements of her span, breadth of thumb, etc.*)

TAUSCH. Perhaps you will allow me to begin with a few words.

AUNT. Just one moment, please. I understood that this was to be some sort of a public discussion. Now it appears to be more like a court martial.

BLAKE. Oh, need we go into that?

AUNT. It is of importance as to who should speak first.

TAUSCH. It is all the same. It makes no difference.

AUNT. Excuse me, it makes a very big difference.

TAUSCH. It is just what you choose to call it. That is of no importance.

AUNT. Herr Tausch, if you call its tail a leg, how many legs do you say a cow has got?

TAUSCH. Really, Miss Dobelle!

AUNT. Answer me, please.

TAUSCH. If you call its tail a leg? Well, five, I suppose.

AUNT. Wrong, four. Because calling its tail a leg doesn't make it one. Blanaid, you're the junior. Begin.

BLANAID. Me? Well, I think it would be a shame to blow them up.

AUNT. Reasons, please, if any.

BLANAID. Because I like Herr Tausch and I think you're all being beastly to him.

BLAKE. For acquittal. Well, that's one point of view. (*Drinks deeply.*)

TAUSCH. Thank you, *Mein Herzchen.* It is not a reason that I had expected, but I appreciate it.

AUNT. Now, Willie?

WILLIE. Ah, sure there's no good asking me. I'm on active service.

AUNT. But if you weren't on active service?

WILLIE. I'm always on active service. I took an oath, you know, and I can't go back on that.

TAUSCH. What kind of an oath?

WILLIE. To obey my superior officers, and not to recognize the Government until the country's free. Isn't this a Government works?

TAUSCH. Pardon me, but what is the difference between the 'Government' and the 'country'?

(*All laugh.*)

DOBELLE. All the difference in the world if you're out of office. I thought I'd made that clear.

TAUSCH. But, pardon me, Willie. If it were not for your oath, do you think that to blow up the works would do a lot of harm to the country?

WILLIE. Ah, it would and it wouldn't. Wouldn't it help a lot of lads out of work if they had for to build them up again? I'm dead against unemployment, d'ye know.

BLAKE. That's enough. Conviction. Who's next?

TAUSCH. But may not the accused speak a word upon his own behalf?

AUNT. Don't interrupt, please. I'm next. And I wish it to be quite clear that I have as yet no personal objection to Herr Tausch.

TAUSCH. I am so glad.

AUNT. He may be a most estimable man for all I know, although he does try to get young girls to go with him to the pictures, and as for his morals, well, they don't concern me. I can be as broad-minded as anybody.

TAUSCH. I beg your pardon . . .

AUNT. Nor have I any objection to any ordinary factory as such. But this building is a power house, which is quite a different thing. Some people, I know, are inclined to scoff at the significance of power houses and to dismiss them lightly as just a small matter. But it is those very people who before they realize it have become dependent on the very thing they tried to laugh off. They think that they can give them up at any time. But they never can. Never.

TAUSCH. The lady is surely speaking of alcohol!

146

BLAKE. But this is eloquence, Aunt Columba. There's not a dry eye.

AUNT. Now once you become dependent upon anything, you are the slave of the man who controls it. Expected to bow the knee to some place-hunting industrialist with a small technical education and with neither culture nor religion to guide them. And if anybody thinks I am going to do that he is very greatly mistaken. I will not be dominated or controlled by anybody, and I am very grateful to Darry Blake for what he suggests, although I don't pretend to approve of him in other ways.

BLAKE. Thank you, Aunt Columba. You see, Tausch, I am appreciated too.

TAUSCH. Really, Miss Dobelle, I am none of these things you call me, I do not expect you to bow the knee.

AUNT. Order, please.

TAUSCH. You misunderstand me, I assure you.

AUNT. You are persistently interrupting, Herr Tausch. Please understand I will not be trampled on by you.

BLAKE. Yes, stop trampling on Aunt Columba, Tausch, and sit down. Now George?

(TAUSCH *shrugs his shoulders and sits down with a glance at the clock.*)

GEORGE. Well, you know I haven't the gift of the gab the way you people have, but when I was in Birmingham I sometimes used to watch all those women and young girls coming in and out of the factories. And, you know, I was touched – more touched than I can say. All those women and young girls having to work night and day, with their poor, pale, pasty faces that they have to make up with rouge and all that, brought tears to my eyes, old man. They ought to be kept out of doors and have proper homes of their own, you know. No life for young girls.

BLAKE. Two up and one to play. (*He stands.*) Well, George, your young girls will have to thank you for their green fields from this out.

GEORGE. Me? How do you make that out?

BLAKE. You and your gun. That's the idea. Why bother with damp cheddar when the Third Evangelist is waiting by the sea wall to do the trick for us.

147

GEORGE. I say, old man, you don't mean you're thinking of actually firing that gun?

BLAKE. Precisely.

GEORGE. Oh, I didn't know that. Did you, Potts?

POTTS. No. I didn't know that.

BLAKE. My dear man, we've been talking of nothing else all evening.

GEORGE. Oh well, I didn't hear you say that.

BLAKE. You don't seem pleased?

GEORGE. Well, it's all very well, you know. But it's a bit of a surprise. After all, those shells. Took a year each to make. And now to see them go up in a flash! And the gun. Four years' work, old man. Supposing something happens to it?

BLAKE. George, you're not trying to back out, are you?

GEORGE. Well, what do you think, Potts?

POTTS. Oh, I didn't know they was going to fire our gun.

GEORGE. We won't get it back, you know. Once they hear about it, it's gone for good.

POTTS. Yes, that's a bit thick, I think.

GEORGE. Anything in reason, old man. But, all these years' work!

BLAKE. George, I'm sorry. We thought you'd be pleased if we used it. But it's too late to change now. That's understood.

GEORGE. Oh, well, I'm against it, then.

POTTS. So'm I.

AUNT. You're in the chair. You've only got a casting vote.

POTTS. Casting what?

AUNT (*shouting*). Vote!

BLAKE. Then it all depends on you, coz. What's the verdict?

TAUSCH. Yes, Mr Dobelle, it depends on you.

DOBELLE. I'm against you.

TAUSCH. *Davor behüte uns Gott!*

BLAKE. Thumbs down!

DOBELLE. My reasons are – (*Enter* AGNES *with a tray. Everybody relaxes except* DOBELLE *and* TAUSCH.)

AGNES. Of course, if you must sit up all night across here in the cold while the fire is roaring in the sitting-room it's no concern of mine. Here's your tea anyway, and you needn't expect me again this evening, for I'm not coming back till poor Mrs Mulpeter is over her trouble.

BLANAID (*taking the tray*). Thank you, Agnes.

AGNES. I've a bottleful of Lourdes water and a string of charmed knots to undo. I've unlocked every door in the house and taken the braids out of my hair. If the tide's coming in, it will be a boy, but once it's over the turn – Who left that brown paper and string there? Was it you, Miss Blanaid?

BLANAID. I'm awfully sorry, Agnes. But I'd like the string to practise a few knots with.

DOBELLE. I would like to give you my reasons . . .

AGNES. You know quite well I must have any brown paper and string. You've no consideration at all. Willie, put that in the drawer of my dresser.

WILLIE. I'm wanted here, Ma.

AGNES. Be off, ye yuck, before I level you.

WILLIE. But Ma, looka . . .

AGNES. Be off, I tell you! (*He runs.*) Goodbye now. The doctor's on his way up, so I must run.

BLAKE. Agnes, just before you go, may I ask you one question?

AGNES. Well, what is it? You'll have to be quick.

BLAKE. We're thinking of blowing up the Power House. What would you say to that?

AGNES. Now there's another thing. The whirring thrum of them mechanicalisms is very disturbing to poor Mrs Mulpeter. You'll have to stop it and the sooner the better. All I say is, whatever you do, do it quietly or you'll hear from me. Good night so. I'll not be back now till it's over for good and all. (*She goes.*)

DOBELLE (*taking his cup*). Some day, God willing, I shall strike that woman.

AUNT. There was nothing to prevent you this evening, was there?

DOBELLE. Nothing to prevent me! Sometimes you ask damn silly questions, Columba.

AUNT. There's no need to be any more offensive than usual. If you can't get on with her, why don't you get rid of her?

DOBELLE. You can't get rid of Agnes. She'd only come back under a different name. Once you surrender to servants you have no right to live.

AUNT. She's a very efficient woman.

DOBELLE. She's a damned dragon.

BLAKE. A dragon? Well, St George, they say, was a dishonest beef contractor. I'll find you one of his descendants, coz.

DOBELLE. I have not given you my reasons yet. This man Tausch comes here with the most high-hatted motives and . . .

AUNT (*giving tea to* TAUSCH *and* BLANAID, GEORGE *and* BLAKE *having refused*). Cold as usual.

GEORGE. I propose a vote of thanks to the chairman for the very able way he has conducted this meeting.

BLANAID. Hear, hear. (*Clapping.*)

DOBELLE. I was once like Herr Tausch here. I too built barrages and constructed power houses, until one day I found myself to be a false friend. So we parted company.

BLAKE. Oh, cheer up, Tausch. You gave me a much better run than I expected.

DOBELLE. I beg your pardon, will you kindly listen to me?

TAUSCH. I am listening, Mr Dobelle.

DOBELLE. But nobody else is. However, I will tell you, Herr Tausch, why we can never be friends. Because you are a servant of righteousness, whilst I have sworn allegiance to the other side.

BLAKE (*to* GEORGE). I didn't even think he'd save his deposit.

DOBELLE. You wish to serve something you call progress. But progress – whatever it is – is never achieved by people like you who pursue it. Progress is the fruit of evil men, with sinister motives. You and your kind can only make misery.

TAUSCH. I am sorry. I do not follow.

DOBELLE. I don't blame you. Very few people will see what I mean.

BLAKE (*studying the Royal Arms over the fireplace*). We have here the eternal struggle of the Gall with the Gael – of the lion with the unicorn. But, while the lion is really a very middle-class animal, the unicorn is a beast of great virility that is subdued to gentleness at the sight of a virgin.

DOBELLE. Have you ever studied Aquinas?

(TAUSCH *rises and listens, a smile spreading over his face.*)

BLAKE. A lonely, chaste and noble beast in many ways very like myself.

DOBELLE. Quite so. Aquinas tells us that in order that the blisses of Paradise may be more delightful to them the blessed in Heaven will be expected to view the tortures of the damned and to rejoice.

(*From outside comes the sound of engines and of distant shouting. Then there is a stampede of men past the window and* BLAKE *springs into activity.*)

150

BLAKE. Christ, the lorries! Where's Willie? Why wasn't he listening?

(*He rushes to the window and shouts.*)

BLAKE. Hi, wait! Fire the gun first, you fools! It's all set! Willie . . . Get back you goddam imbecile. No, in the fuse hole. The other end. Quick . . . you've still got time. All right. Got it? Now give her hell . . . One . . . two . . .

(*He gets down and covers his ears. Several others do likewise. Eventually there is a dull clank as of falling metal. All straighten up and listen, but there is no further sound.*)

BLAKE. I give up! Oh, I give up! Really this is too much.

VOICES (*off*). Hi, you! Put up your hands. Stand back there!

GEORGE. Did anything happen?

BLAKE. Did anything happen! Oh my God!

GEORGE. He can't have put it in right. Ought to do better than that, you know. Come on, Potts, and we'll see.

(*He opens the door. On the threshold stands a soldier in a green uniform. GEORGE and POTTS turn on their heels and walk rapidly off into the adjoining room.*)

Oh, excuse me.

(*The SOLDIER comes in. He is a man of about thirty-seven, with a pale saturnine face and sunken cheeks. His pale blue eyes contrast strangely with the incipient beard and shock of wiry black hair. His expression is one of haunted melancholy. He carries a holster and revolver slung from his Sam Browne belt under his greatcoat which hangs open. The GERMAN greets him with quiet satisfaction. AUNT COLUMBA slips the tea-cosy over the remaining shell.*)

TAUSCH. *Ach, so!*

SOLDIER. Good evening.

BLAKE. Go away Lanigan! You're here too soon.

SOLDIER. Mr Tausch?

TAUSCH. All is well. Commandant, I am so happy that you have arrived in time to prevent any foolishness.

LANIGAN. The works are safe, Herr Tausch. All necessary steps have been taken.

TAUSCH. I am sure. (*The AUNT proceeds to go out.*)

AUNT (*in LANIGAN'S face as she passes*). Scum!

LANIGAN. I'm sorry, but you can't leave here.

AUNT. Detain me! Detain me if you dare! (*She marches out carrying the tray with the hidden shell.*)

151

BLAKE. Lanigan never could cope with the ladies, could he?

TAUSCH. Commandant, I am more than grateful for your so prompt arrival. But I would like to say, now that it is all over, that we have all been the best of friends, and that I will make no charge.

LANIGAN. No charge?

TAUSCH. Let bygones be bygones. Eh, Mr Blake?

BLAKE. Well, well – going to win our hearts by kindness eh?

TAUSCH. I think you and the commandant are old friends, eh?

BLAKE. Friends! Why it was I brought him into the movement in the old days, when we were all one against the British. And now behold my handiwork! A wee State – a Free State, held up by this bile green clothes-prop.

LANIGAN. He has more respect for me than he pretends.

BLAKE. The greatest respect. Don't you carry a gun? (*To* BLANAID.) My dear, once upon a time there was an ass laden with sacred relics. 'Behold,' said the ass to himself, 'how all the people kneel down as I pass by. O noble ass! O excellent ass!'

LANIGAN (*darkly*). All right, Blake.

BLAKE. Come, come. Give Frankenstein his due. (WILLIE *enters.*) Well, if it isn't Liam Reilly, my left-hand man! Where the hell did you go when you were supposed to be on guard?

WILLIE (*indignantly*). Didn't you hear my mother send me on a message? The Staters out there say they have me under arrest.

BLAKE. Naturally.

WILLIE. Under arrest! What's natural about that?

TAUSCH. It is all right, Willie. You go home quietly. I arrange that nothing more will be said.

WILLIE. Go home? But what about the works?

TAUSCH. We will say no more about it.

WILLIE. But do they not go up?

TAUSCH. No, Willie.

WILLIE. You called in the Staters?

TAUSCH (*a little crossly*). That is so.

WILLIE. But that's might against right.

TAUSCH. Well, if you wish to put it that way.

BLAKE. Thus spake Zarathustra.

WILLIE. Oh, that's a terrible thing. Might against right. That's not playing the game, you know.

TAUSCH. That is not a game to me, Willie. It is my business. I have a right to defend myself.

WILLIE. And what about my oath?

(TAUSCH *shrugs his shoulders.*)

Oh, yev tricked us! Without force, says he. Force or unfair influence! Didn't you hear him? And then he calls up the Staters when my back is turned. Oh, there's a thing. But the people of this country can't be cowed by threats.

BLAKE. Oh yes, they can, Willie. Every time. But I'll tell you the right answer to these people. Lanigan can stop us from touching the place tonight. He can lock you and me up if he likes, and in spite of the Bosch. But he can't lock us up for ever. And so long as there's the will in our hearts and the likes of him can only pollute as much of this earth as the area of their own boot soles, so long will the future be before us.

WILLIE. That's right. Up the rebels!

TAUSCH. But what is this? I protest, sir! What right have you to discuss so calmly whether you will blow up my works? They are mine. I have a right to take steps.

BLAKE. Very well. The next time I call, Herr Tausch, we will dispense with the discussion. I shall have nothing more to say to you.

TAUSCH. But I, sir, will have a great deal to say to you.

LANIGAN. Mr Tausch, I suppose that security for these works is essential?

TAUSCH. Essential! Of course it is essential. I do not understand such a question.

(LANIGAN *nods to himself and starts to put* BLANAID *quietly out of the room.*)

BLAKE. Do I see a piano? Well, well. Would anybody be entertained if I were to render the Chinese National Anthem? Those in favour indicate in the usual way.

(BLAKE *commences to play the Introduction.*)

TAUSCH. The Chinese – ! *Lieber Gott!* I will not be treated like this. I refuse to listen. (*Then quietly*) *Ach so.* I understand. You make a joke of me. I am the fool of the family! I should have known better than to respond. It is how I have been treated ever since I have come to this place. But I will not be deceived again. Here you will talk a lot, but it comes to nothing. You and your guns that will never fire. I will not be put out again.

153

BLAKE (*singing*).

> Fu-I loved the green hills
> And the white clouds.
> Alas he died of drink.

TAUSCH. You will discuss this and that, but I am the only one who will ever *do* anything in this place. Mr Blake, it does not matter to me whether you are in jail or not, because you can sing songs and make speeches as well in jail as out of it. And always to the same effect!

BLAKE (*as he plays*). Oh, Willie. Next parade will be the day I come out. And do see that the stuff isn't damp the next time.

> (*Singing next verse.*)
>
> And Li-Po
> Also died drunk
> He tried to embrace a Moon
> In the Yellow River.

TAUSCH. This is no country! It is a damned debating society! Everybody will talk – talk – talk –

BLAKE (*rising after a flourish of chords*). Died drunk! A pleasing thought. But needing a Nero to do it justice. *Qualis Artifex pereo.*

TAUSCH. But nothing ever happens.

> (LANIGAN *without any demonstration shoots* BLAKE *dead. The latter falls with a little sigh of surprise. Then* LANIGAN *slowly puts up his revolver as* BLANAID *appears again in the door and the heads of* GEORGE *and* POTTS *are stuck out of the side door. All are turned to stone.* TAUSCH *springs forward and makes a brief examination.* LANIGAN *turns and walks slowly out, all eyes following him. Then* TAUSCH, *with a sharp intake of breath, rises, bows slightly, and follows him swiftly out. The four other men look on, and crossing to the door, they stare out after them with some excitement.* BLANAID *alone stares at the body on the floor with wide eyes.*)

BLANAID (*coming forward*). Oh!

> (*She sinks down as the men continue to gaze out the door.*)

SLOW CURTAIN

154

ACT THREE

The Scene is the same as Act One. Several hours have elapsed since the conclusion of the previous Act. The hall door is open and the shutters at the window are drawn. The supper things are still on the table and amongst them is the tea-tray from the armoury upon which stands the last shell concealed under the tea-cosy. The picture taken from the armoury is leaning against the wall. POTTS is standing in the open doorway peering out. Presently the model train emerges, and runs round the tracks. AUNT COLUMBA appears at the head of the stairs and comes down. She is wearing a hat but no coat.

AUNT. Somebody has taken my coat from my bedroom. Nobody has any right to touch my things. Nothing is safe in this house. (*She looks around for it and then goes upstairs again, pausing for a moment on the landing.*) You needn't think I don't know where you are.

    (DOBELLE *appears from behind the railway and presently he speaks.*)

DOBELLE. Well, can you see what's happening?

POTTS (*gloomily*). It's gone.

DOBELLE. What? The lorries?

POTTS. Naw. Only one of 'em. Gun's gone.

DOBELLE. But Lanigan?

POTTS. Oh 'im? 'E's still down there postin' guards. 'Orrible fightin' and arguin' there's been.

DOBELLE. What do you mean?

POTTS. That furrin chap. Gone balmy, I guess. Seems to expec' the commandant to arrest hisself or somethin'. (*He spits.*) It's beyond me.

DOBELLE. I see.

POTTS. Pity about that gun.

DOBELLE (*returning to his train*). Well, there's nothing to be done, I suppose.

155

POTTS. Other lorry's still outside. They'll be in 'ere before they go, I guess.

(AUNT COLUMBA *appears once more, this time carrying her coat. She comes down.*)

AUNT. Oh well, if it wasn't touched this time that won't save it the next. I shall have to put a new lock on my door, I can see. All the keys in this house open all the doors. Oh, Captain Potts, please tell George I want to see him before I go. (POTTS *wanders off.*) What time is it? It must be very late. (*She goes and searches the drawers.*) Those are my roller skates, I do believe! How did . . . ? No they're not. I hope people will kindly remember that I have a championship to defend, and if anyone interferes with my skates I won't be answerable for the consequences. Some people don't seem to realize that skating may mean a lot to others.

(*She continues her search. The train runs round and stops in the station. She closes the hall door.*)

DOBELLE (*to the world in general.*) A most peculiar thing! I had quite forgotten the incident, it's so many years ago. I was driving with my uncle in one of those old-fashioned high dog-carts. We were coming back from duck-shooting and a rabbit ran across the road directly in front of us. I remember it distinctly now. My uncle rose from his seat, took a careful aim, and shot the horse through the head. It was a most surprising incident at the time.

(AUNT COLUMBA *stops her searching and presently she crosses quietly behind him.*)

AUNT. Roddy! (*She touches his arm.*)

DOBELLE. Eh – what?

AUNT. I am going away.

DOBELLE. Away. At this hour? Don't be ridiculous, Columba.

AUNT. I can't stay here any longer.

DOBELLE. Where will you go?

AUNT. That doesn't concern you. I shall catch the first train and put my bike in the van.

DOBELLE. Well, you know your own mind best.

AUNT. Roddy, I wish you'd try sometimes to understand my point of view.

DOBELLE. God forbid. I daresay if I understood it, you'd have ruined my life long ago as successfully as you ruined Captain Dopping's.

156

AUNT. I didn't ruin his life. His own dishonesty was quite sufficient to do that.

DOBELLE. Didn't you keep writing him offensive postcards to the mess until he was forced to resign from the regiment?

AUNT. I was only asking for what any gentleman would have returned without question – the mowing machine I gave him. When an engagement is broken off I say it's dishonest not to return the presents.

DOBELLE. I don't suppose the poor fellow had it to return. He had no accommodation for mowing machines. It was a damn silly present to give him anyway. But what's the use of arguing? I don't want to hurt your feelings, and, besides, I'm tired.

AUNT. Well, why don't you go to bed?

DOBELLE. I don't want to go to bed. I have been spending the night reading the *Inferno* and it has upset me.

AUNT (*goes upstairs*). Well, I think you ought to go to bed. (*She vanishes into her room and soon reappears with her bicycle.*)

DOBELLE. Columba, have you ever heard of Antenora?

AUNT. No. What's·that?

DOBELLE. It's the Hell specially made for traitors to one's country. Have you any idea why Ruggieri, the Archbishop of Pisa, should be placed there, while Rahab, the harlot who betrayed Jericho, goes to Paradise?

AUNT. I'm sure there's a very good reason for it.

DOBELLE. It must have been a little difficult to know where one stood.

AUNT (*fixing her attaché case in her basket*). Well, talking of *Inferno,* there is one thing that really makes me uneasy about going away. That child, Roddy. Why don't you try and be nicer to her? Just for a little.

DOBELLE. Please, Columba!

AUNT. It's not much to ask of you. And you're not naturally a cruel person.

DOBELLE. I can't see how I'm being cruel to her.

AUNT. Of course you are. She sees nobody. She knows nothing. And she's just at the age when she needs companionship. She used to say her only friend was that Darrell Blake.

DOBELLE. God knows I don't want to make her life a misery. But I can't see what it has got to do with me. How can I do anything for her?

AUNT. You can send her to school.

DOBELLE. To school! To be taught lies and sophistries! To have illegal operations performed upon all her natural instincts. No, Columba! I'm not quite so cruel as that.

AUNT. But she must be educated somehow. I do my best, but you tie my hands so.

DOBELLE. Another convent, I suppose, is indicated. Perhaps even one on the Danube near Pressburg?

AUNT. There you go again. I know you're against religion, Roddy, but remember they only did what was right by Mary and the child according to their lights.

DOBELLE. I'm not against their religion. I am against their rightness. It is right that a woman should die so that a child's immortal soul should be saved from Limbo, therefore I say that I am against right. It is right that men should murder each other for the safety of progress. I admit it. That is why I am against right and believe in wrong. When I look back over my life, it's as plain as a pikestaff to me. It is always evil that seems to have made life worth while, and always righteousness that has blasted it. And now I solemnly say that I believe in wrong. I believe in evil and in pain and in decay and, above all, in the misery that makes man so much greater than the angels.

AUNT. Maybe you'll have ample experience of it before you're finished.

DOBELLE. Well, what do you offer me instead? A Paradise where I shall be expected to applaud the torment of my friends – who knows, perhaps even those of Mary. Keep it. I prefer to be damned.

AUNT. Mary was a good woman, Roddy. You've no right to talk like that.

DOBELLE. Who can tell? (*There is a knock at the door.*) But here we are arguing again. You'd better go. Come back when you feel better, and I'll do my best by the child in the meantime.

(*He starts the train and follows it out of sight. She stands in thought until the knock is repeated. She goes to the door and peers out. GEORGE and POTTS are there. They have lost much of their buoyancy.*)

AUNT (*letting them in*). Oh, it's you, is it? Been drowning your troubles in drink, I suppose, as usual.

GEORGE. No, but we've been giving them a damn good swimming lesson. Potts says you want to see me.

AUNT. Yes, come in. I have something to give you. Where are the others?

GEORGE. You mean Lanigan and the Bosch? Oh, down below. That German is off his rocker, you know. These foreigners! Anything knocks them over.

AUNT. Why, what's he doing?

GEORGE. Oh, going around. It's been a terrible night. And as if he hadn't done enough already, he's marching round objecting to everything. I declare to God I'd hate to be Lanigan out tonight with that fellow on the loose.

AUNT. Nonsense. They're hand in glove.

POTTS. Could I have . . . glass of water, please . . . voice gone.
   (*She indicates the carafe and he drinks.*)

GEORGE. First we carried poor Darry up to the isolation hospital. And then we came back and tried to reason with those fellows about the gun. It was no good, though. They took it off in one of the lorries. Poor Potts is terribly cut up. On such a day too.

AUNT. And Willie?

GEORGE. Oh, a very bad business. They took him off in the lorry as well. He was raving and swearing that he's going to get Lanigan. You wouldn't believe it was the same fellow. Seeing red.

AUNT. Well, what would you expect?

GEORGE. It's been a terrible night.

AUNT. Terrible. But not so terrible as it might have been. George, I've saved something for you.

GEORGE. Saved something for me?

AUNT. Yes. Trust a woman to be the only one to keep her head in a crisis. If it wasn't for me you'd have nothing left. Look.
   (*She proceeds to raise the tea-cosy. There is a knock at the door and she replaces it.*)

AUNT. What do you suppose that was?

GEORGE. Somebody wants to come in.

AUNT. Well, open it and see.

GEORGE. Me?

AUNT. Yes, go on.

GEORGE. Hadn't you better? It's your house.

AUNT. I will not. You're a man, or supposed to be one.

TAUSCH (*off*). Aal-lo!

GEORGE. It's the Bosch! Good God. what do you suppose he's up to now?

TAUSCH (*off*). Open, please.

(GEORGE *opens the door and* TAUSCH *and* LANIGAN *enter*.)

GEORGE. Both of them!

(*They all stand looking at one another for some seconds.*)

LANIGAN. Is Mr Dobelle about?

DOBELLE (*appearing*). You want me?

LANIGAN. I'm going now. I've told the men at the gate to let nobody through but the lighthousemen and anyone you give one of these passes to.

(*He sits at the table and commences to write.*)

DOBELLE. I see. How long must we have a guard?

LANIGAN. That depends upon headquarters.

TAUSCH. Commandant Lanigan, how often must I repeat that I do not wish to have either you or your men in my works. I do not require the type of protection you provide, and I will not have myself associated with you in the eyes of the public.

LANIGAN. I've told you we're here to stay whether you like it or not. These works are a national affair.

TAUSCH. And to the nation I will answer for them. They are in no danger now except from your presence.

LANIGAN (*to* DOBELLE). I'm leaving you half a dozen in blank. You must fill in the names of your tradesmen and visitors for yourself. I suppose six will be enough?

DOBELLE. I think so.

TAUSCH. Furthermore, I insist upon knowing whether you intend to surrender yourself to the law. It seems to me the most dignified course for you to take and it will save me the painful necessity of having you arrested. If you will not give me your honourable undertaking then I must assume the worst of your intentions.

LANIGAN. Ah, will you leave me alone. Haven't I had enough?

TAUSCH. Mr Dobelle, will you please oblige me with a piece of note-paper and an envelope.

DOBELLE. Try the drawer of the table.

TAUSCH. I thank you.

(*He sits and prepares to write.*)

AUNT. Well, goodbye, Roddy.

DOBELLE. Goodbye.

TAUSCH (*rising politely*). You are leaving, Miss Dobelle?

160

AUNT. I have nothing to say to you.

TAUSCH. To me?

AUNT. I hope for your own peace of mind you have as little conscience as you seem to have. We will not meet again. (*She pushes her bicycle off.*)

TAUSCH. Am I correct in thinking that the lady suggests there is something on *my* conscience?

GEORGE. Well, it was rather dirty work, you know, old man. Willie's right. You tricked those boys into this.

TAUSCH. That is monstrous, sir!

GEORGE. Mind you, I didn't see what happened. I'm no witness. I wasn't in the room at the time. But from what I've heard, it wasn't on the level.

TAUSCH. A crime has been committed. Are you accusing me, sir?

GEORGE. Ah, I don't accuse anyone. But it wasn't straight, you know. Leaves a bad taste in the mouth, old man. No! I'd have expected better. But then, of course – foreigners – you know. Not good sports. (*He shakes his head and, crossing to the table, he sits down silently beside* POTTS *and sinks into gloomy reflections.*)

TAUSCH. I never heard of such a thing. Even Commandant Lanigan appears to have some grievance against me!

LANIGAN (*rising and buttoning his coat*). I only said it was you wanted your works secure.

TAUSCH. I do. But did I ask you to commit a crime? You admit yourself that there is no excuse for what you have done. It is – I can use no other word – it is murder!

DOBELLE. Why not call it war? That's a well-known palliative.

TAUSCH. Pardon me, Mr Dobelle. In war there are certain rules that must be observed.

DOBELLE. I don't see that that's of much importance. From the point of view of the man who dies, it makes very little difference whether he is killed according to rules or not.

LANIGAN. Ah, what's the use of arguing! I was a rebel once. What I've done was war then. Now I'm on the other side and it's murder. I admit it.

DOBELLE. Don't try to explain, Lanigan. Your friends don't want it, and your enemies won't believe you anyhow.

LANIGAN. I'm not trying to explain.

TAUSCH. Well, I must say I admire your frankness, Commandant.

But I do not think that it will assist your position when I have
made my report to the Attorney-General.

LANIGAN. When I took on this job I said to myself: 'Well, I'll
last as long as God allows me.' So make your report and be
done with it. If I don't get what's coming to me for this
business, I suppose I'll be plugged sooner or later by somebody.

TAUSCH (*writing*). You need not be plugged, as you say, by anybody if you do not do these things.

LANIGAN. Somebody has got to do them . . . if the country's to go
on.

TAUSCH. That is quite untrue. How can you say such a thing?

LANIGAN. Ah, never mind. I'm a physical-force man born and
bred in the movement. I'm only doing my job – the job I'm
able to do – the job that always seems to deliver the goods.
There's no excuse for it, I daresay. I don't pretend to be clever
like he was. He was the brains and inspiration of the movement in the old days against the British. But now we seem to
have a damn sight too many brains, and inspiration always
ends in trying to blow up something.

TAUSCH. And so you assassinate that inspiration!

LANIGAN. I suppose you think I enjoy that, when it means a bullet
in my own back sooner or later. But enjoy it or not, I've
always been taught that it's not words but deeds the country
needs, so I'll go on doing what I can, no matter.

TAUSCH. A very fine attitude for young revolutionaries to adopt,
maybe. But you are a man of responsibilities. The State
cannot ignore the forms of justice.

LANIGAN. Forms! Do you think Blake wanted a lot of play-acting
in court to find out what everybody knew already? And then
they'd have tried to break his heart in jail in order to put a
bit more venom into him for the next attempt.

TAUSCH. Ah! Quite a humanitarian, after all!

LANIGAN. I don't know about that. It was he that always had the
wit to find the word for these things. Not me. But I only hope
that when my time comes I'll be plugged fair and clean like
he was, with none of the tomfoolery of law and justice and
the torment they call 'Prepare to meet your God!'

TAUSCH. That is all you have to say before I send this letter to the
Attorney-General?

LANIGAN. Ah, what more is there to be said? I'm a gunman. I

162

always was and I always will be. And if you ask me why, I declare to God I don't know. There's no glamour on my side, nowadays. But God help you all if I wasn't. It may be brains and inspiration that makes the country at the start, but it's my help you're always telephoning for before the end.

TAUSCH. Well, I am amazed!

LANIGAN. There are times when it's best to destroy the things that are nearest to us.

TAUSCH. I have heard that we are supposed to love our enemies in this life. But you would work upon the principle that we must kill our friends, eh?

LANIGAN. If there's any man could answer that, it's the man that has gone. And I believe that if ever I meet him again he'll bear me less ill-will for what's finished and done with, than those that are left behind. So, shot in an attack on the works, is my report. If you know better – well, I won't blame you for saying so. It'll be all the same, I suppose, for *they'll* get me in the end, if you don't. But, by God, they'll not touch this power house again! You'll see that I'm right there. Whatever happens now will be a personal matter between me and the likes of Willie Reilly. The works will be out of it. Good night, gentlemen. (*He goes. The lorry outside is heard to start.*)

DOBELLE. The Moor has done his work. The Moor may go.

TAUSCH. Mr Dobelle, that man is a scoundrel. But do you think that he is sincere in what he says?

DOBELLE. Maybe you are thinking that there are more ways than one in which a man may die for his country?

TAUSCH. Do you feel like that?

DOBELLE. No. I say, let my country die for me.

TAUSCH. Perhaps it would be best for you to make this report, Mr Dobelle. I would do it, but – I am a stranger. Perhaps . . .

DOBELLE. Denounce Lanigan, you mean?

TAUSCH. Some person will have to do so of course.

DOBELLE. There were only three of us there at the time. Willie was committing a felony and can say nothing of any weight. That leaves just you and I.

TAUSCH. I agree. Yes. Just you and me.

DOBELLE. Well, you can rule me out, I don't like the man, but hanging him won't bring back Darrell Blake.

TAUSCH. But murder. It is murder!

DOBELLE. Murder! Yes. The birth of a nation is no immaculate conception.

TAUSCH. But your feelings for your friend who is dead?

DOBELLE. He seems to have been Lanigan's friend too. There is no cure for death.

TAUSCH. Do you try to justify this man Lanigan?

DOBELLE. No. Yet when Lanigan dies he will leave behind him you and your works. When I die nothing will be left but the squabbling of female connections.

TAUSCH. *Das heisst* – you admire him, so?

DOBELLE. No, I hate him. Hate him like poison. But if I were to see him hanged, whenever I turned on your light I should feel more sorry for him than for my friend Darrell Blake. And I could not endure that. I prefer to continue hating him. Besides, would any jury accept the testimony of a man like me against Lanigan's? But they'll believe you, Herr Tausch. Oh yes, they'll believe you every time.

> (TAUSCH *hesitates and then goes on with his letter.* GEORGE *gathers himself together and raises the tea-cosy.*)

GEORGE. Have some cold tea, Captain? We may as well. Oh!

POTTS. 'Ello! Where cher get that?

GEORGE. The last of the Mohicans. This must be what the old lady said she had saved for us.

POTTS. That was decent of her, George.

GEORGE. Not that it's much good, old man.

TAUSCH. A little give and take. A few words around the table. We were good enemies, Mr Blake and I, and we would have come to understand each other before long.

DOBELLE. You would never have understood Blake. He belonged to a different world that had no chance against yours – a world that must inevitably have been destroyed by you. You remember Li-Po? He was trying to embrace the Moon in the Yellow River.

TAUSCH. But I assure you, I would not think of destroying anything. We would have lived, side by side in harmony, respecting each other's point of view.

DOBELLE. Never with him. You'd always have been disturbing the waters with your machinery and drowning his moon in mud. No, in the end you would either have had to kill him or to give up your fight. You remember – he who establishes a despotism and slays not Brutus abideth but a little time.

TAUSCH. I wonder why the people whom we can like most easily are always on the wrong side? Why must Mr Blake be against me and Commandant Lanigan be my protector? Why must I have these monstrous doctrines foisted upon my shoulders?

DOBELLE. I told you, there are monsters in the mists that will glare back at you with your own face.

TAUSCH. Why always talk in parables, Mr Dobelle? You seem to wish to make everything appear unreal.

DOBELLE. If there was anything real in your sense of the word about tonight, was it not Lanigan's shot? That should satisfy even your thirst for reality.

TAUSCH. I see what you are at, Mr Dobelle. You wish me to believe that Lanigan's shot was part of my world – that he and I are truly on the same side.

DOBELLE. More than that. Lanigan is just yourself. He is your finger on the trigger. Denounce him by all means. The tribute to your works is not yet complete. For if he doesn't hang for Blake then Willie will hang for him, and I'm sure you'd like to save Willie. But before you denounce him, I say you must give me an answer to what he has said. And you won't do that. Because there is no answer, and you know it.

TAUSCH. Mr Dobelle, you drive me very far.

DOBELLE. Do you complain of this? What nonsense! Two more lives, Herr Tausch, but what of it! In this welter of blood one great factor will be borne in upon us. The works will remain. Man may perish, but they have been saved. Hallelujah!

TAUSCH. Enough of this.

DOBELLE. The inspiration that threatened them is no more. Nothing remains but the sordid squabble of Willie and Lanigan, in which the works will be forgotten and your programme will go through. I surrender, Herr Tausch. You are the victor after all.

TAUSCH. All guilt must be avenged on earth. I am going to send this letter, Mr Dobelle.

DOBELLE. Then why the delays of the post? The telephone is still at your disposal.

TAUSCH (*after a moment's consideration*). I do not know, sir, whether you regard me as a fool or a lunatic, but whatever may have been the effect of this evening's events upon other

people, I, at least, have retained my common sense. I shall be
glad to use your telephone.

DOBELLE. Do, sir. For the second time this evening.

(TAUSCH *glares at him for a moment and then crosses to the
telephone, and takes up the directory.*)

GEORGE. I say, Potts, let's get rid of the damn thing. It makes
me depressed.

POTTS. Same 'ere, George. I'm sick of the sight of it.

GEORGE. What do you say we chuck it away?

POTTS. Where?

GEORGE. Oh, anywhere. Into the sea. I don't want to see it again.

POTTS. What 'appens when the tide goes out?

GEORGE. Well, over the wall on to the old slag heap. Anywhere
we'll be rid of it.

POTTS. Just as you say, George.

TAUSCH (*after some consideration, has thrown aside the directory
and picked up the receiver*). Allo.

GEORGE (*rising*). Well, bring it along, Potts, old man. I'm bloody
well fed up.

POTTS (*rising and taking the shell*). Only good for the slag 'eap,
I'm afraid. Oh, we've been badly let down. Eight years' work
gone up the spout.

(*They go off leaving the door open, through which the
turbines hum merrily. It is a little lighter outside.*)

TAUSCH. Allo. Is that the exchange? Yes. I want Ballsbridge 586
please. Yes, that is right. No. Never mind. Ring till they
answer, please.

DOBELLE. Until we had the telephone we were quite out of touch
with civilization. (*Pause.*) Certainly if I were the Attorney-
General I'd agree to prosecute anybody at this hour of the
morning.

TAUSCH. Pardon. I speak with the German Legation. It is a matter
for them what steps are taken.

DOBELLE. Oh, cowardly.

TAUSCH. Mr Dobelle, when I have telephoned I am going away
and I do not think we will meet again – socially. I do not
appreciate your satiric neurosis and I do not wish to lose my
temper. But do not think, sir, that I have no answer to what
you say. What I am doing here is greater than any of the
considerations you fling at me – yes, greater even than the life
of a man. I am not afraid to say it, even if that life must be

my own. What is the life of a man beside the future of humanity? There is a purpose in this life, my dear sir, that transcends all personal feelings. Allo. My dear sir, you have only to go outside and look around you. Everything you see has its purpose in the scheme of things. You stand upon the sea wall and look down at the works below. What do you see? Allo. Yes. Yes, I wait still. The great river is there – the granite pier – the navigation lock – the turbine house beside the old slag heap. Everything with a purpose.

DOBELLE. Even the slag heap?

TAUSCH. Yes even – allo. Is that the Secretary? This is Tausch speaking, I have a report for the Minister. Yes, a serious report.

(*Outside there is a livid flash and a roar. In a moment it is followed by the sound of falling masonry. Then the lights go out. When silence comes again the sound of the turbines is no more and a red glow illuminates the sky behind the parapet.*)

GEORGE (*off*). Potts! Potts!

POTTS (*off*). Are you hurt, George?

TAUSCH (*dashing to the door*). The works!

GEORGE (*appearing outside*). It was a good one – a good one, Potts.

POTTS (*far away*). Bet-cher-life!

TAUSCH. What has happened to the works?

GEORGE. Blown to hell. Pure accident. Sorry, must be off.

(DOBELLE *begins to laugh as he lights a lamp.* TAUSCH *seizes* GEORGE *by the collar.*)

TAUSCH. Is anybody hurt? The night shift! Where are they?

GEORGE. Running like hell, old man. Can't be dead if they run like that.

(DOBELLE *picks up the dangling telephone receiver and speaks into it before replacing it.*)

DOBELLE. Did the Minister get that report?

(TAUSCH *releases* GEORGE *and dashes to the sea wall, over which he looks before returning. There is distant shouting from outside.* GEORGE *goes.*)

TAUSCH. *Du lieber Gott!*

DOBELLE. You were telling me – about a purpose – a purpose in this life – a purpose . . . (*He laughs quite hysterically.*) for the old slag heap!

TAUSCH. Please. Please.

167

DOBELLE (*lighting a lamp at the table*). You were explaining to me – your philosophy – excuse me – my satiric neurosis – it overcomes me . . . (*He laughs.*)

TAUSCH. My works! My works!

DOBELLE. Your works! Your memories! Brutus is avenged, O Octavius.

TAUSCH. Isn't it enough that a man has died and that my plant has been destroyed? Must we have laughter and jeers as well?

DOBELLE. It is not I – it is this land – this life. Take your works where they belong. Here is Hesperides – the garden where men may sleep.

TAUSCH. I think I go mad! . . . (*The shouting outside resumes.*) But I forget. Somebody may be injured. I must not give way. I will go down and search in the ruins. I must go at once.

    (*He goes. The red glow in the court is streaked with the first sunlight.* DOBELLE *closes the door behind him as if to shut it all out.*)

DOBELLE. Yes, be off . . . search in the ruins. Search them well. Turn the scorched sod over. It will be all the same in the end. You'll never learn anything, and I'll never do anything. There's no end and there's no solution. (*He picks up the picture of his wife.*) Ah, Mary, have pity on me and on poor Tausch. No, not on Tausch. He's too great to need pity. But me . . . *Ah, Bice – la dolce guida* . . . take away this cursed gift of laughter and give us tears instead.

    (*At the head of the stairs is a white figure in a long night-gown. He sees it with a gasp.*)

DOBELLE. Mary!

BLANAID. I'm frightened.

DOBELLE. Your voice! Why are you standing there looking at me, Mary?

BLANAID. Don't you know me, Father? (*She comes down.*)

DOBELLE. Know you! Why – what am I saying?

BLANAID. I saw a glare and then there was a terrible bang. Aren't you well?

DOBELLE. It's Blanaid! I didn't recognize you. You're so changed, child. You seem to have grown up suddenly.

BLANAID. I am not changed. Only you never look at me.

DOBELLE. I believe I don't. I wonder why. Stay with me for a little.

BLANAID. I was hoping you'd let me. In case there's another bang.

DOBELLE. There won't. It's all over now. (*Offering her a chair.*) Won't you sit down?

BLANAID. Thank you kindly.

DOBELLE (*sitting too*). I wonder what is the proper way to begin on meeting one's daughter for the first time?

BLANAID. I should say, 'Are you staying long in these parts?'

DOBELLE. I rather hope you are.

BLANAID (*kneeling beside him.*) Daddy, why do you never talk to me? Why do you hate me so?

DOBELLE. Because – because I'm an old fool. Because I thought that life had played its last trick on me. (*The lamp flickers.*) I'm afraid there's not much oil in that lamp.

BLANAID. Did I take her from you? (*He smiles.*) I'm sorry.

DOBELLE. I remember. That lock of hair used to do that.

BLANAID. When I grow up I'm going to try to be like her. I think I can. A Guide never gives up. Daddy.

DOBELLE. Yes, my dear.

BLANAID. Will you take my education in hand from now on?

DOBELLE. In what way?

BLANAID. I thought perhaps I might ask you questions from time to time.

DOBELLE. I'll do my best. If they're not too difficult.

BLANAID. May I ask one now?

DOBELLE. Well, only one. Then you must go to sleep and rest yourself. Well, what is it?

BLANAID. Do you know why people aren't happy?

(*There is a pause, during which she settles down and goes to sleep without really waiting for an answer. Through the cracks in the shutters the morning starts to shine.*)

DOBELLE. Well, I think that puts an end to my part in your education. I wonder, after all, do they want to be happy? The trees don't bother and they're not unhappy. And the flowers too. It's only men who are different, and it's only men who *can* be really unhappy. And yet isn't it unhappiness that makes men so much greater than the trees and the flowers and all the other things that can't feel as we do? I used to thank the Devil for that and call him my friend. But there's more to it than that. I suppose the Devil can do nothing for us until God gives him a chance. Or maybe it's because they're both the same person. Those glittering sorrows, eh? Asleep? Well, here endeth the first lesson. (*Pause, while the lamp sinks lower and his head nods.*) Darkness . . . death and darkness. Ah, can anything cure them? . . . I wonder.

(*He closes his eyes. Presently* AGNES *opens the hall door and comes in. It is morning outside and the sunlight floods into the room from behind her. She crosses to the window and opens the shutters with a sigh of intense satisfaction and smiles out at the flowers and the ivy that grow around the frame. Nodding her head, and with an approving click of her tongue, she softly hums a lullaby and surveys a new day. That is the end of this play.*)

CURTAIN

KITZBUHEL, 1930.

Fu - I loved the green hills
(ACT II)

EZRA POUND'S WORDS　　　　　　WILLIAM ALWYN

170

Senza Ped. stacc.

THE GOLDEN CUCKOO

*An irrational comedy
in five scenes*

INTRODUCTION

The Golden Cuckoo is based upon the exploit of an old man called Francis Walter Doheny, who – oppressed as we all sometimes are by a sense of the injustice of life – went out one evening in 1926, and broke the windows of a Post Office in Kilkenny, calling this gesture the Saint-Edward's-Crown-Barker-Parsival-Ironore-Inoco-One-Man-Rebellion. There was a symbolic significance behind each word of this resounding title, and he also made it clear that his action was not inspired by any personal animus towards the Postmistress. Indeed, if he had heard that she had recently suffered the loss of her brother-in-law, he would have postponed his Rebellion to a later date, even at some inconvenience to himself. He then surrendered to a solitary policeman, and was conducted to the local lockup, singing his 'Rational Anthem'.

From confinement, he issued a statement to the Governor-General, the Provost of Trinity College, the Bishop, and the Bar (which is how I came by it) in which he explained the impelling reasons for his surprising gesture. Expecting to go to jail, as other rebels had done before him, he was utterly confounded when a humane and liberal-minded Judge insisted on turning the issue, not upon the injustice of life, but on the matter of Mr Doheny's sanity – an aspect of the case that had never occurred to him.

Now, it seems to me that this whole incident raises problems of some social importance, and all the more so if it raises a laugh. Rebellion against the tyranny of Monarchs and Invaders has long been recognized as a respectable thing. But what about the tyranny of Democracy, which in some of its facets can be even more sinister? At a pinch, Monarchs can be assassinated, but who can assassinate – much less identify – the Common Man? Rebellion is of little avail against the Herd. Yet it can hardly be denied that we live, today, in a community that is fundamentally dishonest, and is getting more so – a society that is subverting

177

the Common Law for the convenience of the Policeman, and that maintains itself by a mass of regulations that have no basis in social morality at all, but are merely there to enable bad laws to operate – the currency and customs regulations, for example.

It is agreed, of course, that laws must be made by somebody, if we are to live in peace at all. It is, however, not so certain that any greater divine right attaches to them if passed by fifty-one per cent of a debating society, rather than by a King in Council. Nor does it necessarily follow that Democracy in office is any less dishonest than the Despot. Indeed, the reintroduction of mass murder as an accepted instrument of international argument, of the torture of prisoners, and of inquisition under penalty, lends colour to the view that the problem of the individual against the State, if it has altered at all, is rather more acute than ever.

In the circumstances, the thesis advanced by Mr Doheny – of the moral duty of the put-upon to break the law from time to time – assumes a significance which grows with the tendency of the State to become, itself, the biggest lawbreaker within sight. Maybe we have not all got the aplomb to select the Post Office windows as the best law to break, but we must admit that his selection was a gallant one, and did nobody any harm except himself.

Whether his personal grievance was legitimate or not is a question that does not really arise. He did what thousands have done before him – thousands who have had statues erected to their memories, without much enquiry into the rights and wrongs of their cause, and many of whose dependants are still collecting profitable pensions. His Independent Republic is a respectable and recognized answer. The only trouble is that Mr Doheny's was a One-Man-Republic, and here the herd instinct in all of us immediately takes offence.

What may be praiseworthy for a thousand men to do in armed conflict – probably slaughtering several harmless bystanders in the process – becomes absurd when it is done by one old man with a flagpole. What would happen – we hasten to ask – if everybody did that sort of thing? But this question is just an alibi. Everybody has not done it, and we need not pose that query until they do. At present, only Mr Doheny has done it. And is the measure of the rightness of his action, the number of people who have backed him up? Is it all a question of mathematics? Yes, says the Functionalist, because Mr Doheny, alone, is bound to fail. And since he fails, he must be wrong. In fact, goes on the Functionalist, I don't think that I like this play at all, because it seems to me to be on the side of failure, which is obviously immoral. The Author has obviously got no moral positiveness. So Mr Doheny suffered the most terrible and subtle of all punishments. He did not go to jail. He went to a lunatic asylum.

This is a subject that we may not wish to have discussed at the present stage of the world's history, but it can hardly be described as puerile. And one of the things that makes me glad that I ever tried to commemorate this heart-breaking old man is the fact that his memorial, in its last act, suddenly proclaimed its independence, too, and refused to accept the so-called happy ending that I originally attempted to impose upon it. I had set out to inveigh against the injustice of Society, and against the fact that its considerable rewards and punishments are largely allotted on a basis of chance. But if the only remedy of the unlucky Man of Resolution is that of a lunatic, this is far from being a happy ending, however one may treat it.

What the play itself proved was that I was wrong in being angry, and that my central character knew better. To a free spirit – he taught me – Justice is really quite a minor matter – a virtue only in the eyes of stock-jobbers and tradesmen, and not something for President Doheny to worry about in the proud security of his One-Man-Republic. It is impossible to punish, or even to be sorry, for one who does not deign to consider himself punished. His victory and his independence are matters of belief, and since he believes in them himself, there is no answer but respectful recognition.

Directors will see that this is actually a very serious play, that will probably go off the rails if allowed to betray the fact that it considers itself to be the slightest farcical. Let the audience laugh, by all means. But it should also be remembered that the highest art of comedy is sometimes to leave people wondering why they ever laughed at all.

The Golden Cuckoo

CAST OF CHARACTERS:

A Boy
Mrs Golightly, the Actress (Letty)
Mr Chaplain, the Newscaster
Mrs Vanderbilt, the Daily
Mr Penniwise, the Lawyer
Mr Hooley, the Cabman
Mr Dotheright, the Obituarist
Mr Lowd, the Editor
Mr Golightly, the Reporter (Paddy)
Mrs de Watt Tyler, the Philanthropist
Miss Peering, the Postmistress
A Policeman
A Photographer
A Detective
A Hospital Attendant

SCENE ONE — Mr. Dotheright's Residence
SCENE TWO — Mr. Lowd's Office
SCENE THREE — Outside Miss Peering's Post Office
SCENE FOUR — A Corridor in a Police Court
SCENE FIVE — Mr. Dotheright's Residence. A month later

This play was first produced at the Dublin Gate Theatre by Longford Productions on Tuesday, 25 April, 1939, with the following cast: —

Mrs Vanderbilt, the help	NORA O'MAHONY
Mr Green, the Corporation official	HAMLYN BENSON
Mrs Golightly, the business woman	VIVIEN DILLON
Mr Pennywise, the lawyer	MICHAEL RIPPER
Mr Dotheright, B.A., the author	NOEL ILIFF
Mr Haybottle, the cabman	RONALD IBBS
Mr Lowd, the editor	ROBERT HENNESSY
Mr Golightly, the reporter	PETER COPLEY
Guard Bullock, the policeman	J. WINTER
Miss Peering, the postmistress	NANCY BECKH
Mme Subito, the foreign visitor	JEAN ANDERSON

Directed by the Author

Its revised version was first produced in the Gaiety Theatre, Dublin, on Monday, 25 June, 1956, with the following cast:—

Mrs Golightly, the Actress	MAUREEN CUSACK
Mr Chaplain, the Newscaster	NORMAN RODWAY
Mrs Vanderbilt, the Daily	MAUREEN POTTER
Mr Penniwise, the Lawyer	JOSEPH TOMELTY
Mr Hooley, the Cabman	SEAMUS KAVANAGH
Mr Dotheright, the Obituarist	CYRIL CUSACK
Mr Lowd, the Editor	NIALL MACGINNIS
Mr Golightly, the Reporter	MICHAEL MURRAY
Mrs De Watt Tyler, the Philanthropist	
	SINNETTE WADDELL
Miss Peering, the Postmistress	ANN CLERY
A Policeman	TRAOLACH O H-AONGHUSA
A Photographer	DONAL DONNELLY
A Detective	P. G. STEPHENS
An Attendant	DEREK HYDER

The production was directed by the Author
with settings by MICHAEL O'HERLIHY

The version printed here has not yet been produced.

185

SCENE ONE

MR DOTHERIGHT'S *residence is a partially-converted stable, containing an odd mixture of books and harness, crockery and sacks, furniture and garden tools. A horse box has been fixed up as a small study, and above this is a straw-filled platform from which comes an occasional cluck. An outer door leads to a yard, and an inner opening to the kitchen. Efforts have been made to make it homely, and it is not by any means uncomfortable. The curtain rises disclosing a small boy who appears to be supervising its ascent. He is as young an age as can be legally procured subject to local regulations and stage experience. He takes a look at the Audience to see that they are all seated and he is at liberty to make some helpful remarks if they are not. A cuckoo clock on the wall utters a single cluck. When all are comfortably seated the boy begins.*

BOY. Good evening. I'm glad you were able to come in time. In case you have not been able to study your programme, this is Act One – an old Coach House partly converted, as you can see, into a not very good residence for Mr Er – Whatshisname. That was one o'clock you heard and in a few minutes the action will begin with a knock at the door. (*Then louder*) A knock at the door. (*The knock comes*). Yes, that's right. And I shall go and let in the (*A goat whinnies off*) Leading Lady, Letty Golightly who has just come to live in the big house across the Yard. Don't mind that goat by the way. And a Mr Chaplain who has something to do with broad –
　　(*He has gone to the door and opened it.* LETTY *steps in. She is young, attractive and fashionably dressed with an air of careless nonchalance.*)
LETTY. Mind your head.
BOY. – broadcasting.
　　(*Chaplain follows her in, bumping his head. He is about thirty and wears a business suit.*)

LETTY. Oh, I did warn you.

BOY. She did you know.

CHAPLAIN. (*in pain*) It's quite all right. I enjoy it, really.

LETTY. You don't look as if you do. Shall I hold it or something?

CHAPLAIN. No thanks. I'll just sit down for a minute. (*He sits*). I say, is this somebody's bed?

BOY. Yes. It's Mr Duthery's bed. He's the Star. Well now that you've started so well, I'll leave you to go on with the Scene.

LETTY. Thank you so much for everything.

BOY. But I'll be back. I have to see about that goat.
    (*He goes off with a friendly salute at the Audience.*)

CHAPLAIN. Who could that be? I mean – this Mr Duthery.

LETTY. Must be the old man the Agent mentioned. (*Looking at some papers*) Name looks like 'Do-the-right'. I understand he goes with the place. How's the poor head now?

CHAPLAIN. Oh never mind that. I'm sure it's good for the moral character.

LETTY. I don't see why . . . (*A cock crows from the loft*) Oh God! (*Pause*) What's good for the moral character?

CHAPLAIN. You'll have to get rid of him of course.

LETTY. I don't see why. Get rid of whom?

CHAPLAIN. The old man you say lives here. You'll probably want it for the car.

LETTY. That's just what I've been wondering. How did you know?

CHAPLAIN. Didn't you say you didn't see why you should get rid of him?

LETTY. No I said that about bumping your head being good for the – Oh do let's stop this conversation, Wystan.

CHAPLAIN. Suits me.

LETTY. You know why I've bought this place, don't you?

CHAPLAIN. (*nodding*) And I'm glad. I don't want to say a word against Paddy. I like him, Letty. Really I do. He's a very brilliant fellow.

LETTY. (*bored*) Yes. (*Pause*) You're always very fair to Paddy, aren't you, Sometimes too bloody fair.

CHAPLAIN. (*with a handsome smile*). Well. One can hardly be too fair to the husband of a woman one adores. Now, can one?

LETTY. (*reluctantly smiling back*) Maybe not. I like the way you have of keeping it from seeming sordid and mean. Thank you for that, Wystan. (*She moves around the room*). Anyhow, it's all over now. I've bought a place of my own at last. It's got to be a clean break. I'm bloody well fed up with Paddy.

(*Her face lights up*). It's like opening a door and letting in – Oh, God, what's that?

> (*The door crashes open and* MRS VANDERBILT *comes in. She hastily conceals a portable radio which she is carrying. She is a rascally old scrub woman in the sixties, wearing an apron under her overcoat.*)

CHAPLAIN. – a breath of cool, fresh air. Eh?

LETTY. Something like that.

MRS VANDERBILT. (*bustling across the room*) Pay no attention to me. I've been out at Confession.

LETTY. We just dropped in to – ah –

MRS VANDERBILT. To pay a call. I know. Suppose I get ya a nice cuppa tea?

LETTY. Oh please don't bother. We were just looking over the place.

MRS VANDERBILT. No bother at all. It'll be wet in a jiffy.

CHAPLAIN. Perhaps we'd better explain what we're doing here. This is the łady who has bought the house across the yard. And I am –

MRS VANDERBILT. Ah sure, amn't I in and out of the place an odd time myself, and heard all about her. I'm Mrs Vanderbilt, and she's the old man's new landlady. Gimme a hand now till I'm free of this Prayer Book.

> (*She places the radio on a side table covered by a newspaper and presses* LETTY'S *hand affectionately.*)

Ah isn't she a gorgeous Mott! Me late husband – God rest his soul – would have had her stripped with a glance!

CHAPLAIN. (*attempting to come to Letty's assistance*) We must get better acquainted, Mrs Vanderbilt. I wish I had connections like you must have.

MRS VANDERBILT. (*looking at him with grave distaste*) Why?

CHAPLAIN. Oh never mind, Ma'am. Just one of my little jests. Er – what exactly was your husband?

MRS VANDERBILT. (*earnestly*) He was a dirty bum. Wait now – the kettle's on the boil. (*She goes into the kitchen*).

CHAPLAIN. What an enchanting inruption! Who do you suppose she is?

LETTY. I can't imagine. But I have rather a fellow feeling for her.

CHAPLAIN. Because her late husband was a bum? (*She smiles mirthlessly*).

189

LETTY. I always like your Gewohnlicherkeit, Wystan.

CHAPLAIN. You're a damn good actress. And I like your German too.

LETTY. (*emotionally*) Oh am I? Paddy says I'm a terrible actress.

CHAPLAIN. Paddy is a dirty bum – to borrow a phrase I've heard.

(*He begins to embrace her, but half laughing, she breaks away as* MRS VANDERBILT *enters and starts to set cups.*)

MRS VANDERBILT. Pay no attention to me. You don't mind your tea as it comes? I've nothing to go in it at all.

LETTY. I prefer it any way, thanks. (*They both sit down as she pours out*). Are you a relation of Mr Do – the – the gentlemen who lives here?

MRS VANDERBILT. Duthery, Ma'am. Duthery is how he pronounces it.

CHAPLAIN. Duthery. I don't think I've heard that name. Is it Scandinavian?

MRS VANDERBILT. (*after a scornful look at Chaplain*) I'm no relation, Ma'am. Just a friend. I do for him, you understand. Just to oblige. And to please Father Feeley, of course.

LETTY. This is Mr Wystan Chaplain. You've probably heard him on the radio.

MRS VANDERBILT. I never listen to that thing.

CHAPLAIN. Come now, Mrs Vanderbilt. Don't tell me you're not one of my public? What's this you've got hidden under the newspaper?

MRS VANDERBILT. Father Feeley was just saying to me – (*He takes the paper off the radio*).

CHAPLAIN. Just as I thought. A radio! A good model too.

MRS VANDERBILT. (*louder*) Father Feeley was –

LETTY. Yes, a very good model. I've got one very like it over at the house.

(MRS VANDERBILT *forcibly puts the paper back.*)

CHAPLAIN. Oh, excuse me. Letty, I believe we've discovered Mrs Vanderbilt's vice. She's a secret listener.

MRS VANDERBILT. (*with sudden venom*) You harness your clapper, you big gowger, or you'll find yourself with an ache where you least expect it.

CHAPLAIN. Who? Me?

MRS VANDERBILT. (*sweet again*) No, you'd hardly know Father Feeley, ma'am, and you a playactress. But he's a very broad-minded man. He wouldn't hold it against you at all.

LETTY. (*taken aback*) Hold it against me!
   (*Another knock on the Door.*)
MRS VANDERBILT. Being on the stage – you know. For all, you're
   a Protestant and respectably married. And your father has
   money too. Though why wouldn't he, and he a Mason.
LETTY. Really!
CHAPLAIN. Mrs Vanderbilt seems to be well-informed on every-
   body's background.
MRS VANDERBILT. Just idle gossip, ma'am. Idle gossip. I pay no
   heed to it at all.
LETTY. Isn't there somebody at the door?
MRS VANDERBILT. Ah, let them . . . (*Then changing her mind*)
   That's right, ma'am. I'd better see who it is, hadn't I?
   (*She opens the door a few inches and somebody sticks a
   foot in.*)
   There's no one at home. The place is empty.
PENNIWISE. (*outside*) Is this where a man called Dotheright lives?
MRS VANDERBILT. No. There's no one of that . . . (*She glances at
   Letty and then opens the door*). Why, yes, sir. That's right.
   Mr Dotheright's residence.
PENNIWISE. I thought so.
MRS VANDERBILT. But he's not in. You'd better call another time.
   (*She tries to close the door, but he pushes in, and she
   abandons the struggle.*)
PENNIWISE. Then I'm going to wait here till he appears. Come on
   in, cabman, come in and sit down.
   (PENNIWISE *and* HOOLEY *enter. The former is a seedy little
   Attorney's clerk in a black suit, and aged about fifty. The
   latter is an elderly cabman in a variety of coats and mufflers,
   with black crepe on his top hat.*)
HOOLEY. Don't mind if I do.
MRS VANDERBILT. You never know what sorts will turn up these
   days.
PENNIWISE. (*to Letty*) Name of Penniwise. Do I know you? Your
   face seems familiar.
CHAPLAIN. (*amused*) It probably is. This lady –
MRS VANDERBILT. She's just a woman that's dropped in.
PENNIWISE. Indeed. Well, I've dropped in too. And here I stay
   till I get what I came for.
MRS VANDERBILT. Listen to that now. He'll be telling us next what
   it is.

191

HOOLEY. He means we've lost the rest of the funeral.

PENNIWISE. That's not what I mean. If you hadn't stopped it would never have happened.

HOOLEY. The old man told me to stop. So I stopped. (*To Chaplain*) Anything wrong with that?

CHAPLAIN. No – so far as we have all the facts before us. It seems quite reasonable.

HOOLEY. (*to Penniwise*) There you are. You heard what the man said.

PENNIWISE. He doesn't know anything about it.

LETTY. Wystan, don't you think we really ought to be going?

CHAPLAIN. My dear, I'm getting more and more interested. What do you suppose will be the next to arrive?

MRS VANDERBILT. Ah, let them be. They stopped for a wet at some pub, and when they came out the hearse was gone.

PENNIWISE. It was not at some pub. It was at a newspaper office.

HOOLEY. The Comet Newspaper.

LETTY. The Comet? That's where my – Oh yes? So you stopped there.

CHAPLAIN. What a small world. We ought to hear some more of this.

PENNIWISE. There's nothing more to hear. Except that this man Dotheright who I'd never seen in my life before, but was sharing the cab with me – this man Dotheright insisted on going inside.

MRS VANDERBILT. I know. They still owe him something.

PENNIWISE. But to stop in the middle of a funeral!

HOOLEY. Well, he'd got to pay for his share of the cab, hadn't he?

PENNIWISE. He had no business to share a cab with me, if he had no money when we started out. And he needn't think he's going to dodge me now. The vehicle is still outside with the fare mounting up. But not at my expense! Here we stop until he produces his legal dues.

MRS VANDERBILT. Tell me, love, what's the time on your gold watch and chain?

PENNIWISE. (*looking at it*) Half-past two. Ttt – ttt!

MRS VANDERBILT. Well, since half the town seems to be dropping anchor here, maybe I'd better put on some sausages. Introduce yourselves.

    (*She goes out muttering*) I don't know who the hell they are at all. (*Shouting*) Take the beast out of my kitchen!

CHAPLAIN. Maybe we had all better introduce ourselves. This is Mrs Golightly – probably better known to you under her professional name.

PENNIWISE. (*suspiciously*) Professional?

CHAPLAIN. Letty Lowe.

(*Puzzled Pause as the* BOY *enters pulling a reluctant goat which he attempts to lead to the Horse Box.*)

HOOLEY. Oh, I know. She's on the movies.

CHAPLAIN. Of course! How smart you both are. (*To Hooley, archly*) You should get a prize. (*Then with some irritation*) Do we have to have that in here?

BOY. I'm sorry but it's not supposed to be in this Act at all.

CHAPLAIN. Then kindly take it away.

(*Now follows some extemporary business and ad-libbing while the animal is pushed and prodded into the horse box where, blocked in, it does whatever it likes for the remainder of the scene.* LETTY *is highly amused at all of this. When all is quiet, the scene continues.*)

BOY. I'm so sorry about this. Please go on.

PENNIWISE. Well – hm. Perhaps we'd better. (*To Chaplain*) May I ask what you're doing here?

BOY. He's a Mr Chaplain.

HOOLEY. That's right. Used to see him on the movies too.

CHAPLAIN. (*Irritated, as Letty laughs*) No, no. Not that Chaplin. Chap-lain. Wystan Chaplain.

HOOLEY. Ah. You're not a bit like the one I remember.

CHAPLAIN. Thank you so much.

BOY. Mr Chaplain is supposed to be a well known News Commentator.

CHAPLAIN. (*with a pained shrug*) "Supposed to be"!

HOOLEY. (*pointing at Penniwise*) He's a Solicitor.

PENNIWISE. Not a Solicitor. An Assistant.

BOY. He means a Clerk. The other one's a Cabman.

(*They shake hands all round with some disdain.*)

HOOLEY. I may only be a cabman, but if I had my rights I'd be living on the fat of the land. Solicitors is no good.

PENNIWISE. We've no time to go into your grievances now. (*To the Boy*) As for you. Maybe you'd be good enough to stop interrupting us with your remarks. Nobody wants you here.

BOY. Oh very well if you want me to go I'll go. But nobody out there will understand a word if I do.

PENNIWISE. (*Looking out where he is pointing*) Out where?

BOY. Oh never mind. Mr Dotheright will be on shortly, and he's the only character that matters. However, call me if there's any more trouble.

(*He goes off, as* MRS VANDERBILT *shouts from the kitchen.*)

MRS VANDERBILT. (*off*) Lay the table, ma'am. And you boys come in here and give me a hand.

LETTY. (*rising*) Really, Wystan, don't you think we'd better be . . . ?

CHAPLAIN. (*to Letty*) My dear, if these are the guests, what the hell will the host be like? I wouldn't dream of going yet.

PENNIWISE. (*calling out*) I don't want anything cooked for me. All I've come for is my . . .

MRS VANDERBILT. (*appearing*) I told you to come in here and lend a hand. D'you want me to raise my voice at you? You parchy old scrivener?

(*She goes again.*)

CHAPLAIN. Come along, Mr Penniwise. We'd better do as we're told.

HOOLEY. May as well have a bite while we're waiting.

PENNIWISE. I suppose you think that's all we'll get. But I've told you – not a foot will I stir out of this house until I've seen that man.

(*The men all go off muttering.* LETTY *lays the table, stopping for a few seconds to look in some puzzlement at the radio. Presently an eccentric-looking little old gentleman enters from the street, and locks the door behind him. He has a hunted look, but shows no particular surprise at the sight of* LETTY.)

LETTY. Oh! (*She pulls herself together*). How-do-you-do?

DOTHERIGHT. Would you kindly shut the window. (*She does so.*) Now put the catch on.

LETTY. (*after doing so*) Are you being pursued by anybody?

DOTHERIGHT. (*taking off his coat and hat*) It keeps out the flies.

LETTY. The flies? I don't quite follow.

DOTHERIGHT. They carry germs, and spread loathsome diseases.

LETTY. So you want the catch on. I see.

DOTHERIGHT. Why are you laying my table?

LETTY. So you're Mr Dotheright. I really ought to explain why I've called.

DOTHERIGHT. Is that your cab outside?

LETTY. (*shaking her head*) No.

DOTHERIGHT. (*disappointed*) Oh. (*Pause*) Then whose is it?

LETTY. I'm afraid it's your cab, Mr Dotheright. Indeed, I ought to warn you – there's going to be a little trouble.

DOTHERIGHT. Oh dear me. Sometimes it's difficult to avoid having a cab.

LETTY. There's Mr Penniwise inside, helping with some sausages, and he says . . . in fact, here he is now.

(PENNIWISE *and* HOOLEY *enter with some steaming dishes.*)

PENNIWISE. Ah, here he is at last. Have you any idea how much the fare is by now?

DOTHERIGHT. We will go into that presently. (*He looks in a dish.*) Sausages.

PENNIWISE. Over two pounds. And you needn't think I'm going to pay it. Here's Hooley the cabman – waiting.

DOTHERIGHT. He will be paid. Suppose we all sit down.

PENNIWISE. Paid, aye, but when?

DOTHERIGHT. Presently. When stockjobbers, shoulder-clappers, horse-copers and writers of scandal sheets begin to use a little honesty in their calling. For the present, we had better all – keep very, very calm.

PENNIWISE. Are you hinting that you have no money?

DOTHERIGHT. I have no money.

PENNIWISE. He has no money!

CHAPLAIN. (*entering*) Who has no money?

HOOLEY. *He* has no money.

LETTY. (*intoning*) Mr Dotheright has no money.

CHAPLAIN. (*putting down the plates*) So this is Mr Dotheright. We've all been getting quite worked up about you, Mr Dotheright, wondering what you were going to be like and – everything. Well, I must say you're all that I personally had hoped for.

DOTHERIGHT. (*To Letty*) Who is this person?

LETTY. Better ask somebody else.

HOOLEY. Why, you know *him*. He used to be . . .

CHAPLAIN. I know what's coming as if you'd said it already. So to avoid any further confusion, you, Mr Dotheright, may call me Wystan.

DOTHERIGHT. Wystan.

CHAPLAIN. Wystan, as a special favour. What is more, if these gentlemen are pursuing you for any money, don't let that bother you. I have some money.

PENNIWISE. (*brightening up*). Well! That makes things look a lot better.

DOTHERIGHT. (*puzzled*) You have some money? What is this money that you have? Mine?

CHAPLAIN. Oh no. It's my own money.

DOTHERIGHT. How did this gentleman's financial position get into the conversation?

PENNIWISE. Mr Chaplain can pay the cabman.

HOOLEY. That's right.

DOTHERIGHT. There, I knew there was some mistake. This gentleman – Wystan – (*he bows*) does not owe the cabman anything. It is I who owe the cabman something.

PENNIWISE. We know. But you can't pay him. He could. He's got money. Lots of it.

DOTHERIGHT. Then of course he could pay him if he has got lots of it. So could the other Mr Churchill. So could anybody for the matter of that.

PENNIWISE. But he will. Then you can pay him.

DOTHERIGHT. Oh. (*Pause*). But surely that shows some confused thinking. If I could pay him for paying the cabman, I would pay the cabman myself.

CHAPLAIN. I say, do let's stop this. The point is, Mr Dotheright, that I can probably spare the cash for a cab more readily than you can. However, I have no wish to force anything on you.

DOTHERIGHT. It had never occurred to me that you intended to use force, sir. May I ask how you come into this matter at all?

CHAPLAIN. Forget it, Mr Dotheright.

DOTHERIGHT. (*graciously*) Not at all. I am always delighted to discuss people's personal affairs if they wish it. Perhaps you would like to tell us what it is that you *do*, in return for all this money?

CHAPLAIN. (*stiffly*) Oh nothing very much. I interpret the news five nights a week, on the radio. That's all.

DOTHERIGHT. What for?

CHAPLAIN. For about a million people.

HOOLEY. That's right. I've heard him. I remember him now.

CHAPLAIN. (*with mock gallantry*) Thank you, Mr Hooley, I knew you were a man of affairs.

DOTHERIGHT. You mean, you tell them what is going on?

CHAPLAIN. More correctly, I help them understand it – to, er, think about it.

DOTHERIGHT. You must be a very remarkable man. So you help people to think. (*Pause*). And do they think?

CHAPLAIN. I would like to believe that I contribute to that end. But if you want the truth, Mr Dotheright, I sometimes wonder.

DOTHERIGHT. If there is any doubt on such a point, I am surprised that they continue to pay you. Unless of course, the fact that you are employed to guide their thoughts is actually to stop them having any thoughts at all.

CHAPLAIN. (*nettled by Letty's smile*) Really, I can't imagine why they employ me at all, Mr Dotheright. I must ask my superiors about it some day. Well, I think we must be going now. It was very interesting to have met you.

LETTY. No, no! I'm interested now. I want to hear some more.

DOTHERIGHT. And who are you, young lady?

CHAPLAIN. She happens to be your landlady.

DOTHERIGHT. Indeed.

PENNIWISE. I'll undertake she doesn't make a fortune out of that.

LETTY. I'm also an actress. A movie actress. Don't ask me what parts I've played, because you wouldn't have heard of any of them. Don't even ask me whether I'm any good or not, because I've never found out so far. And yet, they pay me a great deal. Don't you think that's very peculiar?

DOTHERIGHT. No more peculiar than other matters that have recently come to my attention. Did you by any chance call about the rent?

LETTY. Oh, no. I was only taking a look around.

HOOLEY. You should try one of them Shakespeare plays. They're good.

LETTY. (*to Hooley*) Of course, I'd love to. I've always wanted to play in Shakespeare. But what chance does one ever get? (MRS VANDERBILT *is serving.*)

HOOLEY. There's Ophelia, now. That's a nice part – if you don't mind them songs. They're a bit raw, if you ask me.

LETTY. (*dreamily*) Ophelia. I don't suppose I'll ever get the chance. (*She hums – with a smile at Wystan.*) "How shall I my true love know?"

HOOLEY. No, on second thoughts, not Ophelia. She's crazy.

MRS VANDERBILT. You mop up your slobber, you pauper-house cheat. Never mention the halter when you're supping with the hangman.

(She goes into the kitchen. There is a brief silence.)

DOTHERIGHT. Mrs Vanderbilt is given to these cryptic remarks. Pay no attention. It is best not to follow them up.

PENNIWISE. Look here – to get back to this loan you were offered –

CHAPLAIN. Oh please don't bring that up again. I'm sorry now that I ever suggested it. And really, Letty, I must be going, I have a commentary tonight, and I haven't prepared a line.

LETTY. What's the hurry? Haven't you said it all before?

CHAPLAIN. Maybe I have. But not in a towering rage. That requires a special technique. Well, I see you intend to stay, so maybe I'll see you later. Goodbye, all.

(He goes.)

LETTY. Goodbye, Wystan. And *do* cheer up.

PENNIWISE. *(to Dotheright)* Now you see what you've done. You've upset the man and lost your chance. Is that fair to me – I mean, is it fair to the cabman here?

DOTHERIGHT. The world we live in is unfair. I am, myself, the victim of a grave injustice. Only this afternoon.

LETTY. Is it something connected with that newspaper office?

DOTHERIGHT. Yes, madam.

LETTY. Would you like to tell me about it? Not that I want to seem inquisitive.

DOTHERIGHT. It is a painful story. And we really ought to have something besides these sausages. Ah eggs. I wonder are there any eggs yet. Excuse me. *(He rises and climbs a ladder.)* I have a hen somewhere up here. She hasn't laid as yet, but one of these days – Here, chook chook chook chook.

(An indignant crowing is heard.)

PENNIWISE If it's what I hear, you'll never get an egg out of that.

DOTHERIGHT. *(sternly)* Why not, pray?

PENNIWISE. Because it's a cock.

DOTHERIGHT. That is an allegation that always annoys me very much. I must ask you not to make it again. Where is the bird, and I shall demonstrate. I bought it in the spring from our local postmistress.

PENNIWISE. What as?

DOTHERIGHT. She assured me at the time that it was a fine young pullet. Here – chook chook chook.

PENNIWISE. Maybe she can tell a stamp from a money-order. But

she certainly can't tell a cock from a hen. Or else she cheated
you.

DOTHERIGHT. Sir I believe you are deliberately trying to upset me.
I will not permit it.

LETTY. Oh please don't annoy Mr Dotheright. I'm sure it's a hen.

PENNIWISE. Bosh.

HOOLEY. (*to Penniwise*) What do you know about it, anyhow?

PENNIWISE. I have ears.

DOTHERIGHT. (*who has come down*) You seem to be an unusually
intelligent young woman. Why are you so interested in my
misfortunes?

LETTY. Because I have connections in that newspaper office.

DOTHERIGHT. Personal connections?

LETTY. Yes. Actually – well – yes.

DOTHERIGHT. An arid inhabitant of the outer office? – a young
man in cycling knickerbockers with a quarrelsome face?

LETTY. That description would probably fit my husband.

DOTHERIGHT. (*embarrassed*) Ah. (*Pause*) It seems that I have
committeed a faux pas.

LETTY. Not at all. I don't like him very much myself. What did
he do?

DOTHERIGHT. (*settling down*) I shall tell you, madam. By profession
I am a free-lance obituarist.

HOOLEY. A what?

PENNIWISE. He means that he writes death notices for the newspapers.

HOOLEY. Can he make a living out of that?

PENNIWISE. Obviously not.

LETTY. Never mind. What happened?

DOTHERIGHT. Only the night before last I was going the rounds
of the local shrines of Mercury to find out – in the parlance
of the day – whether there was "anything doing", when this
young man handed me the report of the death of a certain
prominent citizen, by name Boddy.

LETTY. Oh, I know him. At least my father does. He makes
fertiliser.

HOOLEY. Fertiliser! Ah. I've got a horse outside. Called Mac after
a fellow called Macintosh who . . .

PENNIWISE. We are not interested in your horse.

LETTY. Fertiliser and old Bibles.

HOOLEY. (*taken aback*) Horses are the friends of man.

DOTHERIGHT. You seem to be addicted to these truisms. Old Bibles and Almanacks?

LETTY. I didn't realize that Boddy was dead. My father knows him.

DOTHERIGHT. Such was my information at the time. And it was on that basis that I accepted the commission to pay a newspaper tribute to him to the extent of half a column. But on submitting my work to the person concerned, the article was rejected. On the ridiculous ground that the man Boddy was *not* dead, after all.

LETTY. I'm sure he's not. But I thought you said . . .

DOTHERIGHT. I said this to them. I am not concerned, I said, with the question as to whether or not this Boddy is alive. I have been commissioned to execute some literary work, and here it is. I shall expect to see it in print tomorrow morning.

HOOLEY. Fair enough.

PENNIWISE. Hey, wait a minute!

LETTY. And what did they do then?

DOTHERIGHT. They threw me out.

LETTY. Threw you out?

DOTHERIGHT. (*bowing to Hooley*) Both neck and crop. If I may be allowed the use of a cliché myself.

LETTY. You mean to say, they didn't pay you?

DOTHERIGHT. They wouldn't even discuss the matter.

LETTY. I understand the trouble now. You take that very much to heart.

DOTHERIGHT. I regard it as a matter of principle. I do not like being treated in a cavalier manner when I am prepared to adopt a reasonable attitude myself.

LETTY. (*rising*) I think it's a shame, Mr Dotheright. And I'm going to see what I can do about it.

PENNIWISE. What can you do about it?

LETTY. I'm going to talk to the Editor.

PENNIWISE. What good will that do?

LETTY. Probably not much. He's my father. Excuse me if I run along.

(*On her way out she bumps against the radio, and then pauses to examine it. With a dirty look at* MRS VANDERBILT, *who has just entered, she picks it up and carries it out.*)

LETTY. This happens to be my radio.

(*Exit.*)

DOTHERIGHT. What a curious young woman. Did I understand her to say that her father was the Editor of the *Comet* newspaper.

PENNIWISE. Delusions of grandeur. More to the point, whose is that radio she's just snitched?

DOTHERIGHT. Do you know anything about it, Mrs Vanderbilt?

MRS VANDERBILT. Divil a one of me knows. She brought it here herself.

(*She goes out.*)

DOTHERIGHT. Personally I never thought she was quite balanced. She would keep calling me Dotheright.

PENNIWISE. But you are Dotheright.

(*Pause.*)

DOTHERIGHT. Who is?

PENNIWISE. You are.

DOTHERIGHT. (*irritably after a few seconds' consideration*) Of course I'm Dotheright. Then she had no business to be so confusing. Especially when I'm upset over other things.

PENNIWISE. You obviously brought it on yourself – the way you talked to them. You should have kept a civil tongue in your head.

DOTHERIGHT. All my life I have found it difficult to meet with dishonesty and injustice and keep a civil tongue in my head. Whenever I meet with a snake, I know that I must put my foot on it.

PENNIWISE. Aye, and get yourself bitten on the leg.

DOTHERIGHT. Reason often tells us that it is more profitable to suffer wrong in silence. But then a strange childish voice speaks insistently in my ear and says, "Dotheright, you are a coward. You must speak out." And so I speak out.

PENNIWISE. And probably lose your job.

DOTHERIGHT. Invariably.

PENNIWISE. There you are.

HOOLEY. (*to Penniwise*) If everybody agreed with you, would we have done what we did in 1916?

PENNIWISE. I have no knowledge of what you did in 1916.

HOOLEY. (*sententiously*) We marched out into the streets of Dublin and hoisted the flag of liberty over the Post Office. That's what we did.

PENNIWISE. And what did you get for it?

HOOLEY. I got – Well – I got a medal.

PENNIWISE. Hah! Is that all? A medal.

201

HOOLEY. (*producing it from his pocket after some fumbling*) There it is. (*His voice changes.*) But if I had my rights I'd have a pension like all the others. Maybe a good job in the Sweepstakes – for services rendered to the rights of Man.

 (*There is an uncomfy pause until the* BOY'S *voice is heard through the window.*)

BOY. Wear it, Hooley. You're supposed to be wearing it.

HOOLEY. (*suddenly enlightened*) So I am! By Jiminy, why shouldn't I be wearing it?

PENNIWISE. Who is this intolerable interrupter? Take his name, somebody!

BOY. My name is Alexander. (*His voice dies away.*)

HOOLEY. Alexander! That's a name to stir the troops! Look! I'm wearing it!

 (*He pins his medal on to his outer coat. There is another pause while he stands up proudly.* DOTHERIGHT *rises.*)

DOTHERIGHT. This is a very solemn moment, Mr. Hooley – if that is the correct name. May I ask why you did not get your just deserts?

HOOLEY. Because of crookedness and rascality in them at the top. Because of dirty politics – that's for why. And nobody willing to take up my cause with them that matter. Ah, but what's the use?

 (*He sits dejectedly.*)

DOTHERIGHT. Mr Hooley, you must speak out. What position did you hold in this Uprising?

HOOLEY. I was a Lieutenant in the Hibernian Rifles.

DOTHERIGHT. A lieutenant. Then Lieutenant Hooley, I drink a toast to you. (*Raising his cup.*) It is you who shall advise me what a resolute man should do in my position.

HOOLEY. You should go back to that office and kick up hell. That's what you should do.

DOTHERIGHT. Kick up hell. You think that is the proper procedure?

PENNIWISE. Don't be saying such things to the man.

HOOLEY. Well – it'll let off a bit of steam anyway.

PENNIWISE. You'll never get anywhere by causing trouble. If you want to, you can go back and discuss it with them reasonably.

DOTHERIGHT. But suppose they won't listen to reason?

PENNIWISE. There are other remedies – if you have any case at all.

DOTHERIGHT. What other remedies?

PENNIWISE. Well – I suppose you could go and see our Mr Phibbs about it.

DOTHERIGHT. A lawyer.

HOOLEY. Pah! Lawyers is no good.

DOTHERIGHT. You see, gentlemen, we have here two conflicting points of view – the constitutional and revolutionary. Which of them is right? Shall we all go back and find out?

PENNIWISE. What? Now? At this hour?

(*He feels for his watch.*)

DOTHERIGHT. (*crossing to get his coat*) Why not?

HOOLEY. (*rising and buttoning his coat*) That's right! Strike while the iron's hot.

PENNIWISE. (*suspiciously*) What exactly are you proposing? That's funny. I would have sworn I had my watch and chain when I came out.

DOTHERIGHT. Never fear, Mr Penniwise. We will begin with the constitutional. If that fails we will think again.

(MRS VANDERBILT *enters.*)

MRS VANDERBILT. (*briskly*) Well, boys, going out for a nice drink?

DOTHERIGHT. (*as they get into their coats*) No, Mrs Vanderbilt. We are going out to kick up hell – er, if reason fails.

MRS VANDERBILT. Maybe I'd better come too?

DOTHERIGHT. No. I don't think your presence would be any help at all.

PENNIWISE. I would have sworn . . . Um. Oh well, maybe I left it at home.

(*He gets into his coat.*)

MRS VANDERBILT. Whatever you say yourself.

DOTHERIGHT. (*pausing in the doorway*) And Mrs Vanderbilt, we all trust that Mr Penniwise in due course will find his watch again.

(*He waves his umbrella like a sword, and leads the other men off.* MRS VANDERBILT, *smiling blandly, continues to clear the table, humming to herself. The cuckoo emerges from the clock and continues to shout 'Cuckoo' until the Curtain is down.*)

SCENE TWO

LOWD'S *room in the offices of the 'Comet'.*
LOWD *is talking to* LETTY. *He is an expansive person with a firm belief in his own ability to manage other people and get his own way. A smiling wheedler or alternatively a roaring bully whenever it suits him, and yet not devoid of generosity. A bit of a rascal, yet not entirely without a sense of humour. In short, though he might prefer the world to be a better place, he is fully conscious of the fact that it is not, and he knows how to make the best of that state of affairs. He is, in fact, a crook with a conscience that is just sufficiently vocal to force him to justify everything he does in terms of a code of realistic common-sense.* LETTY'S *radio is standing on the floor.*

LOWD. Now, I'm a sane man – a normal, reasonable man-in-the-street. You know that my dear.

LETTY. Yes, father.

LOWD. A bit of an idealist in my own way. But at the same time I pride myself on having both feet planted firmly on the ground, and on being perfectly consistent.

LETTY. I know, father. But this old man says that he was given . . .

LOWD. Never mind him. It's Paddy I'm talking to you about. Are you really determined to leave him, and take this ridiculous place of your own?

LETTY. Daddy, I wish you'd try to understand. It's not just fancy that's making me get out. Marriage is far too important a thing to put up with second best.

LOWD. Of course it's important. That's just what I'm saying.

LETTY. So important that, if it's not right, it's liable to poison your whole life.

LOWD. It never poisoned mine. And, believe me, if Paddy's a crackpot, he's nothing to what your dear mother was.

LETTY. Father, it doesn't make things any better to hear you talking like that about mother.

204

LOWD. O.K. Let's talk about Paddy instead. I admit that he's got the social charm of an orang outang. And his ideas on most subjects seem to be those of an anarchist's apprentice. But you picked him, and you must have liked him once.

LETTY. Paddy's changed.

LOWD. I wish I could believe it.

LETTY. He used to be so sincere. But now life seems to have turned sour on him. He sees a dirty motive behind everything that happens. He says that every decent thing you try to do only turns round and kicks you in the pants.

LOWD. (*reflectively*) I'm sincere too. I think everybody agrees that about me.

LETTY. It's like as if he'd sold his soul to the devil.

LOWD. My dear girl, you must have a poor view of the devil as a business man. He'd never fall for that deal. Do you know something? I think you both ought to go and be psychoanalysed. I can give you an address . . .

LETTY. I don't need to be psychoanalysed. At least not yet, please God.

LOWD. It was only a suggestion.

LETTY. Father, I didn't come here to talk about me. I came to talk about an old man you're cheating. Now don't contradict me. That's the only word for it.

LOWD. Well it's not a nice word to use to your father – particularly after all the words I've avoided applying to your affairs. Now be fair. Is it?

LETTY. It's only a small sum, and he needs it. I'd pay him myself, only he wouldn't take it from me. It's a matter of *amour propre*. He wants to be paid for what he's done.

LOWD. French.

> (PADDY *enters with a pile of proofsheets in his hand. He is a furious-looking young man in the middle twenties, wearing cycling breeches.*)

PADDY. Well –! What's going on here?

LOWD. Come in. Come in. We only need you, Paddy. Your wife's been telling me how to run my business in French.

PADDY. You should never have paid for those extras at St. Chad's. (*He looks at the radio.*) I see you've been having some music too.

LETTY. No. It's like you. Brr-oken down.

PADDY. No doubt that's why you carry it round. Quite a typical state of affairs.

LETTY. Paddy, I'm in no mood for you.

LOWD. Listen – will you please go away – both of you. I've still got work to do.

LETTY. I'll go, father. I see it's no good talking to you any more now.

LOWD. At the moment it would be a great kindness.

LETTY. Goodbye, Paddy.

PADDY. Goodbye, Letty. You're looking tired.

LETTY. I *am* tired.

PADDY. (*handing her a hip flask*) How about a little alimony?

LETTY. (*taking it*) Thanks, Paddy. Maybe I shall.
    (*She goes out, forgetting the radio.*)

PADDY. (*surprised at her acceptance of the flask*) Well! Letty's coming on.

LOWD. She's going to leave you. You know that, I suppose?

PADDY. She *has* left me. (*Pause*) Is this where I'm expected to resign?

LOWD. Because you don't get on with my daughter?

PADDY. I suppose I should resign. Or would you rather give me the sack?

LOWD. Listen, Paddy, when I sack you it'll be for reasons connected with the paper. And God knows, there are plenty of them.

PADDY. (*grinning*) Yes, boss.

LOWD. For instance, how did this damn nuisance start about some unused hack work?

PADDY. Oh, that. I found a report of Boddy's death on your desk. I assumed it called for an obituary, so I handed it out to the first hack who happened to drop in.

LOWD. Damned efficient, aren't you, when nobody asks you.

PADDY. God dammit, you're always bawling people out for waiting to be told. How was I to know it wasn't on the level? It was in your own handwriting.

LOWD. O.K. O.K. Let's forget about it. The rules are the rules.
    (*The telephone rings.* LOWD *picks it up and listens absent-mindedly.*)

PADDY. What did you write it for anyhow? The man's as much alive as we are.
    (LOWD *puts back the receiver.*)

LOWD. Never mind. It should have been left on my desk.

PADDY. You might have warned me. Then it wouldn't have happened. Who was that on the phone just now?

LOWD. Nobody. They didn't answer.

PADDY. Maybe that's because you didn't say hello to them.

LOWD. I didn't want to speak to anyone. Oh, didn't I say hello? Well, maybe it wasn't important.

PADDY. So the old fellow's not been paid?

LOWD. Look, I've had all this out with Letty, and I don't want to hear anything more about it. There are a hundred and thirty-two hacks writing crap for this newspaper, and if any of them don't like to take the rough with the smooth, they know what they can do. Now for God's sake . . .

(*The telephone rings. He lifts the receiver.*)

PADDY. Hello.

LOWD. Oh – Hello . . . Yes . . . Oh, Mrs Tyler. (*He makes a face.*) . . . Delighted you've rung me up . . . Yes, Everything's set for this evening's ceremony. Both press and radio are covering it . . . Very well, just as you like. Tell me all about it . . .

(*The telephone quacks in his hand as he holds it away from his ear, with a look of resignation.*)

LOWD. I know now why the British left America. It was because they were tired of Mrs Tyler.

(*Presently another phone rings, and he lays down the first on his desk, where it continues to quack. He shakes his head and picks up the other phone.*)

LOWD. Yes, Miss Flintwhistle? . . . No, I don't think I can – WHAT? . . . Three gentlemen to see me? Have they an appointment? . . . (*He thumbs rapidly through an engagement diary.*) . . . Professor Somebody. And a Lieutenant? Never heard of them . . . Oh, wait a moment, though. This may be the Rotary Club Party . . . Yes, better send them up. (*He hangs up the second telephone.*) Don't go, Paddy. You may have to look after this bunch. It's about time you learnt how to handle the public.

PADDY. I'll take a few notes on your technique. Got a pencil?

LOWD. On the . . . Funny, aren't you? You'll never make a newspaperman, Paddy. I always said so. You've got the wrong attitude, and, I might add, the wrong trousers.

PADDY. My hands and my brain are the *Comet's*. My legs are my own concern.

207

LOWD. Shaw used to wear things like that. But you're not Shaw. Why can't you go out and turn in a good story once in a while? Just once in a while. Try it tonight. It's not much to ask. But I suppose a real newshawk has to be born.

PADDY. Like you?

LOWD. Yes. Like me. Why should I act coy about it? You've either got it or you haven't. I tell you, Paddy, there's a sort of extra sense that a good newspaperman has. I don't know what it is. But he can smell news before it happens. You've either got it or . . .

(PADDY *is gesturing towards the telephone, which has now stopped quacking.* LOWD *picks it up.*)

LOWD. Ah, yes. Mrs Tyler. Yes. That required a little thought. But I see your point, and I'm sure I agree . . .

(*Dotheright, Penniwise and Hooley file in, and he gestures to them to be seated. They are followed at some distance by the Boy who is carrying a large notebook.*)

LOWD. Yes . . . Yes . . . That's all been seen to. The whole party will be down there tonight. Reporters, photographer and a front-rank commentator It's all been laid on ʌ . . Goodbye, Mrs Tyler . . . Goodbye . . . Goodbye . . .

(*He hangs up, turns to his new visitors with a genial smile.* PADDY *recognizes* DOTHERIGHT, *and is about to speak.*)

Now, gentlemen.

PADDY. Look here. This is . . .

LOWD. That's all right, Mr Golightly. These gentlemen want to see *me*.

PADDY. (*sitting down, with a sardonic grin.*) O.K. They're all yours.

LOWD. (*to the others*) That was Mrs Tyler on the phone – the wife of the American Senator. She's dedicating a memorial to some President this evening and wants us to cover the ceremony too. You made a note of what she said, Mr Golightly?

PADDY. (*arranging chairs*) In duplicate, Mr Lowd. (*He puts on a coat.*)

LOWD. I'll want you to go down and turn in a full report. Now gentlemen, I'm at your disposal. I – er – don't think I caught the names?

DOTHERIGHT. Alphonsus Maria Liguori Dotheright.

LOWD. (*uncomprehending*) Ah, yes, of course. I remember now.

DOTHERIGHT. B.A.

LOWD. And which of you is which?

DOTHERIGHT. That is my name.

LOWD. All of it – just you? Oh I see. I imagined it was everybody. Ha, ha.

DOTHERIGHT. (*grimly*) Am I right in thinking that you are the person in charge here? We want no underlings this time.

LOWD. I'm the Editor if that's what you mean. I presume you gentlemen want to see over the plant? Or – er – perhaps I'm wrong?

(*He starts at the sight of* HOOLEY.)

HOOLEY. (*suddenly*) Why don't you pay him what you owe him?

LOWD. What's that?

DOTHERIGHT. Three pounds and fifty pee.

HOOLEY. Plus tax.

LOWD. I don't follow.

DOTHERIGHT. Pardon my friend's abruptness. The matter arises in connection with some literary work I have been commissioned to execute for your paper.

LOWD. (*stiffening rapidly*) Oh! Is that what you've called about?

DOTHERIGHT. A certain obituary notice.

LOWD. You're not . . .

DOTHERIGHT. Concerning a certain Mr Boddy.

LOWD. Then you're not the Rotary Club! (*Turning on Paddy*) Did you know who these people are?

PADDY. Yes, Mr Lowd. But you said you would attend to them yourself.

(*He sits down and listens with exaggerated politeness, having taken off his coat.*)

LOWD. Take that grin off your face! (*Picking up his papers.*) I'm sorry, gentlemen, but I'm afraid I haven't time to go into that just now. Very busy.

HOOLEY. We won't keep you long.

DOTHERIGHT. I am a man of letters. And at the request of your periodical I have devoted a considerable amount of time to an intensive study of chemical manure – a subject that interests me not the slightest. But I am no longer insisting upon its publication. I am adopting a very reasonable attitude, as everybody agrees.

LOWD. You're not insisting on . . . Listen, I don't know what

209

you're talking about and I'm a busy man. So hurry on. I'll remember you another time.

DOTHERIGHT. That is not what I'm asking for.

LOWD. O.K. It's a free country. Nobody's forced to work for the *Comet* if he doesn't feel inclined.

DOTHERIGHT. My dear sir, you are persistently avoiding the issue, which is the matter of payment for work already done.

HOOLEY. Aye – keep him to it.

LOWD. Are you seriously expecting to be paid for an obituary on a man who isn't dead?

PADDY. We've got dozens of them on the shelves.

LOWD. (*shouting*) Shut up!

DOTHERIGHT. Whether Mr Boddy is or is not dead is a matter quite outside my personal knowledge. Somebody may have made an error of judgement, but –

HOOLEY. To err is human.

PADDY. (*to Hooley*) How do you think of these things?

DOTHERIGHT. But that does not affect the primary question of contract.

LOWD. Listen, Mister, I keep books here. Books. Have you ever heard of them? Places where I write down particulars of the Company's money that I spend. Now, what do you suppose will happen to me if I write down in my books: Paid to Alaphonsius Flinkingirons the sum of three pounds –

DOTHERIGHT. – and fifty pee –

LOWD. – and fifty pence whatever it is –

HOOLEY – plus tax.

LOWD. Damn the tax.

HOOLEY. Oh you can't do that. That's compulsory.

LOWD. Will you kindly let me finish? I'm talking to this gentleman here, about a personal friend of mine who I happen to know is at present enjoying a quiet holiday in Connemara and IS NOT DEAD.

(*To Dotheright*) Do you follow me, my dear sir? Mr Boddy, the well-known Manufacturer of –

DOTHERIGHT. (*nodding*) – of Chemical Manure –

LOWD. Ex-actly. This Boddy is in no need of an Obituary. Nor is the *Comet* Newspaper. We're very much alive, Hah-hah!

DOTHERIGHT. So what?

LOWD. So what! You're not expecting me to pay you out of my own pocket?

210

DOTHERIGHT. Well, will you?

LOWD. No!

PENNIWISE. There you are. You'd better come and see our Mr Phibbs.

LOWD. (*suddenly suspicious*) Wait a minute. What Mr Phibbs is this? How does he come into it?

PENNIWISE. I represent his firm – Messrs. Phibbs and Rooke, Solicitors.

PADDY. The majesty of the Law.

LOWD. (*Stiffening*) I told you to keep out of this. May I ask whether this gentleman is here professionally?

PENNIWISE (*after a cautious pause*) We all came here together.

HOOLEY. In my cab. I'm here professionally.

LOWD. (*after looking around*) That boy over there. The boy with the open notebook. What's he doing here?

PENNIWISE. Oh, he's nobody in particular. Nothing to do with us.

LOWD. What's your name, young man?

BOY. Peter.

LOWD. Peter. (*Pause*) Peter what?

    (*Silence for a moment.*)

HOOLEY. That's not what he told us before.

LOWD. Before what?

DOTHERIGHT. Actually, that answer is not quite accurate. I seem to remember him telling us that his name is Alexander.

PENNIWISE. That's right. It struck me as unusual at the time. Alexander.

BOY. (*quietly*) That was two other fellows.

LOWD. *Two* other fellows? What the hell –?

DOTHERIGHT. There was only one as I remember. And I found him quite inspiring in some ways. Alexander.

HOOLEY. So now he's Peter. Well, all I can say is that somebody's a liar.

BOY. I'm not a liar. In fact I'm the only person in this mess who means exactly what he says.

LOWD. (*heavily*) Par-don me. *I* mean what *I* say. Invariably.

PENNIWISE. Schizophrenia! And at that age too.

LOWD. What are you doing with that notebook?

BOY. Just making some notes.

LOWD. Oh you are, are you. On whose behalf?

BOY. All these other people.

LOWD. What other people?

BOY. (*indicating the Audience.*) Out there. (*Pause while they all stare out and see nothing.*) Why don't you go on with the Play?

DOTHERIGHT. (*quietly*) A bookful of Notes. Peter. That's interesting.

LOWD. (*pulling himself together*) Ah, we've got something more to do than gossip with juveniles. I still want an answer from this gentleman as to whether or not he's here professionally?

DOTHERIGHT. Does it make any difference?

PADDY. Yes, Mr Dotheright, quite a big difference. You see, the *Comet* newspaper, in return for its kindness in allowing people to work for it, considers that it is entitled to steamroll its less-important contributors in small ways from time to time.

LOWD. That's not a bright way of putting it.

PADDY. Only in small ways of course. Let's be frank about this in fairness to Mr Dotheright. If these contributors choose to be nasty and bring solicitors along with them, they're liable to find themselves with no more work after the matter has been adjusted. You understand?

DOTHERIGHT. (*grimly*) Less-important contributors.

LOWD. I never put it that way.

PADDY. No, but we may as well face it. (*To Dotheright*) It's something I'm sure you ought to understand before your friend decides whether he is here professionally or not.

DOTHERIGHT. I don't like being spoken to in this manner.

LOWD. (*suspiciously*) Look here, I don't know what all this is getting at, but I tell you what I'll do. You go away quietly now and I'll find you another one to write.

DOTHERIGHT. May I ask what you mean by "another one"?

LOWD. (*searching on his desk*) In fact, maybe I can give you something right away. (*Pause.*) Yes, here we are. How's that? (*He hands* DOTHERIGHT *some papers.*) See?

PENNIWISE. Ah, that's more like it.

LOWD. Everybody happy now?

DOTHERIGHT. I am always ready and willing to work for a just wage –

LOWD. (*returning to his work*) Good. All the poop's there. Goodbye.

DOTHERIGHT. Nevertheless, the offer of this employment seems to be quite irrelevant to the matter at issue, which, as I said, is payment for work already done.

LOWD. (*irritably*) Look, I'll give you a fiver for the lot, and we'll call it quits. Now be off.

PENNIWISE. Five pounds! Ah-ha! That seems very reasonable.

(*He and* HOOLEY *rise, but* DOTHERIGHT *stops them.*)

LOWD. And you'd better be going too, Paddy.

(PADDY *gets his coat again.*)

DOTHERIGHT. One moment, please. You mean that in consideration of your paper refusing to pay me what it owes me already, I am to continue to work for it at less than half the usual rate.

PENNIWISE. Och, have some sense, man! He's trying to do you a kindness.

DOTHERIGHT. I don't want his kindness. I don't even care very much about his money. All that I demand from him and his paper is a little honesty in their public dealings. Is that too much to ask?

PENNIWISE. Are you mad, Dotheright?

LOWD. Well, I'll be –! Give me back those papers and get out of here, the lot of you.

PADDY. You see! Now you've hurt his feelings. (*Indicating Lowd*).

DOTHERIGHT. I hope so sincerely, although I doubt it very much. But he has hurt my feelings, if that is of any consequence.

(LETTY *enters. She has assumed a new air of defiance. Maybe after a sip of her alimony.*)

LETTY. I've forgotten my – Oh, hello. Quite a crowd here.

LOWD. That's right. Come in, everybody. It's only my private office.

DOTHERIGHT. This room is full of germs. The windows must have been left open.

LETTY. Well I declare it's my old friend and tenant, Mr Dithery.

DOTHERIGHT. Duthery is the correct pronunciation.

LETTY. You've met my father, then? And my husband too. That's my husband over there. The one with the trousers.

LOWD. God give me patience. Paddy, haven't you gone yet?

PADDY. (*Putting his coat on.*) Yes, boss. I'm on my way.

LETTY. I came back for my radio, although why I can't imagine. It isn't working any more. (*She picks it up and puts it on the table where it bursts into crooning.*) Oh, I beg your pardon.

LOWD. Stop that thing!

DOTHERIGHT. We came here to give this gentlemen a chance to explain himself.

LETTY. That was a great kindness on your part.

PADDY. You can see how delighted he is.

LOWD. (*calling*) Flintwhistle! Where's Miss Flintwhistle?

HOOLEY. Pure waste of time. The man seems to be illegible.

DOTHERIGHT. You don't mean illegible, Lieutenant. You mean something else.

(*They cluster around the desk.* LOWD *rises on a chair, appearing above their heads.*)

LOWD. (*shouting*) Golightly! Get this clutch of twirps out of here. And turn that bloody thing off!

PADDY. Pull yourself together, boss. Is that the way to handle the public?

(PADDY *bangs the radio and it relapses into silence.*)

DOTHERIGHT. This paper spends roughly fifty thousand a year on something called Public Relations, and yet it won't pay three pounds fifty that it owes me. It's worse than dishonest, it's inconsistent.

LOWD. (*furious*) I resent that.

PADDY. Now you've done it!

DOTHERIGHT. Completely inconsistent. Not to mention the tax.

LOWD. Listen. I've put up with a hell of a lot but I won't be called inconsistent.

HOOLEY. Then tell us how you're not.

LOWD. I'm damned if I see why I should, but I will. Sit down! And don't you whisper in my office, Letty, it's rude.

LETTY. It would be ruder to say it out loud.

(*They all sit down in a row.* PADDY *takes off his coat as he does so.*)

LOWD. If Mr – Thing – here was a person of importance there's a great deal that I'd do for him. Certainly I would. And why?

DOTHERIGHT. You tell us.

LOWD. Not because I'm inconsistent but because you might be able to do one or two things for me in return. But you're all just like everybody else. You all want something for nothing. So listen here. If you want to be treated as an important contributor go ahead and be one. I'm not stopping you. In fact, I'll be delighted. I'll take you out to lunch at the Company's expense any time you call. But in the meantime

don't blame me if you're treated any other way. Blame yourself for not being important. There now – is that inconsistent?

(LETTY *is about to speak*.)

DOTHERIGHT. No. Let him finish.

LOWD. People are paid what they're worth in this world and it's
a damn good thing they are. I might have given you a few
bob out of kindness. What's-your-name, if you'd gone about it
the right way. But you've called me inconsistent and I'm
damned if I'll stand for that. So now I'm going to be consistent and pay you exactly what you *are* worth. And that's
sweet damn all. So get out of here, the lot of you, and don't
come back till you can make it worth my while to waste my
time. Go on, I mean it.

(*The telephone rings.* LOWD *lifts it. The* BOY *is pulling
agitatedly at* DOTHERIGHT'S *sleeve*.)

PADDY. (*sharply*) Hello.

LOWD. (*shouting into the receiver*) Hello! Oh? I beg your pardon.
Yes?

DOTHERIGHT. We will go, sir.

LOWD. Oh, Chaplain! (*He makes signs at Letty*.) Yes, we're going
to cover your tribute to those superannuated felons. Golightly
is on his way down. He left some time ago.

(*He gestures violently at* PADDY, *who is putting his coat on
again*.)

DOTHERIGHT. Yes, yes! But before taking any further action, may
I inform you, in the vulgar vernacular of the day what I
consider you to be?

LOWD. (*into the phone*) Yes. Yes.

DOTHERIGHT. Thank you, sir. You are a twister.

LOWD. I wasn't talking to . . . (*He lays down the phone*.)
What was that? Did you call me a twister?

DOTHERIGHT. Yes, sir.

HOOLEY. And put that in your . . .

LOWD. . . . pipe and smoke it. I know. I've heard that one too.

DOTHERIGHT. Come along, gentlemen. We will now follow in the
footsteps of our young – what did you say your name was?

PENNIWISE. We'll regret this, I'm telling you. Mr Phibbs will say
we should have taken his offer.

BOY. Actually I'm George! (*He leads them off*.)

PADDY. Where are you going, Letty?

215

LETTY. Out with my gentlemen friends. I don't know where, but I'm going along.

(*She picks up her radio and turns it on.*)

PADDY. Can you give me a lift?

LETTY. It will be a bore, but I will.

(*As they all file out, once again the martial music of the radio.*)

(LOWD *returns to the receiver.*)

LOWD. Flintwhistle, get me Hynie Phibbs at once. God dammit, Chaplain, are you still on the line? Get off! I know how to fix that bastard, Phibbs.

CURTAIN

SCENE THREE

*It is Evening and we find ourselves outside a small SUBURBAN
SHOP-CUM POST OFFICE next door to the entrance to a Pub.
In the window is displayed a mixture of periodicals, trinkets,
toys and cheap ornaments amongst which are a pair of unattrac-
tive china dogs. On the front of the building is affixed a small
plaque, at present covered by a piece of sacking, while over the
shop is the window of the bedroom of* MISS PEERING, *the
Postmistress, at present in darkness.* WYSTAN CHAPLAIN *is
engaged in arranging some boxes into a low platform below the
plaque together with a microphone on a stand and a cuelight
from which cables lead off into the door of the Pub, on the step
of which a cynical-looking Photographer with the fish-eyes of a
permanent hangover is sitting, smoking a cigar. To the side,*
PADDY *is reclining on a street seat, somewhat the worse for drink
and doodling in a notebook, while elsewhere a ponderous* POLICE-
MAN *hovers under a lamp-post, observing* MRS VANDERBILT *who is
seated on the kerb with a metal Supermarket trolley by her side.
Various passers-by pass by, without showing much interest in
these activities, while the Postmistress herself stands outside the
glass door of her shop observing the preparations with sour and
hostile eyes.*

CHAPLAIN. (*tapping the microphone and then speaking*) Hello
   Control Room. Wystan Chaplain testing from the O.B. Point.
   Are you getting me? A – B – C – D – E. Chaplain testing.
   (*A light flashes.*) O.K. We'll give you a voice-test before we
   go ahead.
MISS PEERING. Nobody gets into my Post Office after six o'clock.
   I don't care whose Plaque it is. That's when I close.
CHAPLAIN. Quiet please. We need a couple more boxes . . . And
   that Mrs Tyler ought to be here by now.
MISS PEERING. Nice kind of hour to pick for this sort of thing.
   (*She slams the door behind her.*)

217

PHOTOGRAPHER. Keep an eye on that camera. (*He goes into the Pub.*)

CHAPLAIN. Where's Letty?

PADDY. How should I know? Running around somewhere in a cab with a bunch of creeps.

CHAPLAIN. Oh, not still with that lot!

PADDY. Last I saw of them they were all going into some Solicitor's office. I hadn't time to wait to see them thrown out.

CHAPLAIN. You ought never to have left her with that crowd. (*He goes into the Pub for more Boxes.*)

PADDY. They're just her style.

POLICEMAN. I'm keeping my eye on you.

MRS VANDERBILT. No more than mine's on you, Inspector.

POLICEMAN. I'm not an Inspector and well you know it.

MRS VANDERBILT. You will be soon, my lovely man. I can sniff quick promotion. Oh, there's muscle! That one's a buck of the best. (*She lifts the leg of his trousers. The* POLICEMAN, *in some embarrassment, replaces the trouser leg and grabs her trolley into which he peers.*)

POLICEMAN. Leave my leg alone! What's in this machine?

MRS VANDERBILT. Is them Parkgate manners? If you want me name and address, I'll leave you one of my scrivened visiting cards.

POLICEMAN. Be off in five minutes or I'll call the van. (*The* POLICEMAN *moves off nervously.*)

MRS VANDERBILT. (*Calling after him*) Don't be long, General. You'll be gorgeous in crepe. (MRS TYLER *appears carrying a portmanteau.* PADDY *rises and approaches her.*)

MRS TYLER. Are all the arrangements complete? (*to Paddy.*) Will you take my portmanteau please? (*Paddy takes it reluctantly, half sobered by the majesty of her manner.*)

PADDY. Mrs Tyler, I represent the *Comet* newspaper. How about giving me an outline of what you're going to say on the air?

MRS TYLER. So that you can go away without waiting to hear me say it – eh?

PADDY. (*nonplussed.*) Well as a matter of fact it might catch an earlier edition.

MRS TYLER. I know. You wish to retire to some Public House, and avoid attending the ceremony which you are being paid to report.

PADDY. Well, they're all the same, aren't they?

MRS TYLER. You are a rather impertinent young man, and if you wish to hear what I have to say you must wait and listen. Now be careful with that receptacle. It contains a lot of literature.

(*She moves off to inspect the platform and peep at the Plaque.* PADDY *stares after her indignantly.*)

PADDY. Of all the old –

(*A horse's hooves and the clatter of a cab is heard approaching.*)

HOOLEY. (*off.*) There they are! Whoa up, Macintosh. Steady boy.

(*Presently* DOTHERIGHT *appears and approaches the door where* PADDY *still stands with the portmanteau in his hands.*)

DOTHERIGHT. Ah! A Post Office?

PADDY. Well met Dotheright! Hynie Phibbs showed you the door, I suppose. He wouldn't touch your case, eh?

DOTHERIGHT. (*turning*) He laughed at my case.

PADDY. He was kinder to you than you deserve.

(LETTY *enters.*)

PADDY. (*to Letty*) Hello, Lady Macbeth. Would you mind taking this?

(*He holds out the portmanteau.*)

LETTY. Yes, I would.

PADDY. That's not very wifely. Somebody's got to take it. I can't make any notes with this on my hands.

LETTY. Pooh! (*Letty moves to one side followed by Paddy who abandons the portmanteau, as they converse in undertones.*)

CHAPLAIN. (*entering*) Ah, Mrs Tyler at last! Good evening ma'am. Now look here everyone, I don't mind you looking on if you'll only keep quiet. We'll be on the air from here in a few minutes, and we've just got time to run through Mrs Tyler's routine.

MRS TYLER. Yes, where are my papers? We'll have them here, please.

DOTHERIGHT. Running through Mrs Tyler's what?

CHAPLAIN. (*shouting*) Her routine. Please don't interrupt.

POLICEMAN. (*approaching Mrs Vanderbilt*) Are you still here! Now you take heed, or I'll have to move you on.

MRS VANDERBILT. Quiet, as a mouse.

CHAPLAIN. Now on the cue, which I shall get in my headphones, I shall read the introductory material that will take the

219

programme over from the Studio, and leave it with Mrs Tyler.
Then when I say . . . let me see now. What is Mrs Tyler's cue?

(*Enter* PENNIWISE. *He is met by* DOTHERIGHT.)

PENNIWISE. What's going on here?

DOTHERIGHT. I don't understand it at all. He says he is running
through this woman's routine.

PENNIWISE. I know this place. A Miss Peering is the Postmistress.

POLICEMAN. Ssssh!

(MRS VANDERBILT *slips past carrying the camera. The*
POLICEMAN *grabs it and* MRS VANDERBILT *vanishes.*)

DOTHERIGHT. Whatever it is, it requires absolute silence. Was that
Mrs Vanderbilt I saw just now?

CHAPLAIN. Ah, here we are. When I hear the cue "In the words
of Jefferson: A Rising now and then is a good thing and as
necessary in the political world as storms are in the physical"
– I shall give you the signal, and you go ahead.

MRS TYLER. (*reading from a script*) "Where would we be today
without our Rebels? Would we be living in a free land where
the rule of law guarantees the rights and liberties of even the
humblest?"

DOTHERIGHT. (*interested*) Would you repeat that, please?

MRS TYLER. Where the rule of law guarantees the rights and
liberties of even the humblest?

DOTHERIGHT. Ah. That is what I thought you said.

CHAPLAIN. Pay no attention to this gentleman, Mrs Tyler. I know
him.

MRS TYLER. No, no. I'm interested in his reactions. (*To
Dotheright*) You are probably one of those conventional
people who don't like to admit that our rights and liberties
have been won for us by Rebels?

DOTHERIGHT. No, madam. I took exception to the ridiculous
proposition that the rule of law guarantees us anything.

PHOTOGRAPHER. (*entering*) Where the hell is my camera?

POLICEMAN. Would this be it?

(*They go off, ad libbing.*)

CHAPLAIN. What are you laughing at? I can't hear a word of the
programme above all this chatter and noise. (*To Dotheright*)
And you're the worst.

PADDY. The old boy made a perfectly reasonable remark – the
first we've had this evening. And I propose to report it in full.

LETTY. Shut up, Paddy.

220

PADDY. Shut up yourself.

CHAPLAIN. I shall just have to go and listen for the cue in the car. (*He hurries off.*)

LETTY. You're drunk.

PADDY. Not on clichés anyway.

DOTHERIGHT. Is that corner-boy presuming to compliment me? Because, if so, I do not require it.

MRS TYLER. What is the matter with this person?

PADDY. He's just been done out of a small sum of money by my newspaper. Just a small sum.

DOTHERIGHT. A very small sum – a very small breach of one of the smallest of the Ten Commandments. "Thou shalt not kill" is the only one that is slightly smaller.

MRS TYLER. Well he can sue, can't he?

PADDY. Some solicitor has turned him down.

DOTHERIGHT. These vendors of justice with their writs and their flim-flams, are only valuable because of their hard names, I tell you people, the talons of jailors and attornies are too sharp not to scratch the skin of those who shake hands with them.

PENNIWISE. What do you mean – Vendors of Justice? You don't buy justice. It's free for all.

DOTHERIGHT. That's not what Mr Hynie Phibbs says.

PENNIWISE. Ah, just a small advance for costs, of course. That's reasonable enough when you have no visible assets.

DOTHERIGHT. Just a small advance, and then a long retreat.

PADDY. De minimum non curat lex.

DOTHERIGHT. Latin. (*To the Public at large.*) That means "The law does not bother much about unimportant people".

PENNIWISE. That's not the correct translation.

DOTHERIGHT. May I ask you a question, madam?

MRS TYLER. I suppose we have time. But –

DOTHERIGHT. We live, we are told, in a society where man is rewarded according to his deserts – where wealth is the crown of ability, industry and thrift, and where poverty is the proper penalty of ignorance and improvidence. (*She nods.*) I have got no money, and that is because I have been careless and indifferent, and have not troubled to learn this thing that is called What's What. But what about my friend, Mr Penniwise, who has always played the game, and ought to be better off for it? Are Lieutenant Hooley's services to Society any less valuable than those of my landlady, Mrs Golightly? Yet she, I understand, is in receipt of a salary from the motion picture industry that proves her to be equivalent of two Bishops and three Rural Deans. I have been working this out from Whitaker's Almanack. Or was it Poor Robin? Yes – Poor Robin I think it was that.

LETTY. (*laughing helplessly*) How right he is. And I still don't play Ophelia!

CHAPLAIN. (*hurrying back*) Mrs Tyler, Mrs Tyler, would you please get ready before we hear the cue.

MRS TYLER. Ah yes. We mustn't forget that we have work to do, must we. Would somebody please bring that portmanteau over here.

(*Nobody does, so* CHAPLAIN *grabs it while at the same time trying to adjust his headphones. Various passers-by stop to look on.* MRS TYLER *opens the suitcase and gets out some pamphlets.*)

PENNIWISE. You know, Dotheright, there's something in what you say. It doesn't seem fair, does it?

DOTHERIGHT. It is not fair, my friend. It is a lie that is told to us poor fools who, like the bath-keeper's ass, are content to bring home the fuel that keeps our master's fires alight, and live ourselves on the smell of the smoke.

PENNIWISE. I'm sure the times are hard for everybody.

DOTHERIGHT. Whether the times be hard or good, I have noticed that pimps and jobbers dine better than honest craftsmen should, and that the same cold wind blows through an empty purse.

PENNIWISE. (*thoughtfully*) Maybe I shouldn't have given up my writing?

LETTY. What writing? Is this the secret in your past, Penny?

PENNIWISE. (*stiffening*) Och, a lot of soft nonsense. I've forgotten it now. I was thinking of getting married at the time. She was a bonnie lass – so gay and bright.

(*He looks up at the upper window which lights up.*)

PADDY. (*nauseated*) Lord! Reminiscences!

LETTY. Shut up, Paddy. Why didn't you get married, Mr Penny?

PENNIWISE. Because there was the future to think of. I was going into the professions and had a career to consider. How could I get married?

DOTHERIGHT. And so you took the wiser course.

PENNIWISE. I suppose so.

DOTHERIGHT. And here you are now.

(*Meanwhile* CHAPLAIN *has been getting* MRS TYLER *into position, as she adjusts her glasses.*)

MRS TYLER. Let me see, now.

PENNIWISE. Aye. Here I am now.

CHAPLAIN. Sssh! Quiet please.

MRS TYLER. (*reading*) It is a great pleasure and privilege to be here on behalf of my husband, the Senator, to unveil this Memorial on the wall of the humble birthplace of his distinguished ancestor – the great English Rebel and Reformer of the 14th century, Watt Tyler.

CHAPLAIN. Yes Mrs Tyler, but it should be the 15th century. And that's not the proper opening is it?

MRS TYLER. Oh, are you sure? 15th century?

CHAPLAIN. Definitely but I'll go and check. And I repeat, Mrs Tyler, you mustn't begin until you get the cue from me.

(*He dashes back into the Pub. Some more onlookers gather round.* MRS TYLER *continues, unheeding.*)

MRS TYLER. Our American Revolution which we celebrate once a year on the Fourth of July – don't interrupt – is an expression of protest against tyranny and injustice – where's he gone, that man?

(*As some of her listeners indicate to her what has happened she gets into an inaudible discussion with some of them, and distributes some pamphlets from her portmanteau.*)

MRS TYLER. As our late President Tyler said in – er –

(*She starts to look through the script and makes some marks with a pencil.*)

DOTHERIGHT. You have squandered your days in rummaging the earth for small and unimportant things. And what has it profited you more than any of us?

PENNIWISE. (*in reminiscent mood*)

Lift up your eyes and see the budding hedgerows.

Ours are the meadows and the rowan trees.

This is our Earth. We can rebuild the Heavens,

And in a greener land, reset the seas.

(*Pause, while his Companions look at each other.*)

HOOLEY. (*entering*) I like that bit. "The blooming hedges".

PENNIWISE. (*crossly*) Budding hedgerows.

LETTY. Who's was that, Penny?

223

PENNIWISE. (*with a touch of apology*) Nobody's ma'am. It's just
my own. She was nicer when I wrote it for her than she is
today.
(*He gazes up at the window.*)

LETTY. Not Miss Peering? (*They all look up.*)

PENNIWISE. Yes, Ma'am. (*He sniffs.*)

PADDY. (*after another pause*) Well; I bet there's not a dry seat
in the house.

LETTY. Stop it, Paddy. Stop it!

PADDY. Cheer up, Penniwise. I got married, and you can have my
future.
(*He draws a hip flask from his pocket.*)

LETTY. Oh, I can't bear it. I can't. I can't.
(*She bites back her tears, and runs off, after grabbing the
flask.* PADDY *stares after* LETTY.)

HOOLEY. Is there something the matter with her?

PADDY. Yes. Me. It's nice to be a bit of a shit. Helps you to feel
sort of at home in this world of ours.

PENNIWISE. I think there's virtue in all of us.

HOOLEY. There's only one virtue that matters, and it's Courage.
We learnt that when we occupied the Post Office.

DOTHERIGHT. Yes, Lieutenant, and let us add that there is only
one Evil that matters – Injustice. Injustice is the supreme
sin – not in those who commit it, but in those who submit
to it. For to do so is to ignore the eternal verities and to
admit that Life itself is evil. That is the Sin against the Holy
Ghost.
(*The* BOY *is crossing the forestage leading the Goat on a
tether.*)

BOY. (*with a bland smile*) He's right, you know. You have to
occupy the Post Office. (*He goes off on the other side.*) *Pause.*

PENNIWISE. Was that Alexander?

PADDY. No. It was George – Saint George Washington with his
Dragon.

CHAPLAIN. (*rushing to the Platform*) You're on the air, Mrs Tyler!
Go ahead.

MRS TYLER. (*now completely confused*). When in the course of
human events, no that's not the place, where is it? As our
great President Tyler remarked just a moment please . . . Alas
for the days of heroism. Where are the young men now who
would do as those men did . . .

(DOTHERIGHT *has pushed his way up beside her as she struggles with* CHAPLAIN *over the script.*)

DOTHERIGHT. Excuse me, madam. I have a short announcement to make. I myself propose to hold a Rebellion.

MRS TYLER. I beg your pardon?

CHAPLAIN. Go away! Don't you know we're on the air!

DOTHERIGHT. A Rebellion. The days of heroism have not gone. Would any of you people care to join me?

(*The Onlookers hastily withdraw to a distance.*)

MRS TYLER. Will somebody please do something about this man?

(HOOLEY *and* PENNIWISE *get up beside them.*)

HOOLEY. See here you . . .

PENNIWISE. Dotheright, you'd better come away.

DOTHERIGHT. I will not come away. I agree with everything that has been said. We have been invoking St Peter when what we ought to invoke is Saltpetre. Like the philosopher, Diogenes, we must publicly deface a spurious coinage.

CHAPLAIN. Will you stop interrupting Mrs Tyler?

VOICES. That's right. Ah, get down.

(CHAPLAIN *takes hold of* DOTHERIGHT, *who clings on to something.*)

DOTHERIGHT. I am not interrupting. I tell you, I agree with her. Madam, I appeal to you.

VOICES. Ah, throw him out.

(*Angry Voices rise.*)

(MISS PEERING *looks out of her window and blows a whistle.*)

MISS PEERING. This noise is disgraceful.

(MISS PEERING *goes in again.*)

PADDY. (*excited*) Wait a minute. Wait a minute. Give us a chance of a headline! Any statement, Mrs Tyler, before you throw this rebel out of your revolutionary gathering?

CHAPLAIN. You keep out of this!

PADDY. Be careful now. I'm the Press. Will you not let the man have his say, Mrs Tyler? How many times have you demanded as much for yourself?

MRS TYLER. If the gentleman has a grievance I'm sure he is entitled to ventilate it. But please remember we are on the air.

PADDY. Come on, Dotheright, what do you propose?

DOTHERIGHT. (*with quiet reason*) I propose a Democracy dedicated to the triple slogan, "One Truth, One Law, One Justice" – a

Commonwealth where men shall be given to dignity, and not Dignities to men, and where Liberty and Equity shall be as free as the winds of Heaven.

HOOLEY. (*enthusiastically*) Triple Crown Dotheright; That's him!

PADDY. (*writing madly*) A Bellows full of Angry Wind! How's that for a Headline?

DOTHERIGHT. In furtherance of which I propose to occupy the Post Office.

PADDY. (*after a surprised silence*) Well folks, here's your chance.

CHAPLAIN. What right have you got to occupy a Post Office?

DOTHERIGHT. Precisely the same right as many others before me.

MRS TYLER. This is most extraordinary behaviour.

CHAPLAIN. (*grabbing the microphone*) Cut the whole thing! Do you hear me, Control Room? Cut – Cut – Cut!

VOICES FROM SOME OF THE ONLOOKERS. Let's get out of here. I'm off. So am I. Going to be trouble.

DOTHERIGHT. Don't go, ladies and gentlemen. As participants in this large event, you shall all be given jobs – maybe even in my Cabinet. Mr Hooley here – he has military experience. He shall be Minister for War.

(*As the strains of "Parsifal" are heard approaching from a Radio, he pulls down the awning, half of which remains attached to its rod, which he waves in the air.*)

CHAPLAIN. We'll have to start all over again. Control Room, have you cut?

(*Pause.*) My God! Then do!

DOTHERIGHT. Let us unfurl a new flag, dedicated to Sir Herbert Barker, who in the cause of Science was able and willing to put his own neck out of joint. (*He waves the flag.*)

(LETTY *enters, carrying the Radio and wearing the Horse's hat. Putting the Radio down she distributes straws from the nosebag to the departing Public in a fantastic parody of the mad Ophelia. The* PHOTOGRAPHER *appears from the Pub and hastily starts fiddling with his lens.*)

LETTY. Up the Rebels! That's Rosemary. That's for remembrance.

CHAPLAIN. Oh God! Stop this infernal row. We're still on the air.

LETTY. There's Fennel for you. And Columbine. And there's a Pansy.

PHOTOGRAPHER. (*receiving his*) Are you referring to ME?

MRS TYLER. (*at the mike*) Where would we be without our Rebels? Would we be living today in a land where . . . ?

226

(DOTHERIGHT *has got up beside her and is attempting to take the microphone. The* PHOTOGRAPHER *tries to fix his camera in position.*

MRS TYLER. Let it go. Let it go. Would we be living today . . .

DOTHERIGHT. (*into the microphone*) We must be angry men, unshamed of our anger. We must be mountains who will not be molehills.

(*Continuing to background*) What are our only weapons? They are words – big-bellied words, billowing like galleons out of Espanola – words that strike fire from flint. We shall speak to the great unknowing world how these things came about. (*Meanwhile.*)

CHAPLAIN. Stop behaving like a fool Letty. This is all your fault.

(HOOLEY *makes off with the nosebag and the Hat.*)

HOOLEY. No violence, please. That's Mac's supper. And his Hat!

LETTY. I would give you violence, but it withered all –

CHAPLAIN. Shut up!

LETTY. – when my poor old Father died!

CHAPLAIN. I told you to shut up!

PADDY. (*interfering*) Are you criticising my wife's performance?

CHAPLAIN. Yes!

PADDY. Well, I think it's very good.

CHAPLAIN. Deplorable!

(PADDY *strikes* CHAPLAIN *who goes down like a stone, knocking over the Radio which is suddenly silent, as the voices of the departing public die away.*)

LETTY. (*affectionately*) Did you really like me, Paddy? (*She indicates Chaplain on the ground.*) That much?

PADDY. Absolutely star quality.

MRS TYLER. (*Exhausted*) – when – in the course of human – events –

PENNIWISE. Look out!

MISS PEERING. (*appearing again in the window with some domestic receptacle in her hand.*)

There now! Maybe that will cool your chatter.

(*She empties it over* DOTHERIGHT'S *head, and blows her whistle again.*)

DOTHERIGHT. That, gentlemen, is our baptism by Grace. Here now is our baptism by Fire!

(*He raises the rod and smashes the glass in the doorway.* MISS PEERING *screams and slams her window shut as all the others are galvanised into activity except* CHAPLAIN *who remains prostrate. Police whistles are heard, off, as* PADDY *picks* LETTY *up and carries her off as she shouts*:)

Up with the Barricades. Revolution! Revolution!

PADDY. Out of my way, you nitwits. (*They go off in the opposite direction to the sound of the whistles.*)

PENNIWISE. To the cab, everyone. Quick!

(*He leads the others off – including* MRS TYLER – *towards the Cab.*)

MRS TYLER. Taxi! Taxi!

DOTHERIGHT. I hereby proclaim my Triple Crown Four Man Republic, and occupy the Post Office.

(MRS VANDERBILT *pulls open the door from inside and he enters.* MISS PEERING *reappears at her window. The* PHOTO-GRAPHER *runs madly about trying to find his flashing apparatus, and finally disappears into the Pub.*)

PHOTOGRAPHER. My flash! My flash!

DOTHERIGHT. Mrs Vanderbilt! How did you get in here?

POLICEMAN. (*appearing at last*) What's going on?

(DOTHERIGHT *hastily closes the door and leans against it.*)

MISS PEERING. He's inside! He's the one that did it!

POLICEMAN. (*shaking the door*) Come out of that! Come on. I've got your name!

DOTHERIGHT. (*trying to hold the door against him*) Go away, fellow. We do not recognise you any more.

POLICEMAN. (*pushing*) Well, I recognise you.

DOTHERIGHT. Oh dear me, dear me. To arms! To arms!

(*The* POLICEMAN *slowly pushes the door in and pulls him out by the collar.*)

POLICEMAN. Come on, now. No more trouble out of you!

DOTHERIGHT. (*as he is dragged out*) What? Am I alone? Is it only a One-Man Rebellion?

(*He ceases to resist.*)

POLICEMAN. Are you coming quietly, or shall I call the van?

DOTHERIGHT. No, sir. It is unnecessary to call the van. I surrender. But only to superior force, you understand. (*He hands over his flag.*) You will note, my dear sir, that there are no signs of alcohol upon our person. Report us and our cause aright to the unsatisfied. Now, officer, you may conduct the Republic to the Bridewell.

(*He breathes on the* POLICEMAN *as the* PHOTOGRAPHER, *at last ready, dashes forward to get the final shot, tripping over*

228

CHAPLAIN *and the Radio on the way. As he falls flat on his face the flash bulb goes off, and the overturned Radio breaks forth again into the brassy strains of "Parsifal".* DOTHERIGHT *stalks off with the* POLICEMAN.)

CURTAIN

SCENE FOUR

ANTEROOM OF CENTRAL CRIMINAL COURT

There is a Telephone Box in which PADDY *stands. Beyond this is a bench on which sit* PENNIWISE, MRS TYLER, HOOLEY *and* MRS VANDERBILT – *in that order.*

PADDY. (*looking out of the booth*) When do they reach this damn case?

PENNIWISE. The man said, any time now.

MRS TYLER. Is there still no word that I can go?

PENNIWISE. Mr Phibbs is doing the best he can.

PADDY. (*into the phone*) Any time now. (*He comes out.*) Oh cheer up, Mrs Tyler. You're not being charged with anything – so far.

MRS TYLER. Then why did he take my name?

PADDY. Just as a witness. An important one.

MRS TYLER. I was asked to take part in a broadcast. That was all. Is that an offence in this country? If so my husband, the Senator will have something to say about it.

PENNIWISE. They just want to find out what happened and why.

HOOLEY. We all know what happened but nobody knows why.

(*Pause.*)

HOOLEY. We shouldn't have been caught running away. That's the trouble.

PADDY. Certainly not in that cab. They wouldn't catch *me* doing that.

PENNIWISE. (*irritated*) Look – we've been over all of this already. Let's wait and see what we're asked, and answer as truthfully as possible. The only question that matters will be one of damages. Who broke the glass in that door?

HOOLEY. We all know who did that.

MRS TYLER. Well it wasn't me. And if I'm expected to pay I don't mind saying that there will be questions asked in the American Senate.

PADDY. There'll be questions asked there any way. Who was preaching Rebellion – eh?
(*An uncomfortable pause.*)
HOOLEY. "Mr Dotheright has no money". I seem to have heard that somewhere.
PADDY. In fact, the whole thing was just a dreary little brawl that none of us knows anything about. (*He sighs.*) Oh dear! And I quite enjoyed it at the time.
PENNIWISE. Then you must be as daft as that lunatic.
(MISS PEERING *is shown in by the* POLICEMAN.)
POLICEMAN. Wait in here, please.
(*He goes. There is an uncomfortable silence as they move politely along to make room for her. But she sits down at the end of the line. Realising that she is next to* MRS VANDERBILT, *she then rises and moves along to the other end beside* PENNIWISE.)
HOOLEY. (*after a cough*) We're all sorry, Mum, for what happened last night.
PADDY. Everybody was acting from the highest possible motives.
MISS PEERING. Indeed! I suppose that's why five pounds worth of tenpenny stamps are missing from my till.
MRS TYLER. We never heard about that!
MISS PEERING. (*with added indignation*) Not to speak of two antique china dogs that I can't find anywhere.
PENNIWISE. Believe me, Isa, none of us here knows anything at all about that. We can vouch for everybody, that is . . .
(*He coughs.*)
(*All eyes turn slowly on* MRS VANDERBILT, *who remains blandly composed.*)
MISS PEERING. Is that so?
PENNIWISE. Isa – we're sorry. We had no idea there was going to be anything in the way of – um – larceny.
MISS PEERING. (*a little coyly*) It's a long time since I've seen you, Angus.
PENNIWISE. Yes, Isa. A long time.
MRS TYLER. If there's anything that Mr Penniwise can do, Miss Peering, he'll only be too anxious. Won't you, Mr Penniwise?
HOOLEY. For the sake of ole lang sang.
PENNIWISE. Well – er – of course – mm!
(LETTY *enters briskly with* CHAPLAIN. *He has a black eye.*)
LETTY. Well, thank goodness we've been able to fix that.

PENNIWISE. What have you been able to fix?

MRS TYLER. Are they letting us all go now?

LETTY. Not just yet. But the case is going to be taken by Judge Bland instead of that awful old sour-puss who usually sits in the Police Court.

HOOLEY. Judge Bland. Who's he?

CHAPLAIN. Oh, a very reasonable man. We're lucky to have him. If anybody understands the situation Bland will.

LETTY. Yes, that's what everybody says. If we can arrange amongst ourselves that the damage will be paid for, Judge Bland isn't the kind of person to be hard on the – er, Professor.

PENNIWISE. Hard on him! *We're* the ones to be worried about. Not him.

CHAPLAIN. The Judge is going to see us all in a few minutes. So be ready to come along when I call.

LOWD. (*Entering*) So here you all are – my friends, family and helpmeets! I've been wanting to meet you all ever since I heard that broadcast. One of the most remarkable I've ever listened to. Congratulations, Wystan. Best thing since, "The Fleet's Lit Up".

CHAPLAIN. There are times when I distinctly dislike you. (*He hurries off.*)

MRS TYLER. Mr Lowd, this is no time for flippancy.

LOWD. Don't worry, Mrs Tyler. I'm arranging to do a little personal hunger-strike outside whatever jail they lock you up in. Special comfort facilities have already been laid on. As for you, my friend – (*To Paddy.*)

PADDY. You needn't look at me like that. I'm not being charged. I'm the Press.

LOWD. Not for long, the way you're going.

PADDY. Furthermore, it was I who got your daughter away. Only the people in the cab had their names taken.

LOWD. It was quicker to run, I suppose?

PADDY. Much quicker. But don't bother about them either. Everything is being fixed. Everything except old Dotheright. You'd better see about him yourself; otherwise there's no knowing what he may say about you.

LOWD. You don't have to tell me my business. I know what has to be done. Excuse me.

(*He goes, followed by* MRS VANDERBILT.)

232

LETTY. What do you mean – fix Dotheright?

PADDY. He'll have to be paid what he's owed. And quickly too. Then he can't bring the *Comet* into this mess.

LETTY. But then the whole thing becomes meaningless and absurd.

PADDY. Exactly. As if it wasn't that already.

LETTY. He won't be able to fix Dotheright.

PADDY. Oh yes he will. Maybe it'll cost a little more than the original amount, but he'll be fixed. The *Comet* won't be mentioned.

LETTY. It's not true. The Professor wasn't after money. He was after something far more important.

PADDY. He'll take money just the same.

LETTY. What will you bet?

PADDY. Anything you like, my dear. Against – against a bottle of Irish.

LETTY. It's a bet. Ssssh.

(DOTHERIGHT *enters with the* POLICEMAN.)

POLICEMAN. Wait here. You'll be wanted presently.

LETTY. Good morning, Mr Dotheright.

DOTHERIGHT. (*coldly*) Mr Dotheright regrets that he is not at home.

LETTY. You're not going to give up your Republic, Professor, are you? You still have friends, you know.

DOTHERIGHT. Yes, madam, we still have friends, although I don't see many of them around. I have, for instance, a gallant fighting cock to join my Cabinet. And you have a horse – a horse, if we are not mistaken, called Waterproof.

HOOLEY. Mac.

DOTHERIGHT. An animal of great accomplishments. In the space of a few hours he can effect what it has taken the late Mr Boddy a lifetime of experiment to manufacture. We will appoint him Minister for Transport. The Right Honourable Waterproof.

(PADDY *laughs.*)

PENNIWISE. It's a disgrace for you to be encouraging him.

DOTHERIGHT. Ah, good evening, Miss Peering. Do you know anything about the price of plate glass? I hope that I broke enough to secure a Jury trial.

MISS PEERING. Don't you speak to me, you thief.

DOTHERIGHT. Madam, perjury has not been entirely absent from

233

your own affairs. Neither larceny nor drunkenness had any share in mine.

PENNIWISE. Now, now! You mustn't offend Miss Peering!

DOTHERIGHT. We have noticed that it is usually those who give most offence to others who are the first to be offended themselves. And those whom the world can most easily spare are always the most solicitous about saving their own lives.

MISS PEERING. Angus, I won't stay here and listen to this.

PENNIWISE. Don't pay any attention, Isa. You mustn't take him seriously. Why, he doesn't even understand the laws of economics!

DOTHERIGHT. They say that when Hannibal besieged Casilium, one mouse was sold for two hundred pence, and he that drove the bargain got his price and then died of hunger. He understood the laws of economics, no doubt.

PENNIWISE. Oh, a very high and mighty line. You don't care about money – don't even know what it is, I suppose?

DOTHERIGHT. Yes, sir, I do. It is what we gain on the devil's back and spend under his belly. There are sixty-three ways in which to get it, and a hundred and forty-five ways in which to lose it. If we are covetous we never seem to have it. If we are prodigal we cannot keep it. For it we live in hope of dead men's shoes, damning ourselves to leave our thankless children rich in that which will be worth nothing when to-morrow comes. For it we study to die wealthy rather than to ripen honourably, while all the time honesty is so scarce a commodity that we lay it up carefully to be used only on special occasions.

(LETTY *gives him a round of hand-clapping to which he bows politely.*)

PENNIWISE. Maybe so, but where have your fine ideas led you? What are you now, I'd like to know? An old . . .

LETTY. Oh stop! Please!

DOTHERIGHT. And what are you, who for the sake of this thing, have forgotten how to write your poetry? You are a sorry little lawyer, dancing on a tightrope with a bag of silver in each hand to keep you even for fear of breaking your neck. And under you are lawyers upon lawyers like yourself in their gowns whipped with silk, all staring upwards to see which way the money will fall.

(LETTY *nods approvingly.*)

MISS PEERING. What does he mean, Angus?

PENNIWISE. Och, just a lot of highbrow talk.

DOTHERIGHT. (*reflectively*) What mighty brows we would possess if all men's faults were written on their foreheads.
(*Pause.*)

LETTY. (*quietly*) Now are you answered?
(DOTHERIGHT *crosses and sits down to make a few notes, meanwhile* CHAPLAIN *enters.*)

CHAPLAIN. We've got to go in and see the Judge now, in his Chamber. Not Dotheright – but anybody else who has been called.

MRS TYLER. Now a united front, please everybody. And remember, I have some very important friends elsewhere who had better be kept in mind.

MISS PEERING. Doesn't he want to see me too?

PENNIWISE. Better leave it to me, Isa. You come along and wait outside.

MISS PEERING. I suppose it's the last I'll see of you, Angus?

PENNIWISE. No, no. We've got to have a long talk afterwards.

MISS PEERING. Very well. So long as you remember.
(*As the others go,* LOWD *enters, looking very pleased with himself.*)

LETTY. Don't worry, Professor. It'll be all right.

PADDY. Wait a minute, Letty.

LETTY. What is it?

PADDY. Maybe there'll be some news about our bet. (*To Lowd.*) How about it? Did the old man take his cash?

LOWD. Of course he did.

PADDY. Letty, you've lost. (*To Lowd.*) How much?

LETTY. Oh no!

LOWD. Just a matter of five pounds. No trouble at all.

LETTY. I can't believe it.

PADDY. Make it Bushmills, my dear. And don't worry. You can have a good stiff one out of it, yourself.

LETTY. I don't believe it. I can't believe it!

LOWD. (*crossing to Dotheright with a smile*) Well, my old friend. You're becoming quite an important figure. You'll be having lunch with me, one of these days.

LETTY. If this is true, Paddy, I'll never believe in anything again.

PADDY. Then what a pair we'll be. Oh, cheer up, Letty. I won't be able to enjoy that drink if you don't cheer up.

235

LOWD. We're certainly indebted to you for an exclusive front page story.

DOTHERIGHT. That isn't the only debt you owe me.

LOWD. What's this? Haven't you got it yet?

DOTHERIGHT. Got what?

LOWD. Why, the money of course. I gave it to your wife not five minutes ago!

DOTHERIGHT. You are under some delusion, sir. I have no wife.

LETTY. Oh!

LOWD. No wife – But that queer old lady who goes around with you. I met her in the corridor, and she said she was your wife.

DOTHERIGHT. I have no wife.

LETTY. Paddy, he never took it!

LOWD. But she promised me she'd fix everything with you – said I could leave the cash with her.

DOTHERIGHT. (*after shaking his head*) We have nothing to do with any such transaction.

PADDY. Better try him again – quick.

LOWD. The Confidence Trick! And pulled on me! (*Pulling money from his pocket*) Here, my dear fellow, you must take it now.

LETTY. Careful, Professor.

PADDY. Shut up, Letty. You're trying to foul up our bet.

(DOTHERIGHT *takes the proffered notes, glances at them and hands them back.*)

LOWD. What's this?

DOTHERIGHT. Pieces of paper.

LOWD. (*hardening*) Ah! Not enough, eh? Going to get tough with me. Well, I suppose you're entitled to . . . this once. Well, would an even tenner square us up and leave us friends?

DOTHERIGHT. It would not, sir.

PADDY. Try more.

LETTY. Ssssh!

LOWD. Well, how about fifteen pounds? Not a penny more!

DOTHERIGHT. The correct amount was three pounds and fifty pence plus tax. But I am not interested in that any longer.

LOWD. Look here. Suppose we put it this way. Here I'm giving you three pounds and fifty pee. And I'm also giving you fourteen pounds and whatever-it-is just for yourself.

LETTY. Twelve pounds and fifty pee.

LOWD. O.K. Whatever you say. I'm giving you all that along with it. Understand it now?

DOTHERIGHT. Why?

LOWD. Why what?

DOTHERIGHT. Why are you giving us all this along with it?

LOWD. Why because I like you, Alaphonsius. Because I want to make sure you get a good solicitor.

DOTHERIGHT. Mr Hy –?

LOWD. No, not Hynie Phibbs if you don't want him. You can spend it on Portland Cement for all I care.

DOTHERIGHT. (*thinks for a moment*) Portland Cement. I still see no reason why you should give thirteen pounds and whatever it is for nothing.

LETTY. Twelve pounds and fifty pee.

LOWD. (*shouting*) Never mind the exact amount! I'm getting sick of offering you jobs and money, and having them thrown back in my face. What's the game?

PADDY. Quite simple, boss. He's a sorehead and he wants to have a grievance. If you pay him off he won't have it any longer.

LOWD. Ah!

DOTHERIGHT. That is quite untrue. In proof of which, I shall accept what I am legitimately owed. My One-Man Rebellion does not require a personal grievance to justify it.

LOWD. Here, let's stop this gab. I've got twenty pounds here. But that's the outside limit. Will you take that and shut up about the *Comet* owing you money?

DOTHERIGHT. I will not take twenty pounds or a hundred or a thousand pounds. I will take three pounds and fifty pence and not a penny more or less. – Plus tax.

LETTY. Good for you, Prof.!

DOTHERIGHT. Do not think, sir, because the world is full of money-grubbers who will take anything they can lay their hands on that you can stifle my protest by a larger sum any more readily than by a lesser.

LOWD. (*fumbling in his pockets*) Suffering cheese, what is this? Three pounds, and twenty – thirty – forty – four pounds. Here!

DOTHERIGHT. (*looking at it*) I will not take four pounds.

LOWD. Well, give me change.

DOTHERIGHT. I have no change.

LOWD. Holy smoke, has anybody got change of a pound?

DOTHERIGHT. Why cannot people understand that what I have done is not for purely personal reasons. It is for humanity – and in obedience to my voices.

LOWD. Your what?

DOTHERIGHT. It would be quite impossible to explain such a matter to you without losing my temper. So if you will excuse me I will go and sit down quietly in the next room.

LOWD. Hey, you can't go now. I want to get this fixed up. Wait till I get some change.

DOTHERIGHT. Excuse me please. I have much of real importance to keep in mind. I have shortly to plead my defence at the bar of Society, and then go to jail to prove my point. However, I shall no doubt see you in jail sooner or later. Come and talk to me there, if talking is permitted. Good afternoon.

(He goes off.)

LOWD. What are you sniggering at?

LETTY. Excuse me, father. I think I'll have to go and sit down quietly, too.

(She goes out swiftly after DOTHERIGHT, *as a quiet, soft-spoken man with a thin moustache and an unruffled but sceptical manner approaches* LOWD. *He is a plain-clothes man, but not one of the old stage type, in a bowler hat. He is one of the smoother products, and all the more sinister on that account.)*

LOWD. I've made him the offer before witnesses. That puts me in the clear.

(The telephone rings.)

PADDY. That'll be the news room again.

LOWD. Keep them posted.

*(*PADDY *goes into the telephone box and closes the door as he talks into the phone. But soon he is watching* LOWD.)*

MAN. Excuse me, sir. Are you Mr Lowd?

LOWD. Yes, my man.

MAN. Might I have a word with you? *(He produces an identity card.)*

LOWD. You may have several, if you're not too long about it. *(looks at card.)* Oh! The C.I.D. I didn't know they bothered themselves with Police Court cases.

MAN. Not as a rule, sir. But there's something that puzzles us a little.

LOWD. *(laughing)* I'm not surprised. Mr Dotheright is a tangle of puzzles. Maybe an Alienist would be of more help to you than me.

MAN. Oh, we're not interested in him, sir. But somebody's been looking through his papers and found this.

(*He hands a document to* LOWD.)

Is that your handwriting, sir?

LOWD. Why, yes. (*Pause.*) Yes. It is. (*He hands it back.*)

MAN. This is a draft newspaper report of the death of a Mr Boddy.

LOWD. Ah, yes. I know he was upset over that. It was a silly mistake on the part of somebody in our office. We offered to pay him in full for his work, but he simply wouldn't take the money. Seems to prefer to have a grievance. (*He gives a mirthless laugh.*)

MAN. This report isn't a mistake, sir. Mr Boddy passed away in the West yesterday afternoon.

LOWD. What?

MAN. He's dead.

LOWD. Good Lord. How extraordinary. Poor Boddy. What did he die of?

MAN. We don't know, sir. But it's something we'd like to ask you about.

(PADDY *opens the door slightly and watches through the glass as he telephones.*)

LOWD. Me? Why me?

MAN. This Mr Boddy died yesterday afternoon. But this report of his death appears to have been written by you several days ago. May I ask how you knew he was going to die before it happened?

LOWD. Heavens! You're surely not suggesting that I could have anything to do with his death?

MAN. I'm not suggesting anything, sir. Merely checking up.

LOWD. Well I don't remember anything about it.

MAN. A pity, sir. It's rather important that you should be able to trace the source. Otherwise, I'm afraid . . .

LOWD. Otherwise what?

MAN. Otherwise I'm afraid I shall have to ask you to come along with me to our office, sir.

LOWD. (*getting desperate*) Inspector, I can't possibly come along to your office at the moment. In fact, you've no right to ask me. I've told you all I know about it and you have no right whatever –

MAN. (*interrupting him*) I only asked for your help, sir. Of course you're perfectly within your rights to refuse to give it. Nobody can force you to come to Headquarters without a warrant.

Good morning, sir.

(*He turns to go, but* LOWD *stops him.*)

LOWD. Good God, man, don't take me up like that. You don't have to go and get a warrant.

MAN. I didn't say I was going to do that, sir.

LOWD. No, but I know what you mean. Look, Inspector . . . it's all a little embarrassing, but I see I'd better tell you the truth.

MAN. Yes, sir. Perhaps you had.

LOWD. It really *is* a coincidence, Inspector. I know nothing whatever about Boddy's movements except that he was away on a holiday. It was this that gave me the silly idea of starting a rumour that he was dead. That's literally what happened.

MAN. Indeed!

LOWD. I had no intention of publishing it, of course. But you know, Boddy and I both have – er – had – extensive interests in – er – one or two businesses.

MAN. Chemical manure for instance?

LOWD. Exactly. I'm in that too – although it's not generally known. In fact, I've been recently buying up all the stock I can get. So I thought – you know – er – Boddy being away – er –

MAN. You thought that if a rumour got around the stock exchange that he was dead, you might be able to snatch a block at a bargain price?

LOWD. Well – er – I don't deny that the Market might have been a bit easier. Maybe it wasn't very – er – ethical.

MAN. Maybe not.

LOWD. (*beginning to gabble*) I'm sure you know the Market as well as I do. And after all I did nothing about it and even if I had, that's a very different matter from having him die.

MAN. Of course, sir. In quite a different category.

LOWD. Look here, you do believe me, don't you? You don't suppose I'd invent such a story against myself if it wasn't true?

MAN. I'm sure the Authorities will take that fact into consideration, sir. You'll make a statement of course?

LOWD. Good Heavens, do I have to?

MAN. Yes, sir. There'll have to be a statement. There's rather more in this than Chemical Manure you know.

LOWD. What do you mean? What more is there?

MAN. Well, sir, the Government is very sensitive about anything connected with Nitrates. They make explosives too, you know.

LOWD. Explosives!

MAN. Didn't you know Mr Boddy was in Explosives? I'm afraid
a lot of people will want to know what exactly was behind
his death.

LOWD. God! Take me to the Station at once. I've got to make
a statement about this right away. This can't go any further.

MAN. Very good, sir. I have a car outside.

LOWD. (halting) Not a Black Maria?

MAN. Oh no, sir. Just a taxi. No cause for alarm.

PADDY. (coming out) Boss --

LOWD. You go to the devil.

(As LOWD and the DETECTIVE leave, CHAPLAIN, HOOLEY and
PENNIWISE come in from the other direction.)

CHAPLAIN. Well, thank God that's over.

PADDY. What is?

PENNNIWISE. We're all well out of it.

HOOLEY. A bit of all right, if you ask me.

(LETTY follows.)

LETTY. What's happened?

PENNIWISE. The Judge has had a private talk with us all.

HOOLEY. Very fair.

PENNIWISE. He understood the situation at once when it was
explained to him.

CHAPLAIN. We're all going into Court and he's going to dismiss
the case . . .

PENNIWISE. And any other possible cases.

HOOLEY. And say no more about it.

CHAPLAIN. On terms that the damage is paid for.

LETTY. Oh, thank goodness. They never could have put him in
jail, poor man, could they? That would have been scandalous.

CHAPLAIN. Exactly what the Judge thinks. He seems to be a most
sensible fellow.

PENNIWISE. Mrs Tyler is on her way to the Cunard Line already.

LETTY. Oh, what a relief to know that he won't be locked up.

PENNIWISE. Not in jail, anyhow.

LETTY. What do you mean?

CHAPLAIN. Well, you can scarcely expect them to let him loose,
can you?

HOOLEY. After what he's done?

CHAPLAIN. (defensively) Now listen, my dear, he was really a very reasonable Judge. He doesn't want to punish the old fool if he's not responsible for his actions. And you know quite well that he's not.

LETTY. He is! He is! You've no right to tell the Judge that he's not.

PENNIWISE. What else could we tell him? Do you want to get us all into trouble?

CHAPLAIN. It's awkward enough as it is. And if there's no explanation for what occurred . . .

LETTY. You mean you told the Judge that he was crazy – just to get everybody out of a jam. Is that what you did?

CHAPLAIN. We're trying to do the best for everyone.

PENNIWISE. And he *is* crazy. That's the literal truth.

HOOLEY. As mad as a hatter if you ask me.

LETTY. "Quite a reasonable Judge". And it was I who got the case before him! Oh, what have I done?

CHAPLAIN. There's no other solution. He'll have to go to the . . .
      (DOTHERIGHT enters.)

LETTY. Hush – keep quiet. You mustn't even think of such a thing.

PENNIWISE. Well, somebody's got to tell him.
      (*Pause. The* POLICEMAN *enters.*)

POLICEMAN. Come on, now. The Court is sitting.

CHAPLAIN. Just a moment while we explain the situation to Mr Dotheright. Listen, old man. There's not going to be any question of your going to jail.

HOOLEY. You don't have to do a thing like that you know. Not even for us.

DOTHERIGHT. I am not doing it for anybody else. I have a higher command. I am doing it for Heaven – for my voices.

PENNIWISE. Now don't talk rubbish, Dotheright. Really.

CHAPLAIN. We've managed to explain things to the Judge. He's being very sensible.

PENNIWISE. We've got him to agree that you weren't responsible for your actions.

DOTHERIGHT. Not responsible! But surely the question of drink –

PENNIWISE. Oh no. Not drink.

CHAPLAIN. Even if you do have to go to another place, it won't be for long, I'm sure.

DOTHERIGHT. "Other place" – "not responsible". Why, you talk almost as though I was supposed to be ins – (*He bites back the words.*)

242

(*Pause.*)

PENNIWISE. Yes, that's right. So you see there's no question of your going to jail. Isn't that good news?

DOTHERIGHT. Ins-pired? No? Ins-urgent? Eh? Insolent? Insignificant- Insincere? Then – what?

CHAPLAIN. Dotheright. Let's not mince words. You're insane.

DOTHERIGHT. INSANE!

LETTY. Oh, no!

PENNIWISE. It's the only possible defence.

DOTHERIGHT. Insane! You have been talking to him about me? He spoke of insanity and you did not deny it?

CHAPLAIN. Now look here, we're only doing the best we can for you. You ought to be thankful at getting off so lightly.

DOTHERIGHT. You did not deny it!

PENNIWISE. You won't be long in the asylum.

DOTHERIGHT. Asylum!

LETTY. (*in tears*) Oh, Prof! It's all my fault.

DOTHERIGHT. Asylum! My curse upon you all for pleading so well! You called me mad! You cats-pew on the carpet, you itch in the groin! May the wind make bagpipes of your bones.

POLICEMAN. Come on, you can't shout here.

DOTHERIGHT. I am betrayed. Oh Heaven – betrayed!

CHAPLAIN. Now, listen to me, please. Surely you realise that –

LETTY. Yes, yes – we've betrayed you. All of us. We did it, Professor.

DOTHERIGHT. But my voices – my voices? Do they not want my – my services?

(*He grows very calm as he gazes upwards.*) Is there nobody up there?

LETTY. Oh, be angry, Professor. Please be angry. Roar out and curse us all. I tried to interfere, but Paddy's right. Every decent thing you ever do only turns round and kicks you in the pants.

DOTHERIGHT. (*turning to her grimly.*) No, it is not you that has betrayed me, child. Better for Heaven if it were. It is something far more terrible than that. For men and women can forgive each other. But when the Lord himself chooses to mock His servants, who is there to forgive Him?

(*He lowers his eyes and holds out his wrists to the* POLICEMAN.)

Come, my good fellow. Do your duty. Take me to the mad-house.

(*He moves off with the* POLICEMAN.)

CURTAIN

SCENE FIVE

A few weeks later, Mr Dotheright's *residence again, but now the place has an air of not having been lived in for some time. Amongst the cups and saucers on the dresser two china dogs are unobtrusively standing.* Penniwise *and* Miss Peering *are sitting in silence when* Wystan Chaplain *arrives from the street.* Penniwise *is dressed informally.*

CHAPLAIN. Anybody in?

PENNIWISE. Only us.

CHAPLAIN. Oh, Mr Penniwise.

PENNIWISE. You know my fiancée, Miss Peering?

CHAPLAIN. Your fiancée?

MISS PEERING. (*rather archly*) Yes, Angus has persuaded me to marry him. Aren't we a pair of silly old things?

CHAPLAIN. Well, I can't say I'm surprised. My congratulations, both of you. Where's Mrs Golightly? Did she ask you to come here this afternoon?

PENNIWISE. Yes. We both got postcards.

MISS PEERING. Some sort of a party, we imagined.

CHAPLAIN. I wonder where she can be. Well, never mind. We can wait, I suppose. What are you both doing with yourselves these days?

PENNIWISE. Oh just enjoying my retirement. I've left Mr Phibbs, you know, and after we're married I'm going to settle down in the Post Office.

MISS PEERING. And write poetry.

PENNIWISE. (*modestly*) Well, maybe so. Maybe not.

MISS PEERING. I hope you've managed to come through your little bit of trouble, Mr Chaplain?

CHAPLAIN. Kindly don't mention that deplorable affair ever again.

PENNIWISE. Anyhow, you don't seem to have got the push.

CHAPLAIN. Of course I got the push – as you call it. But only for a week or two. It's beyond me!

PENNIWISE. You mean they liked it?

CHAPLAIN. They detested it. They were raging about it. But it seems to have had the best rating for months. There's even been a demand for a Repeat. So now it seems they're having to have me back. I never heard such nonsense!

MISS PEERING. Oh, you must go back, Mr Chaplain. It wasn't your fault, you know.

PENNIWISE. Of course not. You did your best to stop it. All the same I've heard it said that my fiancée was the hit of the evening. And it was her first appearance too – on the Wireless.

CHAPLAIN. And might well have been my last. However – we'll see. Maybe I shall go back if they give me a rise.

MISS PEERING. It's wonderful how nice everybody has been. Quite restores one's faith in human nature, doesn't it.

CHAPLAIN. Not mine, I'm afraid. And here's the cabman. We only needed him.

(HOOLEY *enters, dressed in a magnificent new coat with brass buttons and braid. Also his medal.*)

ALL. Oooh!

HOOLEY. Well? Whatcher think?

CHAPLAIN. Hooley, you look magnificent. Where does it come from?

HOOLEY. Had it specially made. My own design, too.

CHAPLAIN. I'd know that. You must be doing very well.

HOOLEY. As a matter of fact, I am. I've got my pension now.

CHAPLAIN. A good one, I've no doubt?

HOOLEY. Best that's going. And about thirty years of arrears along with it. Don't know how she managed it.

CHAPLAIN. Who?

HOOLEY. That Mrs Tyler and the Old Comrades Association.

CHAPLAIN. Ah, I see. I see. Santa Claus has been at work. Or is it Aunt Sally?

HOOLEY. I haven't got an Aunt Sally.

CHAPLAIN. Oh yes you have, with a finger that's longer than Coincidence.

(*There is a knock at the door.*)

(*He opens the door and* LOWD *enters. He is dressed in golfing clothes.*)

CHAPLAIN. Ah Hello, Lowd.

LOWD. Is something going on over here? I was at the house looking for my daughter, and I noticed you coming in.

CHAPLAIN. Some sort of a reunion, it seems. Letty asked us over.

LOWD. I wonder what she's up to now.

PENNIWISE. Got quite a holiday look, you have.

LOWD. Why wouldn't I? I've got a holiday – a long one.

MISS PEERING. Well, that's nice, isn't it.

LOWD. I'm glad you think so.

CHAPLAIN. Does this mean you've got the sack too?

LOWD. I prefer to say that I've resigned. Matters became a little complicated over at the *Comet*.

MISS PEERING. You mean, because of this scandal over some swindle on The Stock Exchange?

LOWD. We don't have to go into that again. I'm rather tired of the subject. As a matter of fact, a little rest is doing me no harm at all. Getting some golf at last.

CHAPLAIN. Anyhow, you satisfied the Police. That's something to be thankful for.

LOWD. Of course I satisfied the Police. The man died of a chill on the chest. My contribution was just an unfortunate coincidence.

MISS PEERING. (*Intensely*) How do you know it was that, Mr Lowd?

LOWD. What do you mean?

MISS PEERING. How do you know that when you were thinking out that wicked trick, Providence didn't give you foreknowledge of what was going to happen?

PENNIWISE. That's right. People do sometimes have visions, you know.

LOWD. Visions! Do I look like the sort that has visions? (*Pause.*) Yet, you know, it's a funny thing. I used to say that the sign of a good newspaperman is that he can smell news before it happens. Funny if it turned out that I was right.

HOOLEY. Um. There's many a true word spoken by mistake.

(LETTY *enters.*)

LOWD. My God! An original remark from you!

LETTY. Oh hello everybody. I'm so glad you were able to come. And father too! That's nice.

PENNIWISE. Good afternoon, Mrs Golightly.

LOWD. (*grimly*) What's going on?

LETTY. My, but you're looking fine, Lieutenant.

HOOLEY. Glad you like it.

LETTY. I asked you all over to hear the good news. We're getting the Professor out of the looney bin.

(*General sensation.*)

PENNIWISE. What? He's coming out?

HOOLEY. Well, I'll be . . .

LETTY. Yes, isn't it wonderful? Paddy and Mrs Vanderbilt have got him outside in a car. I've been to see the Judge, and he says that if he's got enough to support him, and if two or three respectable people will join in a bond for his good behaviour, he'll allow him to come home.

PENNIWISE. A bond for his good behaviour? And may I ask who's going to give that?

LETTY. I thought we might all like to join in.

HOOLEY. Us?

LOWD. I expected something like this.

LETTY. For the sake of old times. After all, we're his friends, aren't we?

(*Pause.*) Aren't we?

(*There is a pregnant silence.*)

PENNIWISE. Out of the question as far as I'm concerned. I'm getting married to Miss Peering, and that's enough responsibility of my own, without taking on that sort of thing.

MISS PEERING. Yes indeed. I don't see how Mr Dotheright's future behaviour has got anything to do with us.

LETTY. I see. Well – I'm not really surprised. Congratulations anyhow.

PENNIWISE. Thank you.

LETTY. What about you, Wystan?

CHAPLAIN. (*upset*) Me? Look, I've only just got back my job, and I've got my public to think of.

(*Pause.*) Really, Letty, I don't want to seem narrow-minded, but damn it all . . .

LETTY. That's all right, Wystan. You don't have to explain. If you don't want to, you needn't.

HOOLEY. Now there's no use asking me. I'll tell you that straight before you start.

LETTY. Why not?

HOOLEY. Because it's unnatural – see. I risked all for others once, see. And I've had little enough luck ever since. Now you want me to risk it all again. Maybe you'll think I'm mean, and maybe I am. But it's natural to be mean, see and I'm natural.

LETTY. Well that's a better answer. Thank you, Hooley.

PENNIWISE. What right have you to talk to us in that superior way, as if we hadn't got a right to say no. You're the member of the party with no responsibilities. Why don't you give the bond yourself?

LETTY. Of course I shall, if you all feel this way. And so will Paddy. We can't allow him to go on being locked up.

HOOLEY. That would be too bad.

LOWD. (*approaching*) Excuse me, but why can't we allow him to go on being locked up?

LETTY. Oh, father. I was almost forgetting you.

LOWD. You didn't answer Penniwise's question. What right have you got to make everybody feel mean by putting on that tone of voice to three decent, honest men? Why can't we leave him locked up?

LETTY. You'd like to help him, father, wouldn't you?

LOWD. Me? Help that four-footed friend?

LETTY. After all he's done.

LOWD. "Done" is right! He nearly gets us all into jail, loses me my job, plays hell with Chaplain's career, and now you've got the neck to suggest that I go bond for his good behaviour! What do you take me for?

LETTY. Rather a rascal, father. But a nice one.

LOWD. (*not really annoyed*) Rascal! Well I resent that.

LETTY. Haven't you been saying so to the police at the top of your voice for the past month?

LOWD. That was for a very special reason.

LETTY. Of course – to prove that you were just a nice old crook, and not a murderer. And everyone's loved you for it, daddy. We don't care if it gets you the sack. We love you, daddy, far more than we ever did before.

LOWD. (*backing away*) Well, I care about getting the sack. And you needn't think that you're going to kiss me, and then pick my pocket.

LETTY. Oh, come on. You wouldn't miss twenty pounds or so. Just to keep the old man in comfort.

LOWD. I don't give a damn about the old cod's comfort.

MISS PEERING. Really, Mr Lowd!

LOWD. I've got my own comfort to worry about.

249

LETTY. (*following him*) Now, daddy . . .

LOWD. Besides, I'm a crook. You said so yourself, and that lets me out. You don't go round asking crooks for charitable donations.

LETTY. Of course we do. You used to say that they're the ones who like to have their names at the head of the list. Say forty pounds.

LOWD. No, No! I won't! It's absurd – and completely inconsistent.

LETTY. Of course it's inconsistent – just like all that money you spent on bringing up a thankless child. Wasn't that inconsistent? But you did it, daddy, and I don't believe you're even decently ashamed of it.

LOWD. In your case it appealed to my sense of humour.

LETTY. Well, my goodness, what would be funnier than this? Why, it'll tickle you to death afterwards, every time you think of how you've paid him out for his treatment of you. Come on, where's your cheque book?

LOWD. Look here, if I give you forty pounds . . .

LETTY. Make it fifty.

LOWD. (*struggling with his pocket book*) O.K. O.K. But understand this – I will not go bond for his good behaviour. That's flat and final. Will you take it or leave it?

LETTY. I'll take it.

LOWD. (*flinging the money at her*) Then take it, and let me out of this bughouse before I start acting Napoleon.

LETTY. (*taking it*) But you've ben doing that for years, daddy. Still, thanks a lot for the money. You're a better man than . . .

LOWD. Than Gunga Din – don't say it! I know that's the next to come.

LETTY. Now, daddy, don't shout. You'll make him nervous.

(MRS VANDERBILT *and* PADDY *come in, helping* DOTHERIGHT. *An attendant follows.*)

LETTY. Well, Prof. darling, how are you feeling? Put him down in that big chair.

(*They do so.*)

DOTHERIGHT. (*weakly*) I am Mr Dotheright, and I propose to go home.

MRS VANDERBILT. Of course you're going home, love. Who's got the better right?

DOTHERIGHT. You wouldn't say that if you knew who I was.

250

MRS VANDERBILT. Why, who are you, love?

DOTHERIGHT. (*mysteriously*) Mr Dotheright.

PADDY. And don't you forget it!

DOTHERIGHT. (*to Letty*) Why do your eyes glisten so? Am I to give you sixpence for that tear? Well, I shall see what I can do. Bread also is reserved for those who can pay.

MRS VANDERBILT. Lay out on yer wad, and I'll finger a prayer for you in Saint Adam and Eve's.

PADDY. (*as Dotheright shakes his head*) No penny, no Paternoster.

MRS VANDERBILT. Cheer up, my old fireflint. Next week you'll be skipping round like a gamecock without the loss of a feather. (*To Miss Peering.*) I hear tell you're getting married, ma'am. Well, I've got a nice wedding present for you.

MISS PEERING. A wedding present! That's kind of her, Angus.
(*She is presented with the two china dogs.*)

MRS VANDERBILT. In place of the ones you lost.

MISS PEERING. Angus! Look!
(MRS VANDERBILT *trots out as* PENNIWISE *pacifies his indignant fiancée.*)

PENNIWISE. That's all right, my dear. Thank you, Mrs Vanderbilt.

MISS PEERING. But, Angus, they *are* the ones I lost!

PENNIWISE. Now, now, my dear! Let's not have any more scenes. I lost a watch once; but I say nothing.

DOTHERIGHT. Who is that person who breathes so heavily in the corner?

LETTY. That's my father, Mr Lowd.

DOTHERIGHT. Mr Lowd of the *Comet* newspaper?

LOWD. Mr Lowd, late of the *Comet* newspaper.

DOTHERIGHT. Late?

PADDY. He's lost his job, Prof.

DOTHERIGHT. Tt-tt-tt. I am not surprised. I feared he would come to this. But what is he doing here? Does he wish us to believe that he has mended his ways?

LETTY. Yes, Prof. darling. He's turning out to be quite a reformed character.

DOTHERIGHT. Nonsense! Only the pox converts the whoremaster, and then only when it kills him. But ah, poor fellow, I suppose it is the fault of his environment. Let me see now. (*He feels in his pocket.*) Only fifty pee, I fear. Still, it may assist. Here you are, my poor fellow. You have it. Try not to spend it on drink.

(LOWD *stares at him speechlessly while* LETTY *carries the money over.*)

LETTY. There you are, daddy dear.

PADDY. Aren't you going to thank the President?

LOWD. (*after swallowing several times*) Thank you, Mr Dotheright, for all you've done for me.

DOTHERIGHT. You're welcome. And you had better be off. Respectable employment is often hard to find.

(*He closes his eyes.*)

LOWD. (*slowly*) Perhaps I had.

LETTY. Au revoir, daddy. You're very sweet – really.

(*She kisses him swiftly.*)

LOWD. (*after a pause.*) All merciful suffering Providence! Where's the way out? Where's the bloody –

(*He goes, slamming the door.*)

DOTHERIGHT. (*shaking his head*) Tt-tt-tt. Poor fellow. Poor fellow.

LETTY. And now – what about the rest of you? You'd all better go too. He ought to have rest and quiet.

CHAPLAIN. I'm sorry you seem disappointed in us, Letty. But in the circumstances I really can't see . . . (*He dries up.*)

LETTY. Of course, Wystan. You're much too good a man to see anything as difficult as this. Goodbye.

CHAPLAIN. You mean it? Goodbye?

LETTY. Yes, Wystan.

HOOLEY. Come on. The cab's waiting.

(CHAPLAIN, PENNIWISE *and* MISS PEERING *go out.* HOOLEY *pauses in the doorway and comes back.*)

HOOLEY. Maybe there is something I can give the Professor. Here, you can have it.

(*He removes his medal and gives it to* DOTHERIGHT.)

LETTY. Your medal! Not that, Hooley?

HOOLEY. It's better for him to have it. I'll tell you no lie, ma'am. I never occupied any Post Office.

DOTHERIGHT. What's this?

HOOLEY. Mind you, it's not that I didn't want to strike a blow for freedom. I was always one for doing the kind of thing he did. In theory, at least. But – well, you know how it is, when it comes to the point.

LETTY. Oh, Hooley, I know indeed.

HOOLEY. Maybe I will some day yet. And if I ever do he can give it back to me, Eh?

252

DOTHERIGHT. Well, do not geld yourself when the sun is in Scorpio, or your stones may not grow again by the spring – if at all.

LETTY. Thank you for that, Hooley.

HOOLEY. (*suspiciously*) I wonder what he meant by that? Oh well – the old nag's getting restless. Ta-ta so. (*He goes.*)

LETTY. Well, Prof. darling, it seems that all you're left with are the Publicans and Sinners. The happier people seem to have other things to do.

MRS VANDERBILT. (*re-appearing with cups*) Dirty chancers – that's all they are. Now let's have a nice bite of supper.

PADDY. Still no eggs I suppose from that fraudulent bird up there. (*She proceeds to load the table with many delicacies from her shopping-bag.*)

PADDY. Mrs Vanderbilt, I've always admired your work, but this time you seem to have excelled yourself.

MRS VANDERBILT. Ah, times is good for them that knows where to look for it. I have a job now charring for the Parish Priest. Rest easy there while I go and wet the tea.
(*She goes off again to the side.*)

ATTENDANT. Now what about this bond, ma'am? We're supposed to be on our way to the Judge, you know.

LETTY. Yes, I know. We'll come along in a minute.

DOTHERIGHT. (*struggling up*) I must go home now.

LETTY. But you are at home, Professor. Don't you recognise it?

DOTHERIGHT. No, I am not at home. That place where they put me is my home. It is time for me to go back.

LETTY. No, no, it's all right – truly. You don't have to go back there any more.

DOTHERIGHT. My child, nobody wants your bond, I am going back where I belong. I prefer the company there, if you will forgive my saying so.

LETTY. Please don't talk like that, Professor.

DOTHERIGHT. (*sitting again*) Yes, my dear – very good company. And I may add, they all fully recognize my official position. Indeed, you will be interested to hear that one of my closest friends is the Archbishop of Canterbury.

PADDY. You don't say?

DOTHERIGHT. A most intelligent man, although sometimes a little peculiar in his behaviour.

LETTY. Prof. – I don't know how to explain, but –

253

DOTHERIGHT. (*kindly*) You don't have to explain. You don't believe that he really *is* the Archbishop. You think that he is an impostor.

LETTY. (*confused*) Well perhaps – in a way –

DOTHERIGHT. Like the rest of your world, you believe that you can distinguish the real Archbishop from the false one. But it is harder than you think.

PADDY. By God, he's right! We're all impostors. Every one of us.

DOTHERIGHT. Excuse me, my friend is not an impostor, whatever the other gentleman in Canterbury may be. I know this from certain matters he has let slip in the course of our talks. That is why I propose to go back to him. Goodbye.

(*He rises.*)

LETTY. But you mustn't go back – you mustn't! There's no justice in life if you go back there and get locked up for what you've done.

DOTHERIGHT. Justice? Do you suppose that I care about Justice? Am I a Stockjobber or a Bank Official that I should bother my head over the balancing of payments and accounts? I have left all these things behind.

LETTY. You can't leave them behind. Aren't they what you fought for?

DOTHERIGHT. If so, I have learnt better from my new friends. Justice is of little importance when you know that you have been right.

LETTY. But Heavens above –

DOTHERIGHT. (*sharply*) And please do not mention Heaven to me. That is a somewhat delicate subject. I have offered my services to Heaven, and had my proposal ignored. Very well, If Heaven does not choose to pay its debts any more than the *Comet* newspaper, I have nothing more to say. I shall remain where I have been sent.

LETTY. Oh, Paddy!

PADDY. (*after a pause*) Rather a difficult case, eh?

DOTHERIGHT. As for you young people, let me give you a word of advice before I go. You have not been very happy with each other in the past, and that is because you, also, have been concerning yourselves with justice. You want to love each other in return for your virtues – not a very difficult feat, if I may say so. But you should leave that to your Employers, and love each other for your faults. It may be the advice of a lunatic, but you will find it most rewarding.

LETTY. You're not a lunatic, Professor. You're a Saint.

DOTHERIGHT. I have sometimes wondered about that. Indeed, once or twice I have tried to put it to the test by attempting some simple miracle. But never with any success. As a Saint, I am a failure. But as a Madman – ah, there at least, I am in the forefront of the field. So let us all be happy in the facts, whatever, they may be. For to be otherwise is to die twice. Now, fellow, I am ready.

(*He moves towards the door following the Attendant.* PADDY *follows him.*)

PADDY. (*passionately*) Damn you, Dotheright! How can we be happy in the facts if we have pity? Either the facts or pity, I say – but not both.

LETTY. (*surprised*) Paddy, I never heard you use that word before.

DOTHERIGHT. Why not, my friend? Call Heaven's bluff as I do, and give up neither. That's the only way we have to answer back. Try it and see.

PADDY. (*shouting*) O.K. Don Quixote. I'll try it, if you'll go on trying for your miracle. The one's just about as simple as the other.

DOTHERIGHT. Indeed, you quite inspire me.

(*He pauses in the doorway.*)

LETTY. (*to Paddy*) If he ever succeeds, will you pay me that bet you owe me? I think I've decided what I'll have.

(*She approaches* PADDY *in a menacing manner, and he backs his way into the Horse Box. There is a rustle of straw over-head as the* BOY *sticks his head up and looks down.*)

PADDY. Whatever it is, remember there's got to be a miracle first.

(DOTHERIGHT *solemnly makes a sign of benediction from the doorway, at which an indignant clucking arises from the loft, as the* BOY *drops an egg on* PADDY'S *head below, where it gently breaks.*)

PADDY. God dammit! What the hell . . . ?

LETTY. (*overcome with laughter*) Good old Nick, the King of the Goats has turned up trumps!

DOTHERIGHT. A very remarkable bird!

(*He looks at his hands in some surprise, bows politely and follows the Attendant out as* PADDY *wipes his head, and the clock starts to strike.*)

255

BOY. (*with a wave of his hand to the audience*).
That is the end of this play.
Curtain.

1 August, 1978

THE DREAMING DUST

*A Play Designed for Performance or
Public Reading, not necessarily in a Theatre*

PERIOD PIECE

With the exception of *The Moon in the Yellow River* all my plays included in the present collection are in various ways historical. That is to say, their very divergent plots have each got a factual basis. This detail is not offered as an alibi for any difficulties that you may experience in believing in some of them. The fact that it 'actually happened' is more likely to contribute to the badness of a play than to secure its success. Hollywood is often wise to enlarge on nature.

In the case of *The Dreaming Dust*, however, the hurdle that has taken some years of effort to surmount is not that of satisfying the customers in the auditorium with the truth of my tale. It has been the difficulty of ascertaining what the story actually is. For here, a formidable lobby of scholarship, entrenched for over two hundred years behind a barricade of print, insists on giving us, under the guise of biography, a story that is obviously fictitious.

Let me explain my point further. It would be comparatively easy to draw a stage portrait of the Dean of St Patrick's as a scatological problem-child with a hatred of the sex act and an obsession with lavatories, or as a tormentor of women who drove two of them into the grave, or simply as an unusually angry old man. One might also write quite an amusing satire on the subject of this 'heart burning with hatred against the human race' whose mightiest thunderbolt – *Gulliver's Travels* – was neatly caught by mankind, the target, and metamorphosed into a children's book.

Unfortunately the matter does not end here, as there are other characters to be considered as well as Swift, and if we stick honestly to the data in the case of these also, we soon find ourselves struggling in a Bedlam of eccentrics, from which nothing in the nature of an intelligible play could possibly emerge. What, for example, could any practical dramatist make of a heroine, generally supposed to be the hero's wife, but who is never acknowledged as such, and who never openly objects to this anomalous position, a

259

mettlesome and proud young woman who accepts the charity and support of a man whose relationship to her is questionable in the extreme, who acts as his hostess for over twenty-five years, and who never apparently has a show-down with him on the subject of matrimony?

A character in a play has to be explained sooner or later to the player who is expected to portray it, and this is no easy task if his or her behaviour bears no resemblance to any known pattern of human conduct, or even to some convention of the stage. Yet here we have a set of characters actually taken from life, the oddness of whose conduct is inescapable, whatever their real motives may have been.

So it will not be surprising when I say that the composition of this play has cost me more time and trouble than any other play that I have ever written, thanks to the peculiarity of the material. Its evolution from a frolic on the air into a serious attack on over a dozen authoritative biographies has been described already in the preface to an earlier English edition. Meanwhile the rough treatment of my solution – a roughness directed not so much at the solution itself as at my irritating insistence that it is right – has driven me, at last, to ventilate the whole matter in a biography of my own, entitled *In Search of Swift* – an enterprise that is wholly outside my province as a playwright, and ought to have been undertaken by somebody protected by a Ph.D.

In short, a speculative story invented to account for the peculiar behaviour of a given set of stage characters may perhaps turn out to be closer to the truth than was at first supposed. This may be accounted for by the fact that, while biographers can be intimidated by authorities, playwrights are even more intimidated by the need to make sense that can be explained to a cast.

After a moderately eventful life in various other shapes and sizes, and under at least one other title, the play has now assumed a format in which it may be performed with little in the way of alteration, either on a regularly equipped stage, with full orchestra and choral accompaniment, or as a simple reading without props or scenery, or as a radio play.

Theatrically, it has long since ceased to be as much concerned with the personal problems of Swift, as with the seven deadly sins, their relative deadlines, and the curious phenomenon that it is usually our own particular sin that we find really unbearable in other people. It is an exercise for actors and actresses with a flair for character, who seldom get enough opportunity to display their versatility in the course of one play. In spite of the fact that it is written with a particular eye to touring companies, it has until recently been performed more successfully on television than on the stage. What would probably be its ideal presentation – as an Interlude in St Patrick's Cathedral – is something that I am sure I shall never see.

The Dreaming Dust

The original version of *The Dreaming Dust* was first produced at the Gaiety Theatre, Dublin, by Hilton Edwards and Micheál MacLiammóir on 25 March 1940, with the following cast:

Doctor Swift	HILTON EDWARDS
Charles Ford	CHRISTOPHER CASSON
Doctor Berkeley	EMERTON COURT
Brennan	ROY IRVING
Alex McGee	WILFRID BRAMBELL
John Gay	ROY IRVING
Richard Steele	MICHAEL GOLDEN
The Earl of Orrery	CECIL MONSON
Duke of Ormond	EDWARD BYRNE
Mr. Partridge	TYRRELL PINE
Patrick	DERMOT TUOHY
Verger	ART O'MURNAGHAN
Mr. Harley	JOSEPH SLEVIN
Esther Johnson	MERIEL MOORE
Vanessa	CORALIE CARMICHAEL
Martha Dingley	MAY CAREY
Mrs. Vanhomrigh	DOROTHY DAY
Mrs. Masham	TOSKA BISSING
A hag	KATHLEEN MURPHY
Sir Matthew Dudley	WILFRID BRAMBELL
Addison	PATRICK BYRNE
Pope	MAURICE SELWYN
Meghan	H. KILLICK
Dr. Parnell	JAMES DEVOY

Guests, etc.: Messrs. K. HIGGINS, H. RIND, B. DAWSON, S. O'DONNELL. Misses M. KEELEY, D. HIGGINS, L. MAY, M. MCGLYNN, S. TRAVERS, K. O'BRIEN, P. FITZGERALD, E. DEMPSEY.

In its next form, with a cast deliberately limited to eight or ten characters who appear and reappear in various guises, it was produced at the Provincetown Playhouse, Cape Cod, on 19 July 1954, directed by Tom Newton, and with the following cast:

The Dean — Dr. Jonathan Swift (a leading man) EMILE AUTOR
Stella — Moll (a leading woman) VIRGINIA THOMS
Rev. Dr. Tisdall — John Gay (a character man) FRED LEVY
Vanessa — A trollop (an ingenue) ANNE GERETY
Rebecca Dingley — Mrs. Vanhomrigh CATHERINE HUNTINGTON
  (a character woman)
Charles Ford — (a light comedian) ROBERT BEATEY
Dr. Berkeley — A Ballad Singer (a heavy) THOMAS J. CLANCY
Brennan — The Sexton (a clown) PATRICK CLANCY
Two extra Women

CHARACTERS AND SETTING

THE DEAN
PRIDE
ANGER
LUST
AVARICE
GLUTTONY
ENVY
SLOTH
THE SEXTON
TWO WOMEN CARRYING SKULLS

The action of the play opens in St Patrick's Cathedral, Dublin. In time it opens in the year 1835 but then ranges over many years during the first half of the eighteenth century.

While the stage directions here indicate its more elaborate method of presentation, this play is so constructed that it can be performed with a minimum of adaptation and scenery, either in a church, or in a hall equipped with ordinary stage lighting and with facilities for playing recorded music and effects. If an actual choir and organ are available, so much the better. Otherwise the number of recordings used, and the amount of scenery and properties that are employed, depend upon the taste of the producer and the facilities that are to hand.

With some minor cuts and alterations, it can be presented as a broadcast, lasting an hour and a half. If presented as a reading, without cuts or intervals, it should run for about an hour and three-quarters.

THE PLAY

We are in a section of the south-east end of St Patrick's Cathedral, Dublin, looking across the nave. The area in front of us is divided by the central pillar of two Gothic arches, above which hang some tattered flags. Behind these arches is a side aisle, which in turn is backed by the south wall of the church. Through the western arch (stage left) we can see in this wall a large wooden double door which opens on to the street. Behind the eastern arch is a narrow stone opening through which a flight of steps leads up to the vestiaries. In this section of the wall is a niche containing Faulkiner's bust of the cathedral's most celebrated dean, and to the stage left of this are two plaques bearing respectively the epitaphs of Swift and of Stella. Swift's reads:

HIC DEPOSITUM EST CORPUS
IONATHAN SWIFT S.T.D.
HUJUS ECCLESIAE CATHEDRALIS
DECANI,
UBI SAEVA INDIGNATIO
ULTERIUS
COR LACERARE NEQUIT.
ABI VIATOR
ET IMITARE, SI POTERIS,
STRENUUM PRO VIRILI
LIBERTATIS VINDICATOREM.
OBIIT 19 DIE MENSIS OCTOBRIS
A.D. 1745 ANNO AETATIS 78.

Directly in front of the central column a section of the floor has been taken up, leaving a hole. Beside the column, and also against the rear wall, are tables with hymn books and collecting-boxes. To right and left respectively of the open area in the centre are two lines of simple cathedral chairs, all facing stage right.

267

The organ is playing the introductory chorale to Bach's Passion of St John, and presently the choir enters down the steps from the vestiary, processes down centre, turns right and moves off up what is presumably the centre of the church. They are singing the opening chorus of the oratorio. As they go, two women and a man appear from the right, dressed in the fantastic costumes of some miracle play, and wearing masks, which each takes off as they speak. The organ continues softly in the distance.

PRIDE (*a Leading Woman*). Well, our little masque is over. (*Temptingly.*) I thought you were splendid, Anger.

ANGER (*an Ingénue*). Gluttony cut me out of two of my best speeches. Deliberately, I believe.

ENVY (*a Heavy*). There were no good speeches in that deplorable masque. More people should have been consulted about the script.

ANGER. I daresay that you, Envy, would have liked to have written in an extra Sin or two.

(*Two more men enter, also dressed for the performance, removing their masks as they speak.*)

SLOTH (*a Clown, yawning*). Seven sins are deadly enough for me. Well, now that we've finished our play-acting, perhaps we can all get home to bed.

GLUTTONY (*a Character Man*). Not before the party, Sloth. Isn't there going to be some sort of a party? I mean – after all the work we've had in staging this thing.

(*Another* MAN AND WOMAN PLAYER *follow, unmasking as before. Meanwhile* TWO WOMEN *have entered from the street door, each bearing a round object, wrapped in a cloth. One is a middle-aged woman. The other is a girl. They look around them, and are arrested by Swift's epitaph.*)

AVARICE (*a Character Woman*). A party? Is that all we're going to be given? I would much rather have my expenses.

SLOTH. Avarice has got her eye on the poor box. Better look out!

AVARICE. Don't be ridiculous, Sloth. Still, I do think . . .

LUST (*a Light Comedian*). You look charming, Pride, in that costume. May I help you with it?

PRIDE. No thank you, Lust. I can manage.

A WHISPER. I am that I am.

LUST (*turning*). What did you say?

ENVY. I said nothing.

LUST. I thought I heard a whisper.

PRIDE. So did I.

LUST. Curious. (*Pause.*) Well, let's all go up to the . . .

A VOICE (*with echo, sepulchrally*). I am that I am.

SLOTH. Jaysus! I'm getting out! (*He hurries off.*)
(*The organ stops, and for a moment there is silence.*)

OLDER WOMAN. 'Saeva Indignatio'. There it is. This must be the place.

YOUNGER WOMAN. What a strange epitaph for a clergyman. What does it mean?

OLDER WOMAN. Don't ask me that. Nobody could understand such Latin. '*Virili.*'
(*She points at the plaque. The remaining* MASQUERS *have paused in their disrobing and have turned to the newcomers.*)

ENVY. That is Doctor Swift's epitaph, ma'am. It was you who spoke?

YOUNGER WOMAN. We're looking for his grave.

ENVY. He wrote that epitaph himself.

OLDER WOMAN. Then his Latin was more enigmatic than his English. Where are they laying down the floor?

GLUTTONY. Over here, madam. I'm afraid that you are late for our performance.

OLDER WOMAN. What performance?

GLUTTONY. 'The Masque of the Seven Deadly Sins'.

ENVY. They hope to make it an annual event.

ANGER. Not with me! I've had enough for two years.

AVARICE. What have you got there . . . in that bundle?
(*The* OLDER WOMAN *is removing the wrapping, and there is a gasp of disgust as she exposes a skull.*)

A VOICE (*louder still*). Let the day perish wherein I was born.
(*The* SINS *react more or less in unison.* PRIDE *turns away in silent distaste.*)

AVARICE. Oh, take it away!

ANGER. It's revolting.

LUST. A skull! Where did you get that thing?

ENVY. That voice again! Who is talking?

GLUTTONY. What a disgusting object!

OLDER WOMAN. (*Turning the skull around*). Dr Swift in person, I believe. To be returned again to his proper niche. Is this the hole from which they took it? (*She approaches the hole.*)

PRIDE. No wonder the Dean of St Patrick's is turning in his grave.
(*From below, a dull thudding.*)

AVARICE. God preserve us! What's that?

GLUTTONY. Is there somebody down there?

(A dirty head slowly emerges from the hole. It has the face of SLOTH. AVARICE *and* ANGER *scream.)*

GLUTTONY *(making a closer inspection).* It's a Sexton cleaning out the water. Or – can it be one of us?

PRIDE. There's more than a Sexton in this grave.

SLOTH *(assuming the role of the Sexton).* I doubt it, ma'am. There's bones and there's water down here, and what more is a Sexton? What more is yourself, for the matter of that? Bones and water.

LUST *(with a nervous laugh).* Don't be alarmed ladies. It's only our old friend, Sloth, playing a better part than he had in that Masque.

ENVY. Then let him stop playing the fool. They don't pay you, fellow, for alarming the Friends of the Cathedral.

SEXTON. They pay me for digging, sir. Digging out this, and covering up that.

PRIDE. Then cover it up, whatever it is, and let's be off. I never liked this place.

(The Older Woman hands the skull to the Sexton who lays it on the edge of the hole, facing the Audience.)

OLDER WOMAN. They left it for me to bring back to where it belongs.

SEXTON. After passing it all around Dublin, I'll be bound.

OLDER WOMAN. Yes. It was examined by an eminent corps of phrenologists. *(Turning to the others.)* They were repairing the floor here, and somebody noticed the name on the coffin. Everybody was charmed at such a find . . . even if the verdict of the doctors was a little disappointing.

SEXTON. And what was that?

OLDER WOMAN. Anthropoid in shape, is the report. And sadly deficient in the bump of humour.

SEXTON. Bedad that may be. But he's smiling now.

GLUTTONY. That is in bad taste, sir. Swift has nothing to smile at now.

SEXTON. He has his dreams, your honour. Sure they all have them, down there.

ENVY. That's not a smile. Savage indignation is the phrase he coined, himself. About what, who knows?

(There is a pause, and then the YOUNGER WOMAN *uncovers another skull.)*

YOUNGER WOMAN. The report on the lady is much kinder. A charming skull, they say. A model of symmetry and proportion.

270

AVARICE. Oh not another one! I must go.

LUST. Is this Stella?

(PRIDE *turns away, in profound emotion, separating herself from the others. The* OLDER WOMAN *shrugs her shoulders, as if to echo 'Who knows?'*)

LUST. Because if so, we must make sure that they are returned to the same grave.

ENVY. But that would be most improper. Stella was buried below the end of the buttress . . . over there. (*He points left.*)

ANGER. No, no. This is the woman's grave. He was buried further up the nave. (*She points right.*)

LUST. I don't agree. I am quite satisfied that they were buried together.

ANGER. Never! This is not his grave. It is hers.

LUST. After all, weren't they man and wife?

ENVY. Nonsense. They were never that.

AVARICE. Good heavens, what does it matter now? Does decency demand their separation in the earth?

ENVY. It isn't a question of decency. It's a question of fact. They were never married, and were buried ten feet apart.

ANGER. She here . . . he over there.

ENVY. No. Stella lies below the buttress . . . over there.

GLUTTONY. Wherever they lie, it is apart.

LUST. If he never married her, he must have been a monster.

ANGER. If he *did* marry her, he was a monster.

GLUTTONY. In short, he was a monster in any event – a fact that I have always maintained. So put them back anywhere and have done with it.

LUST. He was nothing of the kind. The people who knew him and were his friends insist that he was no monster.

(*There is general outburst of argument, which is topped by an imperious gesture from* PRIDE.)

PRIDE. Oh, why can't you all be silent? Maybe then they could speak for themselves.

AVARICE. Speak for themselves?

PRIDE. Yes. We all heard that voice. Don't you feel that somebody else is here with us? Somebody very close . . . terribly close.

AVARICE (*after a short, pregnant silence*). Please don't say things like that.

THE SEXTON. Better be careful.

THE DEAN (*who has appeared and is listening*). What are you quarrelling about, my friends.

271

SEXTON. 'Tis about the bones of the dead, Mr Dean . . . a couple of old skulls the doctors have been measuring and taping. And now they're fighting over where they should be thrown.

DEAN (*picking up* SWIFT'S *skull*). I see. You should take better care of your charges, Maguire. These things are the bullion of the Church. Who permitted their removal?

ENVY. You hear what the Dean says. Man is endowed with more than bones and water, as this fellow would suggest.

DEAN. How true. How true Sir Envy. He is, for instance, the inheritor of seven of the most mysterious gifts of the spirit, his sins . . . those things that you ladies and gentlemen have been so ably depicting in your masque this evening. He is born with them. He spends his life trying to escape from them. But in the end one of them kills him. This skull is the symbol of that ritual. And now you are all arguing over where it should be laid to rest. But until you know for certain what was the sin that really killed this man, how can you solve the riddle of his life and death and burial?

GLUTTONY (*sententiously*). Indeed, who are we to judge anybody? We are all sinful.

DEAN. A worthy observation, sir. We are all sinful, as you say. But I have never noticed that a knowledge of that fact enables us to understand our neighbours.

GLUTTONY. I wouldn't presume to contradict you, Mr Dean.

DEAN. You are each, I can see, an authority on one of these human frailties. So let me ask you each in turn what was the sin that overcame this soul? Then, perhaps, we may be able to determine whether these poor relics should be laid together or apart. (*Pause.*) No answer. Perhaps you feel that they should tell their own story. They do, you know. Have you never sat below that column in the evening, and felt that some tormented spirit in this place had something that he longed to say? I have.

PRIDE. So have I.

AVARICE. I think . . . we should be going.

DEAN. One moment, madam. Bear with me, please, for just a moment. Under the pavement of this house of God a tragedy is buried that no masque of ours could ever match. If these skulls could speak, they might tell us what it is; but, as you see, they have no lips. But *you* have lips, my friends.

ENVY. What do you mean, sir?

DEAN. The past is closer than we think. Just four or five feet off, below the level of the floor. And closer still, now that this grave is opened. Lend it your lips, my friends, and let its tenants dream aloud. Listen.

A WHISPER. Yahoos! Yahoos!

> (*They shudder, but remain silent. The organ is heard faintly in the distance as the scene begins to dissolve into a room at the deanery. The* DEAN *places the two skulls on the forestage.*)

PRIDE. Are you quite certain, Mr Dean, that you, yourself, will wish to hear this story?

DEAN (*momentarily taken aback*). What makes you ask that?

PRIDE. The dead are seldom as we would wish them to be. And once they start to speak we must listen till the end.

DEAN (*pulling himself together*). We will take our chance of that. So set the chairs and tables as in the deanery. I will assist in the performance, and we will begin a different masque.

> (*The* PLAYERS *move, almost mechanically, to set the scene under his direction.*)

PRIDE. As you wish. But remember . . . to the end, Mr Dean.

DEAN (*to* AVARICE). Come, Madam Avarice, you shall be Mrs Dingley. Sit over there beside the fire and make yourself at home, while Brennan waits on you. (*He gestures to* SLOTH *with a chuckle.*) This will be good casting. (*Then turning to* GLUTTONY *while the* SEXTON *climbs out and covers the hole.*) And you, Gluttony can let us hear the charge that *you* prefer against this savage shade?

GLUTTONY. As I was saying, sir, it was the worst of sins . . . the sin that degrades the flesh to the level of the brute beast. *He* was the Yahoo . . . not man. An animal . . . a vicious pander to his own degraded appetites . . . a dirty, vulgar fellow.

DEAN. In short, the sin you represented in your masque. So come, Mr Tisdall, to the deanery, through the muddy liberties of St Patrick's. The flickering rushlights in the dingy houses. A stormy night, with the tower of the cathedral outlined against the scudding thunderclouds. That was the kind of night for you to call on Dr Swift.

> (AVARICE *and* SLOTH *have assumed the guise of* DINGLEY *and* BRENNAN, *and now take their places in the scene. The* DEAN *assists* GLUTTONY *into the guise of* TISDALL – *an eighteenth-century clergyman. The organ music changes into a roll of thunder, which continues from time to time throughout the following scene. The other characters melt away to the sides of the stage, from which they watch.*)

273

DEAN. Now, Mr Tisdall, it is time for you to bang upon the great brass knocker of the deanery door.

(*The* DEAN *leaves the stage, as* TISDALL *batters an invisible knocker, which nevertheless resounds through the house.* SLOTH, *as* BRENNAN, *comes grumbling downstage to open an imaginary door. The two skulls remain on the forestage.*)

BRENNAN (*taking* TISDALL'S *cloak*). Ttt-ttt-ttt. He doesn't like water on the carpet.

TISDALL. A most unpleasant evening in the street.

BRENNAN. It'll be unpleasanter here when he gets home from the church.

TISDALL. Who is this lady by the fire?

DINGLEY (*stirring in her sleep*). Eh? What?

BRENNAN. That's only Mrs Dingley. Wake up, ma'am. We've got callers.

(*He takes* TISDALL'S *cloak and throws it on the floor in a corner.*)

DINGLEY (*opening her eyes*). Yes? What was that?

TISDALL. My humble apologies, ma'am. My name is Tisdall.

DINGLEY. Why, Mr Tisdall. I remember you.

TISDALL. Your health, I hope is good?

DINGLEY. As good as can be expected.

TISDALL. And Dr Swift?

DINGLEY. He does not see many visitors these days, but I am sure he will be glad to see *you*. Sometimes he is a little odd in his manner, but you musn't mind it. Hush! Here he comes. I always know his footsteps on the stairs.

(*The* DEAN *enters as* SWIFT).

SWIFT. Take my coat, fellow.

BRENNAN. Yes, Mr Dean.

(*He goes away with it.*)

DINGLEY. Jonathan, don't you see who has called? An old friend – the Reverend Mr Tisdall.

SWIFT. Why, so it is, begad! I thought the room seemed more crowded than usual.

TISDALL. Good evening, Mr Dean.

SWIFT. Good evening, Tisdall. What brings you here after all these years?

TISDALL. I have . . . um . . . been persuaded by my curate to ask a small favour of you on his behalf.

SWIFT. Ah!

DINGLEY. I am sure you would like him to stay to supper, Jonathan.

SWIFT. Let him stay if he wishes. We need some parson to drink the foul wine.

TISDALL. Wine? I never touch wine. At least only medicinally.

SWIFT. That is how this will taste.

TISDALL. I hope I was not mistaken in coming.

SWIFT. That depends on what it is you want for your curate.

TISDALL. My young friend is aspiring to climb the heights of Parnassus.

SWIFT. The heights of where?

TISDALL. He hopes some day to be considered, like yourself, as an author.

SWIFT. Like my friend Mr Congreve, I do not desire to be considered as an author, but as a gentleman. However, if you have brought some of his bum fodder for me to read I shall look it over after the meat. Meanwhile...

TISDALL. Sir, I have not brought any of his work.

SWIFT. Indeed? It might have proved an alternative to conversation.

TISDALL (*getting indignant*). You have always treated me with a certain strain of contempt. But...

SWIFT. Nonsense, Tisdall. You have misunderstood me. I never had any contempt for you.

TISDALL (*mollified*). Ah.

SWIFT. That is why I never troubled to make a bishop of you.

TISDALL (*indignantly*). To make a bishop of *me*. Let me tell you, sir...

(*Raised voices are heard outside.*)

SWIFT. What is all this noise outside in the street?

BRENNAN. Only a couple of beggers was asking after you at the door. I gave them the push.

SWIFT. Indeed! And since when have I given you permission to select my guests?

BRENNAN. Guests? Sure amn't I after telling you, 'tis only...

SWIFT. Go down at once and invite them in.

BRENNAN. Invite them in? An old trollop and a poxy ballad singer?

SWIFT. Both of them, sirrah – unless you wish to join them in the rain.

(BRENNAN *goes off grumbling.*)

DINGLEY. Jonathan, what is this latest nonsense?

SWIFT. Our traditional Irish hospitality, my dear Dingley. Tonight we keep open house. Can I receive one guest and turn away

275

another? Besides, my old friend must meet some of his successors in my affections.

DINGLEY. Inviting in all the rascality of the town. It's scandalous. But there's no use saying anything, I know.

(*A tittering* TROLLOP *appears – played by* ANGER – *and a* BALLAD SINGER *played by* ENVY.)

BRENNAN. Here's your fancy friends. And don't say you didn't send for them yourself, because the company heard you.

SWIFT. Ah, my dear friends. Welcome to the deanery.

(*They titter.*)

SWIFT. Tisdall, I want you to meet my sweetheart.

TROLLOP. God bless you, Mr Dean.

SWIFT. This is Pullagowna, one time my cook until she trapped this poor rogue into matrimony.

TROLLOP. I'm your bully woman, Mr Dean.

BALLAD SINGER. As cushy a mott as ever rattled a gut board on the flags.

SWIFT. A cunning trull for she takes in English, and she pays in French. How is your rascally spouse?

BALLAD SINGER. Poorly, your honour. Very poorly.

TROLLOP. We were thinking that maybe your honour . . .

SWIFT. Then let us hope this sickness will prove a blessing in disguise, and permit the hangman to devote himself to more profitable employments.

(*Raucous laughter.*)

SWIFT. But something tells me that there is a purpose in this visit. What do you want, my friends? A prayer, no doubt. Well, let us all kneel down together.

(*He proceeds to do so.*)

BALLAD SINGER. A prayer!

TROLLOP. What use is Protestant praying?

BALLAD SINGER. The weather's cold, but charity's colder.

TROLLOP. Sure, the Dane knows well what we're after. A few odd coppers, sir.

SWIFT (*rising*). Ah! You will have noted, Tisdall, the wisdom of my sweetheart. She does not look for pity or for pious edification. All that she wants is money, because she knows that without money she may be a pretty but never a proper woman.

TROLLOP. Them's my very words, Mr Dane.

SWIFT. But, madam, have you considered? If I give you money you will become like my poor friend here. (*Indicates* TISDALL.) He cannot sleep out under the hedges as you do, without the fear of having his pockets picked.

TROLLOP. Ah, go on owa that. As if we'd keep it overnight. (*Laughter.*)

SWIFT. An excellent answer, Pullagowna. You are not usurers to store it in your hose. With money well spent, barbarians are tamed and faithful friends are purchased every day.

(*He collects from* TISDALL, *and pours out the contents of his own purse.*)

SWIFT. Come, Dingley.

DINGLEY. Certainly not. These are most undeserving cases.

SWIFT. The more undeserving the greater the charity.

'Where is the man who can this truth deny,
A fishwife hath a fate, and so have I.'

DINGLEY. You can't change the habits of these people either by kindness or by persuasion?

SWIFT. No, Dingley. And even if I did, what would they get for the exchange?

TROLLOP. God will reward you, Mr Dane. For there's little enough we can give you in return.

SWIFT. You can leave me your pitch in Golden Lane.

TROLLOP. I will indeed, your honour. 'Twill be there in my will, settled and sealed by the scrivening bar attorneys.

SWIFT (*to the* BALLAD SINGER). And *you* can sing me the latest ballad on the Dean of St Patrick's. It is the hour of evensong.

TROLLOP. Go on, you scut. Sing when His Reverence tells you.

BALLAD SINGER (*singing*).

'Look down St Patrick, look, we pray
On thine own church and steeple
Convert thy dean on this great day
Or else God help thy people.

This place he got by wit and rhyme
And many ways most odd.
And might a bishop be in time
Did he believe in God.

But fearful as his wrath appears
We'll pray the Lord above
To still the sounds of women's tears
And save us from his love.'

(SWIFT'S *temper boils over.*)

277

SWIFT. Ungrateful rat. Is this the way you repay me?

BALLAD SINGER. I meant no harm, Mr Dane. I meant no harm.

SWIFT. 'Women's tears.' Out of my house, the pair of you. Out, out this instant.

TROLLOP. Holy Jezebel, he'll have us milled.

SWIFT (*driving them forth screeching*). Filthy, crapulous, cankered, mangy, verminous, off-scourings of the dunghill and the jakes.

TISDALL (*horrified*). Dr Swift.

SWIFT. Out, out to the middens that gave you life. Out, you poxy misbirths.

> (*Their voices die away. Door slam.*)

TISDALL. Dr Swift, Dr Swift.

SWIFT. Well, sir? What is the matter with you, sir?

TISDALL. This language is outrageous in a priest. It was you who ordered him to sing.

SWIFT (*bitterly*). They call me a ribald priest, an apostate politician and a perjured lover – a heart burning with hatred against the human race. Tell me, sirrah, is that what you are saying of me?

TISDALL. I do not presume to pass judgment on my fellow-creatures, sir. Anything I say about you keeps strictly to the facts.

SWIFT. What facts, may I ask? The fact, I suppose, that I prevented your marriage to a lady you loved. Eh?

TISDALL. A lady whom you did not condescend to make happy yourself.

DINGLEY. Oh dear, oh dear!

SWIFT (*with icy calm*). So I prevented your marriage! But surely that was a service, my dear Tisdall, to save you from the disappointments of matrimony?

TISDALL. Some consider it a very honourable condition. My curate for instance, who for some reason that eludes me, wishes you to perform the ceremony.

SWIFT. So that is what you're after! I am to play Cupid for your factotum?

TISDALL. An odd way for a clergyman to describe one of his holy offices.

SWIFT. Marriage is an odd condition, my friend. They say, if you want to be blamed you must marry, and if you want to be praised you must die. But never fear, I shall perform the ceremony. Indeed I shall do more. I shall give him a poem for a wedding present. It is called 'Strephen and Chloe' and should be read by every bridegroom. Let me see. Where is it?

(*He opens a drawer and takes out a paper. Dingley begins to get agitated.*)

TISDALL. Dr Swift, if this is one of the poems of which I heard rumours . . .

SWIFT. It is purely instructional, Tisdall, and it may help your young friend. Take these lines, for instance . . .

> 'How great a change! How quickly made!
> They learn to call a spade a spade.
> They soon from all constraints are freed:
> Can see . . .'

(*Dingley rises and starts to search a drawer.*)

TISDALL. Sir, in deference to the presence of one of the gentler sex, I must insist – ahem – on reading this poem by myself.

SWIFT. Do, sir. Take it, and welcome.

TISDALL. There are certain subjects that are not . . . (*He looks at the poem.*) Dr Swift, your work revolts me. Be damned to my cloth, sir, it stinks. *You* stink, sir.

SWIFT. We all stink, Tisdall. It is the fate of the race of man to stink.

TISDALL. No good can come of continuing this visit. It was a mistake from the start. I shall take this poem with me, lest it fall into other hands.

SWIFT. Do, sir. I am sure it will compare favourably with some of the other squibs you keep locked in your drawers for private reading.

(TISDALL *gives a cry of rage.* DINGLEY'S *indignation has been rising. She has now found an envelope.*)

DINGLEY. Jonathan.

SWIFT. Eh?

DINGLEY. Jonathan, I found an envelope today in one of the cupboards. I think it contains something that belongs to you.

(*She gives him the envelope.*)

SWIFT. What's this?

DINGLEY. I have not looked inside. But on the cover is written, 'Only a woman's hair'.

SWIFT (*sobering*). Give it to me. (*He takes it and slams it in a drawer.*) You had no business to pry into my private letters. The visit is over, Tisdall. I hope I shall not look upon your face in this life again.

(SWIFT *goes out, slamming the door.*)

TISDALL. What a foul fellow.

279

(The thunder rolls, and cross-fades into the sound of the organ. The PLAYERS *relax into their original roles.)*

AVARICE. Oh dear! Hardly a fair picture. Swift's real fault was not in that lamentable incident. Mr Tisdall had private reasons for feeling resentful.

LUST *(appearing).* You mean this story about the Dean having prevented his marriage?

AVARICE. Yes, of course. All that Mr Tisdall remembers is a moment in his old age. The Dean was then an embittered man, and used to speak harshly about all the tender emotions. But that was only because he had lost, through his own fault, all chance of experiencing love himself.

LUST. It was Esther Johnson – Stella – of course, whom Mr Tisdall wanted to marry?

AVARICE. Yes, Hetty, Jonathan's ward. The very role for you Pride. Jonathan wanted to marry her himself, you see. And yet he could never bring himself to do so, because of his financial responsibilities. That was his only real fault. He was avaricious in money matters, and in the end this lost for both of them the happiness that they deserved. I have quite a different picture of him from that sour old demon.

LUST. Where would you place the next scene, madam?

AVARICE. In Laracor in the County Meath. Dr Swift was much younger then. A vicar with a country church, planted in a prim Dutch garden. Those were happier days, and he was much more his real self.

(Fade out organ and fade in the occasional twittering of birds. Hold these to background.)

AVARICE. One day Charles Ford came down with news from Dublin. He was the Doctor's closest friend . . . his closest male friend. Such a nice young man – and very popular too. It was a joke of the Doctor's that Charles never got married because he was always in love with somebody else before there was time to put up the banns.

LUST *(as* FORD*) (approaching).* A gross libel, Dingley. I never got married because you ladies were always too busy fussing over Jonathan to listen to my proposals.

DINGLEY. Flatterer!

FORD. Where is Hetty?

DINGLEY. In the garden – talking to Mr Tisdall.

FORD. Ah, I scent a nice bit of scandal here.

(A woman's cry of surprise is heard off.)

DINGLEY. Be quiet, Charles. They're coming.

PRIDE (*as* STELLA) (*approaching with* TISDALL). La, Mr Tisdall. I blush to hear such stories. Where do you learn these things?

TISDALL (*with some relish*). From my choir, Miss Hetty. I listen to their problems from the organ loft.

STELLA. What a world we live in. Why, Don Carlos, what brings you down to Laracor?

FORD. You, dear ladies. You, of course.

DINGLEY. Stuff and nonsense. He has a message for Jonathan from the Archbishop.

STELLA. Mr Tisdall – you know Mr Ford of Wood Park. Mrs Dingley always wrecks his prettiest compliments.

DINGLEY. Only when they are untrue. They want Jonathan to go to London on a political mission. It may mean advancement for him. Think of that, Hetty – advancement.

STELLA (*stiffening*). Indeed? How soon, pray?

FORD. At once.

STELLA. May we expect to lose Presto for some time.

FORD. Who knows? Maybe for months. God knows how long it will take to urge the rights of the Irish clergy upon the Queen.

TISDALL. I am sure that in Dr Swift's capable hands our interests . . .

STELLA. Mr Tisdall, will you and Mr Ford please go and look for the Doctor? I think he is over in the church.

TISDALL. A pleasure to oblige.

FORD (*agitated at such a prospect*). No, no, my dear. I am quite capable of finding Jonathan myself. Please don't interrupt your chat with Mr Tisdall.

STELLA. You will not be interrupting us, dear Carlos. We have finished for the moment and I know that you will enjoy hearing some of Mr Tisdall's views on the problems of his choir.

FORD (*grimly*). You are always so thoughtful for me, my dear Hetty. I must never be left out of anything. Come along, Tisdall. Abominable girl.

TISDALL (*going*). Yes, a delightful girl. What an ornament to any vicarage.

DINGLEY (*as Tisdall and Ford go away*). What *is* that man doing here? On such a day too.

STELLA. Mr Tisdall? He wishes me to marry him.

DINGLEY. To marry him! Oh I wonder what Jonathan will say to this.

STELLA (*sharply*). What has it got to do with Jonathan? Am I his property?

DINGLEY. Now, Hetty, don't get into one of your tantrums. Maybe this is just what is needed.

STELLA. To force Jonathan to ask me himself? I suppose that is what you mean?

DINGLEY. Well, after all, we've been living here in Ireland for more than eight years.

STELLA. Eight years, during which he has never once been with me, except in the presence of a third person.

DINGLEY. Yes, I've noticed that. His discretion is remarkable. Of course he is a clergyman.

STELLA (*indignantly*). And what am I? A trull – that I should compromise his reputation by being found alone with him?

DINGLEY. What a thing to say! I'm sure that's not the reason.

STELLA. Well, whatever the reason is, it doesn't seem to apply to – to other women.

DINGLEY. All I say is that if you don't know his intentions yet, it's high time that you did. And if he's going away to London, it's now or never.

STELLA. I would never condescend to ask him any such question.

DINGLEY. You don't have to ask him. All you have to do is to tell him that you're going to marry Tisdall. And if you won't tell him, I will.

STELLA. Ssssh! He's coming.

DINGLEY. I will not Sssh!

SWIFT (*approaching*). Well, my poppets. Have you heard the news? (SWIFT *is now a man in his early forties, affable and not unkind.*)

DINGLEY. Yes, I suppose you're going?

SWIFT. Of course I shall go. It will be amusing to bait these jacks-in-office.

DINGLEY. Then we must talk over several things before you leave. Come, Hetty. Speak up.

SWIFT. What is the matter with Dingley? I know that look in her eye. It is the eye of a conspirator.

DINGLEY. Never mind *my* eyes, Jonathan Swift. There are others you should be paying attention to.

SWIFT. She reminds me of my late but unlamented guardian, Uncle Godwin Swift – now in Hell.

DINGLEY. In Hell! Indeed, it would be better if you took after that estimable man.

SWIFT. I prefer to believe that I take after my mother – a very genteel lady – one of the Ericks of Leicestershire.

DINGLEY. Ericks of Leicestershire! I happen to know . . .

SWIFT (*with a flash of temper*). Aye, and if any of my poxy Swift relations told you otherwise they lied in their teeth.

DINGLEY. Why Jonathan . . .

SWIFT. A most ancient and respectable connection.

DINGLEY. Why, Jonathan, I was only going to say that Sir William Temple told me his father used to speak very highly of your mother.

SWIFT. That is quite enough on the subject.

(*Uncomfortable pause.*)

STELLA. When do you start for London?

SWIFT. As soon as we have arranged matters with the Archbishop. Charles Ford will come too.

DINGLEY. Mr Tisdall is here.

SWIFT. I know.

DINGLEY. Did you see him?

SWIFT. I had no time for him. What does he want?

STELLA. Now, Dingley!

DINGLEY. No, I will not be silent. He wants to marry Hetty.

SWIFT. The devil he does. Well, I hope you sent him about his business.

DINGLEY. Marriage is not an unnatural state for a woman.

SWIFT. For a woman, perhaps. But for Hetty – scarcely more than a child . . .

DINGLEY. A child . . . fiddlesticks. She's over twenty-six.

SWIFT (*surprised*). Twenty-six . . . Um . . . I suppose she is. Well, tell the fellow he's wasting his time, I wouldn't consider him for a moment.

STELLA. What right have you to talk like that, Jonathan?

SWIFT. Right! I am your guardian – charged with your protection.

STELLA. Jonathan you are not my guardian . . . and you know it.

SWIFT. Sir William Temple on his deathbed . . .

STELLA (*in a challenging tone*). My name is Esther *Johnson*. What has Sir William Temple to do with me?

SWIFT (*after a pause*). But, Hetty, my dear, you are surely not seriously considering Tisdall . . . that . . . that vulgar little . . .

STELLA. Mr Tisdall is not vulgar. He is always correcting vulgarity.

SWIFT. Always collecting it, you mean. His cupboards are stocked with the vulgarities of his parish, laid up in lavender to be brooded on, but never laughed at.

STELLA. He's a very decent man, whose public life is an example to his parish.

283

SWIFT. He is a self-indulgent sepulchre, preaching temperance to his flock, and eating and drinking in the privacy of his closet.

STELLA. What do you know about him?

SWIFT. I know that he's a hypocrite.

STELLA. At any rate, towards me his intentions are unambiguous.

DINGLEY. Which is more than can be said of some.

SWIFT. What do you mean by that?

STELLA. She means . . .

DINGLEY. He knows very well what I mean. We've known each other for twenty years, and we ought to be able to speak plainly. Hetty is a grown woman now, and it is time that she got married. If she is not to marry Mr Tisdall . . .

STELLA. Dingley, I forbid you.

DINGLEY. Very well, I shall say no more. But Jonathan understands.

SWIFT (*dully*). Yes, I understand. I should have foreseen this long ago. You wish to know whether I intend to marry her myself.

DINGLEY. Not an unreasonable question after all these years.

SWIFT. No. I suppose it's not. But, Poppet, these things are some-times not very easy to explain.

STELLA. No explanations are necessary.

SWIFT. I am not the marrying sort, my dear. My circumstances – er – they hardly permit me to support a wife.

DINGLEY. Circumstances – fiddlesticks. You're as well off as any other parson. You're too mean – that's what you are.

STELLA. Don't listen to her Presto. I know the reason, and it is not that.

SWIFT (*startled*). You know the reason? What do you mean?

STELLA. Let's not talk about it any longer. It is entirely my own concern, and I shall marry whom I choose.

SWIFT. Hetty, I insist upon knowing what you meant by what you said.

STELLA. I have nothing more to say.

SWIFT. Hetty, come with me into the orchard. I must speak with you alone.

STELLA. It will make no difference, what you say.

SWIFT. Into the orchard, please, my dear. If I never make any other request, do this for me now.

STELLA. Very well, Presto. If you wish it. But there is nothing more that I want to hear.

SWIFT. We will see. We will see.

DINGLEY. You will see what? What else is there to see, except that we can't go on like this?

SWIFT. No. We can't go on like this.

(*He goes away with* STELLA, *and* AVARICE *reassumes her old role. Fade in organ.*)

AVARICE. But the strange thing is that that is just what they did do. What he said to her we shall never know. But she came back from the orchard with a smile on her calm, proud face, and never mentioned marriage again. No one ever dared to ask them another question. They were the strangest pair of lovers the world has ever known. And believe me, money must have been at the back of it.

LUST. I doubt that, ma'am. Swift loved women more than money. Indeed their company was something that he never could resist. To understand his sin, you must see him in London at the home of Mrs Vanhomrigh, an Irish widow with social ambitions and two lovely daughters. Esther and Moll, one of whom was the real key to his life. (*To* PRIDE.) Come. You must be Moll, my dear. With Gluttony as John Gay.

(*Cross-fade organ to an eighteenth-century string orchestra. The scene assumes the guise of a London drawing-room.* LUST *as* FORD – *is talking with* PRIDE *as* MOLL.)

VOICE (*off*). Sir Richard Steele. The Marquis and Marchioness of Wharton.

FORD. Wonders will never cease, Miss Moll. The Marquis with the Marchioness!

ANGER (*as* VANESSA) (*approaching*). Mr Ford, Where is your parson friend from Ireland?

FORD. Your servant, Miss Essie. I left Dr Swift paying his respects to your mother.

MOLL. A roomful of celebrities to choose from and Essie wants to know, 'Where is Parson Swift'.

VANESSA. Dr Swift has written a book. His conversation is very intellectual.

MOLL. Lord save us. Intellectual! Mr Ford will be wondering what the girls are coming to these days.

VOICE (*off*). Mr Joseph Addison. Mr John Gray.

(GLUTTONY *enters as* GAY.)

GAY. Gay, you fool. Not Gray! Now the imbecile has ruined my entrance. I shall have to make another.

FORD. Come over here, John, and stop playing the fool.

GAY. Charles Ford, the peripatetic Hibernian, on my life! And Miss Essie and Moll. How is your health, miss?

VANESSA. Pretty good, I thank you.

GAY. Pretty and good. There's two very rare things to match together.

VANESSA. You take me up before I am down, sir. Pray, let me rise by myself.

MOLL. Marry, you look as fine as fivepence, but I fear there is more cost than courtesy.

FORD. Moll remarks upon your new clothes, John. You have made an impression after all.

GAY. What? She likes them?

MOLL. Prodigious fine. It is a pity that the worst piece is in the middle.

(*Laughter. The orchestra has stopped.* SWIFT *is tiptoeing by.*)

GAY. Miss Moll, if you cannot be civil to me, I shall take myself home. Ah, here is a kindred spirit masquerading as a clergyman. I shall go and get drunk with him.

VANESSA. Dr Swift, you are not leaving?

SWIFT. Only to another room, miss. Your mother has decreed that one of the ladies is to sing a catch written by a certain Mr Gay. And I cannot abide music, least of all these bawdy ballads.

GAY. B'gad I take offence at that, sir. I am Mr Gay. I must have satisfaction. And do not think that you can shelter behind the breastplate of religion.

SWIFT. Your pardon, sir. Religion is not a breastplate. Religion is a pair of breeches – a necessary covering for nastiness and vice, which nevertheless is easily slipped down for the service of both.

GAY (*amid laughter*). Egad! The parson is a wit. His cloth becomes him as well as a saddle would a sow.

(*Applause off.*)

But listen. They are preparing for the massacre of my offspring. Let us all go and assist at the obsequies. (*Going.*) Come, Charles. Come, Moll.

FORD AND MOLL (*going*). We're coming.

(A WOMAN'S VOICE, *off, commences to sing 'Can love be controlled by advice' from* The Beggar's Opera.)

SWIFT. Now, miss, why do you remain here, when I have insulted all your closest friends?

VANESSA. You have not insulted them, sir. And if you had, it would be no more than they deserve.

SWIFT. You are a woman of discernment, eh? That is very ill done of you.

VANESSA. How is that?

SWIFT. In the economy of nature no woman should be fair as well as wise. How comes it you are not married, miss?

VANESSA. Maybe I shall be, one of these odd-come-shortlies.

SWIFT. And which of the sparks do you fancy?

VANESSA. An' I wed, it will be none of these fly-by-nights, be they ever so witty or so wealthy.

SWIFT. What do you look for in a husband?

VANESSA. I would have a man of genius.

SWIFT. Ah-ha!

VANESSA. Can you find one for me, Dr Swift?

SWIFT. A man of genius, eh? But that is not always a good thing for a young girl.

VANESSA. Why not, sir?

SWIFT. Because your man of genius is not always a man of character. To match happily with a man of genius is as rare as a widow of fifteen or a maid of five-and-twenty. You must walk warily, Miss Vanhomrigh, if that is your intention.

VANESSA. Mercy! You frighten me, Dr Swift. I shall need a friend to give me counsel.

SWIFT. True indeed. Perhaps you have some grave and suitable person in mind?

VANESSA. No indeed. Unless Dr Swift would condescend?

(*The singing is over. There is a patter of applause off.*)

SWIFT (*flattered*). My child, why do you waste your time on me when you have a roomful of wealth and influence next door? I am a poor parson, and have little to offer you, except my conversation.

VANESSA. You have always interested me. You don't seem to mind what the world says of you. You are not like the others – chasing the favour of the Ministers. You are a man of affairs, yet you have chosen Mr Harley as your friend – a mere nobody in the Commons – and you are seen about with Mrs Masham, who is little better than a waiting-maid to the Queen.

SWIFT. My dear young lady, my philosophy is to do what is right and be damned what the world says.

VANESSA. But how can I know what is right? That is what I wish to learn from my tutor. Will you accept the office, sir?

SWIFT. And the fee?

VANESSA. The fee . . . the fee, like the money in poets' pockets, will be invisible.

SWIFT. You are a diverting minx, and will meet with trouble if you are not protected. So if you wish it, you shall have your way.

287

When will we commence the first lesson?

VANESSA. Now, sir. At once.

SWIFT. Now? Here?

VANESSA. Last night I prayed for guidance. Prove to me now that prayer is always answered.

SWIFT. Then when you pray next, pray that you may serve Heaven – not that Heaven may serve you. If you would be my pupil you must learn neither to be a scold, a whore, nor a slut. And, mark you well, the worst of the three is the slut. Remember that however the world goes, a great torch may be lighted at a tiny candle, and a tinker may bring the plague into a city as readily as any member of the House of Peers.

VANESSA. Yes, yes! Go on.

SWIFT. As for ourselves, we cannot be people of consequence unless we have a sound body and live without care. So eat your best plums first and let the rest mend.

VANESSA (*joyfully*). Oh, what drolleries there are upon the earth. We shall laugh at them together, shall we not?

SWIFT. Yes, Miss Essie. We shall laugh at them together – you and I. Laughter is the best fee for your instruction.

VANESSA. Oh, the fee. We were forgetting the fee. What does my tutor need?

SWIFT. I have made it an inflexible rule – a rule I recommend to my pupil – never to require anything of any man.

VANESSA. Nor woman either?

SWIFT. Nor woman either. So set your mind at rest about the fee. No woman has anything to give me.

VANESSA. Not even this?

> (*She kisses him impulsively.* FORD *has reappeared and sees this.*)

FORD. That was a hazardous kiss, young lady.

> (*Swift's embarrassment suddenly turns to anger.*)

SWIFT (*furious*). Charles. What are you doing here?

VANESSA. Forgive me, Dr Swift. Please say that you forgive me.

SWIFT. The lesson is over.

FORD. The first lesson.

SWIFT. I asked you what you are doing here?

FORD. A messenger has arrived from Whitehall. The Lord Treasurer wishes to see you, Jonathan.

SWIFT (*surprised*). Godolphin. To see me?

FORD. Godolphin is no longer Lord Treasurer. The Whigs have fallen, and your good friend Mr Harley is in office. You had better go at once, Jonathan. (*Pause while* SWIFT *stares at* VANESSA.)

SWIFT. Forgive me, Miss Essie, if I go across to Whitehall.

(*Triumphant music from the orchestra.* SWIFT *stalks out, pausing for a moment beside her, for a moment it looks as if he might strike her, but as she cowers away, he relaxes slowly and then he gravely kisses her hand before leaving.*)

LUST. From that moment the vicar of Laracor became one of the most powerful men in England.

(*Fade out music: exeunt. Interval, after which* LUST *enters followed by* DR BERKELEY *and* GAY.)

LUST. You agree with me – er – oh, Dr Berkeley? You consider that I have described the position fairly.

BERKELEY. The British Constitution is a remarkable phenomenon, Mr Ford. I find no mention in it of the vicar of Laracor, yet the pivotal position of Dr Swift cannot be denied.

(AVARICE *enters as* MRS VANHOMRIGH, *followed by* SWIFT, VANESSA *and* MOLL, *played as before.*)

MRS VANHOMRIGH. Ah, gentlemen. I have just been congratulating Dr Swift upon his new deanery of St Patrick's.

SWIFT. Mrs Vanhomrigh is very condescending.

MRS VANHOMRIGH. They say it is a very excellent and profitable appointment.

SWIFT. They are misinformed, madam. I shall be the poorest gentleman in Ireland that eats upon gold plate, and the richest that lives without a coach.

MRS VANHOMRIGH. Still, Mr Dean, we all know that the air of Ireland is very excellent and healthy.

SWIFT. Then, for God's sake, madam, do not mention it here, for if you do they will assuredly tax it. Ah, Dr Berkeley, your servant. I understand that you are looking for a patron for your West Indian project?

BERKELEY. Indeed I had hoped to discuss the matter with you, Mr Dean.

SWIFT. Well, let me see now. Perhaps you will allow me to present Mr Gay.

BERKELEY. I have already met Mr Gay.

SWIFT. So much the better. Dr Berkeley is a philosopher. And do I hear you ask, what is the basis of his philosophy? Well, I shall tell you. He has satisfied himself, for all his imposing bulk, that matter does not exist at all.

BERKELEY. That is scarcely a correct analysis of . . .

SWIFT. He has also a project for a college in the West Indies, dedicated to the washing of Ethiopians – a college where sunbeams shall be extracted from cucumbers, and the natives will be instructed in the art of milking he-goats with a sieve. And you, my friend, I have selected as a proper person to assist in the furtherance of this excellent scheme.

GAY. Me?

SWIFT. Now do not be modest in your demands, Dr Berkeley. Mr Gay has a considerable fortune from his theatrical ventures, and you must not believe him if he tells you otherwise.

GAY. I thank you, for your good opinion of me, Mr Dean. But I really cannot see why I should be selected to assist Dr Berkeley.

SWIFT. Because, my friend, the Scriptures tell us that charity covereth a multitude of sins. Mr Gay is at your service, Dr Berkeley.

BERKELEY. Oh, thank you, Mr Gay. Your patronage is just what we need. But perhaps I may be permitted to correct some of the impressions about my college that Dr Swift may have –

(GAY *ad libs off, protesting, followed by* BERKELEY, *still talking.*)

MRS VANHOMRIGH. How is your chest, Moll? Are you properly wrapped up?

MOLL. Thank you. It is no worse, Mama.

MRS VANHOMRIGH. It is time for you to rest. Perhaps Mr Ford will be so kind as to assist you up the stairs. Not you, Essie. You must stay and entertain the Dean.

FORD. Your servant, ma'am.

MRS VANHOMRIGH. Then come along. Come along.

(*She hustles* FORD *and* MOLL *off, looking back significantly at* VANESSA.)

VANESSA (*laughing*). My dear tutor. You are so cruel to these gentlemen of quality.

SWIFT. Yes, Skinage, I treat them like dirt; for when their day comes I know they will treat me likewise.

VANESSA. Oh, what a glorious time we have had. Tell me that you have loved it too – tell me.

SWIFT. Of course I have.

VANESSA. We have found something together that we must never lose.

SWIFT. That is why I have taken some steps to perpetuate it. You see this paper?

VANESSA. Jonathan – when my mother dies, Moll and I will have an estate in Ireland.

SWIFT. Enough of these gloomy thoughts. Don't you wish to see what I have written?

VANESSA. A house at Celbridge, down beside the river.

SWIFT. I wrote it for you when we were at Windsor.

(*The orchestra starts to play in the distance.*)

VANESSA. Oh! A poem. And dedicated to me. 'Cadenus and Vanessa'. What does that mean? Cadenus?

SWIFT. 'Tis a play upon the word decanus – a dean.

VANESSA. And Vanessa. What a pretty name! Is it me?

SWIFT. Of course, my dear.

VANESSA. Cadenus and Vanessa. You and me.

> 'Vanessa not in years a score
> Dreams of a gown of forty-four,
> His conduct might have made him styled
> A father, and the nymph his child.'

Why, it is our history! Oh, read it to me yourself.

SWIFT. Tut. Not here.

VANESSA. But you must. Nobody will disturb us. Come! Governor Huff insists . . .

SWIFT. Well, you are a white witch and I suppose that Governor Huff must have her way. (*He takes back the m/s.*)

> 'Her knowledge with her fancy grew;
> She hourly pressed for something new;
> Ideas came into her mind
> So fast his lessons lagged behind.'

VANESSA (*taking the m/s*).

> 'I know by what you said and writ
> How dangerous things were men of wit.
> You cautioned me against their charms,
> But never gave me equal arms.
> Your lessons found the weakest part;
> Aimed at the head, but reached the heart.'

Oh, it is true, Cadenus. You never gave me equal arms. (*Suddenly afraid.*) Has your poem a happy ending?

SWIFT. That too is a secret. Will you hear it?

> 'But what success Vanessa yet;
> Is to the world a secret met,
> Whether the nymph to please her swain,
> Talks in a high romantic strain,
> Or whether he at last descends

291

> To like with less seraphic ends;
> Or, to compound the business, whether
> They temper love and books together
> Must never to mankind be told,
> Nor shall the conscious muse unfold.'

(*The orchestra concludes.* FORD *reappears.*)

FORD. Charming. A new poem?

SWIFT (*irritably*). You again, Charles!

FORD. Yes, Jonathan, it is I. I have a letter for you from Dublin.

SWIFT. A letter? Give it to me. You may go, child, I shall follow presently.

VANESSA. You will not be long?

SWIFT. Not long.

VANESSA. I trust you, Mr Ford, not to keep him from me for more than five minutes.

FORD. I promise, Miss Essie.

(*She goes away.*)

FORD. What is the news?

SWIFT (*reading the letter*). Little enough. The ladies play at ombre in Donnybrook.

FORD. It is some time now since you wrote to them?

SWIFT (*irritably*). Since I have been in London, I have written nigh on a volume to the ladies. My journal used to go home to them every week.

FORD. But lately?

SWIFT. Lately there has been no news . . . to speak of. (*Pause.*) May I ask what you are hinting at?

FORD. You know quite well what is in my mind. (*Pause.*) This girl, Esther Vanhomrigh, is very young.

SWIFT (*his temper rising*). She is a grown woman and old enough to have a will of her own. I have asked for nothing that she has not freely offered, and I have promised her nothing in return.

FORD. Of course, Jonathan, I know that. But she is very charming and very tender.

SWIFT. There has been little enough of tenderness in my life.

FORD. Jonathan, I don't profess to understand your life, but surely there is tenderness waiting for you if you desire it?

SWIFT. Charles, you have been a good friend to me, but you have one irritating peculiarity. You will allow nobody to talk to a woman except yourself.

FORD (*his voice rising*). I don't deny that you can downface me,

292

Jonathan. But perhaps you will find it harder to answer your conscience if you choose to listen to that.

SWIFT. What do you mean, sir?

FORD. I mean that this girl, Vanhomrigh, loves you. And before long, she will expect you to marry her. Do you intend to marry her?

SWIFT (*furious*). Marry her? (*Pause.*) Marry her! (*Pause.*) Confound you, sir. Can't you mind your own business?

> (*He walks off as a bell starts to toll . . . Hold to background . . .* ANGER *and* PRIDE *reappear.*)

LUST. Deaf, you see . . . deaf to the voice of reason wherever a pretty face was concerned. There was no mystery about his vice. It was a lusty one that might be forgiven in you or me, but was fatal in a man of God.

PRIDE. At any rate he had to listen to that bell – tolling for the death of the Queen, and the ruin of all his friends in office.

LUST. Yes, it was that bell that drove him back to Ireland – back to his new deanery, to hide himself not only from the spite of the Whigs, but also from love. Poor Swift, he might have survived the Whigs, but he could not survive the Vanhomrighs.

ANGER. Survive indeed! Who was it that survived – Swift or the Vanhomrighs?

LUST. Why, madam, you seem angry?

ANGER. I am angry! You know quite well that he didn't escape either from love or the Vanhomrighs by going back to Ireland.

LUST. Too true, I'm afraid. The flesh is very weak and she could never be persuaded to give him up.

ANGER. Persuaded to give *him* up, forsooth – this shrinking violet, who couldn't escape from the advances of a girl in her twenties! If he had wanted to end the situation, all he had to say was 'I am married to Esther Johnson'.

PRIDE. But what if he wasn't married?

ANGER. If he wasn't married, then he was doubly damned. He was torturing two women, instead of one. Anything he suffered he richly deserved.

LUST. I thought you liked the Dean, young lady?

ANGER. Like him? I hate him, and everything about him. He was a bully and a tormentor. It wasn't the weakness of the flesh that troubled him, but anger and resentment against a world he loathed, and a sex he was determined to humiliate. Love was a sentiment quite foreign to his stony heart.

LUST. Oh, ridiculous!

ANGER. It is not ridiculous. How else could he have behaved the way he did towards both of them? A refinement of torture, I tell you, dressed up in guise of affection. It is in Celbridge that you see the real Swift . . . in Celbridge with Vanessa.

(*Fade out bell.* LUST *vanishes as* ANGER *sits at a desk and commences to go through papers, while* PRIDE, *as* MOLL, *reclines in a chair as if mutely awaiting the approach of death.*)

ANGER (*as* VANESSA). Oh, these papers! These awful papers!

MOLL (*very weak and tired*). After all, it is our mother's estate, Essie. Tell them we can't spend all our days in paying off the debts of the dead. Life is short enough as it is.

VANESSA. Was that a horse?

MOLL (*hardly listening*). No, dear Essie. It was not a horse.

VANESSA. I am sorry, Moll. What were you saying?

MOLL. Shall we stop talking business?

VANESSA. No, no. What shall I say to the attorneys?

MOLL (*with a little twisted smile*). Maybe it was a horse.

VANESSA (*eagerly*). A horse. No, you are laughing at me.

MOLL. Will you see him when he comes?

VANESSA. No. I will not see him. I shall send him away. He hasn't written to me for nearly a month. Oh, Moll, why hasn't he written? Do you think that he loves me?

MOLL. Do you care whether he does or not?

VANESSA. No, I don't care. He is a beast. I hate him!

MOLL (*cynically*). Good.

VANESSA. But if he loves me why doesn't he come?

MOLL. And if he does *not* love you why *does* he come?

VANESSA. Yes, he wouldn't come at all if he didn't love me, would he? Would he, Moll?

MOLL. I suppose not.

VANESSA. Oh, if only I *knew*. (*Pause.*) Moll.

MOLL. Yes, Essie.

VANESSA. This other woman. What do you think she is to him?

MOLL (*not really caring*). Why don't you ask him, Essie?

VANESSA. Nothing would induce me to ask him anything about Mrs Johnson. Never, never, never. Unless of course he chooses to tell me himself.

MOLL. Which he ought to have done long ago. (*Rallying.*) Oh, my dear, dear Essie, can't you be sensible and put him from your mind? Let him go. No man is worth all these heartburnings.

VANESSA. Yes, Mollkins, I can . . . I *will* be sensible. I don't care if he never comes again. He has treated me shamefully. I don't ever want to see him again. If he tries to see me I shall . . . listen, was that a horse? Yes. Yes. It is he! Oh, Mollkins, he has come. Perhaps he has been ill.

MOLL (*shaking her head*). Poor Essie. Poor Essie.

VANESSA. He looks pale. He's coming in.

MOLL. Oh, very well, I shall leave you. It's hopeless to reason with you.

VANESSA (*rushing to the mirror*). I shall be wise and sensible. I promise I shan't pester him with any questions. Oh, I'm so happy. Are my eyes red? How is my hair?

MOLL (*going*). Poor Essie. Poor Essie.

(*She goes, as* SWIFT *enters in a dusty riding habit.*)

VANESSA. Cadenus.

(*She rushes to his arms.*)

SWIFT. My dear.

VANESSA. It's been so long. You look tired. Aren't you well?

SWIFT. It's a wearisome journey on horseback at this time of year.

VANESSA. Give me your coat. Sit down, and let me make you comfortable.

SWIFT. Thank you, my dear. There is a quiet in this house – when Governor Huff isn't on the march. (*He sits.*) I like to talk to you and to recall old times. There's little else in this land of slaves to remind me of those days in London.

VANESSA. Yes, yes.

SWIFT. Harley impeached and imprisoned by the Whigs, the other Ministers fled to the Pretender, and I . . . in exile here – hooted at in the streets by the rabble, insulted by every ignorant buck who chooses to do so.

VANESSA. Forget it all for a little while, Cadenus.

SWIFT. Was it to see me in my degradation that you followed me to Ireland?

VANESSA. Cadenus, I had to come. We had nowhere else to go after our mother died. But let me give you a glass of wine after your long ride from Dublin.

SWIFT. Thank you, my dear. It would be very welcome.

VANESSA. This is the claret that Harley used to like. Do you remember those receptions at my mama's?

SWIFT. I do.

VANESSA (*playing the footman*). 'The Marquis and Marchioness of Wharton.' 'Mr John Gray.' 'Mr Joseph Addison.'
'Pray sir, will you dance with me?' (*She hums a tune.*)

295

'Why, Dr Swift, you are very civil to have come to my little reception.'

SWIFT (*amused*). Your servant, madam. And may I ask who you are now?

VANESSA. Don't you recognize the classical profile of my poor mama? 'We all know, Mr Dean, that the air of Ireland is very excellent.' Go on, sir. Answer me.

SWIFT. What did I say then?

VANESSA. You said, 'For God's sake, madam, do not mention it here or they'll certainly tax it.'

(*She shouts with laughter. He smiles wanly.*)

SWIFT. Oh, we had an abundance of wit, and you were very much in my good graces. I wrote a million fine things upon it though I would let nobody read a word of them but myself.

VANESSA. I have here something else that you wrote. Something that nobody has seen but ourselves, though it is the finest poem you have ever penned.

(*She produces a paper.*)

SWIFT. Cadenus and Vanessa. God grant that nobody ever does see it.

(*He reads.*)

> 'Tis an old maxim in the schools,
> That vanity's the food of fools,
> Yet now and then your men of wit
> Will condescend to take a bit.'

That was nearer to the bone than I imagined. 'Vanity's the food of fools.' Yes, I had some genius when I wrote this poem. And what vanity!

VANESSA. Had! I won't allow you to talk so. You still have all your genius.

SWIFT. And all my vanity too?

VANESSA. You will write poems even finer than this one.

SWIFT. I wonder.

VANESSA. Though none of them will mean quite as much to me. This is our own story, Cadenus – our secret – set down in verse. Do you remember Spring Gardens in the summer?

SWIFT. What a foolish thing is time, and how foolish is man who would be as angry if time stopped as if it passed. Poor Vanessa, you could make use of no other black art besides your ink. It is a pity that your eyes aren't black or I would say the same of them. But you're a white witch, and can do no mischief.

(*She starts to weep.*)

296

SWIFT. Why are you weeping?

VANESSA. Do you love me still?

SWIFT. Of course I love you. Nobody in this world loves and values you more than your friend Cadenus.

VANESSA (*agitated*). My friend?

SWIFT. Yes, your friend. That is what I said.

VANESSA (*emotionally*). Cadenus – is that all? Just your friend?

SWIFT. Remember, my dear. You have promised that there shall be no more of those scenes.

VANESSA. I can't help it. I do my best to be calm, but I can't help it.

SWIFT. Then I must go away. (*She pulls him back as he tries to rise.*)

VANESSA. No, no. I can't bear to be neglected by you.

SWIFT. Vanessa, I cannot tolerate these scenes! If you cannot control yourself . . .

VANESSA. I love you. And you say that you love me. Is there somebody else you love more than me?

SWIFT. No, no! What I've told you is the truth.

VANESSA. Then I can't understand. What is it that keeps you from me? Tell me, Cadenus.

SWIFT. I'm going. (*He struggles to his feet.*)

VANESSA. Cadenus! I must know. I can't bear it any longer. What is this Mrs Johnson to you?

SWIFT. Vanessa, I have warned you.

VANESSA. I don't care. I must know.

SWIFT (*his fury rising*). Mrs Johnson is a friend. Do not mention her name.

VANESSA. Why shouldn't I mention her name? Amn't I good enough?

SWIFT. Be silent, I say.

VANESSA. I will not be silent any longer. Who is she that I mayn't mention her name?

SWIFT. I have told you that . . .

VANESSA. Who is she that she should have a paid chaperone, while my reputation can be flung to the winds?

SWIFT. I will not . . .

VANESSA. What is she to you? Is she your wife?

SWIFT (*thundering*). My wife?

VANESSA. Is that why you won't marry me?

SWIFT (*grimly, after a terrible pause*). Goodbye.

VANESSA. Answer me. For God's sake answer me.

SWIFT. You have disobeyed me. I have told you to be silent. Let me go.

VANESSA. Cadenus, answer me. Oh, Cadenus, Cadenus.

SWIFT. Let me go.

(*He goes out, slamming the door.*)

VANESSA. Cadenus – what is she? Oh, God, I'm going mad! I must know. I shall demand to be told. I shall write a letter.

(*She staggers to the desk, and opens a drawer from which she takes a sheet of paper. Mumbling and coughing she writes.*)

To Mrs Esther Johnson, Ormond Quay . . .

(*Organ, as the lights fade. When they rise again she is gone and* ENVY *is talking to* SLOTH.)

ENVY. Personally, I feel that you are all flattering the Dean. He was not a big man at all, even in his vices. Quite petty, in fact. If he had been a bigger man, he would have made better friends, and might have attained the pinnacle of a bishopric. But he was always criticizing and offending his superiors. He was jealous of everyone who was more successful than himself. That was his trouble.

SLOTH. Mind your foot in the dirt.

ENVY (*moving his foot*). Take Dr Berkeley for instance . . . a man whose writings are still highly esteemed by thoughtful people – much more esteemed than anything the Dean ever wrote.

SLOTH. Why don't you slip over to the deanery like a good man, and go on with your talking there?

ENVY. That is just what Dr Berkeley did do, once or twice in the Dean's later years. His experiences were hardly the same as Mr Tisdall's and they throw some light on the point I want to make.

(*Organ out . . . the scene becomes the deanery.*)

ENVY (*as* BERKELEY). Yes I am Dr Berkeley, my good man. Dr Swift has invited me to supper.

BRENNAN. They'll all be in before long. I'll open a bottle now and have it ready. You take a drop, sir?

BERKELEY. Not in excess.

BRENNAN. Not in excess. Now that's very wise. They put the pledge on you, no doubt.

(*He draws a cork.*)

I never touch it myself.

(*He takes a swig from the bottle.*)

Here's some of them now.

(FORD, DINGLEY *and* STELLA *enter.*)

FORD. Welcome to the deanery, Dr Berkeley. You have met the ladies?

BRENNAN (*going*). I gave him a sup to go on with.

   (*He goes out.*)

BERKELEY. No, Mr Ford. I have not yet had that pleasure.

FORD. Mrs Johnson – Dr Berkeley – Mrs Dingley.

BERKELEY. Your most humble servant, ladies.

STELLA. We have all heard of Dr Berkeley.

DINGLEY. Hetty, is this the man who disbelieves in his own existence and wants us all to live on tar water?

STELLA. Dingley. Don't be ridiculous.

DINGLEY. That's what Jonathan says.

FORD (*hastily*). Mrs Johnson has received a new poem from the Dean. We were just about to hear it.

BERKELEY. Indeed.

STELLA. He always sends one on my birthday.

BERKELEY. Pray read it, madam.

STELLA. With your permission, sir.

> 'Thou, Stella, wert no longer young
> When first for thee my harp I strung.
> Without one word of Cupid's darts,
> Of killing eyes or . . .'

   (BRENNAN *dashes in followed by* SWIFT *who is striking him with a cane.*)

SWIFT (*passing by*). There, sir. Take that, sir. And that. And that. And that.

BRENNAN. Oh, God. Oh, saints protect us. Oh, God.

   (*They disappear.*)

STELLA.

> '. . . of killing eyes or bleeding hearts.'

BERKELEY. Dear me.

STELLA. Did you speak, Dr Berkeley?

BERKELEY. What, madam?

STELLA. You said something, Dr Berkeley?

BERKELEY. Forgive me, madam. I did not intend to interrupt. Was that Dr Swift who passed by just now?

STELLA. Yes. That was the Dean.

FORD. He was only chasing his servant.

BERKELEY. Chasing his servant. I see. Ahem.

   (*He coughs.*)

STELLA. He will be back presently.

FORD. Don't you take any exercise Dr Berkeley?

BERKELEY. Oh yes, indeed, Mr Ford. But er . . .

FORD. But you do not chase your servants?

BERKELEY. Well, scarcely, Mr Ford. But then I'm not so . . . er . . . remarkable a man as the Dean of St Patrick's. Pray proceed madam.

STELLA.
> 'Of killing eyes or bleeding hearts.
> With friendship and esteem possesst
> I ne'er admitted love a guest.
> In all the habitudes of life . . .'

(SWIFT *and* BRENNAN *re-enter. The latter cowers panting in a corner.*)

SWIFT. Now, sirrah, why have you not cleaned my boots?

BRENNAN. Ah, what's the use? What's the use? Sure, they'll only be dirty again by morning.

SWIFT. Ah, an excellent reason. What splendid foresight. Well, my good rogue, I here leave directions that you go to bed tonight without your supper.

BRENNAN. What. No supper?

SWIFT. That is what I said. Why should we waste our good food on you when you will only be hungry again by morning?

(BRENNAN *cries out and the company laugh.*)

Is that Berkeley whom I see?

BERKELEY. I am delighted to meet you once again, Mr Dean, in the quiet of your home.

SWIFT. Why bless my soul. The whole company is gathered. That means it is time for the victuals. Where is my honest cook? Fetch her, Brennan. Fetch her. We must not keep our guests from the food, or they will assuredly drink us out of the house.

BRENNAN. Yes, Mr Dean! . . . I . . .

SWIFT (*shouting*). Cook!

BRENNAN (*shouting*). Cook!

(ANGER *enters as the* TROLLOP.)

TROLLOP. Here I am. Here I am! What is it now?

SWIFT. We are ready to dine, my good woman. Serve the victuals. But first of all, draw for the guests.

BRENNAN. Ah. Draw!

SWIFT. Not you, Brennan.

BERKELEY. I thank you, sir. I do not drink.

(*The* TROLLOP *pours out assisted by* BRENNAN.)

SWIFT. Then fill up your pipe.

BERKELEY. Nor do I smoke.

SWIFT. No bottle? No pipe? Egad, sir, what a poor education you must have had. When I was at Trinity College, drinking and

300

smoking were the first rudiments of learning taught there, and indeed the only ones to survive into later life.

DINGLEY. I think I smell burning.

STELLA. Yes, I smell it too. It is coming from the kitchen.

DINGLEY. Cook!

TROLLOP. Yes, ma'am?

DINGLEY. What is burning in the kitchen?

TROLLOP. I don't know, ma'am, I'm sure. I wonder would it be the matches?

STELLA. Well, I always heard that matches were made in Heaven. But this smells more of the brimstone.

TROLLOP. God save us! It is the meat. The meat for the supper.
(*She hurries off, ad libbing.*)

SWIFT. The meat again. Brennan! Come here. Let me take you by the ear, sir.
(BRENNAN *protests faintly.*)

SWIFT. How fortunate we are to be able to sit here in comfort and luxury while so admirable a staff exerts itself on our behalf. At what hour did you rise this morning, sirrah?

BRENNAN. At six o'clock sharp, your honour.

SWIFT. At six o'clock sharp you interrupted your simple pleasures on my account. If true – which I doubt – that was very civil of you. Remember, Richard, if you ever hope to become a bishop you must rise early enough to cozen the devil.

BRENNAN. Yes, your honour. I'll remember that.

SWIFT. Alas, you will not. For the worse your sty, the longer you lie. Pass round the wine, you rascal. Dingley, were you in church this evening.
(BRENNAN *passes round the wine.*)

DINGLEY. No, Jonathan. I had other things to attend to.

SWIFT. Dingley, I fear you are a godless hussy. Have you never read of the lilies of the field?

DINGLEY. You're no lily, Jonathan Swift, and don't you forget it.

SWIFT. Tut, tut! I am this woman's spiritual adviser, Dr Berkeley, and she rewards me by turning my cathedral into a dormitory for the living as well as for the dead.

DINGLEY. Anyhow, I don't write improper verses about my archbishop. Marry, but I don't. Or have my unfortunate printers prosecuted by the Government.

SWIFT. Doctor, can I not persuade you to join me in an assault upon this iniquitous Government?

BERKELEY. Well, sir, I confess I agree with you in some respects, about the Government. But is the moment opportune to . . . er . . . attack . . .

SWIFT. Maybe not, my dear Doctor. Perhaps it could better be launched from the eminence of a bishopric, later on? Eh?

BERKELEY. That would certainly carry more weight – not that I expect promotion, of course.

SWIFT. I understand. Well, when you get your mitre perhaps you will join me then?

BERKELEY. Maybe so, Mr Dean.

SWIFT. We will see. Take what you can, Dr Berkeley, for Fortune is a drunken whore, stone blind, who sees neither whom she raises up nor whom she casts down. But ho, my friend Brennan! What did I see just now in the pier glass?

BRENNAN. Nothing, your honour, nothing. I was pouring out the wine for the company.

SWIFT. Come, sir. Don't attempt to darn your cobwebs. You were pouring it down your own gullet. Dare you deny it?

BRENNAN. Now, Mr Dean, you know that I never . . .

SWIFT. No, no. I withdraw my question. One commandant is quite enough for any man to break at a time.

STELLA .Come, Presto. Let poor Richard go, and allow us to enjoy ourselves.

BRENNAN. Oh, thank you, ma'am.

SWIFT. Very well, sirrah. I am asked to forgive you, so I forgive you.

BRENNAN. Your honour's most humble servant.

SWIFT. I will merely stop two shillings out of your board wages to pay for your refreshments.

BRENNAN. Two shillings. Oh, merciful Providence, do you hear him? Two shillings.

SWIFT. 'Tis only what you owe me for the drink. You won't deny the tavern keeper his humble score?

BRENNAN. But sir . . . your honour . . . oh, speak to him, you, sir. Two shillings! Oh, I can't pay it, sir. I can't.

BERKELEY. Dr Swift, if I may intervene, to punish the fellow is one thing, but to stop two shillings out of his board wages for twopence worth of wine – surely, sir, that is . . .

SWIFT. Sir, I scorn to be outdone . . . even in cheating. Two shillings it shall be. Be off now, and bring up the food. But not until you have washed yourself. Even though you be a beggar, water is not so scarce that you may not have the use of it on special occasions.

302

TROLLOP (*entering with a smoking dish*). Oh, the meat is burnt, Mr Dean. 'Tis burnt.

DINGLEY. Oh, what a stench.

SWIFT. Begad, so it is. Then take it downstairs and do it less.

TROLLOP. Do it less? Do it less? I can't do it less, and well you know it.

SWIFT. Then what a stupid trollop you are, to commit a fault that cannot be remedied.

(BRENNAN *joins in with him from 'to commit a fault'*.)

BRENNAN. I know that one myself.

SWIFT. Into the dining-room instantly, sirrah.

(*The* TROLLOP *hurries off protesting*.)

SWIFT. She is a woman of great intelligence, and I hope by this means to teach her in a year or two not to burn the meat.

BRENNAN. Excuse me, sir, that was the doorbell I heard.

(*He hurries off*.)

DINGLEY. If you did not interfere so much in the running of the household, things would go much more smoothly. I have given most careful instructions to all your servants, myself.

SWIFT. Which they do not carry out.

DINGLEY. At any rate, they are proper instructions. You have no experience in these matters.

SWIFT. Forgive me, but I have. When I was chaplain to the Lord Lieutenant, I was so poor that I was obliged to keep a coffee house, and all the nobility resorted there to talk treason.

BERKELEY. The Duke of Grafton wished to make me his chaplain when he was Lord Lieutenant. A damned patronizing fellow he was, but I would not accept an appointment from such a man.

SWIFT. I' faith, I never liked him much myself, but when they asked him how he governed Ireland, he used to answer 'I pleased Dr Swift.' Would you care to see all the money that I made when I was advising the Queen's Ministers, Dr Berkeley? Being a thrifty man I have saved the whole of it.

(*He opens a drawer*.)

BERKELEY. But there is nothing here, Mr Dean.

SWIFT. Dingley, see that Dr Berkeley does not steal any of it. Like the money in poets' pockets, it is invisible. Now who used to say that, I wonder?

BRENNAN (*entering*). A letter for Mrs Johnson. 'Twas left in at the door.

STELLA. Forgive me, gentlemen. The handwriting is unfamiliar, and my curiosity overcomes me.

(She tears it open. BRENNAN *goes off.)*

BERKELEY. When the Duke approached me, I said to his emissary, 'Sir,' I said, 'I will not accept the patronage of any bastard. What if his father was a king,' I said, 'his mother was a harlot.'

STELLA *(reading the letter)*. Oh!

BERKELEY. Did I speak well?

SWIFT. Sir, you spoke it in a manner worthy of the House of Peers. Is there anything the matter, Stella?

(PRIDE *walks down to the forestage, and stands there for a moment in silence.)*

DEAN *(following her, in some surprise)*. What is wrong? Why are you stopping the scene?

PRIDE. The rest of the scene makes no sense.

DEAN. Stella . . .

PRIDE. I'm not Stella.

DEAN *(relaxing into* THE DEAN*)*. Maybe not – but for the purposes of our . . .

PRIDE. I am not Stella in any sense of the word. I'm not even a credible woman. What woman in her senses would behave like this?

DEAN *(nervously)*. Your behaviour is perfectly reasonable. A very wonderful woman.

PRIDE. Perfectly reasonable!

DEAN. It has satisfied generations of biographers.

PRIDE *(scornfully)*. Swift's biographers – not hers. It's enough for *his* story that she should be content to live her life as his unacknowledged mistress.

DEAN. No! As his secret wife.

PRIDE. That is worse! If I am your wife, why shouldn't I be recognized? Am I something to be ashamed of? The hostess of your deanery for fifteen years . . . accepting your protection and your money, and yet not good enough to . . .

AVARICE. Oh, no, Hetty, no! We have our own money.

PRIDE. He pretends that it's our own money, but the little we possess doesn't provide half of what we get from him.

AVARICE. Oh, I can't believe that. I can't.

PRIDE. Well, I know it. And the gossips and scandalmongers know it, now that we are dead.

(GLUTTONY *rises from where he has been listening at the side of the stage and approaches.)*

GLUTTONY. Dead? Now look . . . please . . .

304

PRIDE. If it was justified by marriage or by any other reason, then in justice to me that reason should be known.

GLUTTONY. Look – please, don't let us get confused. We are all becoming a little too involved in . . .

DEAN. Of course there was a reason. We know that, Stella. But it is nobody's business but our own. I don't care what they think of me.

PRIDE. But I care what they think of me.

GLUTTONY. After all, you're not really Swift and Stella. Let's not forget that.

PRIDE. Who can say whom we are, now that this grave is open?

AVARICE (*with a shiver*). What a disturbing idea!

PRIDE. If I am Stella, I must be a real woman – not a wraith invented by some biographer to explain *his* behaviour.

DEAN (*sulkily*). The facts are true as we have shown them. You accepted them, and asked for nothing more.

PRIDE (*emotionally*). But that was before they knew so much about this other woman. She was just a silly girl, pursuing an older man. Now they know too much, and yet not enough. What does that terrible scene at Celbridge make of me? . . . a wife who stood silently by, and watched you drive another woman into the grave?

DEAN. There was a reason. What of it?

PRIDE. Yes . . . a reason, which you are still too proud to admit. But what about my pride? Am I just part of the scenery of your life, Jonathan Swift, dying quietly in my lodgings – happy in the role of being your unacknowledged wife? No, no. That is not good enough for me. Stella was not that kind of nonentity.

DEAN (*darkly, after a pause*). What is it that you want?

PRIDE. Before we go on any further with this scene of Dr Berkeley's, we must go back to the garden at Laracor. There was something that was said there that Dingley didn't hear.

AVARICE. Yes, I remember. The conversation that had such surprising results. I could never understand what happened between you then.

PRIDE. There is something missing from the picture . . . something that these graves have never yet disclosed. Without it everything that follows is unintelligible. So come, Presto. I warned you. We must let them have their say. Now that we have begun, we must hear it all.

DEAN (*after a strangled pause*). Very well. Have it your own way.

(*The other characters withdraw into the background, where*

they listen with rapt attention. Once again, we hear the twittering of birds, and the lights on the forestage change.)

PRIDE. I am young again, and it is just before you went to London. (*They reassume the roles of* SWIFT *and* STELLA *as younger people.*)

STELLA. Come, Presto. You want to know what I meant when I said that I knew why we could never be married. Come – we are in the orchard – out of Dingley's hearing.

SWIFT (*reluctantly*). Yes. That's what I asked you.

STELLA. First, I have a question for you, Presto.

SWIFT. What is it?

STELLA. Are you married already?

DEAN. Of course not.

STELLA. That is all that I wanted to know.

DEAN. There could be other impediments besides that.

STELLA. I realize that. Let us not talk about it any longer.

DEAN. What do you mean? Tell me at once.

STELLA. Very well. Since you insist. You know that Sir William Temple was my father. The vicar of Laracor could never condescend to marry a bastard.

DEAN. That is not the reason.

STELLA. Please don't try to make it any easier for me. It's best to face it.

DEAN (*thundering*). That has nothing whatever to do with it. I swear it. At least . . . not in the way that you imagine.

STELLA. Oh why can't you be honest, Jonathan? I understand, and I would never reproach you, if only you would be honest.

SWIFT. That is *not* the reason.

STELLA. Please, Jonathan, I am sorry for allowing the matter to be discussed at all. I don't know what came over me.

(*She turns to go.*)

SWIFT. Stop! Don't go.

STELLA. I can't stay here any longer. I am too humiliated.

SWIFT, I command you to stay. I will not permit you to think such things of me.

STELLA. Please let my arm go. You know you have no right to command me.

SWIFT. I have every right. For the selfsame reason that we can never marry . . .

STELLA. It's not true.

SWIFT. You fling your birth in my face. Very well. My own birth was no better than yours.

306

STELLA. *Your* birth?

SWIFT. Yes, mine. If you were more than a servant at Moor Park
I was more than a secretary.

STELLA. Jonathan!

SWIFT. You have heard me speak of my mother and her ancient
lineage in Leicestershire. Well, the truth is, she was a butcher's
daughter with a post in the household of Sir William Temple's
father.

STELLA. You mean to say that Sir William . . .

SWIFT. I was more than his secretary. I was his brother . . . the by-
blow of an older generation.

STELLA. You . . . too?

SWIFT. What have I got to complain of? They treat their indiscre-
tions well . . . these gentle Temples. The best school in Ireland,
Dublin College and then Oxford. Oh, I was a very lucky fellow.

STELLA. Oh, Presto. You should have told me. Did you imagine
that I would love you any the less for this?

SWIFT. But you must not love me, Poppet. Never, never. Not in
that way.

STELLA. Never?

SWIFT. Don't you understand? I am your blood relation.

STELLA. You mean . . . it is a sin for me to love you?

SWIFT. More than a sin, Hetty. It is a crime . . . a crime against
Church and State. Do you realize what this means in a world
that is filled with bitter enemies? Above our heads hangs the
unspeakable charge of incest.

STELLA. Oh, Presto, but why? Are you sure? Does anybody else . . .
Who knows this, Presto?

SWIFT. I can never be certain of that. It happened so long ago . . .
before the Revolution, and the Wars in Ireland.

STELLA. Then perhaps nobody . . .

SWIFT. But for all we can tell, there may still be somebody – some
servant . . . some mean little attorney's clerk with a long memory . . . who can prove something – who is still waiting his
chance. That is why we must never be found alone together so
long as we both shall live. That is why we must always keep
Dingley with us. Any other course would hand us over to the
threat of blackmail until the day of our death.

(*She broods on this for a while.*)

STELLA. Then there is only one thing for me to do.

SWIFT. Yes?

STELLA. I must marry Mr Tisdall at once.

307

SWIFT. Oh no. Why that? Why that, Hetty?

STELLA. It will make our position clear. Nobody can ever accuse us of these things, once I am another man's wife.

SWIFT. But, Hetty, if you do this I shall lose you.

STELLA. You need never lose anything that you have now, Presto. You will never lose my love. And we can still see each other and be together, can't we?

SWIFT. But consider, my dear, how can we continue to see each other if you do this? I am a priest of the Church, and you will be another man's wife?.

STELLA. Oh!
    (*Then quizzically.*)
Then perhaps you would prefer me not to marry?

SWIFT. I have no right to ask it of you. But . . . oh, my God! the very thought of you married to Tisdall!

STELLA. Presto, if you would rather that I didn't marry, I won't do so.

SWIFT (*surprised*). You mean . . . you would be content to be . . . just my friend? To remain as we are?

STELLA. If you wish it.

SWIFT (*deeply flattered*). You would rather be the friend of Jonathan Swift than the wife of any other man?

STELLA. Long ago when I was a little girl I made a promise to myself. I said that no man would ever marry me except Presto, my dear tutor. I am ready to keep that promise if you want me to.

SWIFT (*exalted*). Esther . . . my star . . . my dear, dear Stella. You are honouring me more than any man has ever been honoured, I am more deeply moved than I can say.

STELLA. Silly. How could I live with any other man after having known you? There is only one thing that troubles me. Suppose some day *you* wish to marry.

SWIFT. Nonsense. What could any other woman mean to me?

STELLA. You are a man, Jonathan, and men sometimes need a love that I will not be able to give you.

SWIFT. I am *more* than a man. I am Jonathan Swift, and I want nothing from any human being that I cannot get from you.

STELLA. Oh, I wonder.

SWIFT. Then stop wondering. I have spoken and there is nothing more to be said. What have we two to do with kisses? Our love is above such cheap embellishments. Come, give me your hand. We will go and look for Mr Tisdall.

STELLA (*going*). You called me Stella. That is a pretty name.
> (*Fade out birds into a roll of thunder. The lights change to those of the deanery.* SWIFT *and* STELLA *return upstage.*)

PRIDE. And now, Dr Berkeley, before I so rudely interrupted, you were saying something about somebody's mother being a harlot weren't you?

ENVY (*confused*). Ahem! I feel, perhaps, that my account had better end at this point.

DEAN (*a little sarcastically*). As you wish, sir. Mrs Johnson may prefer to continue with the story herself, now that she has intervened so effectively. I think I replied that you had spoken in a manner worthy of the House of Peers. Well, Stella? You were reading that letter. Is there anything the matter?

STELLA (*upset*). Nothing, I thank you.

SWIFT. Charles, will you be so good as to take Dr Berkeley and Mrs Dingley in to supper? Mrs Johnson and I will follow presently.
> (DINGLEY, BERKELEY *and* FORD *go off.*)

SWIFT. What is the matter, Stella?

STELLA. This letter is from Mrs Vanhomrigh.

SWIFT. She has written to you! How dare she!

STELLA. She demands that I tell her whether I am your wife.

SWIFT (*furious*). Give it to me at once. (*He takes the letter and reads it.*)

STELLA. What is this woman to you that she has the right to ask such a question of me?

SWIFT. Nothing. She has no right.

STELLA. Is that the truth, Presto?

SWIFT (*after a strangled pause*). No. It is not the truth.

STELLA. Thank you, Presto. It is best that I should know.

SWIFT. What are you going to do?

STELLA. What do you wish me to do?

SWIFT. Tell her that . . . No, you must not do that. Tell her . . . I cannot think!

STELLA. Am I to tell her that I am your wife?

SWIFT. No, no. You must never do that. Never.

STELLA. But why, Presto? What harm can come of it now?

SWIFT. Disaster can come of it. The most unspeakable of charges to overwhelm us both. Both of us . . . don't you understand?

STELLA. But surely that fear must have left you long ago, Presto? It is now almost sixty years since – since those things happened.

SWIFT. That fear will never leave me. It is the torture of all my waking hours. It is right that our friends should suspect our marriage. But for us to confirm it in any way, or to be found alone together . . . no, no! Never.

STELLA. Very well, Presto. I shall tell her then, that we are not married.

SWIFT. Yes . . . No . . . I don't know.

STELLA. If I do so, will she expect you to marry her?

SWIFT (*dully*). I suppose she will.

STELLA. Well? Do you wish to marry her?

SWIFT. I cannot marry her.

STELLA. You mean because of me?

SWIFT. Yes.

STELLA (*very proud*). Do not think, Presto, that I am going to stand in your way. If you love her and wish to marry her I shall not embarrass you in any way.

SWIFT (*eagerly*). Do you mean that it need not make any difference to our relationship?

STELLA (*with a touch of sarcasm*). That I shall remain the hostess of your deanery?

SWIFT. Will you still live near me and accept my protection?

STELLA. You would not have stayed with me if I had married Mr Tisdall. No, Presto. That is too much to ask of me.

SWIFT. Stella, for the love you bear me . . .

STELLA (*bitterly and with great firmness*). Yes, I love you. I always have and I always will love you. That is why I made the choice that I did.

SWIFT (*stricken*). It was I who asked you to make it. I should never have done so. That was my most terrible mistake.

STELLA. You are very cruel, Presto. Has it meant so little to you all these years? Are you sorry now that I decided as I did?

SWIFT. No, no! I am not sorry. You have meant everything to me. You have always been my greatest comfort, my dearest friend.

STELLA. Yet you love her.

SWIFT. That is different. I love you both, miserable man that I am. Can't a man love two women, each in their own way?

STELLA. Love two? Oh no, Presto, no! How can you ask such a question? You must have known how this would end. Why did you ever allow it to begin?

SWIFT. Because I wanted her.

STELLA. What do you mean, Presto? You once told me you would never want anything from any woman that I couldn't give you.

SWIFT. Yes, yes, that was true at the time. It's still true in the sense I meant it, then. But there is something else in me that needs her

. . . as a man needs a woman. Another kind of love. Oh, God, why must I be shut out from that for ever?

STELLA (*painfully*). Presto, are you . . . after all . . . are you only . . .

SWIFT (*stung to the quick*). Yes, I'm only a man – just like other men! Why not? Time and again I asked myself, what before God, is the impediment? Have I wife of my own, that I must fly from her? Am I to chase after trulls and trollops all my life to keep my thoughts from honest women?

STELLA. Oh, my poor, poor Presto. You must marry her at once if this is how you feel. Believe me, there is no impediment. None whatsoever.

SWIFT. How can I marry her if it means that I must leave you?

STELLA. You will have to leave one of us, Presto.

SWIFT. Yes, one or the other. I can see that now. Somebody's heart must crack . . . O God, forgive me.

STELLA (*tight-lipped again*). Please don't be concerned for me. I have my little fortune and my friends, and I shall never reproach you.

SWIFT (*brightening for a moment*). Oh, Stella. Do you mean . . . ?

STELLA. It is my fault too. I should have known better than to hope.
   (*This combination of pity and affectionate superiority completely baffles* SWIFT.)

SWIFT. . . . I . . . I . . . don't know what to say.

STELLA. There is only one thing that I ask of you. It is my only right, Presto.

SWIFT. What is that?

STELLA. If you marry her, I want you to tell the world the truth of what lies between us two.

SWIFT. But, Stella . . .

STELLA (*firmly*). I know what it will mean to both of us. But do you realize, Presto, the things that will be whispered of me, when once you marry her? It's a small request, and my only one. That is all I have to say.

SWIFT (*after a pause*). It's true, Stella. We can never part now and remain silent. We must tell our secret to the world if ever I marry.
   (*Pause.*)
Then I will never marry. No woman on earth shall make me scandalize my mother's name and make a mockery of my best and dearest friend. I shall take this letter back to her, and I shall say . . . I shall say . . .

(The organ fades in with agitated music. STELLA *vanishes, and* VANESSA *appears in a spotlight.)*

VANESSA. Is he coming? Down the turnpike I hear the hoofbeats of his horse. He will be very angry because of my letter but I shall be calm. I know what I am going to say and I have my answers ready.

(Through the music comes the beat of horse's hooves.)

SWIFT *(in another spotlight, cloaked and wearing a hat).* By Kilmainham, by Palmerston, by Lucan, I ride to Celbridge. She knows what she will say to me, but what shall I say to her? Poor child. I must be kind. I shall pledge her to secrecy and then I shall tell her everything. She will understand. I shall say, here is my secret. Now you will understand why we can never marry.

VANESSA. He is mine and I am his. I will never give him up. Never. Never. Never. If he is married I shall kill myself. But no, he could never be such a monster, as to have kept that from me.

SWIFT. I shall say to her, 'Pray you, be my friend. I am doing you this wrong, but pray forgive and keep my secret safe. Think of my reputation and of Stella's.' And she will answer . . . she will answer . . . what will she answer? Trust her, Cadenus, for the love she bears you . . . this love you will not have! God! There is laughter in the skies . . . vile, bawdy, villainous laughter. It is ringing in my ears. It is tearing me to pieces. I shall say . . . I shall say . . .

(The organ music stops and the horse clatters to a halt.)

VANESSA. Listen! I hear him on the stairway. At the door. I'm not afraid. I am ready with an answer for anything he may say.

(They meet in the centre of the frontstage. For a moment he stares at her in baffled torment.)

Cadenus. Oh, Cadenus.

(Pause.)

Speak to me. Haven't you got anything to say?

(He throws down the letter and vanishes out of the light.)

VANESSA *(picking it up and recognizing it with a cry of despair).* Cadenus! My letter. Don't leave me here to die without a word, Cadenus!

(Fade out on her sobbing and coughing into the sighing of the wind. Hold this to background. A spotlight rises on SWIFT, *upstage, reading the Bible.)*

SWIFT. 'These things have I spoken unto you, that my joy might remain in you and that your joy might be full. This is my commandment, that ye love one another – love one another.'

312

(*He pauses and listens to the wind.*)

Oh God, her cry is always in my ears, and there is no escape. What is my sin that I must bear this burden all my life? It is love! this cursed noose that binds men and women together, until they strangle by each other's weight – this harlot rising from the bowels' ooze. I should have shut my ears against her cries, and driven her from my side. But I could not. Because of love! Love! Love! Cursed be love! Cursed be my covinous heart! Cursed be this thing called pity that has damned my soul to all eternity! 'Let the day perish wherein, I was born . . .'

(*Take out wind effect.*)

STELLA (*a ghostly voice*). No, Jonathan. Neither pity nor love. But pride. Love is no sin, and pity brings no punishment. But pride is the sin of Lucifer himself, that loosed all other sins upon creation . . . the sin that cannot bring itself to pray for pardon, and is the most deadly of the seven. That was the thing that destroyed you, Jonathan.

SWIFT. '. . . and the night which said, "There is a man child conceived". Let that day be darkness.'

(*The light widens to disclose the deanery.* FORD *enters.*)

FORD. Jonathan.

SWIFT. Do not interrupt me at my devotions.

FORD. I must speak to you about Miss Vanhomrigh.

SWIFT (*dully*). Miss Vanhomrigh is dead.

FORD. Yes, and you mustn't close your eyes to the fact that she died your enemy.

SWIFT. A little transient fluttering of heartbeats that was a woman.

FORD. Jonathan, I do not presume to instruct you, but her will proves that she hated you.

SWIFT. Vanessa is what I used to call her.

FORD. I know, Jonathan. She has made Dr Berkeley her executor, and has encouraged him to publish all her private papers. This poem 'Cadenus and Vanessa' is already the talk of the town. For your own sake you must tell me whether you have written anything else that may compromise you.

SWIFT. Once I thought every day of death, but now every minute. Yet, I suppose I shall not all die, for half my body is already spent. I shall wither like a blasted elm from the top downwards. But first I shall finish my book. I have a legacy of my own to leave the human race. I shall lash them with scorpions, and dying, leave behind a memorial of my scorn that will last for all time.

313

FORD. Be careful, Jonathan. The human race is a prodigious enemy for one man to challenge. Who knows how it may treat your book?

SWIFT. I shall not care if it burns every copy. That will prove that my thunderbolt has struck home.

FORD. Maybe it will defend itself by subtler means.

SWIFT. No, no! There will be no parrying this blow. There will be no escape from what I say of them here. They shall understand my purpose well enough.

(BRENNAN *enters with* BERKELEY.)

BRENNAN. The Lord Bishop of Cloyne.

(BRENNAN *goes off*.)

BERKELEY. Dr Swift.

SWIFT. Ah, Dr Berkeley. So you have obtained your mitre at last?

BERKELEY. Yes, Mr Dean. Unworthy as I am. But I have called . . .

SWIFT. Accept my congratulations, my lord. And when your lordship has taken your seat in the House of Peers, may we expect that you will at last employ your considerable eloquence in the service of our own country?

BERKELEY. In good time, Dr Swift. My position is not yet as influential as it might be.

SWIFT. I see. Then when your lordship has obtained an even better bishopric you will perhaps become an honest man?

BERKELEY. Most assuredly, Mr Dean. Our mutual friend Mr . . . (*He realizes that he has been insulted*.) What was that, sirrah?

SWIFT. Till then, my lord, farewell.

(*He goes away*.)

BERKELEY. Why, what a scurrilous tongue! What impertinence! What a way to speak of me – who have come here in a spirit of good will! I am highly offended. I shall return home at once.

(*He turns to go*.)

FORD. No, no Dr Berkeley. Don't be offended by Dr Swift. He is a sick and tormented man.

BERKELEY. His troubles are entirely of his own making.

FORD. Maybe so, my lord. But much as we may sympathize with the troubles of the innocent, surely the sufferings of the guilty are fifty times more terrible?

BERKELEY. There can be no excuse for violence and cruelty.

FORD. True, Dr Berkeley, the Dean is a violent and bitter man. But whatever his sins may be, they need no punishment from us. He has full measure.

BERKELEY. This doesn't explain why you wish to see me now.

314

FORD. My lord, you are Miss Vanhomrigh's executor.

BERKELEY. That is true. She has left her fortune to my West Indian project.

FORD. But is it necessary that you publish all her private papers?

BERKELEY. But, Mr Ford, she intended me to do so. In particular this poem, 'Cadenus and Vanessa', which through no fault of mine has gone to the printer.

FORD. Your lordship realizes that this publication was designed by Miss Vanhomrigh with the object of injuring the Dean?

BERKELEY. It seemed to me that they were very excellent and well-written pieces, worthy of notice on their own merits. Otherwise I would never have allowed any of them to leave my hands.

FORD. Your lordship also realizes that these papers will cause – indeed have caused – a great deal of pain to persons other than Dr Swift. To Mrs Johnson, for instance?

BERKELEY. Bless my soul, that side of the matter had not occurred to me. I confess I am nonplussed. Mrs Johnson . . . She must indeed be very upset about it all! How is her health?

FORD. None too good, Dr Berkeley. We fear she has not long to live.

BERKELEY. Too bad. Too bad.

(STELLA *appears, leaning on* DINGLEY'S *arm*.)

FORD. Why, Hetty my dear, let me take your arm.

STELLA. Thank you, Don Carlos. You are very kind.

DINGLEY. She has taken her medicine, and it won't be long now before we have her back at the top of the ladder.

FORD. Of course.

STELLA. I fear I shall be out of breath before I reach the top. Is that Dr Berkeley?

BERKELEY. Your servant, madam. I have come to express my deep regret at . . . er . . . some embarrassment I seem to have caused you unwittingly.

STELLA. You mean . . . the Dean's poem?

BERKELEY. Yes, madam. I had no idea . . .

STELLA. It is a very fine poem. It would have been a great pity if it had been lost to posterity.

BERKELEY (*warming*). Quite so, madam. A most remarkable poem. Indeed, I feel it must have been inspired by a very remarkable person.

STELLA. Maybe so, my lord. On the other hand, the Dean has written very finely on the subject of 'A Broomstick'. You are smiling, Don Carlos. Hetty is herself again, you see.

315

THE DREAMING DUST

DINGLEY. Come, my dear. You must lie down and rest for a little.

SWIFT (*entering*). Stella, what are you doing here? Give her to me.

BERKELEY (*trying to get between them*). No, no! Leave her to me, sir. I shall attend to Mrs Johnson's comfort.

SWIFT. Go away, sir.

STELLA (*politely disengaging herself from* BERKELEY *and giving her arm to* SWIFT). I thank you, my lord Bishop, for your kind intentions. I shall be quite happy with the Dean. He is very good to me. Forgive us if we leave you for a little while.

SWIFT (*going*). And do not disturb us. Come, my dear.

(SWIFT *and* STELLA *go off.*)

BERKELEY. Did you hear? What charity! What magnanimity! It is a lesson in the power of love.

FORD. And yet you remember that poem she read to us?
'With friendship and esteem possessed
They ne'er admitted love a guest.'

BERKELEY. Well, if it is not love, she must be a saint.

DINGLEY. A saint indeed! Hetty's no saint.

BERKELEY. Then the whole affair passes my comprehension.

DINGLEY. Twenty years ago I gave up trying to understand these two. I used to think that I knew something about men and women. But I know nothing. Not a thing! Now I ask no questions and am told no lies. And, Ford, I insist upon my cup of tea.

FORD (*going*). It's in the next room. Let us go.

BERKELEY. I will follow you in a moment.

(FORD *and* DINGLEY *go off.* BERKELEY *hesitates centre and then tiptoes in the direction taken by* SWIFT *and* STELLA.)

BERKELEY. It is inexcusable, I know. But . . . really I must . . .

SWIFT (*off*). Very well, my dear. If you wish it, it shall be owned. Let us tell them the truth, I am willing.

STELLA (*off*). No, Presto. Not now. It is too late.

BERKELEY. Most extraordinary. Oh, my goodness!

(*He hastily conceals himself as* SWIFT *enters in some agitation and kneels centre.*)

SWIFT. O merciful Father, take pity, we beseech thee, upon this Thy poor afflicted servant languishing under the weight of Thy hand. Give her a sincere repentance for all her transgressions . . .

BERKELEY (*indignantly*). Oh!

SWIFT. Accept and impute all . . . Who is there? Charles? Charles

316

– she must not die in the deanery. That would be a most improper thing.

BERKELEY (*appearing*). Die in the deanery! Improper! Is that all you can think about at this moment, you foul fellow?

SWIFT. Dr Berkeley!

BERKELEY. The effrontery – to offer your blasphemous prayers on her behalf. You are her only affliction – not God. How dare you speak like this, most of all in prayer to your Maker? Better ask forgiveness for your own sins.

SWIFT (*calling out in anguish*). Brennan! Dingley!

BERKELEY. This gentle lady, so loving, so lovely, so unhappy, whose tragedy we watch and mourn over, whose grief and sweet martyrdom is your work and yours alone . . .

SWIFT (*collapses, stricken*). No . . . no . . .

BERKELEY. What right have you to pray for her, you wretch, you fiend . . . here on the threshold of the second grave you have dug with your own infamous hands? Wretch! Have you no fear of God's judgment?

SWIFT. Stella!

STELLA (*entering*). Leave him alone. Leave him alone.

BERKELEY. Mrs Johnson!

STELLA. Leave him alone, I say. He is my friend.

BERKELEY. But he has wronged you grievously.

STELLA. He has not wronged me. He is my best and dearest friend. And when I die there will be no reproaches on my lips or in my heart. None whatsoever.

BERKELEY. But surely . . .

STELLA. That should be enough for you. Now leave us, please.
      (BERKELEY *rushes off. The organ and choir are heard faintly in Psalm 10.*)

SWIFT. Oh, Stella! Is it true that I have not wronged you? Did you really mean what you said?

STELLA. Of course, Presto.

SWIFT. If only I had done . . . if only I could do some little thing to repay you for the lifetime of devotion you have given me.

STELLA.

> 'You taught how I might youth prolong.
> By knowing what was right and wrong,
> How from my heart to bring supplies
> Of lustre to my fading eyes.'

SWIFT. That is the poem you wrote for me on my birthday. You are a better poet than ever Presto was.

317

STELLA.

> 'Such is the fate of female race,
> With no endowments but a face;
> Before the thirtieth year of life
> A maid forlorn or hated wife.
> Stella to you, her tutor, owes
> That she has ne'er resembled those;
> Nor was a burthen to mankind
> With half her course of years behind.'

SWIFT. Stella, Stella. No, no! Stella! Open your eyes!

(*The Psalm swells up and then fades out with the lights. When they rise again, all the characters, with the exception of* SWIFT, *are grouped around the grave.*)

SEXTON. Well? Where am I to put back the skulls? Together or apart?

AVARICE. Does it matter – now?

SEXTON. Ne'er a bit. I'll get a box for them both and put in a note to say how they lived in arguments and were buried in arguments, and that I was the last to see them. (*He digs.*) Then I'll close up the floor, please God for the last time, and let them rest there till the Great Day.

ENVY. A brief memorandum of the seven deadly sins.

SEXTON. Sins, moryah! What do any of youse know about his sins, except maybe the one that happens to be your own? That's the only one that nobody can forgive.

LUST. How true. We have each accused him of being ourselves.

PRIDE. Even Stella?

LUST. Stella most of all. He used to say that he scorned to be outdone in anything. But she outdid even him in her pride. That is why they should rest together. They were of the same blood in more ways than one.

SLOTH. If you ask me, there's no man knows a man better than his own man. It was Brennan that did him his last service.

LUST. Brennan! We were almost forgetting you. How would Brennan remember him?

SLOTH. As a lazy, slothful old divil, sitting there in his chair day after day, and not a move or a word out of him, except maybe a curse, or a blow for them that's only trying their best to help him.

(*Doorbell.*)

Excuse me. That was the doorbell.

(*All the characters slip away except* SLOTH *and* AVARICE.)

318

SLOTH (*as* BRENNAN). Good evening, Mrs Dingley, ma'am. So you've come to see the Dean.

DINGLEY. How is he tonight?

BRENNAN. Aw, not a word the wiser. Just sitting there in the old dressing-gown like a man that's dead the week before last. I can do nothing with him at all.

(*He brings her upstage. The light rises on* SWIFT – *an aged imbecile in his chair.* BRENNAN *slips away.*)

DINGLEY. Good evening, Jonathan. (*Pause.*) Good evening, Jonathan – don't you know me? It's your old friend Beccy Dingley come to read to you. Oh, ttttt-tttt. That is no sort of a face to make. There are a lot of people outside, Jonathan. They have come to pay their respects. It's your birthday. You know that, don't you? Your book about Captain Gulliver is still being a great success, I hear. I thought it a little exaggerated in parts – only in parts of course. But they tell me the children love it. In fact, it has become a classic of the nursery. I never would have expected you to write a children's book, Jonathan. Now, now, you mustn't get excited. What would you like me to read today? The Bible? I know that you like the Book of Job best, but I don't think too much of that is good for you. Now here's something nice that we had in church last Sunday.

(SWIFT *grunts.*)

'And Moses said unto God, Behold, when I come unto the Children of Israel, and shall say unto them, The God of your Fathers hath sent me unto you; and they shall say to me, what is his name? What shall I say unto them? And God said unto Moses, I am that I am. I Am hath sent me unto you.' You're not paying attention, Jonathan. Are you taking this in?

(SWIFT *hands her a paper.*)

SWIFT. Read.

DINGLEY. Read this? Why, it's some of your verse. Yes, that ought to be nicer.

> 'He gave the little wealth he had
> To build a house for fools and mad,
> And showed by one satiric touch
> No nation wanted it so much.
> Yet thus, methinks, I hear 'em speak,
> See how the Dean begins to break.'

(*She pauses.*)

Oh, do you think this is a good choice either?

SWIFT. Read.

DINGLEY (*with a break in her voice*).

> 'My female friends, whose tender hearts,
> Have better learned to act their parts,
> Receive the news with doleful dumps.'

(*She pauses.*)

> ' "The Dean is Dead; (and what is trumps?)
> Then Lord have mercy on his soul.
> (Ladies I'll venture for the vole.)"
> "Six deans they say, must bear the pall
> (I wish I knew what King to call)" '

(*With rising emotion.*)

> ' "Madam, your husband will attend
> The funeral of so good a friend?"
> "No Madam, 'tis a shocking sight;
> And he's engaged tomorrow night..." '

(*She bursts into tears and hurries away. The choir can now be heard, at first very faintly in the final chorus of the Passion.* BRENNAN *leads on the others as a group of Dublin rabble.*)

BRENNAN (*whispering*). Whisht, now, all of ye. Be easy and I'll let yez see him. A silver sixpence and yez may have a look at the ould mad Dean. The great Draper on his birthday. There he is now . . . the mad Dean of St Patrick's.

WHISPERINGS.

> Oh glory be to God, wouldn't it scarify you?
> Holy Jezebel, it's like looking into the clay face of death itself.
> Ah, harness your tongue and let me see.
> Well, his dancing days are dimmin'.
> Who said he was asleep?
> He's looking at us.
> He's awake. Oh Saint Larry O'Toole, he's getting up.
> (SWIFT *struggles slowly to his feet.*)

VOICE. He's going to speak.

SWIFT (*with quiet intensity*). I am that I am.

> (*There is puzzled silence.*)

VOICE. But them's the words of the Lord.

SWIFT (*louder*). I am that I am.

> (SWIFT *picks up the great Bible.*)

VOICES. It's blasphemy! Blasphemy!

SWIFT. Yahoos! Yahoos!

> (*He flings the Bible at them. There is a crash of glass and everybody runs screaming from the scene, leaving only the sobbing of one woman –* ANGER *– who is lost somewhere*

320

in the shadows. The voices of the choir grow louder as they approach down the aisle.)

SWIFT. I am ... that I am.

(*He sinks back into his chair. The choir appears, passing in front of* SWIFT'S *chair, where they pause and turn stage right.*)

A VOICE (*chanting off*). May the words of our lips and the meditation of our hearts be always acceptable in thy sight, O Lord, our strength and our redeemer. The Lord be with you.

CHOIR. And with thy spirit.

(*They turn left again, file upstage and pass through the door of the vestiary and disappear.* SWIFT *has vanished too. The organ concludes alone. That is the end of this play.*)

THE SCYTHE AND
THE SUNSET

A Play in Three Acts

UP THE REBELS!

WHEN Sean O'Casey first came to live in London in the 'twenties, he was strap-hanging one late afternoon in a crowded Tube train. After contemplating for some time the unbroken vista of open newspapers, bowler hats, rolled umbrellas and shopping bags, he was finally heard to remark: 'Look at them – all burning with indignation over the Irish question.'

Since that time, a plethora of publishers have sponsored many volumes of Tan War memoirs written strictly from a Flying Column angle, and usually stopping short at the end of 1921, just when the story starts to get interesting. From this fact one might conclude that, outside our verdant island, there is still a widespread excitement over Ireland's military affairs. However, this is an assumption in which I do not readily concur, and I feel sure that some explanation is needed for pushing my way into so congested a district at an advanced stage of the western winter, by writing what has been described as 'another damned play about 1916'.

I was not myself a participant in any of the stirring underground activities that made the New Ireland, principally for a reason that may have contributed to some present sourness on the subject. At the age of sixteen I attempted to join the I.R.A., but did not rise even to the dignity of being blackballed – having failed ignominiously to obtain either a proposer or a seconder, which I was assured by my contacts was necessary. At the age of fifty-four I had much the same experience with the Royal Irish Academy; and these being the only two occasions in my life when I have rashly attempted to join anything without first being asked, I have subsequently affected an air of detachment about both the Academy and the Anglo-Irish War that is understandable, though not wholly sincere. This attitude, however, does not apply to the Easter Rising, in which for a few days I was allowed to play a very minor role as a juvenile civilian internee.

As far as I am aware, only one other play about 1916 was per-

325

formed prior to my own, in spite of all impressions to the contrary. It only seems as if there were more, thanks to the long line of motion pictures glamorizing the later struggle, that have been put out by the film studios. The other Easter Week play is, of course, Sean O'Casey's finest piece of writing, *The Plough and the Stars* – the play of which the title of mine is an obvious parody. Herein any intentional similarity ends, as it would be the act of an idiot for any dramatist to measure his play against such a yardstick as *The Plough*.

Neither in verbiage, plot nor sentiments does this play of mine presume to bear any relation to its magnificent predecessor. The only point in so titling it lies in the fact that *The Plough* is essentially a pacifist play, implying that if only man had 'a titther o' sense', these outbreaks of destruction and bloodshed would never occur. As a quiet man who, nevertheless, is not a pacifist, I cannot accept the fact that, theatrically, Easter Week should remain indefinitely with only an anti-war comment, however fine. So also, it may be noticed that the mouthpiece for most of O'Casey's pacifism is provided by his women; whereas in actual fact the women of Ireland, ever since the Maud Gonne era, have been the most vocal part of its militancy. If I can claim nothing else, I can at least point with some complacency to the fact that – when it comes to the point – both my women are killers.

The Scythe and the Sunset shows every sign of turning out to be one of those elusive phenomena – a play without a public. Apart from whatever intrinsic demerits it may have – and I must confess that I like it very much myself – an antimelodrama on what has now become a sacred subject is distasteful to the sea-divided Gael, and is concerned with a matter that the Sassenach has chosen to forget. As for the Anglo-Irishman, who might perhaps be expected to applaud a few of its less important sentiments, he has become an invisible man, hardly capable of joining in the singing of 'God Save the Queen' in the confines of St Patrick's Cathedral on Armistice Day – an act of defiance that, until recently, was the last kick of this very passé ascendancy.

I have described my play as an antimelodrama, which may require some explanation. Most plays about national uprisings are based upon an assumption that the embattled rebels are always romantic, and that the forces of oppression are totally in the wrong. A dramatist whose historical experience makes it difficult for him to accept these rather shopsoiled axioms as a matter of course, is usually regarded as being either satirical or deliberately confusing, unless he is prepared to waste a lot of time in disproving such conclusions.

I was a schoolboy at the time of the Rising, and for the greater part of three days my home was occupied and fortified by four male members of De Valera's battalion, while we of the family were held, supposedly as prisoners, but actually as hostages. (My father was a judge at the time.) It all sounds more dramatic than it was. Our captors were soft-spoken and apologetic young men who did the least damage they could, compatible with their orders to turn the house into a fort and to prevent us from leaving. On the third day, feeling I suppose that they had by then done enough for Ireland, they stripped off their accoutrements and disappeared through the front gate, shortly before the outbreak of the major pitched battle of the week which began at the other end of the road. I still possess a slouch hat and a bayonet that I saved from confiscation by riding off on my bicycle to a friend's house on the opposite side of the operations, with these incriminating objects concealed as far as possible in a school satchel.

Consequently my recollections of the week are personal and undramatic. Of the rebels, I principally remember their charm, their civility, their doubts, and their fantastic misinformation about everything that was going on. Of the men in khaki there remains an impression of many cups of tea, of conversations about everything except the business in hand, and of a military incompetence of surprising proportions, even to my schoolboy's eye. I could have told them that the best way to cross the Grand Canal was to go round the back by way of another route, rather than by means of a series of frontal bayonet charges against fortified houses, overlooking a narrow bridge. I could also have told them that cavalry in O'Connell Street would be unlikely to get into the General Post Office.

It is a pity that the 'Sinn Fein Rebellion' – as it was wrongly described at the time – has never been properly reported by an objective professional historian. Before long it will be too late to do this from first-hand information, and the accumulating legends, exhibitions of wisdom-after-the-event, and arguments as to who did what (which are so much less interesting than the truth) will have taken command of the record. Until recently little has been written about it from the point of view of Dublin Castle – that symbol of imperial government that was actually in the grasp of the rebels for about half an hour, and could have been completely captured for the first time since its construction by King John, if the intruders had gone on instead of withdrawing. This was the only uprising in the annals of our island of which the secret was perfectly kept beforehand. This triumph of concealment was due to the fact that the rebels had announced so publicly and so often what their belligerent intentions were, that nobody would believe a word they said, and all assumed, as usual, that they were talking through their kepis.

It is not generally known that for the first five hours of the upheaval there was nobody in command of His Majesty's forces in Dublin except a garrison adjutant. Late on Easter Monday afternoon, somebody higher than a major arrived at Kingsbridge from the Curragh, and took charge of the affairs of the Empire. Sir John Maxwell – a soldier who had previously distinguished himself by placing the defences of the Suez Canal on the western bank, I suppose under a mistaken idea that Turkey lay in that direction, and who is generally credited with having suppressed the rising – did not arrive from England until a little more than twenty-four hours before the cease-fire, and barely in time to preside over the least intelligent part of the proceedings – the executions.

Meanwhile, four days were spent in isolating the Post Office by a brigadier with most of the city facilities at his disposal. At which point, fire rather than firing drove the main body of the insurgents into Moore Lane, where they finally gave themselves up. Most of the other strongholds then followed suit – some of them without having been seriously attacked at all. We have also the feat of the gunboat *Helga*, which came up the river to shell Liberty Hall (empty since Monday), and which landed its first projectile in Phoenix Park, greatly endangering the Lord Lieutenant.

Little was done during the first two days to ascertain the dispositions of the Republicans. On the third day a brigade of infantry landed at Kingstown, and proceeded to march up to Dublin by two parallel roads, without either proper reconnaissance, or any other known source of information. A large military barracks stood within one block of their principal hazard. Nevertheless no warning appears to have been given to or asked for by these troops as to what lay ahead, as a result of which one battalion ran up against six or seven valiant Cuchulains, defending a bridge over the Grand Canal, and suffered there most of the casualties of the week, in an engagement that probably had the effect of prolonging the rising from Thursday till the following Sunday.

Indeed it is an eloquent sidelight on the handling of the whole affair by the forces of the Crown, that during the opening days of the fight, the only real road-block in the way of the rebels was provided by the amateurs of the Dublin University Officers' Training Corps, with the assistance of a few colonials on leave, who held their college – and with it a key position in the city – until they were finally reached by the shaken professionals from Kingstown some time on Friday morning.

There are also a few aspects of the conflict from the Republican angle that have been somewhat glossed over. With an exaggerated respect for the prowess of their opponents, they refused to believe that they had captured His Majesty's Under-secretary and the seat of government in Ireland, when in fact they had. They left the telephone system of the city in full working order under the impression that the exchange was heavily guarded – this on the day of Fairyhouse Races! Few of the strongholds that they did occupy had much tactical value, and in several cases had to be abandoned at the first sign of an attack. But most serious of all from their own point of view, they harassed and interfered with the work of the Dublin Fire Brigade – if the word of the Fire Chief is to be believed – thereby sealing their own ultimate fate. For fire turned out to be their greatest – their inescapable, enemy.

But perhaps most interesting of all is a matter that has never yet been commented on at all – the question of Republican leadership. At the end of the week it was P. H. Pearse who surrendered as Commander-in-Chief of the Republican Army and 'President of the Provisional Government'. But how he ever got this lethal office and who, exactly, appointed him (apart from himself) are matters that have never been disclosed.

Before the rising, Commandant Pearse – although a leading light in the military counsels of the secret Irish Republican Brotherhood – was far from being the leader of the Irish Volunteers. He was merely a staff officer in charge of organization, and did not even command one of the city battalions. It would appear from the order of the signatures on the Proclamation of the Republic (printed as late as Easter Sunday) that Thomas J. Clarke, the old Fenian, was originally intended to head the Provisional Government. The person selected to lead in Dublin the combined forces of the Citizen Army and the Irish Volunteers, was James Connolly of the first-named body, while the ranking officer among those of the Irish Volunteers who took the field was not Pearse but Thomas MacDonagh, who commanded the Dublin Brigade. All that Pearse mobilized under his own signature on that fateful morning was a company, which received its directive from him in a handwritten postscript at the bottom of MacDonagh's brigade order. Furthermore, when the main body marched into O'Connell Street to occupy the Post Office, the column was led by Connolly, with Pearse marching in company with others, further to the rear – surely a very odd position for the Commander-in-Chief, and even more so for the President of a forthcoming revolutionary government.

It is also of interest to note that when, at the end of the week, Pearse signed a document accepting unconditional surrender, De Valera refused to recognize it, when it was presented to him in his embattled Mount Street area. He would take orders, he said, only from his military superior, Thomas MacDonagh. Nor would MacDonagh, in Jacob's Biscuit Factory, accept this surrender either, until after 'consultation with Commandant Ceannt and other officers' he agreed to endorse it on his own behalf.

None of these clues gives us any information as to whether Pearse really held the position in which he has been enshrined ever since in the hearts of his countrymen, or, if he did, how and when he got it. Was the office of Commander-in-Chief an unpopular one, once the affair had started to run its fatal course? Was Pearse the only leader present at headquarters who, in the end, was prepared to assume these grave responsibilities, and to offer himself to General Maxwell as a blood sacrifice on behalf of the others? Or was his leadership largely an invention of his own? None of these questions has ever been publicly asked – much less answered.

My lack of personal knowledge of any of the leaders is my principal reason for not presuming to depict any of them by name, or even by implication, on the stage. Nevertheless there is a certain similarity between what one hears of the views and militant idealism of Pearse and some of those expressed by my character Tetley. The circumstances of the surrender, as depicted in my play through the conversations of Tetley and Palliser, are of course fanciful. Nor is there any reason to believe that some earlier efforts to negotiate were actually frustrated by the firing of a machine-gun. Apart from these dramatic inventions, the other details of my play are as factual as I can make them. I have listened to many accounts of those last days, as described to me by men who had to run the gauntlet of O'Connell Street under fire, and I remember very clearly the conversations of the rebels in my own home. But what I recollect most clearly of all is the aspect of Easter Week that is the most happily glossed over today – the intense hostility with which the whole affair was regarded by the Dublin public.

At this distance it is hard to realize the widespread contempt in which the 'Sinn Fein Volunteers' were generally held prior to the Rising. Ireland, as a whole, was enthusiastically in the War on the side of the Allies, and these non-combatant warriors were figures of fun in a world that was engaged on a very considerable struggle elsewhere. It is probable that this contempt was more instrumental in driving the Volunteers into action at that time than any political or economic motives. 'Face', not slogans, is one of the most powerful motivating forces in the breasts of men, and these men had to prove that they were soldiers, or disband in the face of ridicule.

So it is not surprising that the prospect of picking up free sweets from the shattered window of a toffee shop should draw away the bulk of the crowd from the first reading of Ireland's Declaration of Independence. Standing at the corner of Stephen's Green, close to the Shelbourne Hotel, I listened with some youthful amusement to a small crowd of citizens shouting sarcasms at the insurgents behind the railings of the park. From time to time one of the latter would step out and wave a rifle in our direction, at which point the entire mob would scamper off up Merrion Row shouting abuse as it ran, only to return again a few minutes later to its old position, from which the comments were resumed. This sort of thing is not much spoken of today. Everybody is now convinced that he was in the Post Office with Pearse.

In spite of these objections to the official picture it is far from my intention in this play to debunk 1916 – a stupid accusation that I am glad to say is more generally made by those who have never fired a shot in anger, than by those who have. Whether or not we hold that the actual fighting was widespread or of first-rate quality, we must agree that the affair, on the whole, was a humane and well-intentioned piece of gallantry. And the more one sees of how these uprisings have since been conducted elsewhere, the more reason everybody has to be pleased with Easter Week. In those days nobody had much experience of warfare, or of what would be likely to occur if the British Army were challenged in open rebellion for the first time in three or four generations. Nowadays, there is hardly a corner of the globe that has not got plenty of data on this subject, but we must not forget that the Irish Volunteers were the first to try. For this reason alone, the Republicans must be credited with considerable courage in taking the field at all; and in at least two engagements in the course of the week they showed military aptitude of the highest quality, as did, also, the poor old British Tommy, when driven to perform impossible tasks that only tanks would be employed upon today.

331

Brave men are always exciting to write about, particularly when they are afflicted with doubts, and deficient in technical training; and in a wider sense *The Scythe and the Sunset* presents a picture that has been repeated so often in the course of the past forty years that one may legitimately doubt whether its local significance is of very much importance after all. The passing of an imperial civilization in which many of us were brought up is a process that has usually presented the same pattern – although not always so coherently – ever since the opening phase in Dublin. It is not an Irish but a world phenomenon, that the man who loses is often the man who wins, and that each side usually expends as much energy in playing the other fellow's game as it spends in furthering its own.

The conflict of the man with the idea against the man of action is as old as the battle of Pope and Emperor, and what each has to say for himself is as important now as it has been since the trial of Jesus. And whether in Cairo, Delhi, or in Jerusalem, or in Nicosia, I can still visualize some local Palliser rigging that machine-gun in a fury. And I would still be asked afterwards why he did so – this in a world where we not only rig machine-guns for our foes but supply them in bulk to the other side with unfailing regularity.

The fact is, that, outside the theatre, men do not act from logical motives as often as they act under the promptings of the urge that I mentioned before – this thing that the Orientals call 'face'. If it is not permissible to depict this well-known phenomenon on the stage without elaborating the reasons for it, that is the theatre's look-out. Not mine.

The Scythe and the Sunset

This play was first produced at the Poets' Theatre in Cambridge, Massachusetts, on March 14th, 1958, with the following cast:

Dr Myles MacCarthy	JOHN FRID
Roisin	CATHERINE AHERN
Emer Nic Gabhann	SUSAN McCLINTOCK
Michael Maginnis	RAY GIRARDIN, JR.
Endymion	MICHEAL LINENTHAL
Sean Tetley	JUDGE SPRINGER
J. Williams	JACK RODGERS
Liam O'Callaghan	EDMUND ROCHE
Captain Anthony Palliser	JOHN LASELL
Captain Clattering	JOHN A. COE
A Volunteer	JOHN KING

The play was produced by William Driver, the setting designed by Nyna Brael.

The first European production was by the Abbey Theatre Company playing at The Queen's Theatre, Dublin, on May 19th, 1958.

Dr Myles MacCarthy	DENIS BRENNAN
Roisin	CAITLIN NI BHEARAIN (CATHLEEN BARRINGTON)
Emer Nic Ghabhann	DOIRIN NI MHAIDIN (DOREEN MADDEN)
Michael Maginnis	LIAM O FOGHLU (BILL FOLEY)
Endymion	UINSIONN O DUBHLAINN (VINCENT DOWLING)
Sean Tetley	EAMON GUAILLI (EDDIE GOLDEN)
J. Williams	MICHAEL O hAONGHUSA (MICHAEL HENNESSY)
Seamus O'Callaghan	PEADAR O LUAIN (PEADAR LAMB)
Captain Anthony Palliser	TOMAS P. MACCIONAITH (T. P. McKENNA)
Captain Clattering	PADRAIG MACLEID (PAT LAYDE)
Volunteers and others	MICHAEL O BRIAIN (MICHAEL O'BRIEN),
	FRAINC MACMORNAIN (FRANK MORAN),
	DAIRE DE PAOR (DERRY POWER).

The play was produced by Ria Mooney, the setting designed by Tomás MacAnna, the Stage Manager was Seán O Maonaigh (Seán Mooney).

The action of the play takes place in a small cafe in the centre of Dublin.

ACT ONE
    Scene 1   Opens shortly before noon on Easter Monday, 1916.
    Scene 2   Continues about an hour and a half later.
ACT TWO   Tuesday afternoon.
ACT THREE Friday evening.

ACT ONE

Scene 1

An unpretentious restaurant, known as the Pillar Café, one floor up in a building facing on to a wide street. It is the kind of place where, whatever the hour of day, the meals maintain the same quality, centering around bread and butter, bacon and eggs, and strong stewed tea which comes from an urn on the counter. On this counter are also a number of glass-covered stands containing packets of biscuits, chunks of plum cake, currant buns, and jam pots. There is also a dingy showcase exhibiting a mixed collection of chocolate bars, tins of toffee, raffle tickets, and condiments. On the wall behind the counter is stored the crockery, and there is also a hatch, leading through to the kitchen. The room is furnished with a number of small tables covered with stained cloths and surrounded by rickety chairs. On the opposite side to the counter is a low platform on which stands an upright piano with a pile of sheet music on top. A wide window to the rear looks out across the street to an Ionic colonnade, the interior of which is plastered with recruiting posters. Towards the rear, a narrow pillar holds up a portion of the ceiling, and there are two doors: one behind the counter, leading to the kitchen, and the other a swing door on the opposite side, leading to a landing from which presumably a flight of stairs goes down to the street. The whole impression is unappetizing, and should convey the ever-present smell of cabbage-water. Yet there is an air of sordid Latin gaiety mixed with this solid Dublin background, that shows itself in the décor. The flags of what used laughably to be called 'the Allies' decorate the pillar, and on the walls are pinned coloured reproductions of scenes from the Bay of Naples, pictures of Bonzo dogs, Bairnsfather cartoons, religious emblems, and a portrait of Victor Emmanuel.

When the Curtain rises it is a bright, sunlit morning, and two customers occupy adjoining tables. One is a handsome, earnest-

335

*looking woman in her late twenties, plainly dressed in the lower-
middle-class mode of the period. She is wearing dark glasses and is
reading a religious magazine as she finishes her lunch. The other is
a saturnine gentleman in the middle forties whose clothes, although
stamping him as a member of the professional classes, have a
rumpled appearance that suggests that he has not been to bed for a
night or two. From his lapel dangles the admission check to the
enclosure of a race-course. He is studying a menu card with some
distaste. Beside him, waiting for his order, stands a pretty young
shop-girl who is in her street clothes and hat but wears an apron.
Offstage, in an adjoining flat, somebody is playing a piano. It is
actually heard before the Curtain rises, and continues into the
scene. Bartok's 'Evening in the Country' is suggested, but any
music of a similar type that would be considered modern in 1916
will do if the mood is right.*

MACCARTHY (*with a shudder*). Haven't you got anything more suitable for breakfast?

ROISIN. Breakfass? And it ten of twelve?

MACCARTHY. Yes, I know that it's a little late. Would I be patronizing this fly-parlour if breakfast was still to be had in any of the
more sanitary hotels?

ROISIN. You wouldn't be here at all if it was closed the way it
should be a Easter Monda.

MACCARTHY. How true. Today we celebrate the opening of a tomb
in Palestine by closing all the local tombs. Wilde thyme is
blowing now in all the banks, and the officials are at large, airing
their tots on Kingstown Pier. (*He turns to the other customer.*)
What is this lady having? No, don't tell me. I can see for myself.
(*The woman – EMER – gives him a cold glance around her
magazine.*)

MACCARTHY (*politely*). Good morning. (*Then, to* ROISIN.) Do you
suppose that was a snub?

ROISIN. Would that surprise ya?

MACCARTHY (*with a happy thought*). Maybe she takes me for a
masher. Is this music your own selection, madam? Because it
affects my metabolism.
(*EMER stares at him again without replying.*)

ROISIN. That's coming from the nex door. In Miss Garrity's.

MACCARTHY. Miss Garrity's Palm Court Restaurant?

ROISIN. No. It's owney a Servants' Registry. But she does be practising on the pianna when there's no one in. D'ye know.

MACCARTHY. I'm not surprised there's no one in. (*He rises.*) Let us indicate our disapproval to Miss Garrity.

(*He crosses and knocks on the wall. The music stops.*)

MACCARTHY. Results, by God! I wish I was as successful in my practice. (*He returns to his table.*) And now to business before you go off to wherever you're going. Send out the chef.

ROISIN. The which?

MACCARTHY. No. I realize that would be a misnomer. The proprietor.

ROISIN. Oh, the boss. He's off at Fairyhouse.

MACCARTHY. At the races! Dear me. What time did you say it was?

ROISIN. The Angelus will be anny minnit now.

MACCARTHY. There's no need to bring religion into it. Bring me the usual – a cup of stewed, lukewarm tea, a piece of damp toast, smeared with what is alleged to be butter, and half a portion of potato jam.

(ROISIN *tosses her head and goes off to the counter.*)

ROISIN. Ennuf ole guff to float a battleship.

MACCARTHY. I see you have a telephone. (*He rises and goes to where it hangs on the wall near the window.*) Maybe it works. I have a sure tip for the second race, and must engage an outside car.

(*He lifts the receiver as a young man enters rather sheepishly from the street. He is in the uniform of a minor tramway official, and has shiny black hair, long lashes, and a friendly, intelligent expression. In his lapel is a Pioneer shield, bearing the symbol of the Sacred Heart.*)

MAGINNIS. Hello.

ROISIN. So it's you, Mickser Maginnis!

MAGINNIS. *Dias Muire dhuit.* I tought I'd maybe find ya.

MACCARTHY (*at the phone*). Is there anybody there?

ROISIN. I tought you said you was goin route-marchin?

MAGINNIS. They called it off.

(EMER *smiles significantly.*)

ROISIN (*indignantly*). Called it off! Is this the time to be tellin me that?

MAGINNIS (*a little shrilly*). It's not my fault, Roisin. It's not my fault.

ROISIN. I mighta known.

MAGINNIS. It's early yet. Can ya not come now?

ROISIN. Come now is it? An' no one in the place excep meself! (*She slams a plate and a knife on* MACCARTHY'S *table.*)

Let's go to Bray, sez he, a Monda,

Or maybe join the lads at Blackrock Baths.
We might, sez I, for there's a day due te me.
But then, it's No. They've called minoovers for the Volunteers.
Ah, never fret, sez I, I'll work a Monda so
An' save me hollyer for a better day.
So off goes the Boss te the races,
Glad enuff te have me stop behind.
An' out comes the sun,
Te warm the jarvies on the jaunt te Fairyhouse.
An' buckets an' prams on Merrion Strand.
An' chizlers feedin' ducks in Stephen's Green,
Or peddlin' their way up te the Pine Forest.
But once he has me spancelled te the sink
Where are yer man's minoovers now?
Like tealeaves – up the spout.

MAGINNIS. It's not my fault. It's orders from the chief a staff.

ROISIN. That's what I am meself . . . the chief an' all the staff.
There's no playin' at wars for this Judy. It's hard labour for me.
(MAGINNIS *turns petulantly to the window, and looks out.*)

EMER (*who has been collecting her things*). Can I have my bill,
please.

MACCARTHY. This lady speaks, after all. Which is more than can be
said for the exchange.
(*He rattles the phone, and then gives it up.* ROISIN *works out
the bill.*)

MACCARTHY. What's all this pother about a route march? This is
not a military uniform, is it?

ROISIN. The Flyboy Fusiliers.

MAGINNIS. Ah, dry up for God's sake.

ROISIN (*pursing her lips*). Ninepence the spaghetti . . . threepence
the bread an' butter . . . and three ha'pence the cuppa tea.
One . . . an' a penny ha'penny.

MACCARTHY (*to* EMER). Clearly the course of true love is not running
smoothly. May I sit down here for a moment?

EMER. No.
(*She pays the money which* ROISIN *takes to the cash register.*)

MACCARTHY (*sitting down*). Thank you. You are a stranger in this
country, I expect. So you will hardly understand the difficulties
we Irish are up against in our sex relationships.

EMER (*enigmatically*). What makes you think that I'm a stranger?

MACCARTHY. There is an air of mystery behind those enigmatic
glasses. Something tells me that you are a beautiful spy. Nobody

but a stranger to our city would look for a feast on a Feast Day.

EMER. Then why are *you*?

MACCARTHY. My circumstances are very special.

ROISIN. Been on the tiles, I'll be bound.

MACCARTHY. On the tiles!

ROISIN. How well I know the signs. He's afeared to go home.

MACCARTHY. A neo-Thom-cat descending from the chimney-pots after a night of what is laughably called sin. Please don't scold me while I have this taste of linoleum in my mouth.

EMER. What you need is a good purgative.

MACCARTHY. My dear lady, medical advice is quite useless to me. I am a doctor myself, and I know how unreliable it is. You're not a member of the D'Oyly Carte Opera Company, by any chance, required to rehearse this glorious afternoon?

EMER. No, I'm not.

MACCARTHY. 'Full to the brim with girlish glee.' No? Well then perhaps you will share a car with me to Fairyhouse?

EMER (*going through her bag*). No.

MACCARTHY. Too bad. My wife can't stand me, either.

EMER. I'm really not interested.

MACCARTHY. I suspect it's much the same with Marie Bashkirtseff behind the samovar. She also finds her lover unsatisfactory.

ROISIN. Now don't be puttin' me into one o' me tantararums.

MAGINNIS. What's that you said?

MACCARTHY. Notice? You might suppose they were objecting to the word 'unsatisfactory'. But it's not that at all. It's because I referred to them as lovers.

MAGINNIS. You'll be finding yerself in trouble one a these days.

MACCARTHY. You see. They love each other, but it only embarrasses them. I often wonder how this race of ours has managed to propagate itself at all, with the age of consent at thirty-five. Good God, man, there's nothing derogatory in being her lover! The birds and the bees do it too.

MAGINNIS. I'm not askin' about any birds or bees.

MACCARTHY. Because you disapprove of any rumours you have heard on the subject.

MAGINNIS. Would you like a puck on the gob?

MACCARTHY. Don't be deceived by our charm, madam. None of us are any damn good as lovers. No regard was taken of our native peculiarities when the formula of passion was being worked out. Dr Yeats, our national poet, expressed it clearly. (*He intones.*)

'What's the use of kissing your girl
Only once a night?
Only once a night.
You know it isn't right.'

EMER (*sarcastically*). Dr Yeats, indeed!

MACCARTHY. Printed, I assure you, by the Cuala Press, with hand-coloured illustrations by a hairy fairy. I'll send you a copy if you leave me your address.

ROISIN. That one has a great nose for other people's business.

MACCARTHY. This sort of bullying is every Irishman's business. Because he doesn't sweep you off your feet, he's blamed for everything else – even when his friends fail to turn up for a route march. Er . . . what is this organization, by the way?

MAGINNIS. The Volunteers.

MACCARTHY. Which of the many varieties?

ROISIN. A Mickey Dazzler – that's what he is, drillin' for Ireland in the Banba Hall.

MAGINNIS. And what's wrong with that?

ROISIN. Oh, nuttin at all. You'll be a gineral with that lot before yer brother's a serjeant in the Munsters.

MACCARTHY (*to* EMER). My confusion is due to the fact that we have so many armies in this country – north and south – in addition to His Majesty's. Five, I believe, is the actual number at present.

MAGINNIS. It's not Ireland's war.

MACCARTHY. The only thing that they all have in common is the fact that they do not take part in any fighting. The Boy Scouts are the only independent belligerents in the present war. You follow this, I hope, Miss . . . er . . . what did you say your name was?

EMER (*looking at her watch*). Smith.

MACCARTHY. Smith. Oh well, keep it a secret if you insist. One incognito is as good as another.

EMER (*with a grim smile*). As a matter of fact, it *is* Smith.

MACCARTHY. I understand your caution, however much I feel personally hurt about it. Mary Smith, I suppose.

EMER (*with some distaste*). They once christened me Pearl, believe it or not.

MACCARTHY (*delighted*). The snowy-breasted Peril! How sensible you English are! Micheál here has got to live up to the moniker of an archangel, but you are content to nestle in the modest oyster. It's a pity our two races can never communicate. Yours is the world of 'Keep the Home Fires Burning' – of cupie dolls and *Nash's Magazine.* You have Billy Bunter to rag and slackers to give white feathers to. You have your Empire and your House of Lords to provide you with endless amusement. You don't give a damn whether you are an Angle, a Saxon or a Jute, and you are fortunate enough to be fighting for your bloody lives. Here we have only a land of saints and cemeteries that laughs at nothing but itself, and where even the route marches to glory never come off.

EMER. Before long you're in for a big surprise.

(MACCARTHY *goes back to the telephone carrying a milk jug.*)

MACCARTHY. You must have a word with my wife. You won't like her, but she's English too, and it may divert her attention from me. A penny? Ah yes.

(*He feels in a pocket, holding jug and receiver in one hand.*)

ROISIN. Lippin' full, at this hour!

MACCARTHY (*into the telephone*). Hello.

MAGINNIS. As well oiled as Kelly for Bykes if ye ask me.

ROISIN. All you was asked was if ye'd be free for Easter Monda.

(MAGINNIS *turns away rather shamefacedly to the window.*)

MACCARTHY. 2663 please. Sorry to disturb you at your devotions.

(ENDYMION *pushes open the street door causing MacCarthy to spill the milk over the side of his face. He is a fantastic figure wearing an old-fashioned small bowler hat with a string attached to it, a long-skirted sports coat, and a very high hard collar. His trousers are tucked into leggings. He wears an eyeglass and carries a bundle of sticks, umbrellas, and a sword in a scabbard, all of which are tied together with red tape and with a seat card reading 'Engaged'.*)

ENDYMION. Did you want to speak to me?

MACCARTHY. Ow!

ROISIN. Jeesus Mary Joseph!

ENDYMION. Endymion. At Home today. R.S.V.P.

MACCARTHY. Never startle a man when he's in a certain condition.

ENDYMION.

        I just dropped in to see
        That all is ready for the party.

MACCARTHY. Then drip out again. Nobody wants you here. (*Into the phone.*) Oh hello, my love. Sorry I can't speak to you now. My ear is full of milk.

(*He hangs up.*)

ROISIN. It's owney Endymion. He put the heart across me.

EMER. Is he one of your patients?

341

MACCARTHY. Not any longer, so don't encourage him. He'll have no parties at my place.

EMER. What is this place of yours?

MACCARTHY. The Little Flower Refuge for Nervous Complaints. Drop in any time.

ENDYMION. St Vitus's Ballroom.

EMER. Does this mean you're mental?

MACCARTHY. Not personally, of course. But some of my patients are.

ENDYMION.

> At twelve noon.
> Uniforms and desecrations will be worn
> And half the Civil Service will be there.

MACCARTHY. That's a damnable lie about the Civil Service. At least half of them were never at my place.

ENDYMION.

> Carriages in six days' time.
> And for the few who will not leave,
> Beds are provided by the Lord Lieutenant.
> I hope to see you all.

(*He bows and stalks out.*)

MACCARTHY. It's always a pleasure to see the last of him.

ROISIN. Why do they let the poor *omadhaun* wander in the streets at all?

MACCARTHY. He's quite harmless . . . a personal friend of the Chief Secretary and a very gallant fellow in his day. As a matter of fact, we do sometimes have very pleasant little parties out at my place.

EMER. I suppose nobody can distinguish the guests from the patients?

MACCARTHY. Bless you, we don't mix socially with the patients. They only serve the drinks. I wish you'd come to one.

EMER. Can you do ordinary doctoring? Regular work, I mean?

MACCARTHY. My dear young lady, I am one of the best-known doctorers in Dublin, and as for my regularity, it is . . . very good indeed.

(*She rises, looks at her watch, and puts another bag on the table.*)

EMER. Well, maybe you can be of some use.

MACCARTHY. I can indeed. To begin with, I can show you the sights of the city. Guinness's Brewery – the corpses in St Michan's – Lady Gregory . . .

EMER (*opening her bag*). You don't have to show me around Dublin.

MACCARTHY (*going to the window*). Now here we have the finest street in Europe, not forgetting the Nevsky Prospect . . . immortalized in folk-lore and ballad as 'The Meeting of the Waters'. You know the song, no doubt?

EMER. I know the song, and it has nothing to do with O'Connell Street.

MACCARTHY. Yes, O'Connell begins it in person. To the left – our Liberator, standing on his pedestal, surrounded by his large illegitimate family, looking out over the water. Next we come to the effigy of a nonentity who is said to have brought the water-supply to Dublin . . . a memorial to an unknown plumber. And here, to the right, between us and the public urinal, presiding over the entire vista – Lord Nelson . . .

(*The tramp of feet is heard behind his voice.*)

ROISIN. What's that I hear?

(*As the Angelus starts to ring,* EMER *blesses herself.*)

MAGINNIS. It's the Angelus. (*He blesses himself.*)

ROISIN. No, listen.

MACCARTHY. . . . . Lord Nelson who made his name on the water . . .

ROISIN (*pushing him aside as she goes to the window*). Eggscuse me, It's marchin' I hear.

MACCARTHY. . . . . a one-eyed English sailorman with an eye for only one thing . . .

ROISIN. No minoovers how are ya! What's that I see comin' down the street? The Christian Brothers, I suppose, on their way to a sodality?

MAGINNIS (*looking out too*). What's on ya at all?

MACCARTHY. . . . . a sailorman with a bacchante by Romney, pregnant in every port. Don't push me.

MAGINNIS. The Volunteers! But they tole me . . .

ROISIN. They tole me this. They tole me that. The war's put off till half pass five. Don't shoot till ye see the green in the white of me eye.

MAGINNIS. Roisin, they tole me it was off. I don't understand it at all.

ROISIN. The warrior's late for the battle. The bombadier has missed the boat. Oh, wait till I tell the brother an' he home on leave. He'll burst his britches with the laughter. An' you callin' him a renegade not two years ago for joinin' up with the fightin' men.

MAGINNIS. Roisin, will ye listen to me . . .

ROISIN (*bitterly*). Ah, youse ones give me the sick. I'd be ashamed

343

te be seen walkin' out wid ya an' the men in kharki dyin' in Flanders Field.

MAGINNIS (*hysterically*). I'll leave the Volunteers that's what I'll do. I'll not be made a mock of any longer. I'm no flyboy fusileer.
(*There is a crash of glass outside in the street, following a shouted command. A confused babble of voices is next heard. In the room there is a sinister pause. From the room next door, the piano is heard once again. Albeniz's 'Cordoba' is suggested.*)

EMER (*finally*). Has it started?

MACCARTHY (*looking out of the window*). Most extraordinary.

ROISIN (*who is back at the bar*). Well? What's the latest from the front?

MACCARTHY. Most extraordinary thing I ever saw.
(EMER *is taking off her glasses and hat.*)

MAGINNIS. Begob, they're in action.

MACCARTHY. Swarming into the Post Office . . . breaking the windows, and turning the people out into the street.

ROISIN. Janey Mac, let's have a luk at this. Turning the people out?
(EMER *starts to pull some of the tables over towards the window.*)

MAGINNIS. Posted in Orders so it was. All minoovers is cancelled by the chief a staff.

MACCARTHY. If those are Minoovers, give me a night at the Tivoli.

MAGINNIS. If they're goin' inta action why wouldn't they let me know?

MACCARTHY (*covering his eyes and coming away*). Maybe they just want to buy some stamps.

EMER. Move over please.

ROISIN. Ay, what are ya doin' with them tables?

EMER. We want this place. They'll be in here shortly.

MAGINNIS. There's two of them coming over now.

MACCARTHY (*sitting down and closing his eyes*). Pardon me . . . the feet . . . painful . . .

ROISIN. Whatja mean – want this place? Who are you anyways?

MACCARTHY. Don't ask her. Let's forget it and start looking for a cuke buke.

EMER. I'm sorry we'll have to disturb you. But this is war.

ROISIN. War?

MACCARTHY. About a hundred men with a cab. Yes, I saw a cab too. And a couple of drays filled with pikes and guns. No. I saw nothing.

344

MAGINNIS. Why wouldn't they tell me? Do they take me for an informer or a scab?

EMER. I told you to expect a surprise.

(*The piano stops, and two men enter from the street, dressed in green uniforms, with felt hats fastened up at one side. The first is the younger of the two – TETLEY – a quiet, clean-shaven man in the thirties with a square, resolute jaw and far-away eyes. He wears a greatcoat over his Sam Browne belt. The other – WILLIAMS – is a stouter man in his forties, with a bushy moustache, and a revolver on his belt. He has no overcoat. EMER turns to them expectantly.*)

TETLEY. Is this the place?

EMER (*her eyes shining*). Yes, Commandant.

WILLIAMS. Is there any way through to the rear?

EMER. You'll have to knock a hole through the wall of the kitchen. In there. (*She points*).

WILLIAMS. That's simple.

TETLEY. I'll send up a couple of men with a crowbar. (*He bows politely to those present*). Excuse us, please. (*He goes out*).

WILLIAMS. And you'd better collect your equipment from the dray.

EMER. I know what I have to do.

(*She takes off her overcoat, disclosing a green tunic and skirt. Putting the overcoat on a chair, she takes a hat from her bag and leaves the room. WILLIAMS goes to inspect the kitchen.*)

ROISIN. Knock a hole with a crowbar? In the name of God what's goin' on?

MAGINNIS (*grimly*). Well, if that's the way it is, it's nuttin te do wit me.

MACCARTHY (*his eyes closed*). Corporation officials – that's all they are.

ROISIN. Carryin' guns?

MACCARTHY. Perhaps they intend to raise the rates.

(*A shot is heard outside. Everybody jumps.*)

MACCARTHY. There! They've raised the rates.

MAGINNIS (*sarcastically*). A Risin' – that's what it is. But owney for them that's let in on it.

MACCARTHY (*opening his eyes*). Once it was too many strangers in the house. Now it's a damn sight too many friends.

(*TETLEY enters followed by two VOLUNTEERS carrying tools and a crowbar.*)

MACCARTHY (*wincing and closing his eyes again*). Suppose we discuss drink. In Singapore, I hear, the climate makes them sweat, so rendering whiskey auto-somatic.

TETLEY (*with grave politeness*). I'm sorry to have to disturb you people, but we're taking over this entire block. There's no cause for alarm.

MAGINNIS (*hostile*). Who's alarmed?

MACCARTHY. I am. Definitely.

(WILLIAMS *enters. He speaks much more brusquely.*)

WILLIAMS. Across here in the kitchen. Be sure a passage goes through to the rear. And all the window glass will have to be broken.

ROISN (*getting in their way*). You will not! Not in my kitchen.

TETLEY. Any damage will be repaid in full by the Irish Republic.

ROISIN. Irish Republic how are ya! No yuck in fancy dress is taking a crowbar inta my kitchen excep the plumber.

WILLIAMS. Keep out of the way, girl.

ROISIN. I will not.

MACCARTHY (*hastily rising*). Now listen, my dear, let's not forget these men are dying for their country.

ROISIN. Let them die somewhere else so, an' give their country a chance.

WILLIAMS. Look, I'm warning you . . .

MACCARTHY. Please, please, let's have no acrimony, please. Why not begin by telling us in simple language just what this Irish Republic is?

TETLEY. It will be proclaimed in a few minutes' time.

MACCARTHY. Proclaimed? Who by?

TETLEY (*after a brief pause*). As a matter of fact . . . I've got to arrange about that. Thanks for reminding me.

(*With a swift, charming smile he hurries off.*)

WILLIAMS (*motioning impatiently to the* VOLUNTEERS). Out of the way now, miss. Go on in, men. (*As they hesitate.*) Ach, will I have to shift her myself?

(*He grabs* ROISIN *and pushes her aside. She struggles and tries to slap his face. As the two* VOLUNTEERS *slip by into the kitchen* MAGINNIS *interferes, and* WILLIAMS *turns on him, his hand on his gun.*)

ROISIN. Leave go of me ye scut or ye'll find there's more scrappin' in me than in the whole of yer windy militia.

MAGINNIS. Leave that girl alone.

WILLIAMS. Keep off me – you!

ROISIN. Easy, Mickser. Can't ya see he has a gun?

346

(*As they freeze for a moment into inaction,* MACCARTHY *hastens to the piano.*)

MACCARTHY. Let's have some gay music. I hate hearing my teeth chatter.

(*He raps on the wall without any result. From the kitchen comes the sound of hammering and smashing, which continues at intervals till the end of the scene.*)

WILLIAMS. Who are you?

MAGINNIS. A volunteer.

WILLIAMS. Then why aren't you outside with the men?

MAGINNIS. Because I take me orders from the chief a staff. Whose orders am I supposed to take?

WILLIAMS (*with a contemptuous laugh*). I don't know anything about your chief of staff. If it wasn't for us in the Labour movement the Volunteers would still be forming fours. But you're in it now, all right. We're all in it together.

(EMER *enters staggering under a folded stretcher and several boxes of medical supplies. She drops the stretcher on the floor, and carries the boxes to the counter, where she takes out a Red Cross apron and starts to unpack.*)

EMER. We've taken the Castle and three barracks. Two brigades of Germans have landed in Kerry. The whole country has risen.

MAGINNIS. My God, is this true?

WILLIAMS (*nodding his head*). There'll be no going back on this. (*He turns his head as scattered cheers come from outside.*) Oh, are they reading the Proclamation? I suppose I'd better go down.

(*He goes out without any great show of enthusiasm.* EMER *flies to the window, as a voice outside is heard reading the Proclamation.*)

EMER. To think that I've lived to see this day! A new flag flying over the Post Office!

MACCARTHY. I suppose it's too much to hope that there's a policeman somewhere?

EMER (*jubilant*). No more police! We're free of those bosthoons for ever.

MACCARTHY. Woman, you have been deceiving me. You *are* a beautiful spy after all. My God, what did I say to her that I shouldn't? Guinness's – the corpses – Lady Gregory . . .

EMER. This place is picked as a dressing station, and . . .

MACCARTHY. And I am to be your Christian slave. I see it all now.

347

EMER. If you're really a doctor there'll be plenty of work before long.

MACCARTHY. I love work. I can sit looking at it for hours.

ROISIN. Two peep-o'-day boys making poor little Belgium outa my kitchen! Can nobody stop them?

EMER (*at the window*). Be quiet girl, and let me hear the words of the Proclamation.

ROISIN. If that fella could suck as well as he can blow they'd give him a job at the waterworks.

(*She stares indignantly into the kitchen, as* MAGINNIS *sits down gloomily.*)

EMER (*banging on the window*). Oh, cheer, everybody! What's the matter with them all? Why can't they cheer? Don't they know they're free?

(*There is a crash of glass, followed by some scattered cheering.*)

ROISIN (*turning*). What's that?

MACCARTHY (*pointing sardonically out of the window*). The Birth of a Nation.

EMER (*sinking down in despair*). Oh, no!

MAGINNIS. Well anyway, the crowd is cheerin' him at last.

MACCARTHY. I'm afraid not. They're only breaking into Noblett's toffee shop.

(*The hammering continues from the kitchen, as the cheering grows from outside.*)

CURTAIN

Scene 2

It is about an hour later. The glass in the window has apparently been knocked out, and some of the tables and chairs have been piled in front of the aperture to make an ineffective barricade. EMER – *now wearing a Red Cross apron – is unpacking bandages and bottles of disinfectant on the counter, and clearing away the cups and cake stands to make room for them.* MAGINNIS *is still sitting gloomily in a chair with his hands in his pockets, while* ROISIN *and* MACCARTHY *are gossiping near the window.*

348

ROISIN. Will I ever forget the night this body-builder outa Maguire and Gatchell's used te be oxin' his way up an down Henry Street with the string a hurley medals he fecked from Moran's on the Quays doin' His Lordship with a strap with straw hair how are ya up from Tullamore oh beef te the heels ye'd tink soap an wather cost a fortune. (*She raises her head and listens.*) Lissen! It's my belief som'in's comin'.

(EMER *is now putting a Red Cross flag on a pole.*)

EMER. What is it?

MACCARTHY. Whatever it is, it'll still be pleasanter than home. Heigh ho. There's no place like home . . . for which we can be heartily thankful.

ROISIN. The people are clearin' off the street.

(*Horses' hooves approach.*)

MACCARTHY. Hark, I hear hooves!

ROISIN (*gleefully*). It's horses . . . an' men on them. Fightin' men for wonct.

MAGINNIS (*hurrying to the window*). Let's see.

ROISIN. Them's the lads . . . the real McCoy at last.

MACCARTHY. My God, you don't mean proper soldiers?

ROISIN (*as the hoof-beats grow louder*). It's the Lancers.

MACCARTHY. Lancers! Woman, give me that flag.

ROISIN. A whole troop a them.

(MACCARTHY *struggles to take the flag from* EMER.)

MACCARTHY. Have you no morals, woman? Don't you realize the importance of hanging out this rag? Don't crowd me.

(*He obtains possession of it, and sticks it out of the window.*)

ROISIN. Will ye look at them . . . gallopin' straight at the Post Office . . . flags flyin' on their lances . . . cobbles sparkin' under the hooves! Them are the boys'll banjax the lot of them!

MACCARTHY. There now.

ROISIN (*shouting*). Up the Lancers! Up the Royal Irish!

MACCARTHY. Thank God, we're safe now.

(*There is a volley of shots, followed by some confused shouting and the hooves then gallop off.* MACCARTHY *appears to swoon.*)

MACCARTHY. Is anybody still alive?

(*Distant cheering.*)

ROISIN. Oh God! They opened fire from the Post Office.

EMER. Can't you act like a man?

MACCARTHY. I have no intention of acting like a man.

EMER. Well at least pull yourself together.

349

MACCARTHY. I am perfectly pulled together. In fact I'm in a knot.
Don't tell me that ammunition was real?

EMER. What did you expect? Confetti?

ROISIN (*incredulously*). They fired on them! . . . fired on the men
and the horses!

MAGINNIS. One o' them is down. Will ya look.

ROISIN. The poor horse! Lyin' there in the middle a the road. Oh,
the murderin' blagards.

MAGINNIS. Here come the Volunteers. They're pickin' him up.
They're carryin' him over here.

MACCARTHY. What? The horse?

MAGINNIS. No, ye eediot! The Lancer.

MACCARTHY. You're quite sure? I have no experience as a vet.

EMER. Get that door open.

MACCARTHY (*peering carefully out the window.*) What's happening
now? Aren't the soldiers still there?

ROISIN. They've ridden off up the street. I can't see them now.

> (*A third rebel – O'CALLAGHAN – and one of the* VOLUNTEERS
> *carry in a British officer –* PALLISER *– whom they place on the
> stretcher. This rebel is more exotic and striking than either
> of the others whom we have seen. He has the high colour and
> burning eyes of an invalid. Around his neck is wound a white
> scarf, and he coughs frequently. From one side of his belt
> dangles an enormous pistol in a hanging holster. On the other
> side he carries a sword. His uniform is neat and complete,
> and on one of his wrists is a slave bangle. He is highly strung,
> and over-dramatic in his gestures.* PALLISER *– who appears to
> be unconscious – is a man of about twenty-five, with a clipped
> military moustache.*)

O'CALLAGHAN. Can't anybody lend a hand?

> (MAGINNIS *runs to their assistance, and the other* VOLUNTEER,
> *when relieved of his burden, hurries off again.*)

MAGINNIS. Here. Let me.

ROISIN. Oh, the poor fella.

MACCARTHY (*suddenly becoming businesslike*). Don't carry him like
that, unless you want to break his neck. Get him down on the
stretcher.

ROISIN. Is he killed?

O'CALLAGHAN (*fanatically*). We got him with the first volley! Then
all the rest turned tail and galloped off like rats. Lord, it was
magnificent.

350

MACCARTHY (*rapidly examining the body*). Galloping rats indeed! Get me hot water – quick.

(MAGINNIS *runs for it to the counter.*)

ROISIN. You've killed him, ya scut!

O'CALLAGHAN (*exalted*). The insolence of them – riding up the street like that . . . expecting that we'd all come out with our hands up, I suppose. But we showed them something. We showed them.

ROISIN. Have ya no shame on ya for what ya did?

O'CALLAGHAN. This is war, girl. War!

MACCARTHY. Never mind what it is. Just hand me one of those napkins.

EMER. You don't need them. I've got dressings.

MACCARTHY (*taking them*). Clean, I hope.

O'CALLAGHAN. Who is this man?

EMER. He says he's a doctor.

O'CALLAGHAN. We'll need doctors. Let him carry on if he's willing.

ROISIN. Murderers – that's what youse are . . . you an' yer dirty . . .

PALLISER (*opening his eyes*). Goddam and blast. Damn. Damn. Damn.

MACCARTHY. Quite a coherent corpse.

ROISIN. Is he not dead at all?

MACCARTHY. He's dislocated a knee. Must have been knocked out, falling off his horse.

PALLISER. Hell and damnation blast it.

O'CALLAGHAN. Don't swear like that. There are women present.

MACCARTHY. Let him swear if he likes. He probably thinks he's at home .Cut the rest of that puttee off. And gently!

ROISIN (*going out to the street*). What about the poor horse? Some-thin' must be done about it.

PALLISER. Horse be damned. How did it throw me?

MACCARTHY. It didn't throw you, old boy. It just passed out with a bullet in the bum. There now. Hold him steady, you people, and I'll set it right away.

(*As* MAGINNIS *and* O'CALLAGHAN *hold his arms, and* EMER *holds his head,* MACCARTHY *sets the leg with a deft jerk.*)

PALLISER. Ow! What the hell . . . ?

MACCARTHY (*with a friendly pat and a smile*). There. All over now. Old Macan used to say, 'Always get the worst over before the patient knows what happening.' Now, a tight bandage and a couple of splints and you'll be all fixed up.

(*He snaps his fiingers at* EMER, *who fetches splints and ban-*

351

dages. Meanwhile MacCarthy *feels him over with expert fingers.*)

PALLISER. Call yourself a doctor?

MACCARTHY. Quite some time now since I've had the chance to do a bit of surgery. I always liked it. Keep that leg steady till I . . . No, you don't seem to have anything else.

O'CALLAGHAN. Will he be all right?

MACCARTHY (*putting on the splints with* EMER'S *help*). He'll not be able to get around for a bit, but he'll be all right.

O'CALLAGHAN. In that case, don't forget, everyone, that he's our first – no, our second – English prisoner.

PALLISER. Who are you calling English?

O'CALLAGHAN. Well, whatever you are there's no need to worry. You'll be treated strictly in accordance with the Hague Convention.

PALLISER. You mean the Geneva Convention.

O'CALLAGHAN (*stiffly*). I said the Hague Convention.

MACCARTHY. Just settle for the Firemen's Convention, and hand me a pair of scissors.

PALLISER. What happened to the rest of my troop?

O'CALLAGHAN. They turned tail and fled.

PALLISER. Oh, they did, did they.

MAGINNIS. They're still down there somewheres . . . hidin' behind the Parnell Monument.

O'CALLAGHAN. Wondering, no doubt, what hit them.

PALLISER. I shall stop somebody's leave for this.

O'CALLAGHAN. We mustn't be too hard on them. They little knew what they were up against. (*He offers his cigarette case.*) Cigarette?

PALLISER (*looking him over quizzically*). Well . . . that's very handsome of you. Thanks. (*He accepts one. Then, to* MACCARTHY.) Quite a fellow.

MACCARTHY (*fixing the splints*). Give him a light.

O'CALLAGHAN. You'll give your parole, of course?

PALLISER. What does that consist of?

O'CALLAGHAN. You know. Your honourable undertaking not to try to escape if we don't lock you up.

PALLISER. From all accounts, I'm not likely to get very far with this leg.

O'CALLAGHAN. Then you agree?

PALLISER. Certainly . . . if the alternative is to be locked up.

(*The telephone rings.* MACCARTHY *goes to it irritably.*)

MACCARTHY. Yes, yes, I'm coming. Who is it? As if I care a damn. No, it's not the Pro-cathedral. This is the Hell Fire Club.

(*He hangs up.*)

O'CALLAGHAN. Has that telephone not been cut? Can nobody carry out the simplest instructions?

(*He wrenches out the wires.*)

MACCARTHY. Now that was a tiresome thing to do. I still have several calls to make.

O'CALLAGHAN. Well, you can't make them from here.

(MACCARTHY *remains behind for a little while examining the severed wires, before returning to his patient.* TETLEY *appears in the door, carrying a machine-gun.*)

TETLEY. See what I've got.

MAGINNIS. A machine-gun!

O'CALLAGHAN. Splendid. How did you capture it?

TETLEY. Someone found it in the Post Office.

O'CALLAGHAN (*excited*). You mean to say they had that when we stormed the place?

TETLEY. Well – yes. It was somewhere upstairs.

O'CALLAGHAN. But this is tremendous. (*To the others.*) Look – we've captured a machine-gun.

TETLEY (*with a ghost of a wicked smile*). Well – yes. There was no ammunition. That's probably why nobody fired it.

O'CALLAGHAN (*disappointed*). Oh.

TETLEY. But we have some ourselves. That's why I brought it over. To see if somebody could tell us how to work it.

(*He gives a sly look at* PALLISER.)

MACCARTHY. Look here, you can't fire that thing from here. Don't you see the Red Cross flag?

TETLEY. We can't fire it at all unless somebody can put it together. Can you, Seamus?

O'CALLAGHAN. My battalion never had one. Don't you know anything about it?

TETLEY. How should I? I got my military training in the Board of Works. (*He looks at* PALLISER.) Pity.

PALLISER (*after a pause*). There's no good looking at me. I'm a prisoner.

TETLEY. Oh, of course. We could hardly expect an Englishman . . .

PALLISER. Listen. I was born and brought up in Greystones.

TETLEY. Oh, I beg your pardon. Then you certainly won't want to help us. I have an idea that it goes in this way.

MAGINNIS (*interested*). No, no. It goes the other way round.

O'CALLAGHAN. It does not! The belt obviously has to be on the other side.

MACCARTHY. Look – please will you leave that thing alone. Just to oblige me.

O'CALLAGHAN. Don't interfere. I happen to know that it must be this way up.

PALLISER. As a matter of fact, you're all wrong.

TETLEY. Oh?

PALLISER. For a bunch of alleged soldiers, I've never seen such ignorance.

TETLEY. There you are. I told you it goes the other way. He knows.

PALLISER. That nut on the left has to engage the . . . Here, pull it over here somebody. (*They do so*). It has to engage with this thing here.

MACCARTHY. Look here, this is all most improper. Who's rigging this machine-gun for what?

PALLISER (*stopping his work*). He's right. Why the hell should I be showing you how to fix it?

TETLEY (*with an amused shrug of his shoulders*). Why indeed?

PALLISER. I'm a prisoner. He told me so himself.

O'CALLAGHAN (*to* MACCARTHY). Why do you have to stick your nose into this?

MACCARTHY. Because I have some respect for the sanctity of my profession. That's why.

TETLEY. Never mind. We'll leave it here, and get Williams to fix it for us, when we can find him.

O'CALLAGHAN. I'll send for him. I think he's trying to get into Trinity. (*He goes.*)

MACCARTHY. My difficulty was to get out of Trinity. It took me seven years.

MAGINNIS. There's a man in my battalion was in the Boer War.

TETLEY. I suppose they had machine-guns then. Who are you, by the way? A Volunteer?

MAGINNIS. I was. But I'm going to leave.

TETLEY. That's too bad. Why?

MAGINNIS. Why yourself? Why wasn't I mobilized?

EMER. He's a renegade if he's leaving now.

MAGINNIS. It's well for you you're not a man – callin' me that.

TETLEY. I'm sure he's not that, Miss Nic Gabhann. He probably got the countermanding order.

MAGINNIS. I got me orders from the chief a staff. If I was wanted why wasn't I mobilized?

EMER. The chief of staff is to be ignored. He's not fit to lead a thing like this.

MAGINNIS. Ignored? What sort of an army is it where yer tole te ignore the chief a staff?

TETLEY. Not a very orthodox one, I'm afraid. We're all acting according to our lights. Nobody will blame you afterwards if you obey the chief of staff.

EMER. Nobody except all true Irishmen.

TETLEY. You mustn't be so bitter, Miss Nic Gabhann. I'm sure the chief of staff is doing what he feels is best for the country. It's we who are being insubordinate.

EMER (*passionately*). There you go again . . . trying to save the face of everybody but yourself! When you're the last man left in that Post Office, you'll die trying to find excuses for the others that have walked out on you.

MAGINNIS. I'm not walkin' out on anyone. All I want to know is whose orders I'm supposed to take.

TETLEY. You'll have to work that out for yourself. All I can say is that some of us have decided that now is the time to strike. If we wait any longer there'll be no Volunteers left, and this generation will go down in history as being as craven as the last. Personally I'm not going to accept that.

MAGINNIS. But have we any . . . any . . .

TETLEY. Do you mean, have we any chance?

EMER. Of course we have a chance. It's now or never. France is out of the war for want of men. The old enemy is on the run at last.

TETLEY. Well, we hope so, at any rate. As for France – we only have rumours to go on. But some people tell us that if we can manage to hold out for a certain number of days we'll have the right to be recognized as belligerents at the peace conference.

MAGINNIS. Is that the truth?

TETLEY (*with a shrug of his shoulders*). I hope so. But all I can say is this: that the greatest war in history is being fought – a war in which millions of men are laying down their lives for their countries. And as I'm a soldier too, I'd feel pretty mean if I didn't seize the opportunity of fighting for mine. That's all.

EMER. In years to come, every decent man in Ireland will be wishing he could say 'I was in the Post Office in 1916.' You have your chance now, Maginnis. Are you going to take it, or are you what that girl called you – a Mickey Dazzler?

(ROISIN *enters in some excitement.*)

ROISIN. The chizlers is all over the street eating sweets from Nob-

355

lett's. The women are dancing jigs in Talbot Street. I've never seen the like in all me born days.

MAGINNIS. Where can I get a gun?

TETLEY. Over in the Post Office. What's your unit?

MAGINNIS. C Company – Third Battalion.

TETLEY (*putting a hand on his shoulder*). Then they'll be wanting you out at Ballsbridge. I hope you're not going to regret this.

MAGINNIS. I don't give a damn if I do.

TETLEY (*laughing*). A lad after my own heart. Come on. I'll see to your orders myself.

ROISIN. Mickser – where are you going?

MAGINNIS. Where no one will call me a Mickey Dazzler.

(MAGINNIS *and* TETLEY *go out, followed by* EMER. ROISIN *runs to the window to look after them. Next door, the piano starts to play again. This time it is Satie's 'Gymnopédie, No. 3'.*)

ROISIN. Mickser!

MACCARTHY (*rising from his final bandaging*). There. That should repair itself if you give it a chance. Now how about another cup of your abominable tea, my dear?

PALLISER. Suits me too. Who's the pianist?

ROISIN. The oul wan next door. They ought te get her out.

(*She goes thoughtfully to the urn and pours out three cups.*)

MACCARTHY. And some of those nice Digestive Biscuits. We won't have them if they're not digestive. (*He lifts the receiver.*) Oh, hello! Are you there already? 2663 please. Of course it's an official call. This is the Chief Secretary speaking.

PALLISER. I thought he pulled out the wires of that thing.

MACCARTHY. Yes, but I stuck them back again. I suppose it's too much to hope that my home has been burnt to the ground. No – somebody answers. A penny? Oh! I would have thought that official calls were free. However . . . (*He puts a coin in the box.*) let's not be captious in such times. Ah – is that my love? This is your Tristram. I just wanted to tell you that I can't get home because of this er . . . this revolution . . . Yes, I said revolution . . . haven't you heard? Blood is flowing in the streets, my darling. And I . . . what? Now don't be vulgar, Margery. As a matter of fact I did have milk in my ear. Listen, darling, the most frightful things are happening in Sackville Street . . . dead horses everywhere. Well I'm damned. She doesn't believe me! (*He hangs up.*) It just shows the importance of never telling the truth.

ROISIN. (*bringing the cups*). Do youse take sugar?

PALLISER. No thanks.

(*Another crash of glass is heard, followed by cheering.*)

MACCARTHY (*feeling in his pockets*). Do you suppose that could be a tobacconist's? I'll come back for my tea after taking a peep. (*He goes.*)

PALLISER. Wouldn't you like to go too? I'll be quite all right, you know.

ROISIN. Are you sure, now? I've half a mind to go and see what's happening to Mickser.

PALLISER. Off you go, and take your time. I can look after myself now that I've got my tea.

(*She goes.* PALLISER *puts down his cup and pulls himself across to the window, where he takes down the phone, and looks out.*)

PALLISER. Hello. Hello. Put me through to the Royal Hospital . . . Certainly it's a military call. Hello. (*He puts in a penny.*) Yes. Get me Colonel Kennard quickly. Captain Palliser speaking. No . . . Kennard. K – E – N – the garrison commander . . . There must be somebody in charge of the British Empire, even if it is a bank holiday . . . Hello . . . Oh, it's you, Bunny. I thought I recognized the adenoids. (*He settles down cosily.*) I know this is going to be a surprise to you all in Intelligence, but there's some sort of a rebellion going on. (*A voice yaps indignantly in reply.*) All right, you know already. But you may not know that this is your old friend, Tony Palliser – yes, 6th Reserve Cavalry, and I'm here in an O.P. right opposite the G.P.O., from which point I am going to direct you in cleaning the whole thing up, before any red tabs come back from the races. Now listen, Bunny, you can settle it with a company if you come through the right way . . . No, not over the bridge. They're barricading Elvery's. Try Beresford Place and in by the back of Clery's. I'll keep you posted . . . And Bunny, send me down a packet of Players, there's a good chap . . . No you can't ring me here, but I'll ring you whenever I can . . . Now Bunny, listen while I explain . . .

THE CURTAIN HAS SLOWLY FALLEN

ACT TWO

It is a dull, showery afternoon, a day later. The place is in a mess, and someone has removed the flags of the Allies, and drawn a full beard on Victor Emmanuel. The unmounted machine-gun still stands on the floor near the window. PALLISER *is reclining on a bed improvised from a few chairs, and is smoking a cigarette as he reads Emer's religious magazine. He has a crutch beside him.* MACCARTHY *and* ROISIN *are sipping cups of tea at one of the tables. From the street comes an occasional crash and sometimes some distant shouting. Next door, the piano is playing Granados's 'The Maiden and the Nightingale'.*

MACCARTHY. Actually, I once did have a patient who thought he was Napoleon. Very rare, you know, that Napoleon business, although it's what loonies are usually supposed to do. Usually they go in for more up-to-date selections.

ROISIN. Like Charlie Chaplin?

MACCARTHY. Yes – or somebody really amusing, like Lloyd George. This Napoleon was very popular with the students until one day Endymion got hold of him and taught him to say, 'I'm Johnny Doyle of Drimnagh'. Imagine my embarrassment before a whole classful of tittering medicals. 'Now tell us who you are,' I said. And the bloody fellow answered, 'I'm Johnny Doyle of Drimnagh.' And the annoying thing is that he wasn't Johnny Doyle either.

ROISIN. So it was after that, you put out poor Endymion?

MACCARTHY. Of course. Couldn't have that sort of sabotage on the premises.

(ROISIN *starts to examine the tealeaves in her cup.*)

PALLISER. That woman next door is still there. I thought they took her out yesterday.

MACCARTHY. So they did. She must have come back.

ROISIN. D'yever read the cups?

358

MACCARTHY. I can't say that I do. I'm usually apprehensive enough about the future.

ROISIN. There's some queer things in this one.

MACCARTHY. I once had my horoscope cast by a Parsee Graduate in Surgeons. He warned me against taking part in an official ceremony where a platform would collapse under me. I never liked to make any further inquiries.

PALLISER. Obviously a hanging.

MACCARTHY. An interpretation that had also occurred to me. But I don't think it's very nice of you to mention it. Why don't you concentrate on your magazine?

PALLISER (*putting it down*). I've already read it twice through including the advertisements for altar wine.

MACCARTHY. It ought to be very good for you. However, we'll send across to Eason's and loot you a lot of old newspapers. Then you can brood over happy bygone days that you spent in the trenches.

PALLISER. You might get me a few books.

MACCARTHY. Make your choice. You'll never have a chance like this again. Anything from Bertha Ruck to William Blake.

PALLISER. I think I'd prefer the last.

MACCARTHY (*surprised*). Blake? Really? Mightn't it seem a little affected to sit there reading Blake during a rebellion?

PALLISER. No better time to understand him.

ROISIN. Hey-ho. I wish I understood meself.

MACCARTHY (*indulgently*). So do we all, my dear. And those who succeed don't usually enjoy the discovery.

ROISIN. I'd like to ask you a question, all the same.

MACCARTHY. Why pick on me, my dark Rosaleen?

ROISIN. I dunno. Mebbe it's because what you say is sort of . . . original. D'ye know.

MACCARTHY. Original? My dear, I pride myself on never having made an original remark in my life.

ROISIN. That's a queer thing to be proud of.

MACCARTHY. The only people who make original remarks are my patients. They're all completely original.

ROISIN. All the same I'd like to ask you something I've offen wunnered. Mebbe you'd tell me, an' you married all these years, an' . . .

MACCARTHY. And had the nerve taken out. Go on.

ROISIN. Is there . . . is there such a ting as true love at all, Doctor Mac? D'ye know what I mean?

359

MACCARTHY. I know just what you mean . . . unfortunately.

ROISIN. Is there such a ting at all? Or is it something the bukes and the pictures has cuked up to cod us? You know, Doctor Mac, like . . . like Christmas.

MACCARTHY (*sadly*). So Christmas is only a cod.

PALLISER. She's right, you know. There is no Santa Claus.

ROISIN. Ah, it is an' it isn't . . . that's no matter now. But I wish you'd tell me about the other, Doctor, for I wudden want to be disappointed in that. D'ye know.

MACCARTHY. I find such a question disturbing, after my Easter celebration.

ROISIN. Ah, ye know I'm not talkin' about anyting nasty.

MACCARTHY. Really! The arrogance of these women over the problems they arouse themselves! Did you hear how she described my Easter?

PALLISER. I did, and I dare say she's right. You would say that the lust of the goat is the bounty of God.

MACCARTHY. You mean Blake would say it. I only wish I still had some of the goat's problems. Of course I had them all in T.C.D. and enjoyed them enormously. But now, alas, I have only a few simple complexes left, and they haven't even got the glamour of looking ridiculous.

PALLISER. Too simple by half, I'll be bound.

MACCARTHY. Well, all great art is simple. That's why second-rate people sneer at it.

ROISIN. What does he mean, Captain? Who's trying to sneer at what?

PALLISER. You wouldn't understand, Roisin. You're a woman, and have a soul above the gymnastics the Doctor is talking about.

MACCARTHY. Exactly. She's a woman. All she wents from life is just the sky and the moon.

ROISIN. An you mean I'll . . . never find them?

PALLISER. Here's hoping you will, my dear.

MACCARTHY (*determinedly*). She'll never find anything until she accepts the fact that no primula can live that isn't planted in a reasonable amount of dirt. But no woman ever will.

ROISIN. Will what?

PALLISER. He means that life itself is a dirty business, and we've got to put up with it.

MACCARTHY. I mean nothing of the sort. What I'm trying to convey is the fact that love is a vegetable that must be planted in a bed pan, and watered with a nice supply of disappointments.

ROISIN (*primly*). There's nuttin' nasty about true love.

MACCARTHY. Then for God's sake don't say so. Nature has wisely provided that most of the important things we have to do seem wicked. There is great wisdom in that. So don't disabuse us of the idea, or we may lose interest in Nature, and stop doing them.

ROISIN. I mighta known I'd never get an answer. It's Mickser and me I wanted to know about . . . not either a yous.

PALLISER. We should have remembered. But all we do is talk about ourselves.

MACCARTHY. I suppose the next question is: 'Can Galahad be Galahad if he's only a boy employed by the tram company?'

ROISIN. It's not his job I mind. Sure what better am I meself? But . . .

MACCARTHY. But you know in your soul that you are a heroine. Where, on the other hand, are the heroes?

ROISIN. Well, I wouldn't put it that way.

MACCARTHY. No. But you mean it.

PALLISER. One of the things about my profession is that it sometimes enables us to find out who the heroes are.

MACCARTHY. My dear fellow, even in your profession it needs influence to be a hero. How often have you been allowed to try?

PALLISER. Not very often. But perhaps that's just as well. People shouldn't be encouraged to pursue these second-rate ambitions.

MACCARTHY (*dumbfounded*). Heroism? A second-rate ambition?

PALLISER (*crisply*). Certainly. Just another form of self-advertisement.

MACCARTHY (*after a pause*). I think the trouble is that most of us are in the wrong occupations. Palliser, here, would probably have made an ideal tramways official if his family had allowed him to take it up, while Mickser is the real military genius.

PALLISER. Thanks. Thanks a lot.

MACCARTHY. After all, who but a tramways official would have thought of leading a cavalry charge against the General Post Office? Mickser would never have tried that.

ROISIN. Cavalry charges, moryah! That's all I hear about, an' me wonderin' whether it's love I feel.

MACCARTHY. If you want to know whether you're capable of that emotion, take him across to Holyhead on the mailboat. If you can contemplate each other being seasick without losing interest, then you are both ripe for parenthood. Not before.

ROISIN. Ah, I knew I'd never hear any sense.

(*She takes the cups over to the counter. The music concludes.*)

PALLISER (*who has been slightly offended*). Isn't it about time you went home? If you don't go soon, all your patients will be getting better.

MACCARTHY. I am quite aware of that possibility. (*He rises and goes to the telephone.*) Hello.

(ROISIN *screams as* ENDYMION *enters from the kitchen. He has donned a pair of celluloid cuffs on his ankles.*)

ENDYMION. You *do* want to speak to me.

MACCARTHY. Never again. (*Then, into the phone.*) This is the head of the Fire Brigade. Get me 2663 at once.

ROISIN. Where did you come from?

ENDYMION. Through the official funk-holes.

PALLISER. You should blow a horn or something.

ENDYMION.

Some day I shall be heralded by horns.
Enter Endymion – Chorus to these large events,
Coming to limn the progress of the offstage scene.

PALLISER. Well, what's happening?

ENDYMION.

High preparations.
Colonels and brigadiers, coralled from the Curragh
And from the better types of house of ill repute,
Will soon be planning operations in the Castle yard
To burn the city to the ground.

PALLISER. Don't be absurd. Why should they?

ENDYMION.

Because they have artillery.
Would you expect them not to use it –
Affirming the royal peace with great explosions?

PALLISER. Nonsense. None of that is necessary. I've told them myself how to . . . I mean, I . . . (*He hesitates in some confusion.*)

ENDYMION. I know. You've spoken to them on the telephone.

MACCARTHY. The telephone! Why you sly old fox! You know you're not allowed to use the telephone. Hello. (*He drops a coin in.*) Got you that time, my dear. Yes darling. It's me again.

ENDYMION.

And they have called you in return to say
That not an item of the news has changed.
Verdun holds out.
No Prussian sole has bruised the soil of Kerry.

362

PALLISER. I know. It's only a matter of time.

ENDYMION.

        Till what?

        Haha! Till what?

PALLISER. Till it's all over.

ENDYMION.

        Till generals and ministers arrive

        Bringing a bloody sunset from the east.

MACCARTHY. I thought I'd better warn you, my love, that the end of the world has begun, so you'd better start packing. On second thought, don't bother to pack, for the same reason.

ROISIN. Tell us what's happening to the rebels.

ENDYMION.

        They, too, are doing their best to earn unpopularity.

        Out near Ballsbridge, a few old men

        With wooden guns that will not fire

        Have been shot down.

ROISIN. I don't believe it.

ENDYMION.

        The issue's knit,

        And every fellow plays the other fellow's game.

        The Green makes murder and the Crown makes martyrs,

        And the great and unwashed Liberated loot.

        Victory's the crown, my friends, for him

        With the least power to engineer his own defeat.

        In short, the situation's normal.

PALLISER.

        Marry, here's grace and a codpiece;

        That's a wise man and a fool.

ENDYMION (*staring at him coldly*).

        No, I will be the pattern of all patience;

        I will say nothing.

        I am Endymion – beloved of the Moon.

        I wear my cuffs upon my ankles.

        So, in a world that's upside down,

        I walk upon my hands.

        Good afternoon.

    (*He stalks off towards the street.*)

MACCARTHY. Margery, that's no way to talk to a man who's doing his bit . . . B – I – T . . . No, I wasn't referring to you. Dammit, she's rung off.

PALLISER (*pointing after* ENDYMION). There's your hero for you.

The most gallant gentleman in Ireland. And what has it profited him?

MACCARTHY. Some day the worm will turn. But nobody will notice. Who knows one side of a worm from another? You were saying?

PALLISER. I said he was a hero. A man who met with fate in Guinness's.

MACCARTHY. So they say. But that was twenty years ago.

PALLISER. Leapt into a vat to save a drowning man, and struck his head. So now – a hero and a lunatic!

(*He bursts into a sardonic laugh, as* WILLIAMS *enters from the kitchen.* MACCARTHY *hastily replaces the receiver, which he has still been holding.*)

WILLIAMS. Who came through this passage?

PALLISER. Only Field-Marshal Endymion.

WILLIAMS (*suspiciously*). I thought I saw someone else. (*He goes to the telephone.*) Has anyone been using this telephone?

MACCARTHY. I'm afraid I did, my dear fellow. I have to keep the wife posted.

WILLIAMS. Why weren't these wires pulled out?

MACCARTHY. They were, old boy. But I pushed them back again.

(WILLIAMS *wrenches them out and takes the receiver under his arm.*)

WILLIAMS. You'd better not do that again. You must be looking for trouble.

MACCARTHY. Looking for it! You obviously don't know my wife. She's beginning to show her age. (*To* PALLISER.) She's already got some grey hairs in her moustache.

ROISIN. Is it the trut you plugged some old G.R.s out at Ballsbridge?

WILLIAMS. Who told you that?

ROISIN. Never mind. Is it the trut?

WILLIAMS (*looking at* PALLISER). Has anybody else been using this phone?

MACCARTHY. Rather a silly question! Who else would want to talk to my wife?

WILLIAMS (*to* PALLISER). If you've been playing the spy – Oh, never mind. I'm going to call a meeting over here.

PALLISER. Why over here?

WILLIAMS. Because it may concern you.

PALLISER. That's very cryptic. Isn't the war going too well?

WILLIAMS. It's going fine. What makes you think it isn't?

PALLISER. Oh, nothing. Those Huns . . . soon be here?

WILLIAMS. You'll see. (*Then to the others, as cheering breaks out quite close.*) We've taken three more barracks, and there's a German submarine out in the bay. Men from the country are pouring in every hour.

ROISIN (*sceptically*). Game ball. You'd think he had seven toes.

MACCARTHY. Actually he has. (*Then with a deprecating laugh.*) Though not all, of course, on the same foot.

(EMER *comes in from the street in some excitement.*)

EMER. Something will have to be done about that crowd. Now they've broken into the shop downstairs.

WILLIAMS. No one can stop the workers from taking a few of their needs.

EMER. Who's talking about their needs? If it was food or blankets I could understand. But toffee shops and fancy dancing shoes, hats and children's toys . . .

WILLIAMS. What do you expect us to do? Fire on them? (*Then, with a slight laugh.*) If a few chizlers get a bag of sweets or a teddy bear, it'll be the first time they've ever had something for nothing.

EMER. Next thing it will be drink.

MACCARTHY. Drink? Where? Tell me, woman.

EMER. In Meagher's round the corner. Somebody broke in during the night and set it on fire.

MACCARTHY (*agitated*). On fire! My God, this must be put out at once. (*He prepares to go.*)

ROISIN. It's all right. The Brigade has put it out.

MACCARTHY. But is the place still open?

ROISIN. How should I know?

MACCARTHY (*making for the door*). Will you excuse me, folks. I think I'll . . .

EMER. Where are you off to?

MACCARTHY. Just to get a few medical supplies. We need them, you know.

PALLISER. Bring me back a quart while you're at it.

EMER. Is it liquor you're after?

MACCARTHY (*pausing in the doorway*). What an abominable suggestion! When I'm only going to call on a little chemist round the corner. A teeny-tiny chemist.

EMER. I'm going along to see what you're up to.

MACCARTHY (*in mock horror*). Ah, the peasant mind! Always full of suspicion.

WILLIAMS. The bourgeois mind. Not one of you understands the poor.

PALLISER. I do. I'm absolutely broke. Make it Scotch.

MACCARTHY. I have no idea what any of you mean. Goodbye.

(*He hurries off followed by* EMER. *The piano is heard next door, playing from Griffes's 'White Peacock'.*)

EMER (*To* WILLIAMS *as she goes*). How can we have a government of our own if we don't have law and order?

WILLIAMS (*suddenly losing his air of confidence*). Ah, what does it matter what they take? It'll all be up in flames by morning.

PALLSER (*alarmed*). In flames? Why?

WILLIAMS (*viciously*). Because your people are bringing artillery on to the Quays. That's why.

PALLISER. Artillery! So that's the game.

WILLIAMS. It may be a game to you but it's no game to the people.

ROISIN (*mockingly*).

'So-wil-jers are we
Whose lives are pledged to Eye-er-land.

WILLIAMS (*turning on her*). Ah, will you dry up!

ROISIN. Who's banjaxed now? Slattery's Mountain Fut.

WILLIAMS. Get out of here, woman. Go and join your friends if that's the dirty fighting you admire.

ROISIN. Me friends is me own concern. I'll go an' warn me friend Miss Garrity to mind the fire.

WILLIAMS (*rather pompously*). Yes. Get her out of there. Get all civilians out of the area.

(ROISIN *tosses her head and walks out by the street door.*)

PALLISER. Funny how indignant you civilians always get whenever you find that there are two sides to every war.

WILLIAMS. Are you calling me a civilian?

PALLISER. Well, aren't you acting like one? If you want to have a fight you must expect to get hit.

WILLIAMS. With big guns! Against a few lads with shotguns and scapulars!

PALLISER. Ttt-ttt. I know. And all of them so difficult to keep clean. Of course, it's always unfair to be beaten.

WILLIAMS (*passionately*). Yes it is when it's done by holding women and children to ransom.

PALLISER. You're not only a civilian. You're a journalist.

WILLIAMS. I'm not exaggerating. Your people are getting ready to blast the whole city to hell in order to get at us.

PALLISER. That was one of the hazards of starting it in the city.

366

WILLIAMS. I'm not going to argue with you. I want to see your commanding officer. Do you know him?

PALLISER. I know the present one. But he won't·be here for long.

WILLIAMS. I'm going to get some of our leaders. So don't attempt to escape. We may want you. (*Indicating the telephone receiver.*) And this I'll take with me.

(*He goes out by the street door. As* PALLISER *stands up on his stiff leg, a British Captain* – CLATTERING – *also rises, from behind the counter. The piano stops.*)

PALLISER (*startled*). God!

CLATTERING. About time that bloody fellow went.

PALLISER. Bunny! Where the hell have you come from?

CLATTERING. Through·those dashed little holes. Why the devil haven't you been keeping in touch? The Colonel is furious.

PALLISER. I can't keep in touch while they're here, and they're here all the time. Now he's taken away the telephone.

CLATTERING (*going to the window with a notebook*). Good thing I came to see for myself. Had quite a ride on a fire engine.

PALLISER. Why didn't you send those men yesterday?

CLATTERING. My dear chap, we could hardly start off before everyone was back from the races. Then we got a better idea. I say, they've made quite a mess of the old Post Office, haven't they?

PALLISER. Who got a better idea? Who's in command now?

CLATTERING. Oh, some brigadier from the Curragh. Not a bad sort. Of course all the usual jobbery and backbiting is in full swing – you're lucky to be out of it, old boy. But I think we've got him to see the light.

PALLISER. Bunny, is it true you've got some guns on the Quays?

CLATTERING. Yes, old boy. That's the new idea. In fact, that's why I'm here. To take a look-see before we open fire.

PALLISER. But Bunny, that's crazy. If you open fire with artillery you'll burn half the town.

CLATTERING (*still busy taking notes at the window*). Got to do something fast, old boy. Two brigades from home are due at Kingstown some time tonight. By tomorrow that ass Hempenstall will have them all marching up the Rock Road with drums beating and colours flying. If we don't do something ourselves before that crowd turns up, we'll find ourselves in Q jobs in Liverpool – you as well as me.

PALLISER. But Bunny, this mustn't be treated as a military operation.

CLATTERING. I know they're only a bunch of Sin Feeners, but . . .

PALLISER. I tell you, they're just about ripe to be plucked. I've talked to them. If we can only bluff them into coming out with their hands up, it's all over.

CLATTERING. Who cares where their hands are? About time we did a bit of shooting ourselves.

PALLISER. But Bunny, you don't undertsand. A lot of fireworks will only make them look important.

CLATTERING. I don't follow.

PALLISER. Let's march them through the streets without their pants, and ship them off in a cattle boat to their friends – the Huns. That'll put 'paid' to the whole business.

CLATTERING. Sounds to me as if you want to make everything look damn silly. What's the idea?

PALLISER. I want to make *them* look damn silly.

CLATTERING. A bit fanciful. What?

PALLISER. It's the answer. I know this country.

CLATTERING (*becoming rather arch*). Ah, yes. Scratch a Paddy and you're all the same, no matter what uniform you're wearing.

PALLISER. What the devil do you mean by that?

CLATTERING. I mean, old boy, frankly – you don't mind my being frank, do you?

PALLISER. No, I don't mind you being frank.

CLATTERING. Well what I'm getting at is this. You're a horseman and I'm a gunner. And basically – one can't shut one's eyes to the facts – basically you fellows always hate to see a gunner firing his guns. Isn't that so?

PALLISER. It is not so. You can fire your blasted guns to your heart's content. But not just now. Don't you understand?

CLATTERING. Pity you can't be frank, like me. But you Paddies! (*Archly.*) Always love a spot of intrigue, don't you? Do you know what that fellow Braithwaite tried to do?

PALLISER. God, give me patience.

CLATTERING. Tried to get me taken off the circulation list. Me, of all people! I don't know who these old dug-outs think they are. Haven't heard a shot fired since Ladysmith, and now they're hand in glove with the Territorials, trying to run the show as if they owned it. Of course your crowd in Marlboro Barracks doesn't come under that heading, but we all know what camp you're in.

PALLISER. I'm not in any camp. I just want to get this thing licked.

CLATTERING. Oh come now. You're not going to ask me to believe that you're not up to the neck in that Bisley business?

368

PALLISER. What has Bisley got to do with it?

CLATTERING. We all know who you fellows have been backing for captain of that shooting team.

(PALLISER *pulls himself together, and drums with his fingers for a short time, while* CLATTERING *returns to the window, having triumphantly made his point.*)

CLATTERING. What do you suppose has happened to the populace? Gone to ground in the pubs, I suppose, now that a little bit of shooting has begun. How's morale? Fairly low, you say. And their O.P.s . . . where did you say they are?

PALLISER. None of them even know what an O.P. is. Listen Bunny. I can tell from your remarks that you're a pretty astute fellow.

CLATTERING. Uh-uh! Flattery. What's coming now?

PALLISER. Nothing about the guns, Bunny. But I've been thinking over what you said about the Bisley team.

CLATTERING (*interested*). Oh?

PALLISER. You don't mind me speaking frankly, do you?

CLATTERING (*really interested*). No, no. Be as frank as you like. Only don't try to pull the wool over my eyes. I know.

PALLISER. Well, I'm ready to admit that we've been backing the wrong horse.

CLATTERING (*gratified*). Ah!

PALLISER. But I'm not going to admit it in public without a *quid pro quo*. That's frank, isn't it, Bunny?

CLATTERING. Yes. We know where we are now. Nothing like being frank.

PALLISER. So I'll do a deal with you.

CLATTERING. Well, what's the proposition? Do come on.

PALLISER. I'll back you up over the Bisley team, if you hold up on those guns till tomorrow. My God, there's somebody coming! Hide!

CLATTERING (*reluctantly going back behind the bar*). I never could understand how anyone could imagine that a fool like Wilbraham-Northwood could – Oh, excuse me.

(*He sinks from sight, as* O'CALLAGHAN *enters from the street.*)

O'CALLAGHAN. Who was talking?

PALLISER. Nobody. I was just talking to myself.

O'CALLAGHAN. I thought I saw somebody else at the window.

PALLISER. You must have been mistaken.

O'CALLAGHAN (*looking around*). About this parole of yours . . . you realize what it means, of course?

PALLISER. That I'm not to leave here without your permission.

369

O'CALLAGHAN. That you're not to take any further part in this business in any way. You've undertaken that, on your honour as a soldier.

PALLISER. Have I?

O'CALLAGHAN. You don't seem certain. Do you realize what may happen if you break your parole?

PALLISER. The whole subject is rather a dull one.

O'CALLAGHAN. You forfeit your rights as a prisoner of war, and are liable to be shot.

PALLISER. Why keep on about it?

O'CALLAGHAN. Because Williams thinks, and I agree, that both you and the enemy know a damn sight too much about what's going on, ever since this thing started.

PALLISER. Maybe it's just natural intelligence.

O'CALLAGHAN. Maybe it's intelligence that goes by the name of spying. Is this your hat?

(*He picks up* CLATTERING'S.)

PALLISER. Yes.

O'CALLAGHAN. I thought you were in the Lancers.

PALLISER. O what the hell! Maybe it's somebody else's I borrowed.

O'CALLAGHAN. I don't remember you having a hat when we carried you in.

PALLISER. Miss Garrity found it in the street, and very kindly brought it up.

O'CALLAGHAN. I see.

(H*e looks around the room, and even over the counter, but apparently sees nothing.*)

O'CALLAGHAN. Well, maybe I'll leave you now. Goodbye.

(*He goes out by the street door.*)

PALLISER. Goodbye. (*Then, after a pause.*) Are you still there?

CLATTERING (*reappearing*). I've been thinking that over about the Bisley team. What exactly is it that you want?

PALLISER (*in a low voice*). I want you to have that brigadier standing by to treat with these fellows. It may come quite soon – perhaps even this afternoon.

CLATTERING. You know he can't give them terms without first talking to the frocks.

PALLISER. Yes he can if he likes. To hell with the frocks.

CLATTERING. Oh, I agree with you there. All the same –

PALLISER. Get them in the bag on any terms you like while the spirit's low. Then we can talk about the next step. But no shell-fire till we see how they're going to jump. Keep those guns quiet, no matter what the Castle says. Have the wrong ammunition. Tell everybody all the lies you like, but let's get them in the bag first.

CLATTERING (*after a pause*). About the team . . . of course I don't care much who's adjutant.

PALLISER (*impatiently*). All right – Bertie's adjutant. Is it a deal?

CLATTERING. Not that I want to be unreasonable. But it does seem obvious that if somebody isn't in command who has a lot of pull in Whitehall, everybody's going to get the wrong end of the stick, the most ghastly quarters to begin with and . . .

(O'CALLAGHAN *is standing in the doorway with revolver drawn.*)

CLATTERING. Oh. This fellow's back again.

O'CALLAGHAN. Put up your hands.

CLATTERING. Put up what?

O'CALLAGHAN. Your hands.

CLATTERING. I shall do nothing of the sort.

O'CALLAGHAN. I'll shoot you if you don't.

CLATTERING. Stop behaving like a cowboy, my man. As I haven't got any weapons the idea of putting up my hands is absolute nonsense.

O'CALLAGHAN. I warn you. You'll be plugged. I mean it.

CLATTERING. Don't be ridiculous. You can't shoot an unarmed man.

(*Very deliberately, he turns his back. After a dreadful pause,* O'CALLAGHAN *dashes to the window and shouts.*)

O'CALLAGHAN. Hey, below there! Send up some men. Hurry – I've caught a spy.

PALLISER (*to* CLATTERING). Quick. Now's your chance.

(CLATTERING *leaps out by the kitchen.* O'CALLAGHAN *is about to run after him, but collapses across the counter in a violent fit of coughing.*)

PALLISER. You should take something for that.

O'CALLAGHAN (*almost in tears*). Damn you! Damn you!

PALLISER. Why didn't you shoot? No ammunition, I suppose.

O'CALLAGHAN. None of . . . your damn . . . business.

(MAGINNIS *runs in from the street carrying a rifle.*)

MAGINNIS. What is it?

O'CALLAGHAN. Enemy spy – through there – catch him . . .

(*As* MAGINNIS *runs to the kitchen door he collides with* MAC-CARTHY *coming in, and grabs him.* MACCARTHY *has a number of bottles which he struggles to get behind the counter.* PALLISER *shouts with laughter.*)

371

MACCARTHY. Don't touch me, you guerrilla.

O'CALLAGHAN (*still between his coughs*). Not him – officer – in uniform . . .

MACCARTHY. Not with the child in my arms.

> (MAGINNIS *runs off after* CLATTERING, *and* WILLIAMS *hurries in from the street.*)

WILLIAMS. What's happening?

MACCARTHY (*concealing the bottles*). Everybody's dashing about – wearing different uniforms. I can't keep track of what side I'm on.

O'CALLAGHAN. Enemy spy.

PALLISER. A spy in full uniform! Don't be absurd.

WILLIAMS (*drawing his revolver*). Where is he?

> (O'CALLAGHAN *tries to point.*)

O'CALLAGHAN. Someone's gone . . . after him.

MACCARTHY. If it's the gentleman who hurried past me, he seemed to be going to the cloakroom. (*He throws a book to* PALLISER.) There's what you asked for.

PALLISER (*delighted*). 'The Marriage of Heaven and Hell.'

MACCARTHY. You'll never guess where I found it.

O'CALLAGHAN. He was talking to . . . (*He points at* PALLISER.)

WILLIAMS (*grimly*). Ah, I see. Passing information.

MACCARTHY (*to* O'CALLAGHAN). That's a terrible cough. Let me see.

WILLIAMS. And over the telephone as well. I see it all now.

MACCARTHY (*looking at* O'CALLAGHAN'S *throat*). Have you ever had T.B.?

WILLIAMS. Why hasn't he been kept under proper guard?

O'CALLAGHAN. Can't get away . . . Gave me . . . his . . . parole.

MACCARTHY. Stop trying to talk.

WILLIAMS. Well, he's under guard from now on till we decide what to do with him.

> (*He draws a pair of handcuffs from his pocket and, putting away his gun, he pinions* PALLISER'S *hands around the pillar.*)

PALLISER. If you're all so damned incompetent as to leave a telephone in a place like this, what do you expect?

WILLIAMS. Shut up.

O'CALLAGHAN. I cut . . . it. Somebody . . . fixed it . . . again.

MACCARTHY (*authoritatively*). Sit down at once and let me have a proper look at your throat.

> (O'CALLAGHAN *obeys, as* TETLEY *comes in, following* EMER. *He has lost much of his vigour and seems to be deeply depressed.*)

EMER (*pointing at* MACCARTHY). There he is! How well you gave me the slip.

MACCARTHY (*snapping his fingers*). About time you appeared, nurse. Give me a swab, and then hold my torch.

> (*After a moment's surprised hesitation she hurries obediently to his assistance, and presently* O'CALLAGHAN'S *coughing subsides, as swabs are taken and examined.*)

TETLEY (*looking at* PALLISER). What's happening to this officer?

WILLIAMS. Whatever's supposed to happen to spies and informers. Everybody knows their fate.

PALLISER. And the fate of civilians who try to play at soldiers.

WILLIAMS. He's been in touch with the enemy ever since yesterday.

PALLISER. Talk about me charging the Post Office! They don't even know enough to occupy the telephone exchange.

TETLEY (*incredulously*). But surely this isn't possible? This officer gave his parole.

WILLIAMS. You must be even simpler than I thought. But there's other things more urgent at the moment. You know they're bringing artillery on to the Quays?

TETLEY (*tonelessly*). Yes, I know.

WILLIAMS. Once they open fire with that it's goodbye to both the city and the population.

TETLEY. It's happening to a good many cities besides this one. Does it matter very much?

WILLIAMS (*loudly*). Does it matter?

TETLEY. If we hadn't considered that possibility, why did we ever start?

WILLIAMS. We started it to make a public protest – not to force the workers to commit suicide along with us. Now we've made that protest.

MACCARTHY. These instruments are a disgrace. Take them and . . . No, not you. Where's that Roisin girl?

EMER. I don't know.

PALLISER. Next door talking to a piano player.

> (MACCARTHY *strides to the wall and bangs on it.* MAGINNIS *re-enters, out of breath.*)

MAGINNIS. He got away. There's an enemy barricade across Marlboro Street.

WILLIAMS. Damn it, are they on that side now? Well, this just confirms what I think.

MACCARTHY (*shouting*). Roisin Whateveryouare, I want you.

> (*He returns to* EMER *and* O'CALLAGHAN.)

TETLEY (*to* MAGINNIS). I thought you'd gone to the Third Battalion?

MAGINNIS (*rather sulkily*). The men on the canal don't understand their orders. They sent me back to ask is this a war or is it not?

TETLEY. What's this all about?

WILLIAMS. I told them off for opening fire on a detachment of Veterans.

MAGINNIS (*indignantly*). They were marchin' into Beggarsbush with guns on their shoulders.

WILLIAMS. Those aren't the people we're fighting. It's had a very bad effect.

MAGINNIS (*shrilly*). A bad effect!

WILLIAMS. They ought to have had more sense. But it all adds up to the same thing. Artillery . . . this trouble at Beggarsbush . . . and now this fellow being allowed to get away.

MAGINNIS. That wasn't my fault.

TETLEY. What's in your mind?

WILLIAMS. I was going to suggest that this man (*indicating* PALLISER) should be sent across to find out what terms we can get.

EMER. Terms?

WILLIAMS. Now it will obviously have to be somebody else.

TETLEY. I thought it was going to be something of this sort.

O'CALLAGHAN (*weakly*). The Provisional Government will never agree to ask for terms.

WILLIAMS. The Provisional Government needn't know about it, until I can tell them what the terms are.

MAGINNIS. Terms? Does he mean surrender? And we not in action for two days yet?

WILLIAMS (*confidently*). In those two days we've accomplished a great deal. We've captured five barracks and nearly taken the Castle. The country's up . . . alive and kicking. There's nothing dishonourable in discussing terms after that.

PALLISER. You've taken no barracks.

WILLIAMS. Keep out of this please.

PALLISER. You've taken no barracks. Not a county has risen, except for a skirmish in Wexford. Two brigades of infantry are landing at Kingstown, and will be marching on the city within twelve hours. These are the facts. But don't let them bother you. You'll be given terms – good ones – if you're quick about it.

TETLEY. Captain Palliser, is it in your role as a parole-breaker that you have all this information?

PALLISER. Never mind how I know. Is it true or is it not? That's the question.

WILLIAMS. Pay no attention to him.

TETLEY. I don't know anything about reinforcements arriving at Kingstown. As for the rest – according to my information, it's perfectly true.

EMER (*astonished*). True?

WILLIAMS. Don't be a fool, Tetley.

TETLEY. It's perfectly true. Let's be realistic about this for once, now that we're talking about the future. We've driven off a very determined attack on the Mendicity Institute, and we've scattered a small party of idiot Lancers . . . if our prisoner will forgive the expression. As for any offensive operations against armed men, we have not – so far – taken and held as much as a sentry box.

WILLIAMS. We took the Magazine Fort.

TETLEY. Are we there still?

EMER. We took Dublin Castle.

MACCARTHY. Are you assisting me, nurse, or are you talking politics?

TETLEY. We took the Castle – yes – and we came out again as soon as somebody fired a pistol out of one of the windows.

WILLIAMS. What kind of a way is this to talk?

TETLEY. It's a very good way. I'm not blaming the men. They have all shown great courage in being with us at all, and what we've failed to do is simply a matter of ignorance. Dammit, we're only taking on the British Empire in open warfare for the first time in three generations. It takes us a little time to learn. But we'll never learn by pretending that we've done things that we haven't.

MAGINNIS. What about the Germans? Haven't they landed in Kerry?

TETLEY. At least we've been spared that indignity. Nobody else is going to come and save us.

MAGINNIS. Jaze!

WILLIAMS. Tetley, we've got to keep up morale.

MAGINNIS. D'ye mean by that we've got to be tole a lot of lies?

WLLIAMS. Everybody does it, Maginnis. Look at the 'Official War News'. Men won't fight unless they think they're winning.

TETLEY. Men won't fight until they believe that all is lost. Why must we imitate the enemy even in his illusions?

MAGINNIS. I don't give a damn whether we're winnin' or not. I just don't like bein' tole a lot of lies.

WILLIAMS. It was never a question of winning. It was a matter of making a protest, and that we've done.

ROISIN (*entering from the street*). Well, I got ole Miss G. to go home at last.

MACCARTHY. There you are, you tiresome girl. Put on some boiling water and sterilize these disgusting implements. I'm going out to get some proper equipment.

(*He rises and starts to jot down a list.*)

ROISIN (*to* MAGINNIS). Aw, wait till ye see Napoleon! What brings you back from the Gran' Canal?

MAGINNIS (*sulky again*). There was nuttin' doin' out there.

ROISIN. Nuttin' excep for te plug a few ole gorgeous wrecks. Murderin' blaggards!

MAGINNIS. God forgivus is there no pleasin' that one at all? If I stop out of it I'm a flyboy. When I go into it I'm a murderin' blaggard. They call us soljers and' send us into action, and when we loose off at the red, white an' kharki they say it has a 'very bad effect'.

WILLIAMS. I said that, in this case, your target was unfortunate, that's all.

MAGINNIS. Unfortunate is right. It's unfortunate we ever got inta it. But I'll tell ya this, when I go back an' tell the men at the bridge that they're to inquire the name, address and occupation of every man in kharki before they open fire, I know what they'll do. They'll go home to their tea that's what they'll do an' small blame to them. An' for God's sake will ye give me a cup now.

(*He goes indignantly into the kitchen after* ROISIN, *passing* MACCARTHY *on his way out towards the street.*)

WILLIAMS. Where are you off to?

MACCARTHY. To Jervis Street Hospital.

WILLIAMS. Don't you know they're shooting down that way?

MACCARTHY. That melancholy fact has not escaped me. However, if I can't get to Jervis Street, I shall borrow what I need from His Majesty.

WILLIAMS. His Majesty! Look here, whose game are you playing?

MACCARTHY. Don't adopt that tone with me. Whose game is everybody playing? It's painfully obvious from all the nonsense I've heard that nobody knows whose game is what. My patient Endymion was perfectly right when he said that this campaign will be won by whoever manages to do the least for the other side.

376

WILLIAMS. Listen to me. If you're game enough to go as far as the British barricades, would you go further – and come back?

EMER. Don't be an eedyet. The man would never go near a barricade. Sure he's scared to death already.

MACCARTHY. Madam, do I look like the kind of man who is scared at the call of duty?

EMER. Yes.

WILLIAMS. Well, are you?

MACCARTHY. Certainly I am, you miserable shop steward. (*With a change of tone.*) What do you want me to do?

WILLIAMS. I want you to get through to the British commander and ask him to me by the O'Connell Monument in about half an hour.

EMER (*passionately*). No! Not that!

MACCARTHY. Supposing he's having cocktails in the Shelbourne?

EMER. Don't let him go, Sean.

TETLEY (*with a calming gesture*). Easy.

WILLIAMS. In that case have one with him, and bring me back word of his alternative.

EMER. You fool – once he gets over there, he'll never come back.

WILLIAMS. Is it clearly understood that whatever the answer is, you'll come back with it?

EMER. He'll just give away more information.

MACCARTHY. There is no information of the slightest interest to anybody, if it's what I've been hearing. However, I shall be your dove, on the strict understanding that it's kept quiet afterwards. I don't mind a bullet, but I'm not going to run the risk of knighthood over this.

WILLIAMS. Then off you go.

(MAC CARTHY *leaves by the street door.*)

EMER. Fools! Fools! That's the last you'll ever see of him.

MACCARTHY (*looking in agcin*). I'm going now. But I shall come back, my dear Peril, if only to show you how to put on a roller bandage without wrecking the circulation of the blood. Well, *au revoir*, everybody.

EMER (*to* TETLEY *and* O'CALLAGHAN). Haven't you two got anything to say about this?

O'CALLAGHAN (*rising*). I think . . .

MACCARTHY (*reappearing*). I'm going now. About half an hour. At the O'Connell Monument? Is that right?

WILLIAMS (*roaring*). Yes. And hurry up.

MACCARTHY. Bye-bye. (*He goes.*)

377

O'CALLAGHAN. I was about to say that this is not something any of us can decide. It's a matter for . . .

MACCARTHY (*reappearing*). It was proved by statistics that under the age of forty-five we live longer than over it. Isn't that encouraging?

WILLIAMS (*throwing the magazine at him*). Will you get out of here!

MACCARTHY. I'm going now. Let me be the first at your post mortem. (*He goes.*)

TETLEY. Yes, Seamus? What were you saying?

O'CALLAGHAN. I was trying to say that . . . (*He pauses and looks at the door, but nobody reappears.*) Trying to say that I'm going across to the Post Office to call a meeting.

EMER. Yes – call a meeting. The Council will soon vote this down.

WILLIAMS. We'll see. I'll go with you. What about you, Sean?

TETLEY. No. I'm going to stay here.

O'CALLAGHAN. Why?

TETLEY. Because I feel that way.

EMER. Aren't you going to vote?

TETLEY. No.

WILLIAMS. Oh very well. Stop here and sulk if you must. But when we get before the Peace Conference ask yourself what was it that got us there? My realism, or your sulks.

O'CALLAGHAN (*at the door*). The firing's got bad in the street. We'll have to run.

WILLIAMS. All right. Off you go.

PALLISER. Hi. What about me?

WILLIAMS. We'll deal with you later, when we have time.

PALLISER. Supposing I want to leave the room for a certain purpose?

WILLIAMS (*throwing the key to the handcuffs to* TETLEY). Here. You look after him. Take the damn key.

O'CALLAGHAN. You go first. I'll be the slowest.

WILLIAMS. All the more reason for you to get a good start.

O'CALLAGHAN. I don't see that at all. Surely if . . .

PALLISER. Ah, let me give you a tip. The one that starts first will be half way across before they start shooting. It's the one behind that gets it.

WILLIAMS (*stiffly*). That was not what was in my mind.

O'CALLAGHAN (*laughing*). Oh come on. I'll race you neck and neck.

PALLISER (*shaking his head*). Amateurs!

(*They both disappear.* MAGINNIS *watches from the window, his cup of tea in his hand.*)

378

EMER. Why wouldn't you go too?

TETLEY. Because I never take part in votes if I'm not sure that I'm going to accept the decision.

EMER. Your vote might have made all the difference.

TETLEY. I don't think so. Williams can be very convincing – under certain circumstances.

MAGINNIS. They're running. An' not a shot bein' fired.

ROISIN (*from the bar*). Who'd waste bullets on men bound for Mountjoy?

EMER. Then you think . . .

TETLEY. I don't know what to think. I'd fight to the last building and the last man if I was sure of only one thing – that I was fighting for my country and for my people, and not just for my own satisfaction.

EMER. Do you doubt that?

TETLEY. I'm afraid I do. Look at that girl over there. You know how she feels about us. Are we fighting for her?

ROISIN. Ye are not.

EMER. Who would mind her? She's only a West Briton – a shoneen.

ROISIN. Call me that again an I'll gut ye for garters. I'm for John Redmond an there's no yella streak in our flag.

TETLEY. You see. She's the people. It's their hostility that's really shaken me – not any question of whether we're going to win or lose. I was watching their faces during the reading of the pro-clamation, and there was nothing but derision in those eyes – derision, and that murderous Irish laughter. It was as if we were putting on a rather poor entertainment for them, and they wanted their money back.

EMER. They'll change. We'll show them.

TETLEY. Show them what? That they're downtrodden? You can't show people that if they don't feel it. There we were – in our hands, the first declaration of our independence for the past seven hundred years. But there was no sign of understanding in those eyes. And then . . . at the words 'Ireland through us sum-mons her children to the flag and strikes for her freedom' . . . that crash of glass, and that terrible shout of 'Noblett's toffee shop'.

(*He sinks into a chair and covers his face with his hands.*)

TETLEY. Oh, these moments of doubt and self-examination! I can stand anything but them. Do I have to pretend to myself that I'm another Jesus Christ – that everyone's wrong except me? Endymion thinks like that. But I'm a sane man – amn't I?

379

(EMER *comes to him and is about to touch his head with her hand. We realize for a brief moment that she adores this man. But then something holds her back, and for a while she stands there in silence.*)

ROISIN. What we all need is a good square meal.

MAGINNIS. Game ball.

ROISIN (*going off*). Come an' lend a hand while I whip up what I can. Mr Vitali can charge it to the Irish Republic.

MAGINNIS (*getting out cups*). I never cared for that Citizen Army. I suppose we'll all be hanged now.

TETLEY (*pulling himself together*). No, Mickser. I don't think you'll be hanged. Maybe just a little . . . penal servitude. (*He smiles and* MAGINNIS *smiles back.*)

MAGINNIS. Penal servitude. I've offen wunnered what that's like.

(EMER *moves slowly away and sits silently beside the machine-gun near the window.*)

PALLISER. Pity you never attended an expensive public school. Then it would hold no surprises for you.

TETLEY. Tell me, Captain, was it at your expensive public school that you learnt to break your word?

PALLISER. That seems to be weighing on your mind.

TETLEY. It is, because it puzzles me. I always imagined that whatever we might say against the British Army, it had a certain code – a canon of good form, if you like to put it that way – that included a respect for the laws of war.

PALLISER. Indeed.

TETLEY. You don't wish to enlighten me? Am I wrong, or are you just an exception?

PALLISER. You have me at a disadvantage, Tetley. Make the most of it while you can.

TETLEY. Oh? I beg your pardon. Allow me to unlock this thing. (*He does so.*)

PALLISER. Thank you. I hope this doesn't get you into trouble. I understand that I'm to be court-martialled, or something.

TETLEY. Oh, I don't think that any of them will bother about you at the moment. In fact, if you'd like to go, I'm sure Maginnis will help you to a place of safety.

PALLISER (*puzzled*). Go?

TETLEY. Better now than later. The going may not be good, but it's still tolerable.

PALLISER (*suspiciously*). Are you inviting me to escape? What's the idea?

380

TETLEY. I suppose it's because I'm just a damned amateur. If I had your professional attitude, I'd let them shoot you as you probably deserve. But what's the point, now?

PALLISER. I don't see much point in being shot at any time. All the same I don't think I'll go just yet. Perhaps I'll stay and join you in that bite of food.

TETLEY. Stay if you like. But if you've no better explanation to give, I don't think *I'll* join *you*, Captain.

PALLISER (*taken aback*). You what? Is this a snub?

TETLEY. Maybe they'll be back later to shoot you, if you insist . . . and they haven't forgotten.

PALLISER. You sound rather patronizing. I believe it *is* a snub.

TETLEY. Interpret it any way you like. One thing I would be grateful to know. Is there really a column of reinforcements landing at Kingstown?

PALLISER. Yes. You haven't a hope, I'm afraid.

TETLEY. That's not why I asked the question.

PALLISER. Maybe you want me to pull a few strings for you?

TETLEY (*stiffening*). What do you mean by that?

PALLISER. I mean, about your own future – after you've surrendered I dare say I could get you off, if we concocted a good story now, and both stuck to it.

TETLEY (*offended*). I don't need to have any lying done for me, thank you.

PALLISER. It's tit for tat. After all, isn't that why you're letting me go?

TETLEY (*with a flash of temper*). I always suspected that you weren't a gentleman, but I'd no idea that you'd presume to think the same of me.

PALLISER (*furious*). What the devil do you mean? Whatever I am, I'm a gentleman.

TETLEY. Would a gentleman disregard his parole?

PALLISER. I disregard no promises that I give myself. I do disregard promises that are thrust on me by other people for their own convenience.

TETLEY. An officer and a gentleman is not supposed to break the laws of war. There's no getting away from that.

PALLISER. If you were a real soldier and not a sham one you'd know that all soldiers break the laws of war continually. They couldn't fight a war if they didn't. The whole art of war is to know when to break the rules intelligently. And it has nothing whatever to do with being either an officer or a gentleman. The fact that you don't know this, classifies you – both socially and professionally.

EMER (*rising in a fury*). How dare you talk to him like . . .

PALLISER. How dare he adopt that superior tone to me?

TETLEY (*calmly*). Now, don't let's get annoyed, please. We all know that Captain Palliser and his friends have a monopoly of a certain tone towards people like us.

PALLISER. I'm damned if I'll be patronized.

TETLEY (*to* EMER). So naturally he's annoyed at my offering him his life, and then not allowing him the satisfaction of saving mine.

(EMER *sits down again, silently.*)

PALLISER (*with a sneer*). So you think your life's in danger, do you?

TETLEY. Well, I would imagine so – after this. Of course there's no knowing what the Castle will do. But I imagine that some of us will have to be hanged or shot.

PALLISER. And you hope it's yourself. That would be so much easier than fighting to the last ditch.

TETLEY. On the contrary. Fighting to the last ditch seems to be extremely easy. Your profession is quite terrifying, Captain – it's so simple. It requires no special qualities, except an indifference to one's personal fate that I find rather pleasant.

PALLISER (*sarcastically*). Indeed?

TETLEY. In fact. I've found since yesterday that soldiering gives one a great feeling of release – especially when you're bound to be beaten. I suppose that's why so many stupid people make a success of the Army. It doesn't require much courage to be shot at.

PALLISER. So far, you've had damn little data on that.

TETLEY (*ignoring him*). But to be hanged is quite a different proposition. I'm very much afraid of that, because I don't know how I would react. It's easy to be brave up here in the mind. But what will the body do? Will it let you down? Will the stomach turn to water, no matter how often it's told that it mustn't? Who knows, whether hanging's a difficult thing to take, or if it's not?

PALLISER. All these doubts would be swallowed up in the enormous pleasure of being a martyr.

TETLEY. Now there you show your ignorance, Captain. I know that's what you think I'm after, but I don't want to be a martyr at all, and I'm sure I'd make a rotten one. But what can I do? If we were to 'concoct' some story – as you say – to get me off, it would have to take the line that I had had nothing to do with this rising, and disapproved of it.

382

PALLISER. Well, why not? It's a flop, isn't it?

TETLEY. Whether it's a failure or not, it has at least expressed the purpose of my life. You could hardly expect me to repudiate that.

PALLISER. Do you seriously mean to say that you know the purpose of your life?

TETLEY. Of course. Don't you?

PALLISER. Good lord no. What's more, I'd hate to, almost as much as I'd hate to know the date of my death. Is the purpose of your life to show that about seven hundred years of history have all been a mistake?

TETLEY. If you like to put it that way.

PALLISER. That's a bit pompous, isn't it? May I ask where you got these ideas from?

TETLEY. Oh, I don't know, really. Mainly from my father, I suppose.

PALLISER. I see. (*Pause.*) Your father, I suppose, was an old Fenian ... a charming old failure, crippled from long years of imprisonment?

TETLEY. No. As a matter of fact, he was an English Nonconformist.

PALLISER. A what?

TETLEY (*with a smile of recollection*). And he was far from being a failure. He made quite a good living out of manufacturing rosary beads. That's how he came to this country and met my mother.

PALLISER. Well to hell with the English! I always said they were at the back of Ireland's troubles.

TETLEY (*cryptically*). That's why you're in the English Army, I suppose?

PALLISER. I'm in the army that we Irishmen have officered in all its most important victories.

TETLEY. I know. That puzzles me too. Why do you people enjoy fighting everybody's battles except your country's?

PALLISER. Look here, my friend, it's not the professionals who enjoy fighting battles. As a soldier, I believe in peace on earth – goodwill towards men. Can you say as much?

TETLEY. That's a well-known Protestant mistranslation. What the Vulgate says is 'Peace on earth to men of goodwill'. Quite a different thing.

PALLISER. Well, are you a man of goodwill?

TETLEY. I don't know. I suppose – since I've always hated evil and wanted to fight it – that I can't be a man of goodwill. Maybe that's why I have never been wholly devoted to peace on earth.

PALLISER. It's odd, then, that you're not going to fight it out.

TETLEY. How can I, if the others decide . . .

PALLISER. Blake says that if the fool would only persist in his folly. he would become a wise man. (*He rises and limps over to the piano.*) You should read Blake. He belonged to the Middle Nation . . like you.

TETLEY. I'll probably not have an opportunity for much more reading.

PALLISER. If I had my way, you'd have more opportunity than you expect. Now I'm beginning to wonder if that might not be a pity.

TETLEY. Are you hinting that I ought to persist in what you call my folly? May I ask why?

PALLISER. A fight that doesn't get fought out has a way of stinking afterwards. Besides, I'd rather like to see how much of a soldier you really are. There's more to it than this, you know. (*He gestures towards the window.*)

TETLEY. Much more, I'm sure. *I'd* also like the chance of finding out.

PALLISER. Even if you're licked?

TETLEY. Whether we lose or win is a matter that only God can decide. How we behave is something that depends upon ourselves.

ROISIN (*entering*). There's baked beans now, on the stove.

TETLEY. Thanks. I'll come in and get some.

(*He goes into the kitchen. From the next room the piano is heard again. This time, Respighi's 'Notturno' is suggested.*)

ROISIN. Will ya have some too?

PALLISER (*listening to the piano*). Yes.

ROISIN. Well lissen te that now! The ole one's back again. I tought I had her out for good an' all.

PALLISER. What's she like – this Miss Garrity? Another Maeve of Connaught, harping her warriors against Muirthemne?

ROISIN. Ah, not at all. She's an ole Loyalist in black bombazine, with a picture of King Teddy on the whatnot. (*She goes back into the kitchen.*)

PALLISER. Good for her! A diehard! As a neighbour, I salute Miss Garrity.

(*He strikes a few chords in harmony with the playing next door. EMER rises from her seat and approaches him.*)

EMER. Captain Palliser, will they really hang him if there's a surrender now?

PALLISER. I don't know. That depends on who's in charge.

EMER. You've been planning something else for him? Haven't you?

PALLISER (*with a laugh*). A fate worse than death.

EMER. But why? What is it that you've got against him?

PALLISER. Nothing – except that he's my enemy . . . that he wants to destroy most of the things that my country means to me. Isn't that enough?

EMER. Are you afraid of him?

PALLISER. Not as a soldier, certainly. As a corpse – well, that might be a different matter.

EMER (*thoughtfully*). Yes, you hate him. Is it because he said you weren't a gentleman, and wouldn't have tea with you?

PALLISER. Don't be ridiculous.

EMER. I think it must be that. Or else you hate him because he's got a purpose in life, and you haven't.

PALLISER. Life is much too complicated to define a purpose.

EMER. Except to the saints.

PALLISER. I don't know that I like saints.

EMER. That's what I said. You hate him.

PALLISER. I don't remember when I invited you to discuss my feelings with me, Miss Smith. You say that I hate him. What would you say if I were to suggest that you love him?

EMER (*getting upset*). I'd say you were a very impertinent man.

PALLISER (*interested*). By God, I believe you do! You're blushing (*She turns away her head.*) Don't worry, I won't tell.

EMER. It wouldn't matter if you did. It isn't with any woman that he's in love.

PALLISER. More fool he.

EMER. He's not a fool. Even if he did offer to let you go.

PALLISER. Yes, he offered to let me go. But I didn't go, Emer. At least not yet. So you needn't start asking me to save him in return.

EMER. It's *you* that's the fool if you think I'm asking you to save him!

PALLISER (*surprised*). You mean, you want to make sure that he's hanged?

EMER (*emotionally*). That's a cruel way of putting it.

PALLISER. It's a cruel thing to want.

EMER (*passionately*). I don't want him to be hanged, but I want his life to have its meaning – the meaning that he puts on it himself. I don't want him to have . . . whatever it is that you've been planning for him.

PALLISER. What's it got to do with me . . . what you want? We're not friends, are we?

EMER. No. Maybe that's the best reason for you to help him – just because you aren't friends. Isn't that what your Blake would say?

PALLISER. Help him? How?

EMER (*earnestly*). Don't let them make him surrender now. Don't let them. You can do something, can't you?

PALLISER. So that's what you call helping him! By making sure that he dies. You want a holocaust, do you, so that your lover can win the only crown he's fit for?

EMER. You *are* afraid of him – afraid most of all to see him die.

PALLISER. Why should I be afraid to see him die?

EMER. Because you know, for all your talk, that you couldn't face it the way he could.

PALLISER. So you think not?

EMER. What's death to him or me, so long as it's a good one? But, oh, what's the use of talking? Nobody can ever understand that, who hasn't got the Faith!

PALLISER. What invincible ignorance. Do you suppose that only a Catholic can die? You're like a child I once knew who couldn't understand why I didn't kill and rob when I hadn't got the Church to keep me good.

EMER. How could you ever understand death the way we do?

PALLISER (*furious*). My God, what do you suppose I am?

(*He takes a step towards her, colliding with the machine-gun on the floor.*)

PALLISER. Damn that thing. I nearly broke my . . . (*A pause, while he looks at the machine-gun, and then out of the window, where something else attracts his attention.*) Listen, my good girl. I've had about enough play-acting from you and your friend from the Board of Works. You want to know what war is, do you?

EMER (*doggedly*). We're ready to learn.

PALLISER. It's about time you did – calling yourselves soldiers. If I was to show you how to start a fight that may teach you more than you've bargained for, would you thank me for it?

EMER (*dully*). Yes.

PALLISER. I wonder. (*Pause.*) Well, let's see who's best fitted to look Azrael in the face – the saint or the unbeliever. Come over here to the window. Do you see our friend MacCarthy down there

386

beside the O'Connell Monument? That's my C.O. along with
him. They must have come to discuss terms with Williams.

EMER. I suppose so.

PALLISER. Well, here's your chance to turn wind into wonderment.
(*He lifts the machine-gun into the window, and makes a few
rapid, businesslike adjustments.*)

PALLISER. A lot of damned incompetence. Simplest thing in the
world to rig a machine-gun. Now my dear, if you really want to
open the Book of Revelation, all that you have to do is to (*He
limps away.*) ... press the trigger.

EMER (*her eyes full of tears*). Thank you.

PALLISER. No thanks are expected. (*He turns and looks at her with
a slight smile.*) Better wipe the eyes first.
(*He hands her his handkerchief, which she takes and applies
to her eyes.* PALLISER *limps to the bar with a nonchalant
shrug of his shoulders.*)

PALLISER. I say, everybody. The doctor's down the street.

ROISIN (*entering with a plate of beans*). Then let him stop there.
I've no beans for that wan.

PALLISER (*taking the plate*). All prepared for high negotiations.
Thank you, my dear. And do be careful of that thing, Miss
Smith.

EMER (*blessing herself*). *Quam oblationem tu, Deus, in ominibus
quaesumus, benedictam, adscriptam, ratam, rationabilem,
acceptabliemque facere digneris.*

PALLISER (*eating*). Nothing like a nice plate of ...
(*The machine-gun blazes out of the window. Amid general
shouting,* TETLEY *and* MAGINNIS *rush in. The piano has
stopped.*)

TETLEY. What the deuce ...

MAGINNIS. What's up?

PALLISER. My God! She fired it!

TETLEY (*shouting*). Turn that damn thing off!

PALLISER (*shouting back*). She doesn't know how.

TETLEY. Then you do something.

PALLISER. Then get out of my way.

TETLEY (*to* MAGINNIS). Take in that flag, Maginnis.
(*The gun stops firing, as* MAGINNIS *struggles with the Red
Cross flag.*)

PALLISER. You really are a very careless girl.
(*He touches the gun again, and it bursts into action once
more. Both he and* EMER *appear to struggle with it.*)

387

TETLEY. You fool! Can't you see we have a Red Cross flag hanging out?

PALLISER. Sorry. My mistake.

(*The firing stops, but outside in the street is a confused noise of shouting and considerable rifle fire.*)

ROISIN. Will ye look at the doctor runnin' like a hare?

MAGINNIS (*rolling up the flag*). That'll be the last we'll see a him.

ROISIN. Bedad, you'll see him shortly. He's runnin' this way.

MICKSER (*dropping the flag and joining her at the window*). This way!

TETLEY. What possessed you to touch that thing? Not only is this a hospital, but they had a flag of truce.

PALLISER. Yes, the Brigadier will be furious. Two more laws of war gone down the plug hole.

TETLEY. How did it get fixed?

PALLISER. You'd be surprised, old boy. But not so surprised as me.

(MAC CARTHY *enters breathlessly amidst a roar of shooting.*)

PALLISER (*to* EMER). Now see what you've started.

MACCARTHY. What idiot fired that damn blunderbuss? Has nobody any respect for my cloth?

PALLISER. Nothing personal old man.

MACCARTHY. It was you, you miserable Horse Marine. Give me a drink, somebody.

MAGINNIS (*getting out a bottle*). He said he'd come back and bedad he did.

MACCARTHY (*pouring out*). If I hadn't known it was the shortest route to alcohol I would never have chosen it. Do you know, I had just said to the Brigadier – a somewhat ill-informed individual – that . . . (*Some artillery opens up.*) Cripes!

ROISIN (*flinging herself into* MICKSER'S *arms*). Jaze! What's that?

PALLISER. Artillery. (*Then, to* EMER). Yes, you do seem to have started something. Congratulations, and apologies.

TETLEY (*quietly*). I suppose we're for it now.

MACCARTHY. Let this be a lesson to everybody. Though I'm damned if I know what it is.

TETLEY (*crisply*). Maginnis, can you get through with a message to the men on the Canal?

MAGINNIS. I can try, sir.

ROISIN. Don't leave me, Mickser.

MAGINNIS (*disengaging himself tenderly*). It's all right, Roisin. I'll be back.

TETLEY. Tell the Commandant there's a column on the road from

Kingstown. Tell him to open fire and to keep firing while the buildings last. Tell him to fire at everything in an enemy uniform – armed or unarmed. Tell him that if he does that I'll see that nobody blames him afterwards.

MAGINNIS (*delighted with himself*). I'll tell him.

TETLEY. And Mickser. Tell him it's a hopeless cause. But to put up a bloody good fight.

MAGINNIS (*dashing off by the kitchen*). That's the kind of an order the lads will unnerstan'.

ROISIN (*in distress*). Mind yerself, Mickser.

TETLEY. As for me, I'm going across to the Post Office.

(*He strides off towards the street.* EMER *watches him go from the window.* PALLISER *limps slowly to the piano, and* ROISIN, *open-eyed, goes back behind the bar, covering her mouth from time to time as a heavy gun continues to fire.*)

MACCARTHY (*refreshed*). Ah, I feel a new man. Now how about another half for the new man?

CURTAIN

ACT THREE

The piano is heard playing 'There's a long, long trail awinding'.
The Curtain rises upon the same scene, on an evening three days
later. The street outside is lit by the red glow of fires that grow
more intense as the Act proceeds.
EMER is bandaging the shoulder of a wounded VOLUNTEER *who lies*
on the stretcher while PALLISER *is strumming the tune on the piano.*
ROISIN *stares out of the window. There is the occasional rattle of*
rifle-fire from outside.

ROISIN. When do you tink will Mickser come?

PALLISER. What makes you think he'll come at all?

ROISIN. He'll come.

EMER (*to the* VOLUNTEER). There now. Is that easier?

ROISIN. The fire is the worst this side a the street. It'll be up here
before long.

PALLISER. Then you'd better be going. We need no virgins on this
burning deck.

ROISIN. I wouldn't go without a word a Mickser.

PALLISER (*ending his playing*).
    Weep not for Ferdia, trusting bride.
    He lies embattled by the ford,
    Drunk with the bloodied waters of the Grand Canal.

ROISIN (*to the* VOLUNTEER). Did ye hear any news a the men at the
bridge?

EMER. Don't be bothering him with questions. You'll hear soon
enough.

ROISIN. If owney I knew what's keepin' him.

PALLISER. Here's someone coming now.

ROISIN (*excited*). Where?
    (MACCARTHY *appears from the kitchen with more bottles,*
    which he places proudly on the counter, in full view.)

ROISIN (*disappointed*). Ah, it's owney him.

390

MACCARTHY. Only me! What more did you expect, woman? King William the Third on a camel? You should shout 'Hooray!' The MacCarthy Mor is still on his feet. (*He counts the bottles.*) A few more beakers full of the warm south.

(EMER *is noticeably less hostile towards* MACCARTHY, *and even gives him the flicker of a frosty smile.*)

EMER. So you've been looting again?

MACCARTHY. 'Salvaging in Wynn's Hotel' would be a nicer expression. Everything seems to be on fire. Let me see what you've been doing to that man.

(*He goes swiftly to the stretcher and begins a businesslike examination.*)

EMER. I suppose you can't help it. You're made that way.

MACCARTHY. Mm. Not bad, my love. Give me another dressing. How did he get this?

EMER. Fighting his way back from Mount Street. They've been fighting there for over two days.

MACCARTHY. As if anybody could be unaware of Mount Street. Mm. You seem to have done this quite well. Yes, very well. (*Rising.*) It has come to my attention, sister, that you can be a ministering angel in spite of a forbidding bedside manner.

EMER. You're not so bad yourself – in spite of some other things I won't mention. (*She smiles.*)

MACCARTHY. My God! A smile from Granuaile. Fellow, we're both going to pull through! The sun has come out on this blood-red evening. What about a little refreshment all round?

PALLISER (*promptly*). Yes, please.

EMER. Why do you have to spoil it all with drink? Nobody's supposed to touch that.

MACCARTHY (*opening bottles*). That is one of the seamier sides of this uprising. Do you know, some idiot locked up the bar of the Coliseum Theatre, as a result of which the entire contents have gone up in smoke! Bismarck was right. He said that the Irish and the Dutch ought to swop countries. In a few years – he said – the Dutch would make a garden out of Ireland, and the Irish would begin to neglect the dykes.

(*He hands round glasses.* ROISIN *and* EMER *refuse.*)

EMER. No thanks. You know my views.

MACCARTHY. After all I've been through to bring a hiccough to those rose-red lips! (*To the* VOLUNTEER, *who is hesitating about accepting.*) Doctor's orders. (*Then, taking a glass himself.*) Still . . . a Pearl of great price. However desperate the situation, she always manages to look as if she's just had a nice cup of tea. Why can't you be a little craven from time to time, if only to keep me company?

EMER. As a coward you're as big a fraud as ever.

MACCARTHY. But I *am* a coward! I am. Fear is such a healthy emotion. If only we could manage to be afraid together, we would both be in each other's arms for all time.

EMER. A nice ambition.

MACCARTHY. We must have met before – maybe in some past existence, half a hundred guilts ago. And now we have so little time left.

> Swift speedy Time, feathered with flying hours
> Dissolves the beauty of the fairest flowers.

EMER. You must be a terrible trial to your poor wife.

MACCARTHY. Is this a moment to bring her up? Under your left breast you keep a heart. Does it never beat a fraction faster when I appear? Or don't you like me at all?

EMER. I don't dislike you.

MACCARTHY. Come on. Be specific. Mention just one of the things you like about me.

EMER. I don't see why I should.

MACCARTHY. Because it would be good for my morale. Just one little thing. Do you like my nice white teeth, for instance.

EMER. They're all right.

MACCARTHY. They damn well ought to be. They cost me thirty-five pounds. Do you like my hair?

EMER. Ah, will you stop this nonsense.

MACCARTHY. That, at least, is genuine. Would you like me to give you a lock of it?

(*He picks up a pair of scissors*).

EMER (*indignantly*). I would not!

MACCARTHY (*disappointed*). You don't want a lock of my hair?

PALLISER. If she won't have it, I will.

MACCARTHY. No, sir. To have one of these you have to be not only civil but sober.

PALLISER. You flatter yourself that I could ever get drunk on what you provide.

MACCARTHY. If you don't like what we have in stock, you can take your custom somewhere else. You don't find me sitting around here, like an accident waiting for somewhere to happen.

PALLISER. Dammit, I've got a crack in my knee.

MACCARTHY. And ants in your pants. Well, anything you've got, you

must have brought in with you. These premises are inspected
annually by the Corporation.

(MAGINNIS *enters from the street, covered with dirt and
glory.*)

ROISIN (*running to him*). Mickser, yer back!

MACCARTHY. Is this a moment for clichés?

ROISIN. What happened to ya?

MAGINNIS (*exalted*). We fought them at the bridge since Wensda
afternoon. Seven of us.

EMER. Against hundreds.

MAGINNIS. I dunno how many. We weren't countin'.

EMER (*with grim satisfaction*). But there's fewer now.

(*She turns to the wounded man and works on one of his
dressings.*)

MAGINNIS (*transported*).

> Like the sea on the beach at Bray,
> Wave after wave lappin' the bridge
> Then rollin' back an' comin' on agin.
> Water that knows no better.
> Brown breakers turnin' red,
> An' bayonets flashin' in the sun.
> They flung Mills bombs inta the garden of the house,
> Roarin' bloody murder.
> We fought from twelve till dusk
> Dodgin' from winda te winda
> With the Tommies' bullets playin' chunes in the pianna,
> Till the fire druve us up over the roofs
> And behind the chimney pots.
> The gun was red-hot in me hands
> An' I cooled it off with oil from a tin a sardines.
> The smoke'd catch me by the troat
> And tear the eyeballs from me face.
> But it was them went back – not us . . .
> Back, an then on agin,
> Till all the terrace was a hell a flames
> And the lead was rain runnin' from the gutters.

ROISIN. Glory be to God, how could flash an' blood stand the like a
that?

MAGINNIS (*matter of fact*). I declare te God, I dunno. I wudden'
reckernize meself.

ROISIN. It woulda put the heart across me. Were ye not scared te
death?

MAGINNIS. At first I was scared, Roisin . . . scared that I was goin'
to be afeared. D'ye know. But when it all got goin', I forgot. An'
then when I remembered, I sez to meself, 'Begob, I forgot to be
scared.' An' at that, God forgive me, I started to laugh, an' the
most unholy joy come over me, for I knew then I was a soljer,
an' nuttin' could ever take that from me. (*Pause.*) Has no one
got a Woodbine?

EMER. Here. Take the package.

(*He lights up, as* MACCARTHY *pours out a bottle of stout.*)

MACCARTHY. You shall have more than a Woodbine, Mickser. You
shall drink a flask of your own family beverage – Gwine's
Twenty.

MAGINNIS. What the hell is that?

MACCARTHY. You probably only know it by the Milesian pronunciation. Maginnis is the more ancient and honourable form of
the name.

(*He holds out the glass, which* MICKSER *takes.*)

MAGINNIS. I'll have it, begob, Pioneer or not.

MACCARTHY. Let nobody stop you. And after we have drunk, we
will dally with the women.

ROISIN. You'll what?

MACCARTHY. Girl, do you not know that nature devised you to be
the recreation of the warrior?

ROISIN. A nice warrior you are!

MACCARTHY. If I am not in Mickser's class, I am the next best thing
– a bard.

(*The piano is heard off, playing Debussy's Piano Duet,
'Minuet'.*)

PALLISER. There she is again!

(*He joins with her in the duet.*)

MACCARTHY. Dance with your doxey, Mickser, while I describe her
bosom in a *villanelle*.

ROISIN. Me what?

MACCARTHY. Your . . .

ROISIN. Never mind, if it's what I tought I heard.

MACCARTHY. Here, there are no such things as bosoms. The female
frontispiece is only a plaque for medals, holy and Celidhe. (*To*
EMER.) Well, shall I ignore anatomy and write about Cuchulain's much neglected bride?

EMER (*ignoring him, to the* VOLUNTEER). Are you comfortable now?

MACCARTHY. I can do it through the medium, if you insist, *acushla
geal mochree*, my admirable *Feis Ceoil*, my darling little *Cruis-*

keen Lawn. You see, I am a native speaker. (ENDYMION *appears from the street.*) Oh, go to hell, Endymion!

ENDYMION.

> Is this the last dance?
> Then may I have the pleasure?

EMER (*to* MACCARTHY). These are no times for foolery.

MACCARTHY. These times are fortunate – honoured above all other times in being ours. Be brave. My wife will never know our secret.

PALLISER. Your wife can find your secret written up in privies.

MACCARTHY. Pay no attention to the licentious soldiery. (*As he turns away.*) Oh very well. Nobody cares.

> (*He claps his hand to his brow, and moves off in the throes of composition. Meanwhile* ENDYMION *has commenced a grave and dignified minuet with an invisible partner.*)

ENDYMION.

> Goodbye, my love.
> Familiar things must now be put away.
> Hard-riding squires
> Drink the last stirrup-cup of power.
> Another lordship's here to stay.

PALLISER (*as he plays*). Ladies to the centre.

ENDYMION.

> Spring's a raw season,
> Boisterous with words we do not know.
> We must pack up forbidden memories
> With the court suits of dead solicitors,
> And send the bundles to the prop rooms.

PALLISER. Swing your partners. Bow and retire.

ENDYMION.

> The April wind blows cold on royalty,
> Swift, Grattan, Sheridan, Wellington and Wilde,
> Levees on Cork Hill,
> The tramp of crimson sentries in the colonnade.
> No more of Suvla Bay or Spion Kop.
> The bunting under which we spilled our colours on the globe
> Shall hang in gaunt cathedrals
> Where no one goes.

> (PALLISER *suddenly crashes his hands on the piano in a loud discord.*)

PALLISER. Be off, old zany. Who wants to hear your prophecies?

> (*He breaks into a jig-tune, drowning out the playing from the*

395

next room. ENDYMION *stops dancing and surveys* PALLISER *before speaking.)*

ENDYMION.

You changed the tune –
Tired of the other, I suppose.

(PALLISER *stops playing, and* MISS GARRITY *is heard again.)*

PALLISER. About time too. I've had enough of you and old Miss Garrity.

ENDYMION.

And tired, beyond all thinking, of ourselves,
A paradox that nobody
Will ever understand.
So, let us make our bows together –
Baron Hardup, the Prince and Cinderella.

PALLISER, I'll make my bow when I choose.

ENDYMION (*placing a hand on* PALLISER.)

This is my beloved son
Who sees more ways from Sackville Street than one.
So take the road, my lad,
With my permission and my Gaes –
That when you go, you never let them see you run.

(*There is an outburst of rifle-fire from outside. All freeze for a moment.* ROISIN *with her head on* MICKSER'S *shoulder. The piano next door has stopped.)*

PALLISER (*noticing the silence*). She's stopped.

ENDYMION. Carriages at midnight.

(*He bows and stalks from the room by the kitchen.* TETLEY *carries in* O'CALLAGHAN *from the street. The latter's tunic is splashed with blood, and his eyes are closed.* MACCARTHY *and* EMER *spring to his assistance, and the wounded man is laid on the floor.*

MACCARTHY. Here, let me take him.

MAGINNIS. What happened to him?

TETLEY (*serious, but not too emotionally*). We were running across the street – more than half way over before they opened fire. He was just in front of me when I noticed the little hole in the back of his tunic. Suddenly there. Just a little hole. But he kept on running – ten – fifteen – twenty steps, before he seemed to realize what had happened. Then I caught him just as he was falling, and carried him the rest of the way over. Is he gone?

MACCARTHY. No. But it won't be long. Water – quick!

(ROISIN *brings a glass of water and holds it to* O'CALLAGHAN'S *lips.* PALLISER *strikes a chord on the piano, and listens for the answer. There is none.*)

PALLISER. I think . . . Miss Garrity's . . . in trouble too.

MACCARTHY (*to* EMER). Do you know an Act of Contrition? (*He rises and crosses to the bar, his hand over his eyes.*) I wouldn't trust myself . . . to remember it.

    (PALLISER *strikes another chord, and listens.* EMER *whispers into* O'CALLAGHAN'S *ear. He opens his eyes and smiles.*)

ROISIN (*to* PALLISER). Sssh! Is this a time to be playin'?

O'CALLAGHAN. Don't stop him. Why are you all so . . . glum.

ROISIN. Don't try to talk. Let you listen to the Act of Contrition.

O'CALLAGHAN. I've said it myself . . . every day . . . for the past year. I'm ready.

MACCARTHY. Then you knew?

O'CALLAGHAN. I knew. If it wasn't this . . . it'd be . . . something else. Ah, cheer up, for God's sake. Look at Sean there. He knows who's . . . well off.

TETLEY. You think so?

O'CALLAGHAN (*gathering strength for a little*). It was a . . . good fight. Why don't you play something, Don Quixote? Are you in mourning for your horse?

PALLISER. Are you addressing me?

O'CALLAGHAN. Yes. I'm surprised to find you haven't run away.

PALLISER. You never told me I could go.

O'CALLAGHAN. As a soldier, you never used to have much difficulty . . . about breaking your word.

PALLISER. As a soldier who never carried any ammunition, you needn't be so smug.

ROISIN (*angrily*). That's no way to talk to . . . to a . . .

PALLISER. To a dying man. Why not?

ROISIN (*astounded*). You oughta have some respect. Is this a time for spite?

O'CALLAGHAN (*with a grin*). No, don't be spiteful, Captain. Just one thing . . . I'd like to let you know.

PALLISER. Well?

O'CALLAGHAN. I had ammunition . . . plenty of it.

PALLISER (*surprised*). Then why didn't you shoot?

O'CALLAGHAN. I'm glad . . . I didn't. I'd be thinking of him . . . now . . . if I'd killed him. Now I can . . .

PALLISER. Leave thinking to others? If you mean me, don't speak too soon. I haven't run yet.

O'CALLAGHAN (*sinking fast*). Bet you . . . I'll be here . . . after . . . you . . .

(*He closes his eyes.* MACCARTHY *returns swiftly for a brief examination.*)

EMER. Is he gone? (MACCARTHY *nods. The Catholics cross themselves.*) May God grant peace to his great soul.

(*They all rise except* PALLISER. MACCARTHY *goes behind the bar to have another drink.* EMER *goes to the window, and looks out.*)

ROISIN (*looking down at* O'CALLAGHAN). What's he smilin' at?

PALLISER (*savagely*). Why wouldn't he smile? He was going to die, and he knew it. We're all going to die, only we don't know it.

ROISIN (*softly*). Is it always like that?

TETLEY. I'd like to think so.

ROISIN (*turning on* EMER). It's all your doin'. But for you it mighta been over a Tuesda.

EMER. Keep out of this.

ROISIN (*shrilly*). I'll not keep out of it. Wasn't it you that fired that gun?

EMER. You know nothing about it.

ROISIN. But for you there's many a man would be still alive.

EMER (*contemptuously*). Alive for what?

PALLISER. Ah, leave her alone.

ROISIN. She fired the gun an' she supposed te be a nurse. What kind of a woman is that? Drivin' men te slaughter an' the flames. She fired it.

TETLEY. Maybe she did. But how did it get fixed in the first place? (*Pause while all eyes but* EMER'S *turn on* PALLISER.) Can you help us, Captain?

PALLISER (*to* ROISIN). Why are you glaring at me? I'm not the one you used to glare at.

ROISIN. It was you that fixed it. Why?

PALLISER. Why? Because . . . because Montaigne tells us that a glass of water night and morning is the best cure for constipation.

MACCARTHY (*gloomily*). That is not at all certain. (*He returns to his drink.*)

ROISIN. You did it because you didn't want the trouble to be ended. You wanted to see them all slaughtered.

EMER. You're a fool, girl. Why can't you keep your mouth shut?

ROISIN. Because I'm sick a killin', that's why.

PALLISER (*looking at* O'CALLAGHAN). Even the killing of killers?

ROISIN. Who did he ever kill? He was a better man than any a youse.

PALLISER. We always are, once we're in his condition. Strange . . . this importance of the dead.

ROISIN. Will ya stop sneerin'! I've just seen a man die for his country – his country an' mine.

PALLISER. And so you're going to change your views about the whole business?

ROISIN. What de ye expec'? Oh, I dunno what to tink.
  (*She turns away to* MICKSER, *covering her face with her hands.*)

PALLISER. A pity that it wasn't me. I like my country too.

TETLEY. Captain Palliser, I hope we all like our country, however differently we may express it. I suppose you've heard you have a new commanding officer?

PALLISER. No. Who's that?

TETLEY. He landed this morning in the small hours. I don't know his name, but they say he's a soldier of the old school.

MACCARTHY. I know all about him. He was out in Egypt defending the Suez Canal. Only nobody told him who his opponents were, so he arranged matters to have the Canal defend him.

TETLEY. Yes, I think that's the man.

MACCARTHY. It's a damn scandal, that's what it is. We're entitled to a sledgehammer and they send us an oats-crusher. Another injustice to Ireland.

TETLEY. We hear, however, that he's very stern. The situation requires measures of the utmost severity.

PALLISER. Oh, God.

MACCARTHY. There *are* some acute Saxons, but these obtuse Angles are all we ever get over here. (*Pause.*) Personally, I thought that rather a good remark. I suppose you'll laugh at it next year.

PALLISER (*despairingly*). No, we laughed at it last year.

TETLEY. Dr MacCarthy, I really think we've had enough of you. Do you suppose you could get that wounded man out of here, to a place of safety?

MACCARTHY. Over to the Post Office . . . from the fire into the frying pan?

TETLEY. No. To Jervis Street Hospital. We've evacuated the Post Office, and broken our way through to the small shops in Moore Street. That's what we came over to warn you about. The Post Office has become quite untenable.

PALLISER. It was untenable from the start. I could have told you that.

TETLEY. It served us well enough against cavalry charges. But you see how we're all learning from experience. Maginnis will help you with the stretcher, and somebody else had better take that Red Cross flag.

MAGINNIS (*finishing his stout*). You'll need me in Moore Street.

TETLEY. Yes, you'll be needed Maginnis, but not in Moore Street. These are your instructions. You're to dump your equipment, and after you've got your man to the hospital, you will retire from these operations altogether, and keep out of internment if you can. (*With a smile.*) In particular, avoid being identified by Captain Palliser. It's absolutely essential that as many men as possible should remain at large. Is that understood?

MAGINNIS. You mean, this isn't the end?

TETLEY. I mean that it's up to you to see that it's only the beginning. Report to a Staff Captain Collins.

MAGINNIS (*delighted*). Come on youse.

ROISIN. I'll carry the flag.

> (*He salutes, and* TETLEY *returns his salute.* ROISIN *takes* TETLEY'S *hand, and kisses it fervently, much to his embarrassment.* MACCARTHY *and* MAGINNIS *pick up the stretcher, and carry it out, following* ROISIN, *who carries the flag.* EMER *goes to the window to watch.*)

MACCARTHY (*as they go*). Now don't push me. You know I'm a very nervous man. It's all due to a governess who gave me complexes by insisting that I wear button boots when I was three. Ever since then whenever I see a button . . .

> (*There is no firing as they go.*)

PALLISER. So there's going to be more fighting?

TETLEY. Yes, Captain. But of a different kind. We live – some of us – and learn.

PALLISER. From behind hedges, I suppose. You'll never get to the Peace Conference with that kind of fighting.

TETLEY. Oh who cares about the Peace Conference. That's just another illusion we're well rid of. The boys who come through this will have to do their own fighting. Only next time it will not be strictly in accordance with the rules.

PALLISER. I thought you loved the rules.

TETLEY. Somebody told me once, that the sign of a good soldier is his readiness to disregard the rules in an intelligent way. The boys will be better at that than we of the older generation. By the way, I hope they got across!

EMER (*turning from the window*). They got across. Are you not going yourself?

TETLEY. Yes. But only on my way to another destination.

EMER. Where's that?

TETLEY. The Post Office has served its purpose. I had intended to stop in it till the end, but I've since thought that maybe we can win this war after all.

EMER. What do you mean?

TETLEY. Now that Captain Palliser has a new commanding officer, there's a better use I can make of the last few days of my life than by being burnt to death like a rat. So we're going to surrender.

EMER (*horrified*). Surrender! But if you do that they'll only hang you!

TETLEY (*with grave simplicity*). Yes. I hope I can face up to it. I think I can.

PALLISER (*disturbed*). That's not a soldier's end.

TETLEY. Then maybe you were right, Captain. Maybe I'm not much of a soldier after all. (*Then with a slight smile.*) Perhaps I'm something more significant.

PALLISER. You needn't think you'll get off, after this week's work.

TETLEY. If I thought there was any danger of that, I'd take the pleasanter course and fight it out. But this new man of yours seems to be quite a hangman. He'll hang the entire Provisional Government. He'll hang innocents for being related to us. He'll probably take the wounded from hospital and hang them too. There'll be court martial after court martial, and you, Captain Palliser, will be subpoenaed, I'm afraid, as a star witness for the Crown.

PALLISER (*grimly*). Indeed! So that's the role you've picked for me.

TETLEY. It's not my casting, Captain. It's Heaven that provides us with our roles in this fantastic pantomime.

PALLISER. Well Heaven can't ballyrag me. I pick my own parts.

TETLEY. I'm afraid you can hardly get out of it. And I'm sorry; because you did us a great service once.

PALLISER. *I* did?

TETLEY. Of course. I know who fixed that machine-gun. I believe you did it because you didn't want to see your countrymen climb down without putting up a good fight.

PALLISER (*vehemently*). I did it for no such melodramatic reason. (*He glares at* EMER *before turning back to* TETLEY.) And if you're proposing to thank me for anything, I shall take it as a damned impertinence.

TETLEY. Then why did you do it?

PALLISER. For no reason that I intend to discuss with you.

TETLEY. Why? Are you ashamed of what you've done?

PALLISER. Who wants to be thanked for letting himself be talked into playing the other fellow's game? But we always do. (*Gloomily.*) We deserve whatever's coming to us.

TETLEY (*shaking his head*). Look at him. I believe he's suffering from some absurd sense of guilt over having acted like an Irishman.

PALLISER. You go to hell.

EMER. Be careful Sean. He'll be crowing over you if you surrender now.

PALLISER (*lying viciously*). Yes, I'll crow! Cock-a-doodle-do!

TETLEY. I don't think so, Emer. You saw how that shopgirl behaved over poor O'Callaghan. What will she feel – what will the nation feel! – when fifteen or twenty of us have been treated to what will be called our 'just deserts'?

EMER. But he mustn't be let feel that he's won.

PALLISER. No! Don't let me feel that!

TETLEY. I am not concerned with what the enemy feels . . . any more than with the Peace Conference . . . now. What matters to me is that this week can be turned from a disgrace into a triumph – that all our mistakes and incompetence can be made of no importance whatever by giving ourselves up to some fool of a general.

EMER. But how do you know it will end that way? This has got to be your triumph, not his. (*She points at* PALLISER.) You mustn't weaken now.

TETLEY (*with a wry smile*). I wish to God it was weakening, but it's not. If you will do something for me now, you'll soon see how it will work out.

EMER (*aghast at what she knows is coming*). *I'm* to?

TETLEY. Yes. I want you to go out with a white flag, and offer your commanding officer to that general.

EMER (*passionately*). No! It's unnatural! Let the others climb down if they have to, but let you and me stop in the Post Office.

TETLEY (*firmly*). No, Emer. We can do better than that. If he offers you any terms, we may have to fight on. But if he insists on unconditional surrender, bring me back the good news at once to Moore Street. I shall be over there, trying to convince the others.

EMER (*bursting into silent tears*). No! I'll carry no white flag.

TETLEY. My dear, I know what I'm doing. (*Surprised.*) And crying does not become you.

EMER. Your dear! Don't call me that. You'd never ask me to do such a thing if you didn't know that it's never been true.

TETLEY (*puzzled*). What has never been true? (*She turns away her head.*) I don't understand. (*Pause.*) Do you want me to ask one of the other ladies to oblige? (*Pause.*) Well at any rate will you wish me good luck and goodbye?

(*He holds out his hand, but she turns away abruptly, pausing for a moment to glare at* PALLISER, *before going out by the kitchen. The smell of smoke begins to become noticeable.*)

EMER. No. But I'm ready to wish *him* goodbye.

PALLISER. Me?

EMER. I think *we've* managed to look Azrael in the face. What about you?

TETLEY. What are you two talking about?

PALLISER (*meeting her eye, gravely*). Quite a killer. Mm.

EMER. Now's *your* chance to turn wind into wonderment.

PALLISER. Fair enough. (*Pause. Then suddenly.*) Goodbye.

EMER. We'll see if it's goodbye.

(*She goes.* PALLISER *stares after her. Then he gives a little mirthless laugh.*)

TETLEY. Some women can never understand politics.

PALLISER. Some men can never understand women. I wonder which is the more ignorant.

TETLEY. This is hardly the time for enigmas, Captain. Let me help you to a place of safety before I go.

PALLISER. No, thanks.

TETLEY. I smell smoke. Come along. I can carry you if necessary.

PALLISER (*louder*). No, thanks.

TETLEY. But the fire will be here in five or ten minutes.

PALLISER. Will you kindly mind your own business and allow me to mind mine?

TETLEY. What's the idea? Are you proposing to commit suicide?

PALLISER. I have no such second-rate ambitions. I leave those to your sort.

TETLEY (*offended*). A prisoner of war who is judicially murdered does not commit suicide.

403

PALLISER. You don't have to be murdered. In fact, I'll give you a fair offer. If you'll undertake to let me save your life, I'll give you the satisfaction of saving mine.

TETLEY. You mean, I'm to join in some lies, that you will tell at the court martial?

PALLISER. Yes.

TETLEY (*indignantly*). I shall do nothing of the sort.

PALLISER. O.K. Off you go, then.

TETLEY (*distressed*). I've *got* to go through with this. Can't you see? But you've got nothing to die for by stopping here.

PALLISER. And nothing to live for except the honour of playing Judas to your Jesus. What do you take me for?

TETLEY. A professional in the service of the big battalions. Your own choice.

PALLISER. If you think I'm going to be a witness at your apotheosis you can think again. I've made you a fair offer, and if you won't take it, you can be the fellow who runs. Not me.

TETLEY. What earthly good will that do you?

PALLISER. It will show you and that bitch who's killing you for not marrying her that there are other people who understand as much about death as you do. And there's no pie in the sky to make it any easier for us.

TETLEY. So that's at the back of it! Palliser, you're a fool. It's not me she's killing, but you. If this is just a matter of showing off, I'm at least doing something the world will know about. But if you stop here until the building collapses, nobody will know about it except me.

PALLISER. Thank you. I shall know about it myself.

TETLEY (*after considering him for a moment*). And this is the fellow who had the nerve to call me pompous for knowing my own mind. I would never have believed in such vanity. But don't think that you can bully me out of my destiny. I warn you that if you insist, I shall leave you this bonfire for whatever satisfaction you can get from it.

PALLISER. Goodbye.

(TETLEY *goes to the door, and turns.*)

TETLEY. Listen, Palliser, I know that you people have a pride in your past. But isn't it our turn now?

PALLISER (*softening*). Of course it is. I know what's coming, and there's no hard feelings so long as I don't have to be part of the audience. When we built an Empire, Tetley, we didn't have much in the way of big battalions. But we had life and an interest in ourselves. Now we're tired of being what we are, and we play the other fellow's game because we're sick of winning. I see it all as if it had happened already. Ireland's only the start. We're going to go on winning every war, but piece by piece we're going to give it all away – not because we're licked, but because we're bloody well bored. So don't be too proud of yourselves. It won't be the first time that people like you have loosened the foundations of a civilization – and at Easter too, by gad. You'll have it in chains again, as you had it before. But not me.

TETLEY. In chains? We, who are fighting for liberty?

PALLISER (*with a smile*). You don't give a damn about liberty. All you care about is a cause. And causes always let you down. Your admirers will find that out before they've finished.

TETLEY (*after a pause*). Perhaps it's just as well you won't be around. I think I shall defeat your general, but I must admit that in some ways you defeat me. Well, I must go now.

PALLISER. You'll walk across, I suppose. Just to show off.

TETLEY. No. I shall run like hell, as any soldier should. I've got a better use for my life than that.

PALLISER. You ought to walk. It'll come to the same thing in the end.

TETLEY. It may be the same end, but it will not be the same thing.

PALLISER. They're rotten shots. I know. I taught them.

TETLEY (smiling). I don't think I'll risk it all the same. Goodbye, Julian Imperator.

(*He salutes.* PALLISER *turns away abruptly and stares out of the window. With a little shrug of the shoulders,* TETLEY *leaves. When he has gone,* PALLISER *turns round and salutes.*)

PALLISER. See you shortly, Commandant General.

TETLEY (*off*). Thanks. I heard you.

PALLISER. Eavesdropper! Listener at doors! (*He returns to the window.*) Don't run, cowardy custard. Blast it, don't run. Shoot you fools, shoot! Not a bloody shot! (*Shots.*) Ah! Oh damn, damn, damn! He's got across. I always knew those musketry courses were no damn good.

(*From next door, the piano is heard once again, leading up to the crashing finale of Ravel's 'Le Jardin Feerique'.*)

PALLISER. Well I'll be . . . ! (*He turns to the body of* O'CALLAGHAN.) You hear, my friend? We're neither of us the last to go. (*He shakes his head.*) Winter gives back the roses to the frost-filled earth.

(*He goes to the piano, and joins in his part of the duet. For a time they play, as the glow of the fire grows deeper. Then there is a crash and the other piano stops.* PALLISER *continues alone. Presently the central pillar falls with a shower of plaster.* PALLISER *is still continuing to play as the Curtain slowly falls. That is the end of this play.*)

SOUTH HADLEY, 1957

A SELECTED CHECKLIST

compiled by Joseph Ronsley

1. Plays

*The Moon in the Yellow River and The Old Lady Says 'No!':
Two Plays,* with a foreword by C. P. Curran, (Jonathan
Cape), London, 1932.

The Moon in the Yellow River, revised version, (Jonathan
Cape), London 1935.

Storm Song and A Bride for the Unicorn: Two Plays,
(Jonathan Cape), London, 1935.

The Golden Cuckoo and Other Plays, (Jonathan Cape),
London, 1954. Contains *The Golden Cuckoo; The Dreaming
Dust; A Fourth for Bridge.*

The Collected Plays in 2 volumes, (Jonathan Cape) London,
(Little Brown) Boston, 1960. Contains, in Vol. 1, *The Old
Lady Says 'No!', The Scythe and the Sunset, A Fourth for
Bridge;* in Vol. 2, *The Moon in the Yellow River, The
Dreaming Dust, 'Strange Occurrence on Ireland's Eye'.*

The Golden Cuckoo, revised version, (Proscenium Press),
Newark, Delaware, 1971.

The Dramatic Works, Vol. I, (Colin Smythe), Gerrards Cross,
Bucks., (Macmillan of Canada/Maclean Hunter) Toronto,
1977. Contains *The Old Lady Says 'No!'; The Scythe and the
Sunset; Storm Song; The Dreaming Dust; 'Strange Occurrence on Ireland's Eye';* with general introduction and
an introduction to each play.

The Dramatic Works, Vol. II, (Colin Smythe), Gerrards Cross,
Bucks., (Humanities Press) Atlantic Highlands, N.J., 1979.
Contains *A Bride for the Unicorn; The Moon in the Yellow
River; A Fourth for Bridge; The Golden Cuckoo; Nine
Rivers from Jordan; Tain bo Cuailgne,* with a general intro-
duction and an introduction to each play.

The Dramatic Works, Vol. III. Announced but not yet
published. (Colin Smythe), Gerrards Cross, Bucks.,
(Humanities Press) Atlantic Highlands, N.J. To contain
plays for radio and television.

2. Prose

Nine Rivers from Jordan: The Chronicle of a Journey and a

Search, revised version of *Dionysia,* (D. Verschoyle), London, 1953, (Little, Brown), Boston, 1955.

In Search of Swift, (Hodges, Figgis & Co.), Dublin, 1959.

John Millington Synge, (Columbia University Press), New York and London, 1965.

The Brazen Horn, (Dolmen Press), Dublin, 1976.

3. Collaborations

Blind Man's Buff, A Play in Three Acts, by Ernst Toller and Denis Johnston, (Jonathan Cape), London, 1938.

4. Contributions to Books

'The Making of the Theatre', in *The Gate Theatre — Dublin,* edited Bulmer Hobson, (The Gate Theatre), Dublin, 1934.

'Television: The Present and the Future', in *Penguin Parade,* 2nd series, no. 1, edited by Jack Morpurgo, (Penguin Books), West Drayton, Middx., 1947.

'A Short View of the Progress of Joyceanity', in *A Bash in the Tunnel,* edited by John Ryan, (Clifton House), Brighton, 1970. Originally published in *Envoy* (Dublin) April 1951.

"Introduction' to *The Voice of Shem: Passages from Finnegans Wake,* by James Joyce, freely adapted for the theatre, by Mary Manning, (Faber & Faber), London, 1958.

'Did you know Yeats? And Did You Lunch with Shaw?' in *A Paler Shade of Green,* edited by Des Hickey and Gus Smith, (Leslie Frewin), London, 1972. American edition titled *Flight from the Celtic Twilight,* (Bobbs-Merrill), New York, 1973.

'Myles na cGopaleen' in *Myth and Reality in Irish Literature,* edited by Joseph Ronsley, (Wilfrid Laurier University Press), Waterloo, Ontario, 1977.

[On 'The Dublin Gate Theatre, 1928–1978'] in *Enter Certain Players: Edwards-MacLiammoir and the Gate 1928–1978'* edited by Peter Luke, (Dolmen Press), Dublin, 1978.

6. Contributions to Periodicals

'Sean O'Casey: An Appreciation', in *Living Age* (Boston), April 1926.

'A National Morality Play', in *Motley* (Dublin), March 1932. Under pseudonym E. W. Tocher.

'Towards a Dynamic Theatre', *The Gownsman* (Cambridge), 8 June 1935.

'Yeats as Dramatist', in *The Irish Times* (Dublin), 13 June 1935.

'Theatre or Cinema', in *The Listener* (London), 11 September 1935.

"The World we Listen in', in *Radio Times* (London), 23 October 1936.

' "The Young Roscius": A Boy Genius of Regency Days', in *Radio Times* (London), 12 February 1937.

'The Theatre in Ireland', in *One Act Play Magazine and Radio Drama Review* (Boston), October 1937.

'Public Opinion: A National Morality Play' [open letter], in *The Bell* (Dublin), March 1941.

'Shaw: The Man and His Work', in *The Irish Times* (Dublin), 26 July 1941.

'Dublin Theatre', in *The Bell* (Dublin), November 1941.

'Drama — The Dublin Theatre', in *The Bell* (Dublin), February 1942.

'Juno and O'Casey', in *Radio Times* (London), 3 May 1946.

'Mr. Shaw, We Wish You Well', in *The Listener* (London), 1 August 1946.

'It's So Good There'll be Trouble', in *Radio Times* (London), 13 September 1946.

'Behind the Television Cameras', in *English Digest* (London), October 1946.

'Sean O'Casey: Realist or Romantic', in *The Listener* (London), 17 October 1946.

'Television and the BBC', in *The Spectator* (London), 22 July 1949.

'A Decade in Retrospect, 1939–49', in *The Month* (London), vol. 3. no. 2, 1950.

'Joxer in Totnes', in *Irish Writing* (Cork), December 1950.

'Waiting with Beckett', in *Irish Writing* (Cork), Spring 1956.

'Letter to a Young Dramatist', in *The Listener* (London), 30 August 1956.

'Our First Film', in *Creation* (Dublin), November 1958.

'What Has Happened to the Irish', in *Theatre Arts* (New York), July 1959.

'That's Show Business', in Theatre Arts (New York), February 1960.

'The College Theatre — Why?', in *Theatre Arts* (New York), August 1960.

'Humor — Hibernian Style', in *New York Times,* 5 February 1961.

'Needed: New Perspectives for the Theatre', in *Theatre Arts* (New York), December 1962.

'Dream Theatre', in *Smith Alumnae Quarterly* (Northampton, Mass.), Winter 1963.

'Sean O'Casey', in *The Nation* (New York), 5 October 1964.

'Policy for the Abbey Theatre', in *Hibernia* (Dublin), 15 May 1970.

'Brian Friel and Modern Irish Drama', in *Hibernia* (Dublin), 7 March 1975.

'Giants in Those Days of Shaw, De Valera and Sir William Haley', in *Irish University Review* (Dublin), Spring 1978.

8. Librettos for Operas

Six Characters in Search of an Author (Theodore Presser Co.), Bryn Mawr, Pa., 1957. Music by Hugo Weisgall.

Nine Rivers from Jordan (Theodore Presser Co.), Bryn Mawr, Pa., 1968. Music by Hugo Weisgall. Reprinted in *Dramatic Works* vol. 2, with revisions.

9. Unpublished Plays

Ulysses in Nightown. Performed in New York, 1958. Adaptation of part of James Joyce's *Ulysses.*

Finnegans Wake. Performed in New Haven Conn., 1959. Adaptation of Joyce's novel.

Riders to the Sidhe: A Musical Synge-Song. Performed in Cambridge, Mass., c. 1960.

10. Radio Plays (with date of first broadcast).

The Call to Arms. 19 December 1936, on BBC National Service.

Death at Newtonstewart. 7 October 1937, on BBC National Service.

Not One Returns to Tell. 24 December 1937, on BBC Northern Ireland Regional Service.

Lillibulero. 30 March 1938, on BBC London Regional Service.

The Parnell Commission. 31 May 1938, on BBC London Regional Service.

Weep for Polyphemus. 18 June 1938, on BBC London Regional Service.

Multiple Studio Blues, with John Cheatle. 24 November 1938, on BBC London Regional Service.

The Face of Courage, with Stephen Potter. 31 December 1939, on BBC Home Serevice.

Nansen of the Fram. 23 December 1940, on BBC Home Service.

High Command, with Igor Vinogradoff. 4 August 1941, on BBC Home Service.

The Gorgeous Lady Blessington. 21 August 1941, on BBC Home Service.

Amanda McKittrick Ros. 27 July 1943, on BBC Home Service.

11. Radio Adaptations of Stage Plays
The Moon in the Yellow River. 14 May 1935, on BBC London Regional Service.

A Little Trouble in Court ['*Strange Occurence on Ireland's Eye*']. 7 December 1937, on BBC Northern Ireland Regional Service.

A Bride for the Unicorn. 22 March 1938, on BBC National Service.

Blind Man's Buff (Toller and Johnston). 22 August 1949, on BBC Home Service.

12. Television Plays
Weep for the Cyclops [version of *The Dreaming Dust*]. 21 August 1947, on BBC Television.

The Moon in the Yellow River [version of stage play]. 16 October 1947, on BBC Television.

Death at Newtownstewart [version of radio play]. 4 January 1948, on BBC Television.

The Unthinking Lobster [version of *A Fourth for Bridge*]. 18 August 1948, on BBC Television.

The Call to Arms [version of radio play]. 10 June 1949, on BBC Television.

The Glass Murder. Telefis Eireann. 5 February 1963.

13. Biography and Criticism
Denis Johnston, by Gene A. Barnett (Twayne/G. K. Hall), Boston, Mass., 1978.

Denis Johnston, by James F. Carens, (Bucknell University Press), Lewisburg, Pa., 1976.

Denis Johnston's Irish Theatre, by Harold Ferrar, (Dolmen Press), Dublin, 1973.

Denis Johnston, A Retrospective, edited by Joseph Ronsley (Colin Smythe), Gerrards Cross, Bucks., and (Barnes & Noble Books/Littlefield Adams), Totowa, N.J., 1981.

Acknowledgements

The author wishes to thank the following for permission to reprint copyright material:

Macmillan & Company, Ltd, and Michael and Anne Yeats for the stanzas from *Cathleen ni Houlihan* from *The Collected Plays* and *Into the Twilight* from Yeats's *Collected Poems*.

Faber & Faber, Ltd, for 'Fu-I loved the Green Hills' from 'Epitaphs' in *Personae* by Ezra Pound. Also William Alwyn for permission to publish and perform the music score of this poem.